Keeping Your School Safe & Secure:

A Practical Guide

Center for
Education & Employment Law
CEEL

Center for Education & Employment Law
P.O. Box 3008
Malvern, Pennsylvania 19355

ISBN 978-1-933043-28-9

Published 2007   by: Center for Education & Employment Law

Application for Preasssigned Control Number pending.

Cover Design by Patricia Jacoby

Other Titles Published By
Center for Education & Employment Law:

Students with Disabilities and Special Education
Private School Law in America
Higher Education Law in America
U.S. Supreme Court Education Cases
Deskbook Encyclopedia of American School Law
Deskbook Encyclopedia of Public Employment Law
U.S. Supreme Court Employment Cases
Deskbook Encyclopedia of Employment Law

TABLE OF CONTENTS

CHAPTER ONE
Access and Building Security

CHAPTER TWO
Emergency Preparedness and Response

CHAPTER THREE
Student Issues

CHAPTER SIX
Extracurricular Activities

CHAPTER SEVEN
Health Issues

CHAPTER EIGHT
Statutes and Regulations

CHAPTER NINE
Forms

INTRODUCTION

We are excited to introduce this edition of *Keeping Your School Safe & Secure: A Practical Guide.* Designed for the busy education professional, this easy-to-use resource presents a unique combination of materials designed to help administrative professionals formulate and implement a comprehensive plan to keep schools a safe place to learn. Case summaries, source materials, forms, checklists and practical guidance are organized into chapters by subject area for easy reference. A comprehensive index and case tables make it easy to quickly find the information you need.

Now more than ever, school security and related issues predominate the education landscape. Rely on *Keeping Your School Safe & Secure: A Practical Guide* with confidence as a valuable tool to avoid legal liability and protect the health and safety of your students.

ABOUT THE EDITORS

Curt J. Brown is the Group Publisher of the Center for Education & Employment Law. Prior to assuming his present position, he gained extensive experience in business-to-business publishing, including management of well-known publications such as *What's Working in Human Resources, What's New in Benefits & Compensation, Keep Up to Date with Payroll, Supervisors Legal Update,* and *Facility Manager's Alert.* Mr. Brown graduated from Villanova School of Law and graduated magna cum laude from Bloomsburg University with a B.S. in Business Administration. He is admitted to the Pennsylvania bar.

Steve McEllistrem is the senior legal editor at the Center for Education & Employment Law. He co-authored the deskbook *Federal Laws Prohibiting Employment Discrimination* and is a former managing editor of *Employment Law Report.* He graduated *cum laude* from William Mitchell College of Law and received his undergraduate degree from the University of Minnesota. Mr. McEllistrem is admitted to the Minnesota bar.

James A. Roth is the editor of *Legal Notes for Education* and *Special Education Law Update.* He is a co-author of *Students with Disabilities* and *Special Education Law* and an adjunct program assistant professor at St. Mary's University in Minnesota. Mr. Roth is a graduate of the University of Minnesota and William Mitchell College of Law. He is admitted to the Minnesota bar.

Thomas D'Agostino is a managing editor at the Center for Education & Employment Law. He graduated from the Duquesne University School of Law and received his undergraduate degree from Ramapo College of New Jersey. He is a past member of the American Bar Association's Section of Individual Rights and Responsibilities as well as the Pennsylvania Bar Association's Legal Services to Persons with Disabilities Committee. Mr. D'Agostino is admitted to the Pennsylvania bar.

Elizabeth A. Wheeler is editor of the monthly newsletters *Private Education Law Report* and *Classroom Management & Education Law Update.* A graduate of Macalester College and Capital University Law School, she is a member of the Massachusetts bar. Before joining the Center for Education and Employment Law, she was legal editor for three employment law and two education law newsletters; one focused on public school law, the other on special education.

HOW TO USE YOUR GUIDE BOOK

We have designed the *Keeping Your School Safe & Secure: A Practical Guide* in an accessible format for both attorneys and non-attorneys to use as a research and reference tool toward prevention of legal problems.

Research Tool

As a research tool, our guide book allows you to conduct your research on two different levels – by topics or cases.

Topic Research

♦ If you have a general interest in a particular **topic** area, our **table of contents** provides descriptive chapter headings containing detailed subheadings from each chapter.

> ➢ For your convenience, we also include the chapter table of contents at the beginning of each chapter.

Example:
For information on MRSA infection, the table of contents indicates that a discussion of this topic begins in Chapter Seven on page 203:

CHAPTER SEVEN
Health Issues

HOW TO USE YOUR GUIDE BOOK

◆ If you have a specific interest in a particular **issue**, our comprehensive **index** collects all of the relevant page references to particular issues.

Example:
   For information on entranceway security, the index provides references to all of the text dealing with building security instead of only the text dealing with entranceways:

Building security, 2-28
    Cases, 17-28
        Intruders, 17-18, 18-19, 22-23, 24-25, 26-28
        Student searches, 19-22
    Coordinating with first responders, 15
    Doors, 9-10
➡   Entranceways, 10-13
        Biometrics, 12-13
        Card readers, 12
        Closed-circuit television (CCTV), 11
        Metal detectors, 10-11
        PIN codes, 12
        Security personnel/greeters, 11-12

Case Research

◆ If you know the **name** of a particular case, our **table of cases** will allow you to quickly reference the location of the case.

Example:
   If someone mentioned a case named *Daniels v. City of New York,* looking in the table of cases, which has been arranged alphabetically, the case would be located under the "D" section.

D

D.F. v. Board of Educ. of Syosset Cent. School Dist., 64
D.O.F. v. Lewisburg Area School Dist., 130
➡ Daniels v. City of New York, 18, 36
Danso v. Univ. of Connecticut, 86
Davis v. Monroe County Board of Educ., 80, 89, 93, 94

✓ Each of the cases summarized in the guide book also contains the case citation, which will allow you to access the full text of the case if you would like to learn more about it. *See How to Read a Case Citation, p. 327.*

♦ If your interest lies in cases from a **particular state**, our **table of cases by state** will identify the cases from your state and direct you to their page numbers.

Example:
   If cases from California are of interest, the table of cases by state, arranged alphabetically, lists all of the case summaries contained in the guide book from California.

→ **CALIFORNIA**

Avila v. Citrus Community College Dist., 163
Elk Grove Unified School Dist. v. Workers' Compensation
   Appeals Board, 75
Flores v. Morgan Hill Unified School Dist., 92
Garcetti v. Ceballos, 43
Hemady v. Long Beach Unified School Dist., 171
In re Johnny F., 121
In re Jose Y., 136

✓ Remember, the judicial system has two court systems – state and federal court – which generally function independently from each other. *See The Judicial System, p. 323.* We have included the federal court cases in the table of cases by state according to the state in which the court resides. However, federal court decisions often impact other federal courts within that particular circuit. Therefore, it may be helpful to review cases from all of the states contained in a particular circuit.

We hope you benefit from the use of the *Keeping Your School Safe and Secure: A Practical Guide.* If you have any questions about how to use the guide book, please contact Thomas D'Agostino at tdagostino@pbp.com.

TABLE OF CASES

TABLE OF CASES

TABLE OF CASES BY STATE

TABLE OF CASES BY STATE

CHAPTER ONE

Access and Building Security

I. INTRODUCTION

An important key to maintaining school safety and security is controlling access to school facilities. A variety of tools are available to help schools ensure that access to school facilities is gained only by authorized personnel. A one-size-fits-all approach to controlling school access is inappropriate. Although some issues relating to school access are common to most schools, an individualized assessment must be undertaken to determine which specific security steps are best-suited for your particular facility.

Several factors should be taken into consideration when determining how best to ensure safe access to school facilities. These include:

- the grades that the school serves
- the layout of the school campus
- the enrollment level
- the location of the school (e.g., urban vs. suburban or rural)
- the crime level in the neighborhood where the school is located

II. ENVIRONMENTAL DESIGN

It is important to note the value of incorporating environmental design elements that ensure school safety and security to the maximum extent possible. While this is a benefit that can be most fully utilized by incorporating environmental design principles into new facilities at the design stage, some of these design elements can also be incorporated into existing school campuses. In addition, expansion and reconstruction plans create a valuable opportunity to increase school safety by incorporating environmental design elements that take school safety into account. In all of these cases, the likelihood of crime can be reduced via an effective use of the school's physical environment.

A. Crime Prevention Through Environmental Design (CPTED)

An approach to increasing safety called Crime Prevention Through Environmental Design (CPTED) recognizes the important role that the design of the built environment can play in reducing the risk of criminal activity. CPTED is not intended to replace traditional crime prevention approaches. Instead, it should be thought of as a complementary tool that can be incorporated into an overall comprehensive plan to make schools safer.

The CPTED approach incorporates several concepts that are applied to increase the security level of the studied facility. The approach has been used to provide an increased measure of security at facilities such as government buildings, commercial complexes and parks. Although not originally developed specifically with schools in mind, the approach is particularly useful in school settings, partly because application of its principles can substantially increase the safety of the school environment while preserving a welcoming environment and avoiding a prison-like atmosphere. Another strong advantage of CPTED is that it is relatively cost-effective.

CPTED has a strong record of success. The Broward County, Florida school district experienced a dramatic reduction in crime after implementing CPTED, and some state legislatures have mandated its use in schools.

The CPTED approach involves several discrete components, including natural surveillance, natural access control, and territoriality.

1. Natural Surveillance

The natural surveillance component of CPTED seeks to maximize the safety advantage that is gained when the environment's physical features keep obstacles to surveillance to a minimum and enable authorities to observe the facility's entire physical environment without undue interference and without a need to resort to advanced technological measures. Essentially, this component seeks to maximize the ability of authorities to observe the environment, in general, and especially higher-risk areas, such as parking lots and building entrances. Several potential barriers impede the ability to maximize surveillance capabilities, such as solid walls, overgrown shrubbery, and inadequate lighting.

2. Natural Access Control

Natural access control, a second important component of CPTED, refers to the benefit obtained by taking steps to design the facility's physical environment in a way that deters criminal activity by creating a perception of risk to potential offenders. This is accomplished, for example, by constructing the physical environment so that visitors are guided through the physical space of the facility by means of clear routing, signage, and other steering features.

3. Territorial Reinforcement

A third component of CPTED is territorial reinforcement. This component seeks to create an environment that encourages authorized users of the space to develop a sense of territoriality or ownership over the space. When authorized users develop this sense of territoriality, potential offenders are discouraged from engaging in criminal activity. An example of a design feature that encourages territoriality is clear border definition of property lines.

Professional resources are available to aid schools in conducting a CPTED analysis. School personnel also can perform a CPTED analysis by undertaking a comprehensive study of criminal behavior and other misconduct that occurs on campus. This study is intended to identify and categorize the types of problems that take place and to ascertain whether patterns exist with respect to time and/or location. Ideally a comprehensive study will yield information that can be used to change the physical environment in a way that reduces the incidence of criminal behavior or other improper conduct.

4. Case Study: Effective Use of CPTED

The Broward County, Florida school district was one of the first in the country to effectively utilize CPTED concepts in the school environment. After completing an evaluation, the district applied a number of CPTED strategies in the school environment. Based on the assessment, the district considered changes relating to vehicle access and border definition. It also considered relocating parking lots and replacing restroom entrance doors with open mazes. In addition, it evaluated strategies relating to the maintenance of landscaping and the effective use of lighting and color in and around school facilities. The district's use of CPTED techniques resulted in a significant reduction in school-related crime.

B. Specific Environmental Elements

The following are examples of ways in which schools can help prevent crime in the school environment by controlling specific environmental elements in ways that increase the security of entrance areas.

1. Entrances

A basic key to maintaining a safe school environment is controlling access to the school campus. The school campus should be designed (or redesigned) so that students and visitors must pass through a particular designated entrance or entrances. The school's main entrance should be the school entrance that is closest to the school's main parking lot. It should be clearly marked and in the front of the school near the administrative areas of the building. By locating the main entrance in this manner, visitors will be steered toward it and not to another less prominent entry point. In addition, main entry points should be located in areas of high visibility so people entering and exiting can be observed easily by school personnel. Glazing of windows and doors enhances the ability to conduct effective surveillance. Windows should be kept free of announcements and other postings that impede the ability to conduct effective surveillance of the entrance area. It is preferable for both the entrance area and the parking area to be observable from the school's administrative area. The entrance should be wide enough to minimize pedestrian traffic congestion during peak periods. For many schools, an opening of at least 20 feet will be required to enable smooth ingress and egress.

Minimizing the number of entry points is a critical key to maintaining building security. Providing just one entry point is not a feasible option for most schools and, in fact, can be counterproductive to the overall effort to maintain safety. Decisions relating to the number of entrance points that should be provided in addition to the main entrance must be made with reference to each school's particular characteristics, keeping in mind that it is desirable to maintain a number of entry points that allows for manageable ingress and egress without unnecessarily creating the added risk that each additional entrance point potentially represents. Secondary entrances are an area of particular concern, and they require special attention because they are often a problem area. Secondary entrances should be placed in visible locations and should be monitored. They should be subject to all the security controls that apply at the main entrance point.

CHECKLIST – ENTRANCES

- The main entrance is located close to the school's main parking lot.
- The main entrance is marked by clear and adequate signage.
- The main entrance and parking lot can be easily monitored by administrative personnel from inside the school building.
- Windows and doors near the main entrance include glazing.
- Windows are kept free of postings and other impediments to visibility.
- The entrance is wide enough to accommodate pedestrian traffic at peak times.
- The number of entrances is kept to a minimum.
- Signage steers visitors to a particular entrance.
- Secondary entrances are monitored.

2. Traffic Control/Parking

School parking areas require extra attention because they frequently are locations where vandalism and other crimes take place.

It is important to control access to the school and its parking areas by limiting the number of entrance and exit points to the school campus. The number of access points to parking areas should be limited. This reduces the likelihood that the school's parking area will be perceived as a public space. Vandal-proof lighting in parking areas should be provided, and the use of gates to limit or prevent access to parking areas during low-use times should be considered.

Controlling the flow of both vehicular and pedestrian traffic is of critical importance. Vehicular and pedestrian traffic should be routed in a manner that separates the two and minimizes congestion while also enabling easy observation. Where feasible, traffic lanes of ingress and egress should be separated by a landscaped median. In addition, automobile traffic should be separated from bus traffic once entry to the school campus is gained. Bus parking should be configured so that buses can maneuver the lot without needing to back up to park or turn. It is preferable to avoid long and straight stretches of roadway on the campus. Avoiding long straight stretches helps to keep down the speed of vehicles and reduce the risk of injury to pedestrians. Where appropriate, traffic-control devices, such as speed bumps, can help keep reduce the probability of vehicles traveling at excessive speeds on the school campus.

Visitor parking should be designated as such via proper signage, and signage should further define authorized uses within the parking area. The ability of students to gain access to parking areas at times other than arrival time and dismissal time should be restricted. In addition, parking areas and vehicular routes should be observable from a point or point within the building's interior that includes administrative areas and/or classrooms.

It is necessary to maintain proper access routes for emergency service personnel. Service and delivery routes should be separated from other traffic routes.

CHECKLIST – TRAFFIC CONTROL/PARKING

- Vehicular routes and parking areas can be observed from administrative areas and/or classrooms inside the school.
- Access to parking areas is restricted to a limited number of entrances.
- Automobile traffic is separated from bus traffic by barriers and/or routing.
- Pedestrian traffic is separated from motor vehicle traffic by barriers and/or routing.
- Undesignated spaces within parking areas are minimized.
- Traffic control devices are used when necessary to control speeds.
- Long, straight stretches of roadway are minimized.
- The parking area includes signage that sets out the authorized use of the assigned space.
- The parking area has vandal-resistant lighting.

3. Signage and Sightlines

Signage serves the dual role of helping to control access and providing notice of prohibited behavior.

The campus should include clear signage that directs all visitors to the school's main office, where they can be screened to make sure they have a legitimate reason to be on the campus. Preferably, the main entrance should be visible from both the administration area and main point of vehicular access.

Maintaining open sightlines is another important key to campus security. Building placement, landscaping, the placement of signage and lighting should all take into account the need to maintain open sight lines. This is especially true in higher-risk areas of the school campus, such as parking lots, pickup/drop-off points, bus stops, hallways and stairwells. These higher-risk areas can be identified by analyzing the school's incident history.

Borders within the school's campus should be clearly defined.

CHECKLIST - SIGNAGE

- There is a sign or marquee that identifies the school by name and is visible from a point beyond the school's physical borders.
- Signs include large lettering.
- Signs are well-lit.
- Directional signage is used as needed to control traffic flow.
- Signage directs visitors to a main point of entry.
- Signage does not create a place to hide.
- Signage does not block lines of sight.
- Signage indicates restricted areas.
- Signage indicates bus-loading and drop-off zones.

4. Preventing Roof Access

A number of steps can be taken to reduce the likelihood of unauthorized access to the roof of a campus building. Access to rooftop areas should be available only from inside the building, preferably from a locked point. Placement of landscaping and trees should not enable access to the roof of any building.

Covered walkways should be designed in a manner that does not create opportunities for unauthorized access to a building's roof or other upper-level area. In addition, if the campus includes columns that potentially could be scaled to gain unauthorized access to a roof or upper-level area, the columns should be made from smooth building materials. Alternatively, a slippery finish or coating should be applied to the columns. Campus walls and other architectural features should be designed in a manner that does not allow for footholds or handholds to create an ability to gain unauthorized roof access. Niches in exterior walls should be avoided or eliminated, as these can create hiding places for unauthorized and dangerous materials.

5. Landscaping

As previously noted, landscaping should take into account the need to maintain open sightlines and to deny unauthorized access to rooftop areas. There are additional important points to keep in mind regarding the important role that landscaping can play in maintaining building security. It generally is advantageous to delineate space throughout the school campus both internally and externally. This is because delineating space as a defined area with a particular purpose helps to remove any perception that the space is available and open. It also makes it easier to assign security responsibilities for specific areas within a school's campus. One way to delineate space in the outside areas of a school campus is through the effective use of landscaping.

Landscaping can be used to define the outer boundaries of school property without the use of fences. Where fences are used, landscaping can be added to help create a more welcoming look while maintaining the security that the fences provide.

It is important to make sure landscaping is maintained so that it does not create hiding places. Shrubbery should be trimmed to a height of less than two feet. Tree canopies should be kept at a minimum height of eight feet, and hedges should be kept low enough to avoid serving as a hiding space. Controlling the growth of landscaping plants is also important to enabling clear lines of sight. Landscaping also can serve as a way to direct and control traffic, giving direction to vehicles and pedestrians, or limiting access to particular areas.

CHECKLIST – LANDSCAPING

- The school's landscape design does not create hiding places.
- The school's landscape design maintains open sight lines.
- The school's landscaping is well-maintained and is not overgrown.
- The school's landscaping does not block lighting.
- Shrubbery is kept at a maximum height of less than two feet.
- Tree canopies are trimmed to a minimum height of eight feet.

III. TRAINING AND EDUCATION

School staff, students and parents all play an important role in preventing criminal activity that results from unauthorized access. All school staff should be trained to intercept strangers and to report them to administration if they do not feel safe approaching a stranger on campus. Students should be instructed not to open doors or otherwise enable access by strangers. Students also should be instructed that they are not to assist other students in circumventing prescribed access procedures or routes. Parents should be provided with detailed information regarding the access control strategies that the school utilizes. Parents need to understand the importance of following the school's rules and procedures governing access to school facilities.

It is helpful to take inventory of particular skills or expertise staff members possess that would be useful in the event of an emergency, such as experience in firefighting, or search and rescue. Such individuals can be added to the school's crisis team. For examples of forms that can be used to conduct a staff skills inventory and to create a crisis team member list, see Form I-1 and Form I-2 in chapter nine.

The Pennsylvania Department of Education has set out school safety recommendations that encourage school staff and students to be watchful for and to report suspicious activities, including the following:
- an unusual interest in entry points, security points
  and/or access controls

- an interest in gaining site plans, bus routes, attendance lists or other sensitive information
- an unusual degree of interest in personnel or vehicles approaching or leaving facilities or parking areas
- observation of security drills and procedures
- prolonged surveillance by people appearing to be vendors or others not usually seen in the area, and
- an unexplained presence of people in areas where they should not be.

IV. WINDOWS AND DOORS

A. Exterior Doors

Exterior doors should be designed to prevent unauthorized building access. The National Clearinghouse for Educational Facilities offers a checklist that lists a number of desirable attributes for exterior school doors, including the following:

- Doors should have a minimal degree of exposed hardware and should be installed using non-removable pins.
- Although exit-only doors do not need outside locks and handles, access should be possible in some manner in an emergency, such as by using a proximity card.
- Doors should be made from steel, aluminum alloy, or solid-core hardwood. If constructed of glass, doors should be fully framed and equipped with tempered glass that is breakage-resistant.
- To prevent doors from being pried open, door frames should be installed without excess flexibility.
- Exterior locks should be mounted flush to the door surface and should not rely on protruding lock devices such as a key-in-knob device.
- Exterior swinging doors should be equipped with a deadbolt lock that is at least one inch with a one-inch throw bolt and hardened steel insert, as well as a free-turning glass or steel-tempered guard, and double-cylinder locks if glass is located within 40 inches of the locking mechanism.
- Panic bar latches should be protected by pick plates.
- Panic push bars should be equipped with tamper-proof deadbolt locks and a metal plate covering the gap between the doors.
- Strike plates should be securely fastened to door frames.
- If the door is key-controlled, it can be equipped with contacts so it can be tied into a central monitoring and control system.
- Double doors should be equipped with heavy-duty, multiple-point long flush bolts.

- If a door is particularly vulnerable to unauthorized use, consider installing door alarms or delayed opening devices, or using sensors or cameras to monitor it from a central location.

In addition, exterior doors should permit a view of the outside via narrow windows, sidelights, fish-eye viewers or cameras, while being configured so that an intruder cannot open the door from the inside by breaking a window or sidelight.

B. Windows

School administrators who want to provide staff and students with the advantages afforded by natural lighting should do so with an awareness of the security risks that windows can create, especially with respect to unauthorized entry.

Placement of windows plays a key role in minimizing unauthorized entry. Ideally windows are placed where they enable easy surveillance of school grounds, and especially higher-risk areas. For example, it is important to include windows that enable staff to monitor the school's main entrance. These windows should be kept free of announcements or other postings that create an obstacle to effective surveillance.

Of course, windows that are operable (that is, ones that can be opened and closed) should have locks that can secure them in a closed position. Window film can be used to reinforce window glass and hold it in place should it be subjected to impact. Second-floor windows should be inaccessible from the outside. Ideally each room should include at least one designated window that can be used as a means of escape in the event of an emergency.

Basement windows are an area of particular concern and should be protected by window well covers or grills.

V. SPECIFIC MEASURES AT ENTRANCEWAYS

The specific security measures implemented at entrance areas will depend on a number of factors, such as budget and incidence history. These measures are not undertaken singly but are part of a comprehensive overall security plan.

A. Metal Detectors

The use of metal detectors at school entrance points is an extreme measure that can help prevent unauthorized access but is often subject to criticism. Walk-through metal detectors can be utilized in conjunction with handheld detectors, which can be used to investigate further when an individual triggers the walk-through detector. Use of a walk-through detector requires a significant investment of space. The detector itself will typically fill a space approximately three-feet wide and two-feet deep. Of course, the staging area is much larger. It must allow enough room to provide a comfortable environment for those waiting to pass through. Space also is needed for people who are being scanned to place items in a pass-through container and to turn around and pass through a second time if needed. Care must be taken to locate the system in an area where it will not be subjected to potential sources of interference, such as nearby electromagnetic equipment or even plumbing in the walls.

Opponents of metal-detector use complain that such use is overly intrusive and creates an atmosphere of fear. Because metal detectors cannot distinguish between items that are dangerous (such as a knife) and items that are not (such as a set of keys), trained personnel are needed to operate and monitor them. This need, in combination with the cost of the detectors, the cost of hiring trained personnel to man them, and the fact that the layout of many schools makes it difficult to efficiently implement a metal-detection system, makes metal detection an impractical security tool for many schools. But metal detectors can also be an effective tool for reducing the likelihood of an unauthorized intrusion.

B. Closed-Circuit Television (CCTV)

Closed-circuit television technology can be used strategically to deter unauthorized access and to help prevent crime throughout the school campus. A CCTV system intended to prevent access by intruders must be designed with reference to, and in coordination with, conditions that exist at the school with respect to external lighting and landscaping conditions. When cameras are placed at external locations, steps should be taken to minimize the likelihood of compromises to performance that can arise due to vandalism and exposure to outdoor elements. These systems typically monitor entrance points and parking areas, recording images that can be preserved electronically. Decisions relating to placement are made with reference to the level of risk associated with particular areas. Although full-time monitoring of CCTV cameras is not financially feasible for many schools, CCTV creates a record of any suspicious or illegal activity and can serve as an effective deterrent.

C. Security Personnel/Greeters

The use of security guards and/or greeters is a low-tech but effective tool for preventing unauthorized access to a school's campus. Located at entrance points, security guards can check identifications and respond immediately to suspicious activities. Greeters, who are often parent volunteers, can serve a similar function at entrance points. Grandparents, caregivers, and retired community members also serve as good sources of greeters. The greeter's role is not to directly intervene to stop criminal activity. Instead, greeters can determine whether a visitor has a legitimate reason to be on the school's grounds and can direct the visitor to a specific location where he can complete applicable sign-in procedures. Ideally, greeters should also receive training relating to the school's evacuation plans and emergency procedures. Students should not be used as greeters.

D. Card Readers

Access-control card systems can be used to help keep track of who is entering a school facility. When this technology is used, an identification card is encoded and recognized by a card reader. When the reader recognizes the card, access is gained, such as by lifting a mechanical arm to permit access to a parking area. This system carries the advantage of not requiring live personnel to operate. But there are also potential drawbacks. Cards can be passed from one person to another person, and more than one individual or vehicle may be able to enter at the same time using just one authorized card.

E. Use of PIN Codes

Access can also be limited by requiring individuals to enter a personal identification number (PIN) code into a keypad in order to gain entrance to a designated area of the school. The use of PIN codes is more effective as a security measure when it is combined with the use of identification cards and card readers. Their use includes potential drawbacks, including a vulnerability to vandalism and the ability of authorized users to permit entry by unauthorized personnel.

F. Biometrics

Biometric devices permit access only upon identification of a particular physical trait associated uniquely with the authorized user. Examples include fingerprint readers, systems that verify identity by measuring the size and shape of the entering individual's hand, and technology that reads retinal impressions. This technology works in essence by collecting data relating to a specific individual's physical or behavioral characteristics and comparing it to data that already is on file. These devices carry the advantage of allowing authorized users to enter without having to remember any type of identification card. Because they rely on unique individual characteristics, they also carry the advantage of being more reliable than identifiers such as identification cards. Although biometric devices are more commonly used in applications that require the highest level of security, such as prisons and international border points, they may become more prevalent in school applications as technologies improve.

A 2006 evaluative study of an eye-scanning system used in three New Jersey elementary schools highlighted the advantages and shortcomings of relying on this particular type of biometric technology as an access security measure in the school setting. Teachers and staff, and more than 700 school parents, had their eye images scanned into a computer system. To gain access to the school, they were required to have a camera on school grounds scan images of their irises. Five cameras were placed in exterior locations, and another six were placed in interior locations. The study found that the system provided an accurate identification and unlocked the door 78% of the time. Another 6% of attempted entries were properly denied because the individuals' eye scans were not in the computer. But 16% of the time, there were problems with scanning due to outdoor lighting conditions or a failure of the individual to line up his eyes properly with the camera. Despite the shortcomings, parents and staff indicated a perceived increase in school security.

VI. LIGHTING

Proper illumination of entry areas and parking areas is a key to preventing unauthorized access to facilities. Because light fixtures are vulnerable to vandalism, they should be mounted as high as possible and covered with a material or housing that prevents breakage of lenses. Lighting fixtures can be controlled by clocks or by photocells that turn them off at dawn and on at dusk, although a manual override feature should be included. Lighting controls and switches must be protected, and the accessibility of electrical panels must be restricted.

Lights should be placed in a manner that minimizes glare and the creation of shadows. Ideally, the lighting near entrance points should cast a pattern of light horizontally rather than vertically. Flush-mounted or recessed light fixtures should be used when possible. Because light-colored surfaces reflect light more efficiently than dark-colored surfaces, the presence of light-colored surfaces at entry points will increase the overall level of entry-point security. Maintaining a fixed schedule for maintenance of all outdoor lighting, including lighting at entrance points, is another important safety key. Decisions relating to the provision of lighting must be made with reference to the need of lighting to work effectively with other security measures that may be in place, such as the use of closed-circuit television.

CHECKLIST - LIGHTING

- There is a regular schedule of maintenance for outside lights.
- Special attention is paid to adequacy of lighting at entrance points and other high-risk points of potential intrusion.
- Light lenses are protected by an impact-resistant material.
- Lighting fixtures do not provide handholds that can be used to climb into the building.
- Exterior lighting minimizes glare and shadows.

VII. CONTROLLING ACCESS BY VISITORS

A detailed procedure for controlling access to the school by authorized visitors is an essential component of a school safety plan. Visitors should be steered to a main entrance by clear appropriate signage and by the layout of the school's exterior. Ideally, they will be intercepted by a greeter or security officer outside the school building before they can proceed to sign in at a main office, where school personnel can verify that they are at the school for a legitimate purpose. Schools should strongly consider implementing a requirement that visitors produce photo identification to verify identity. Visitor badges, which must be located outside the reach of visitors in a secure area, should be dated and issued once authorization for the visit is confirmed. The date, time, name, purpose, and intended destination of the visitor should be recorded in a log that each visitor should sign. School personnel should accompany visitors to the specific area of the visit. An important but sometimes overlooked feature of a visitor access policy is the incorporation of a "checkout" procedure whereby the visitor surrenders his pass or badge before leaving and the time of the visitor's departure is noted in the school's log. The log should be checked periodically during the day to determine whether any visitor appears to be remaining at the school for an inordinate amount of time. For a sample authorization to release a student, see Form I-3 in chapter nine.

CHECKLIST – VISITOR POLICY

- School entrance points include signage that steers visitors to an office location.
- Sign-in areas are adequately staffed.
- Visitors must produce photo identification.
- Visitors are required to wear dated visitor passes or badges once authorization is confirmed.
- Visitors are escorted to their specific visit location.
- Visitor identification passes and badges are kept in a secure area.
- Visitors are required to sign a log indicating date, time, and intended destination.
- Visitor identification passes and badges are collected from visitor upon exit.
- Time of building exit is recorded in a log.

For steps key personnel should take in response to a school intruder, see Form II-12 in chapter nine. Information about specific steps to take in situations involving a weapon, and in potentially violent situations in general, can be found on Form I-4 and Form I-5 in chapter nine.

VIII. COORDINATING WITH FIRST RESPONDERS

Coordinating with first responders, such as police, fire and EMS personnel, is an important component to maintaining building security. In September 2007, the Attorney General of Pennsylvania introduced an innovative and novel tool that schools can use to improve coordination between schools and first responders in the event that security at a school's entrance is breached and an emergency response is required. The Attorney General's Office created a School Safety Project CD-ROM. Based on a program that was developed by a local school district within the state, the CD-ROM helps schools create building safety plans that first responders can access on Web sites in the event of an emergency. The CD-ROM helps districts create a secure Web site that includes information relating to many aspects of the facility, such as floor plans, photographs of school grounds, and a contact list of school administrators. The program on which the Attorney General's guide is based was developed by the Susquenita School District at a cost of approximately $1,000. First responders can access a password-protected Web site and view floor plans, school access roads, and photographs of classrooms and corridors. First responders can even access a real-time view of classrooms and offices, as the Web site includes images taken from school security cameras. This feature enables first responders to gain an inside view of the school building before entering.

IX. EFFECTIVE LOW-TECHNOLOGY ALTERNATIVES

Ideally, technological measures designed to protect entry points should be combined with less technical, but effective strategies and techniques to decrease the risk of criminal behavior. The U.S. Department of Justice's Office of Justice Programs has compiled the following list of low-technology but effective tools for deterring unauthorized entry to school facilities. Some of these measures are discussed elsewhere in this chapter. Utilizing the combination of them that best fits a particular school's needs can have the effect of increasing entry-point security.

- Post signs warning that unauthorized trespassers are subject to arrest.
- Post signs indicating that all vehicles on campus are subject to search.
- Provide a guard to check identifications at the main entrance to the school.
- Provide authorized vehicles with parking stickers so that unauthorized vehicles can be more easily identified and removed.
- Require student uniforms so that outsiders can be easily identified.
- Implement a school policy that bars hats; shirts that include messages related to alcohol, drugs, violence or gangs; and exposed tattoos.

- Provide greeters at all open entrances.
- Provide a minimal number of entrances.
- Implement a policy under which students walking around the school campus during class time are challenged for a pass and are potentially subjected to search.
- Close off the main student parking lot during the day.
- Provide fencing that defines school property and discourages casual intruders.
- Implement a policy under which the student identification cards of students who are suspended or expelled are confiscated and his or her photograph is made available to security staff.

X. CASE STUDY: INSTALLATION OF FACILITY MANAGEMENT SYSTEMS

The Harrison County School District Two, located near Colorado Springs, Colorado, serves more than 11,000 students and has 23 schools. In 2002, the district decided to upgrade its security systems at all of its schools, which included elementary schools, middle schools, high schools, alternative schools and charter schools. After soliciting several proposals, the district decided to install a security system that included closed-caption television, digital video recording, and card access control.

Early on in the installation, a vendor installed card readers on perimeter doors of schools and all staff members were issued combination identification badges and access cards. All exterior building locks were re-keyed, and key distribution was limited to a very small number.

A digital video recording unit was installed at every school in the district. Front lobbies in all schools were outfitted with cameras. Surveillance was added for exteriors and some interior areas. Digital video recorders replaced VCRs, and some secondary buildings were outfitted with pan-tilt-zoom cameras.

A policy was implemented whereby all perimeter school doors, except the ones at front lobby entrances, remained locked at all times. Cameras began recording all activity at lobby entrances at all times, with monitors enabling school staff to observe those areas. Each school's security system was linked to a central location, where monitors at all the school facilities could be viewed at all times. The installed system also enabled administrators and security personnel to view video from a remote location by using a Web browser.

The system was installed in a way that enabled it to interface with the district's pre-existing burglar alarm system. This alarm system alerted the district's private security company whenever an alarm was triggered after hours.

In cases of a security breach, the system enables personnel to export video clips to a CD-ROM for delivery to local law enforcement authorities.

The system includes an authentication process which verifies that stored video has not been altered.

A lockdown capability is also included. Staff can activate a button in the front office that locks perimeter doors and deactivates card readers. When a school is placed in lockdown, entry can occur only via the front door after staff has had the opportunity to view the person or persons seeking access, and chooses to permit access by manually unlocking the door.

The system also provides wireless personal panic control devices that are distributed to key personnel. These devices can be activated to signal a need for assistance from any location on the school grounds. When activated, the devices cause a white strobe light to turn on in the school's front office and send e-mails and pages to members of a designated response team.

The district reported tremendous success with the new system. Soon after installation was completed, an individual who entered three different school buildings during a lunch hour, and stole cash and credit cards from teachers' purses was caught on tape. The system also reduced fighting and vandalism.

XI. LEGAL DECISIONS

◆ A father drove his 12-year-old son to the premises of a Jesuit high school that the 12-year-old and his brother attended. The father waited outside in the car while the 12-year-old entered the school to find his brother, who was participating in a school event. The 12-year-old was accosted by a convicted sex felon who had gained unauthorized access to the school. He was taken to an unlocked men's restroom, where he was sexually assaulted. The incident took place on a Saturday, when school was not in session. The parent sued the school, its president and its principal, **claiming they were negligent in leaving the school doors unlocked and unattended during school-sponsored activities**. The court upheld a ruling against the parent, finding that he failed to show the defendants owed him a duty of care. There is generally no duty to protect others from the criminal acts of third parties. Although a duty may be found to exist when there is a special relationship between the defendant and the plaintiff, potentially including the relationship between a school and a student, a special relationship giving rise to a duty did not exist in this case. School was not in session, and the 12-year-old was not participating in any school-sponsored event at the time of the assault. In addition, the parent did not show that the assault was foreseeable. As a result, the decision against him was affirmed. *Roe v. Univ. of Detroit Jesuit High School and Academy*, No. 264269, 2006 WL 475285 (Mich. Ct. App. 2/28/06).

◆ A high school physical education teacher sued the city that employed her after an intruder entered her classroom and assaulted her. While teaching a volleyball class, the teacher noticed two young men come into the gym. She recognized one as a student at the school, but she did not recognize the second man. When the teacher walked toward the men and blew her whistle, the unknown man struck her in the left temple. The man left but returned a short time later and punched her in the back of the head, causing her to lose consciousness. She suffered serious injuries. **The teacher sued the city, claiming it was negligent as a landlord of the high school when it allowed the attacker to gain unauthorized access to the school.** She also claimed the city breached a special duty to protect her from harm and breached a contract with a teachers' union by failing to properly implement a school safety plan. The court granted the city's motion for summary judgment. Because the city was acting as a public government entity and not as a landlord when it undertook efforts to provide security at the school, it was immune to the teacher's claim of negligence. The court also rejected the teacher's claim that the city breached a special duty it owed to her when it allegedly failed to implement a school safety plan and protect its teachers. Neither the maintenance of a comprehensive security system nor school officials' representations that they "take security seriously" created a special duty. Finally, the court rejected the contract claim because the city could not be held liable to individual teachers for any alleged contract breach between it and the teacher's union. The city's motion for summary judgment was granted. *Daniels v. City of New York*, No. 04-CV-7612 (CM), 2007 WL 2040581 (S.D.N.Y. 6/26/07).

◆ While leaving her high school following her last class for the day, a student inadvertently bumped shoulders with another student. The second student told the first that "she was going to kill her." The first student then met her sister, who also attended the school, in another area of the school. She attempted to report the incident at a security office, but she received no response when she knocked at the door. She and her sister were then assaulted as they attempted to leave the school. **The second student struck one of the sisters in the head and elbow with a hammer, and the second student's brother, who was not a student at the school, stabbed the other.** The sisters sued the city's board of education and others, claiming negligent supervision. A jury returned a verdict of $50,000 for one of the sisters and $750,000 for the other. A lower court set aside the verdict and dismissed the complaint, finding that the evidence did not prove negligent supervision. On appeal, the court reinstated the verdict, finding that the jury could permissibly find that the board failed to provide adequate supervision when it was most needed. *Mirand v. City of New York*, 190 A.D.2d 282 (N.Y. App. Div. 1993).

◆ While providing instruction in her classroom, a teacher was confronted by four intruders. One of the intruders accused the teacher of having physically abused a student. The intruder then assaulted the teacher with a metal chair, causing back injuries. **The teacher sued the board of**

education, claiming it was negligent because it failed to monitor and control the people who entered the school. The teacher also claimed that the school negligently failed to provide proper security and created a dangerous condition. In addition, she claimed the board breached a union contract that required school principals to develop safety plans. The court granted the board's motion for summary judgment. The board was immune to the negligence claim because the provision of security was a governmental function rather than a proprietary function. The court rejected the teacher's claim that the school assumed a special duty to protect her and thus was not immune to the negligence claims against it. The teacher alleged that this special duty arose when the school's principal told her not to worry because she was "in a good school." She also alleged that a special duty arose based on the collective bargaining agreement between the teachers' union and the board. The court held that neither the principal's statement nor a collective bargaining agreement provision requiring principals to develop safety plans created a special duty. Therefore, the teacher's negligence claims failed and summary judgment was awarded to the board. *Genao v. Board of Educ. of the City of New York*, 888 F.Supp. 501 (S.D.N.Y. 1995).

◆ The parent of a high school student complained to the school's principal after the student broke his leg during a school football practice. The parent claimed that the student received no medical attention from any of the coaches present at the practice. Two years later, the parent complained to the principal again after the student was inserted into a football game even though he was feeling ill. A short time after he made the complaint, the principal barred the parent from entering any school district property except to drop off and pick up his son. The principal also circulated a memo stating that he physically feared the parent and that the parent was "the most out-of-control parent [the principal] had witnessed in 31 years of education." The parent later sued the school district, claiming it violated his constitutional rights by barring him from school property. The court granted the district's motion to dismiss the claim. The court was unable to locate any authority for the proposition that the parent had a constitutional right to enter school property. To the contrary, **school officials have a right to assure that parents conduct themselves properly while they are on school property**. The parent did not show that the decision to bar him from school property violated his constitutional rights. *Van Deelen v. Shawnee Mission Unified School Dist. #512*, 316 F.Supp.2d 1052 (D. Kan. 2004).

◆ As he entered his public high school in Philadelphia, a student was instructed by a school employee to remove his coat and place his book bag on a table to be searched. The employee then scanned the student with a metal detector and patted him down. All entering students were subjected to the same scan and pat-down procedure that day. When the employee felt a bulge resembling a knife in the student's coat, he searched the coat and found a box cutter in one of its pockets. The student was later arrested and charged with possession of a weapon on school property. At the criminal trial, his motion to suppress the physical evidence was denied, and he was convicted and placed on probation. He appealed, claiming the physical evidence should have been suppressed because he had been subjected to an unlawful search and seizure. **The student claimed the search and seizure were unlawful because there was no reasonable suspicion or probable cause to believe he had violated any law or school regulation.** The court held that that the search did not violate the student's constitutional rights. Administrative searches are permitted even in the absence of individualized suspicion when they are conducted as part of a general regulatory scheme to ensure public safety. The search was reasonably related to the school's interest in promoting student safety, and it was justified because of the high rate of violence that was present in the Philadelphia public schools. In addition, all students were subjected to the search, and the uniform procedure that was followed assured that officials would not improperly exercise discretion with respect to the searches. The order adjudicating the student delinquent was affirmed. *Ex rel. S.S.,* 680 A.2d 1172 (Pa. Super. Ct. 1996).

◆ A public high school in Philadelphia periodically subjected all students to a point-of-entry search for weapons. When the searches were conducted, students were required to stand in line and empty their pockets while their backpacks, coats and other personal effects were searched. Students were also scanned by a hand-held metal detector. During one such search, a student removed a Swiss army-type knife from his pocket. He was arrested for bringing a weapon onto school property and was adjudicated delinquent after a juvenile hearing. After a court affirmed the disposition, the student appealed again. On appeal, he renewed his argument that the evidence should have been suppressed because the search was made without any individualized reasonable suspicion. The court rejected the argument and affirmed the lower court's decision. **The search was justified because it affected a limited privacy interest and was minimally intrusive.** In addition, the student population and parents were notified of the purpose of the search and the manner in which it was conducted via a school policy and procedure manual, mailings, and notices that were posted throughout the school. The purpose of the search – to keep weapons out of public schools – was compelling. Therefore, the search did not violate the student's constitutional rights. *Ex rel. F.B.,* 726 A.2d 361 (Pa. 1999).

◆ A high school subjected its students to random searches for weapons using a hand-held metal detector. The school provided students and their parents with notice of this practice before it was instituted. On one day, the school decided to search all students who entered the attendance office without hall passes or who were late. A knife was found in the pocket of one of the students who was searched, and she was charged with the crime of bringing a knife onto school grounds. The trial court denied her motion to suppress the evidence and sustained the petition against her. She appealed, challenging the denial of her motion to suppress the evidence. The appeals court affirmed the lower court's decision. **Special needs administrative searches can be conducted without individualized suspicion so long as the government need is great, the privacy intrusion is limited in nature, and it would be unworkable to require a more rigorous standard of suspicion.** In this case, the searches were minimally intrusive, and it would be unworkable to institute a system that relied more on suspicion. Therefore, the search did not violate the student's rights under the Fourth Amendment. *People v. Latasha W.*, 70 Cal.Rptr.2d 886 (Cal. Ct. App. 1998).

◆ An alternative learning center, which was attended by students who had been removed from other school campuses due to disciplinary problems, subjected all students entering the center to a search. **The search, which was conducted every day, required students to pass through a metal detector, be patted down, remove their shoes for inspection, and empty their pockets.** All students and parents attended an orientation session that included a description of the search policy. During a search, an examining officer found a marijuana cigarette inside the shoe of a student. At a trial held to determine whether he should be adjudicated delinquent, the student filed a motion to suppress the evidence. The motion was denied, and the student was adjudicated delinquent. He appealed, renewing his argument that the evidence should have been suppressed because it was discovered as a result of an unlawful search. The court rejected the student's argument and affirmed the lower court's decision. Even though the search was not conducted based on individualized suspicion, it was justified by the school's need to maintain a safe learning environment in a high-risk setting. Public school students are subject to a greater degree of supervision than adults, and the state had a compelling interest in maintaining safe schools. In addition, the uniform nature of the searches guarded against an abuse of discretion by administrators. The search was an administrative search that intruded on the privacy of students only to the extent necessary to satisfy the state's interest in maintaining safety. The lower court's ruling was affirmed. *In re O.E.*, No. 03-02-00516-CV, 2003 WL 22669014 (Tex. Ct. App. 11/13/03).

◆ A school chancellor adopted guidelines for searching students as they entered public high schools. Under the guidelines, several schools were selected for periodic scanning. At the start of the school year, students at the selected schools were told they would be subjected to a search at some point. The students were not told ahead of time precisely when the searches would take place. Although all entering students were potentially subject to being searched, the guidelines allowed personnel to limit the search, such as by searching every second or third student. Any student chosen to be searched was asked to place bags and parcels on a table, and to remove any metal objects from pockets. Students were then scanned with a metal detector. When a bag or parcel activated the detector, students were asked to open the bag or parcel. If a body scan activated the detector, students were again asked to remove metal objects. Students were taken to a private area if a second body scan activated the detector again. They were then asked a third time to remove metal objects before being subjected to a pat-down search. A student who was subjected to a search under the guidelines was arrested after a metal detector activated on her bag and a knife was discovered inside. She filed a motion to suppress the evidence, arguing it was discovered in violation of the Fourth Amendment. The court denied the motion. **The search was permissible because the need to maintain school safety outweighed the minimally intrusive nature of the searches.** In addition, the searches were permissible even though the guidelines did not include any provision requiring administrators to gain the consent of students before conducting a search. Children are required to attend school, and a consent element "would be all but impossible to administer." The motion was denied. *People v. Dukes*, 580 N.Y.S.2d 850 (N.Y. Crim. Ct. 1992).

◆   To prevent students from entering with weapons, a public high school set up metal detectors that students passed through shortly after they entered. A student entered the school and turned around to leave when he saw other students lined up to pass through a metal detector. When he was stopped by a police officer and told he would be required to go through the detector, he raised his shirt to reveal a pistol and said "someone put this gun on me." The student was arrested, and he filed a motion to suppress the evidence. The trial court sustained the motion, finding that **the student could have turned around for innocent reasons that were unrelated to the metal detector**. The state appealed, but the reviewing court affirmed the lower court's decision. A person is seized when his freedom of movement is restrained, and the student's detention constituted an illegal seizure. Although the state argued that the officer was performing an administrative search, the cases it relied on to support its argument did not prevent people from choosing not to pass through a checkpoint. In addition, the officer did not have a reasonable suspicion to believe the search would turn up incriminating evidence. Instead, the decision to order the student to pass through the detector was based on a hunch. The order suppressing the evidence was affirmed. *People v. Parker*, 672 N.E.2d 813 (Ill. App. Ct. 1996).

◆   The parent of a student who was fatally shot at his high school sued the city, the board of education and others. The parent claimed the city and board negligently allowed people who were armed and dangerous to gain unauthorized access to the school and failed to use metal detectors at the school on the day of the shooting. The parent further claimed that by placing metal detectors at the school, the city and board voluntarily assumed a duty to provide special protection against criminal acts by third persons. In addition, she separately claimed that the city and board owed a special duty to the student because he was in their direct and immediate control and because they were uniquely aware that he was at risk. A lower court issued a ruling against the parent, and she appealed. The appeals court affirmed the lower court's ruling. The city's decision to use metal detectors at the school did not negate the immunity it enjoyed under a tort immunity statute. Nor did a special duty exception to immunity apply, because the parent did not show that a special relationship existed between the city and the student. For similar reasons, the decision favoring the board was affirmed. **The decision to use metal detectors did not make the board an insurer against all criminal activity.** In addition, there was no showing that the decision not to use the metal detectors every day increased the incidence of crime at the school. The lower court's ruling was affirmed. *Lawson v. City of Chicago*, 662 N.E.2d 1377 (Ill. App. Ct. 1996).

◆ The father of two children sought a divorce from his wife. The wife obtained a temporary restraining order splitting custody of the children. A school policy allowed students to leave with their parents provided the approval of the principal was first obtained. The date and time of student departure and return was to be recorded with the reason for leaving school. The father became upset when he came to school and learned his mother-in-law had taken the children to their mother. The mother told staff not to release the children to their father, but a staff member said that would require a court order. The next day, the father came to the school for both children. The reasons he gave for signing them out were "keeping promise by mother" for the daughter and "pay back" for the son. The son's teacher read the reasons after he left and notified the principal. However, the father had already left with both children. Police arrived at his house to find it ablaze. The father brandished a knife, and the police shot him to death. The children's bodies were found inside the house. The mother sued the school board in a state court for negligence.

The court held for the board, and the mother appealed. The state court of appeals held that schools, teachers, and school administrators have a duty to exercise ordinary care for student safety. The board was not liable for negligently violating its own sign-out policy. There was no evidence that staff knew about a dispute until the mother called the day before the murders. The trial court correctly held that a school has no legal duty to follow the instruction of one parent not to release a child to the other parent without a court order to that effect. The court affirmed judgment on a claim based on the father's violent nature. However, failure to read his reasons for signing out the children was evidence of breach of the duty to exercise ordinary care for the children's safety. **The court rejected the board's claim that it had no legal duty to examine a parent's reason for signing out a child.** The reasons the father gave for signing out the children might cause a reasonable person to suspect he intended to cause them harm. The state Governmental Tort Liability Act did not protect the board, since the decision to release the children did not involve planning. The decision was reversed, and the case was remanded for further proceedings. *Haney v. Bradley County Board of Educ.*, 160 S.W.2d 886 (Tenn. Ct. App. 2004).

◆ A parent who was visiting a school got into a confrontation with a school employee. A school safety agent witnessed the confrontation and attempted to separate the parent and the school employee. The school safety agent advised the school employee to walk away from the confrontation. The school employee walked to a staircase to return to her classroom. Moments later, the parent followed the school employee into the stairwell and attacked her. The parent sued the board of education to recover for the injuries she sustained. A trial court denied the board's motion for summary judgment, but the appeals court reversed the trial court's ruling. **The appeals court held that the parent did not show that the school safety agent had assumed an affirmative duty to act to prevent the attack.** The parent did not show that the school agent was aware that the parent posed a threat of violence. Therefore, the board was not liable for the school employee's injuries. *France v. New York City Board of Educ.*, 834 N.Y.S.2d 193 (N.Y. App. Div. 2007).

◆ A deranged convicted felon entered a school building holding a picture of a young girl. The school principal confronted the intruder, who then left. The school subsequently instituted a new access control policy. An individual was stationed in the school's lobby to screen people entering the school, and people entering the school were instructed to sign in at the principal's office. The policy further required staff to monitor visitors through a floor-to-ceiling window in the principal's office. Approximately one year following the incident involving the intruder, a different intruder gained unauthorized access to the school. **The intruder walked between 100 and 150 feet into the school before stopping in a school hallway and attacking a 10-year-old student with a hammer. The attack caused serious injury.** The student's parents sued the school's principal, the county school superintendent, the board of education and others, alleging they were negligent in failing to develop a school safety plan as required by state law and allowing the attack to occur. A trial court granted the defendants' motion for summary judgment, and an appeals court affirmed the trial court's ruling. The school had prepared and put into place a school safety plan before the attack on the student took place. Because the school safety plan was in place before the attack occurred, the defendants were entitled to official immunity on the negligence claims raised against them. The ruling of the trial court was affirmed. *Leake v. Murphy*, 644 S.E.2d 328 (Ga. Ct. App. 2007).

◆ A high school secretary noticed a neatly dressed man carrying what appeared to be flower boxes near a school entrance. The secretary asked the man if she could help him. He uttered an incoherent response, thanked her, and moved along. A short time later, the man was observed by an individual who worked at the school as a water safety instructor. At the time, the man was standing between a swimming pool and bleachers. **The layout of the school building made it easy to become disoriented, and it was not unusual for male visitors to become disoriented and walk through the girls' locker room.** The water safety instructor, who also believed the man was delivering flowers, concluded that he had reached the area by walking through the girls' locker room. She began to walk toward him to ask why he was in the building. While doing so, she met a school custodian who had also seen the man exit from the girls' locker room into a lobby area. When the custodian saw the man, he commented that it was odd to see someone coming out of the girls' locker room. The man again uttered an incoherent remark and moved on. About an hour after the secretary first saw the man, she observed him again near a school entrance. This time, the man was talking to a student. She did not confront him, even though she later admitted that he did not belong in that location because it was not the school's main entrance. A short time later, the man sexually assaulted a student in the locker room. The student's parents sued the school district, claiming it failed to provide adequate supervision and security. A lower court granted immunity to the individual school employees but not to the school district, and the school district appealed. The appeals court affirmed, finding that the school district was not entitled to immunity on the parents' claims. **The employees engaged in discretionary acts which deserved the protection of official immunity. However, this immunity did not extend to the school district. If it did, the district would be rewarded for failing to develop and implement a basic security policy.** The lower court's ruling was affirmed. *S.W. v. Spring Lake Park School Dist. No. 16*, 592 N.W.2d 870 (Minn. Ct. App. 1999).

◆ A high school teacher brought a 14-year-old special education student to the assistant principal's office, stating that she had found the student walking in the school's hallways. The assistant principal claimed that the student failed to correctly identify herself by name. The student was unable to provide her home address, student identification number, or telephone number. The student did provide the telephone number of a man she said was her uncle. The assistant principal decided to suspend the student for truancy and insubordination. **School policy barred the release of students to anyone other than a parent, legal guardian, police authority, or a person designated in writing by a parent. Nonetheless, the assistant principal allowed the student to call the man she identified as her uncle to arrange for her to be picked up from school.** Although he told the student he needed to meet with the supposed uncle before she could be released, the assistant principal then left the student alone in the lobby of the school's main office without assigning anyone to supervise her. He then forgot about her. At some point during the day the man identified by the student as her uncle picked her up from school and allegedly sexually abused her at his home. The student's mother sued the vice principal and the school district, asserting due process and state law claims. A magistrate judge granted summary judgment in favor of the assistant principal, finding that he was immune from suit. The mother appealed. The appeals court affirmed the decision in favor of the assistant principal. The assistant principal was entitled to qualified immunity on the student's federal claims because the student did not adequately allege a violation of substantive due process. The student claimed the assistant principal was liable to her on her federal claims because the assistant principal had a duty to protect her from third-party violence due to the existence of a special relationship between her and the assistant principal. The assistant principal was not obligated to protect the student due to a special relationship. The student could not prove her claim that the assistant principal had a duty to protect her because he created the danger that led to her alleged harm. The student could not prove this claim because the assistant principal did not restrain the student in a way that created a constitutional obligation to protect her. In addition, he did not act with deliberate indifference. The student's state-law claims failed as well, because the assistant principal's actions did not result in the student's alleged injury. The decision of the lower court was affirmed. *Doe v. San Antonio Independent School Dist.*, 197 Fed.Appx. 296 (5th Cir. 2006).

◆ A high school student sued a board of education, a high school and others after she was raped in a school bathroom by a non-student intruder. **The student alleged that the defendants wrongfully failed to provide security guards in the area of the alleged attack and near the exterior doors of the school building.** The student claimed that students frequently opened exterior doors of the school to allow other students to enter from the outside. The board of education, high school and private security firm appealed a trial court's decision to deny their motions for summary judgment. The appeals court reversed the trial court's ruling. The alleged security deficiencies arose from the allocation of security resources, which was a governmental function. Because decisions relating to the allocation of school security resources are in the nature of a governmental function, the district and high school could not be held liable unless they had a special relationship with the student that created a special duty to protect her. No special duty existed in this case, as there was no direct contact between the student and the school defendants before the alleged attack. In addition, the school defendants did not have notice of prior sexual assaults at the school and had no reason to anticipate that an intruder would enter the school to commit a violent crime against a student. Finally, the claim against the private security firm failed because the school defendants controlled the security guards at the school. The lower court's ruling was reversed. *Doe v. Town of Hempstead Board of Educ.*, 795 N.Y.S.2d 322 (N.Y. App. Div. 2005).

◆   A substitute teacher sued a board of education after she was attacked by a school intruder, claiming the board negligently failed to provide adequate security. The court reversed a trial court's decision to deny summary judgment to the board. The court explained that **because the provision of security against attacks by school intruders is a governmental function, there is no liability unless there is a special duty to protect**. In this case, there was no special duty to protect the substitute teacher. The implementation of security measures did not create a special duty, and the board made no special promise of protection to the substitute teacher. The trial court's decision was reversed. *Bain v. New York City Board of Educ.*, 702 N.Y.S.2d 334 (N.Y. App. Div. 2000).

◆   A teacher selected one of her fourth-grade students to supervise a classroom of second-graders while their teacher went to retrieve supplies from another part of the building. While the teacher was away, the fourth-grader was lured from the second-grade classroom by an intruder. The intruder exited the school with the student by proceeding through an unlocked rear door and through an open gate of a security fence. He then forced her into a wooded area, where he raped her. The student's mother sued the school district, claiming negligence. A jury found in her favor and awarded nearly $251,000 in damages. The district appealed, arguing that it could not be held liable in negligence because the actions of the intruder were not foreseeable. The appeals court rejected the argument and upheld the jury's verdict. There was enough evidence for the jury to find that school officials were on notice that students were in danger of being assaulted by intruders. The school was located in a statistically high crime area, and there had been sexual assaults and other violent crime in the surrounding area. In addition, school security was deficient in several ways. **The gate on a security fence at the rear of the school was left open and unlocked, and a set of doors at the back of the school did not close and lock properly due to an alignment problem. Doors at the front of the school did not close properly, and an intercom system was not functioning properly at the time of the assault.** Further, unaccompanied and unknown adult males were permitted to roam school hallways. All of these things raised a factual issue of foreseeability that was properly submitted to the jury. The trial court's judgment was affirmed. *District of Columbia v. Doe*, 524 A.2d 30 (D.C. Ct. App. 1987).

◆   A teacher at a day care center was killed when a local resident with a history of mental illness entered the center through an unlocked rear entrance and shot her. The center was operated out of a wing of a local high school. The rear entrance was open because it was being used by several contractors who were working on construction projects at the high school. The teacher's husband sued the school district and owner of the day care center under 42 U.S.C. § 1983, claiming they created the danger that resulted in the teacher's death by unlocking the back entrance for the contractors. A trial court ruled against him, and he appealed. The appeals court affirmed the ruling against the teacher's husband. The state generally has no obligation to protect citizens from the violent acts of private individuals. Although an exception to this rule applies when the state creates a danger that causes harm, the exception was not applicable in this case. **The district could not have foreseen that allowing construction workers to use the back entrance would result in the shooting, and it did not willfully or deliberately disregard a foreseeable danger.** The trial court's ruling was affirmed. *Morse v. Lower Merion School Dist.*, 132 F.3d 902 (3d Cir. 1997).

CHAPTER TWO

Emergency Preparedness and Response

I. INTRODUCTION

Within a span of 10 years we have had Columbine, September 11th, and the hurricanes Katrina and Rita – in addition to numerous other disasters that threatened the lives of students and staff and seriously impacted the ability of schools to do their job of educating the young.

In response to the growing threats of violence and terrorism, as well as increasingly brutal natural disasters, most school districts have developed crisis management plans. In fact, 95% of them have, according to a 2007 report by the GAO (Government Accountability Office), the agency that acts as the investigative arm of Congress.

This chapter will first consider the state of the law on these plans and then discuss their basic elements before providing more detail about the crisis management issues that government agencies believe still need to be addressed if schools are to provide the best possible protection for students and everyone else at school.

II. LAWS AND DECISIONS CONCERNING SCHOOL CRISIS MANAGEMENT PLANS

School crisis management plans are governed primarily by state law. Although the federal government has provided a wealth of information and advice to schools concerning crisis management and does expect schools to achieve National Incident Management System (NIMS) compliance as part of wider local government NIMS compliance, the only federal mandates for districts are attached to the receipt of federal funds – such as Readiness and Emergency Management grants offered by the U.S. Department of Education's Office of Safe and Drug-Free Schools.

Most school districts across the United States have followed federal advice to prepare detailed plans for handling emergencies at school, but not all states have passed laws that require them to do so. Some states have laws requiring these plans at schools, but those laws vary from state to state.

There is less variation and more common ground in the legal rules developed through case law in the courts. Although school crisis management plans have not been around long enough to generate a large body of case law, the legal claims that students, teachers and others have raised based on a school's adoption of school safety planning have been analyzed under pre-existing legal rules – such as rules governing state and federal constitutional claims, school liability for personal injury, disability discrimination, employment and libel. Generally speaking, students and teachers are almost never successful in holding schools responsible for the injury or loss that they allege was caused by the school's failure to have an adequate safety plan in place.

A. Laws

No act of Congress requires schools to have crisis management plans. Laws that require written plans are all at the state level – but not all states have them. When Congress asked the GAO to look into schools' emergency preparedness, only about two-thirds of the states – 32 – told the GAO that they had specific laws or policies requiring the creation of crisis management plans.

Even though state and federal law may not obligate them to do so, an overwhelming majority of school districts – 95% – have written crisis plans in place. And 85% of all U.S. school districts are subject to some type of requirement (either a state law or a district policy) that requires schools to develop their own plans.

As high as these numbers are, the National Association of Attorneys General's Task Force on School and Campus Safety would like to see them go even higher. The task force has recommended that states condition school funding on whether schools have emergency management plans in place. The task force would also like states to make it a requirement that schools conduct regular crisis drills of the plans and include staff, students and the community's emergency responders in these drills.

But because there is no federal law addressing school crisis management plans, there is no uniform set of rules that applies to every school crisis management plan at every school in every state. State laws vary greatly from one state to the next – which makes sense, given the significant state-to-state variations in culture, weather conditions and geographical features.

B. Conducting a Risk Assessment

Recognizing this diversity, the U.S. Department of Education encourages districts to begin crisis planning by taking local conditions into account to anticipate disasters they are most likely to face. The Model Emergency Plan for the Schools, posted at the National Incident Management System Web site, nimsonline.com, was created by a team in California's San Francisco-Oakland Bay area. Not surprisingly, in addition to the other emergencies it specifically addresses, this plan contains a special extended section on earthquakes.

Plans in other states focus on disasters that are more likely to occur in their areas based on particular characteristics relating to weather or the physical environment. For example, in the Midwest tornados are a concern. The Gulf States have already faced devastating hurricanes. Other parts of the country are prone to relatively harsh winters or an increased likelihood of severe flooding. For a form outlining steps key personnel should take in the event of a weather emergency, see Form II-1 in chapter nine.

Some schools are located in the vicinity of man-made risks, such as nuclear power plants or factories that produce toxic materials. Because of the wide range of potential crises, and because the risks vary greatly from place to place, school crisis management plans must be tailored to address the likely risks facing each school.

While districts are encouraged to start their planning by engaging in specific risk assessment, the Federal Emergency Management Agency warns school officials not to assume that they know all the local dangers. They suggest that those involved with planning visit fema.gov or contact their state emergency management office to find out if there are non-apparent natural or man-made disaster risks in the area, such as nearby railroads or highways where hazardous chemicals are regularly transported.

C. Plan Requirements

There is variety in the crisis-planning requirements in the laws of the states, but there are also plenty of common threads. Some typical state requirements for school plans include:

- holding training drills (approximately 21 states, including Florida, Nevada, New Jersey and Alaska)
- planning for the disasters the law specifies (approximately 18 states, including Utah, Vermont, Illinois and Massachusetts)
- reviewing and revising the plan regularly (approximately 18 states, including South Carolina, Mississippi, Maine and Indiana), and
- using input from police, fire departments and other emergency services providers to develop the plan (approximately 16 states, including Georgia, New York, Ohio and California).

Although the laws governing the details of school crisis plans all exist at the state level, schools can be required to follow specified federal standards for their plans as a condition for receiving federal funds.

For example, 91 school districts in 32 states were awarded Readiness and Emergency Management for Schools grants in 2007. Ranging from $83,000 to $773,500, the grants were authorized by the Office of Safe and Drug-Free Schools.

Before filling out their applications, grant applicants were instructed to review the office's publication *Practical Information on Crisis Planning: A Guide for Schools and Communities.*

To be awarded a grant, applicants had to agree to:

- develop their crisis management plans by working with five community-based partners (law enforcement, public safety, public health, mental health, and the head of the local government)
- demonstrate that their plans addressed the needs of individuals with disabilities, and
- include written pandemic plans that included disease surveillance and data gathering, their protocol for deciding whether to close schools, their plan for continuing instruction if school was closed, and their plan to keep the school's essential functions operational during and after the crisis.

The grant recipients also agreed to follow their state or local Homeland Security Plan's requirements and meet all National Incident Management System (NIMS) requirements by the end of the grant period.

NIMS is the uniform U.S. system for responding to emergencies. Created by a Homeland Security presidential directive in 2004, it specifies standardized methods that state and federal emergency responders must follow.

Because school districts don't fall under the traditional definition of emergency responders, public school personnel aren't generally required to take NIMS' IS-700 introductory course or comply with NIMS requirements unless the school district's local government requires compliance. But as with all the requirements listed above, state compliance that would otherwise only be discretionary can be made a condition for receiving money from the government.

D. Legal Decisions

Crisis management plans have been around long enough to generate some court cases. There is more uniformity in the judicial decisions than there is in the state laws, probably because most of these cases have been decided based on precedent set by earlier lawsuits against schools. The largest subset of cases involves injuries at school, i.e., cases raising state law claims of personal injury or federal allegations that an injury amounts to a constitutional deprivation.

1. Safety Plans Do Not Create Duty

Generally speaking, students and teachers have not been able to hold schools responsible for injuries caused by other students – or even intruders – by arguing that the school's crisis planning somehow created a duty to ensure their safety.

One basic rule in these cases is that courts virtually never find the state (here, the public school or the police) legally responsible for the violent acts of private individuals.

There are two very narrow exceptions to this rule. The first exception is the **state-created danger (or enhanced danger) doctrine**. The second is the **special relationship doctrine**.

Under the **state-created danger doctrine**, the state can be held responsible for a person's injury if the state's actions either created the danger that caused the injury or somehow made that danger significantly greater. This is an extremely widespread doctrine in the United States. The only federal circuit court of appeals that hasn't adopted it is the Fifth U.S. Circuit Court of Appeal, which has jurisdiction over Louisiana, Mississippi and Texas.

Under the second exception, the **special relationship doctrine**, the injured party can prevail by showing that the government took actions that created a legal duty to protect him or her.

The decision in a case filed after the Columbine shootings clearly illustrates the operation of the legal framework described above. The court that dismissed most of the personal injury lawsuits brought by students and teachers in the wake of the Columbine shootings almost always followed the rule that the state was not legally responsible for private individuals' violent acts. But this same court refused to dismiss the following case, in which both the state-created danger and special-relationship exceptions to the rule applied.

◆   The police created a legal duty to protect a Columbine teacher who bled to death after medical attention was delayed for four hours. **The police interfered with the teacher's ability to save himself and took actions that increased his danger of bleeding to death.**

A teacher was standing outside a cafeteria packed with early lunch period students when he saw two students approaching with guns. The teacher went into the cafeteria and shouted for the other students to run. He lagged behind until the last of the students escaped up a stairway. As he was urging the last ones up the stairs, one of the gunmen shot him twice in the back. The teacher managed to shepherd approximately 50 students into an upstairs classroom before he collapsed.

The teacher had spotted the gunmen at approximately 11:35 a.m. and was shot about five minutes later. Perhaps half an hour after that, rooftop police sharpshooters with high-powered binoculars saw the gunmen commit suicide in the library.

Although the officers in command knew about the suicides almost immediately, they incorrectly characterized the state of affairs inside the school as a "hostage situation" and followed "hostage situation" procedure by allowing no one in or out of the building – including the firefighters and SWAT team that wanted to rescue the teacher and the emergency medical staff that wanted to provide him onsite care.

Inside the classroom, another teacher and several students applied makeshift compresses to staunch the injured teacher's bleeding. By 12:30 p.m., at least two people had made 9-1-1 calls – which were relayed to the responding officers – to report how seriously the teacher had been injured and to tell emergency responders exactly where to find him. They also hung a large sign in the window reading: "1 BLEEDING TO DEATH."

An uninjured teacher spent the afternoon keeping 9-1-1 operators informed of the deterioration of the injured teacher's condition. Starting at around noon and continuing for more than three hours, the 9-1-1 operators kept relaying the police's message that help was "on the way" and would arrive soon, and that no one should leave the classroom to seek medical help.

At around 2:00 p.m., a 9-1-1 operator alerted the police that the people in the classroom were threatening to throw chairs through the windows to attract help for the injured teacher. Although the police knew the gunmen were dead, they told the operator to say this plan was more likely to draw the gunmen than medical help. About half an hour later, an uninjured teacher tried to leave the school to find a medic, but a SWAT team member, acting under police orders, forcibly pushed him back inside.

Once rescue personnel did enter the building, the injured teacher was the last wounded person they reached – even though he was the only person identified as someone who could be saved by emergency medical treatment and they had been told exactly where to find him. A SWAT team finally reached him at 4:00 p.m. By that time, his originally survivable injuries had become fatal. He died.

The deceased teacher's personal representative sued the board of county commissioners, the sheriff's department and several individual officials, alleging deprivation of life in violation of the deceased teacher's right to due process. The United States District Court for the District of Colorado denied the government defendants' request to dismiss the suit.

The district court explained that the U.S. Supreme Court held in 1989 that the Fourteenth Amendment's Due Process Clause does not impose a duty on a state to protect individuals from private acts of violence. Its purpose is "to protect the people from the State, not to ensure that the State protects them from each other." *DeShaney v. Winnebago County Dep't of Social Services*, 489 U.S. 189, 109 S.Ct. 998, 103 L.Ed.2d 249 (1989).

However, the district court continued, the Tenth U.S. Circuit Court of Appeals – which has jurisdiction over Colorado – had adopted two exceptions to this rule, both of which applied here. The special relationship doctrine applied because the government created a duty to protect this teacher by interfering with his ability to save himself, falsely assuring those caring for him that help was coming soon and ordering them not to seek other aid. The state-created danger exception also applied because the police took actions that increased the teacher's danger of bleeding to death by keeping him from the medical treatment that could have saved his life. *Sanders v. Board of County Commissioners of County of Jefferson, Colorado*, 192 F.Supp.2d 1094 (D. Colo. 2001).

Most personal injury cases that focus on schools' crisis planning follow this framework. Courts have not been persuaded by injured students' and teachers' arguments that schools should be held legally responsible for their injuries because of the fact that the schools had – or didn't have – a crisis plan. Instead, to hold the schools liable, courts have insisted the injured parties must establish that either the special relationship doctrine or the state-created danger exception applies.

◆   A gym teacher who was hospitalized after an intruder's attack couldn't sue the city for her injuries. **The court rejected her argument that the city created a special relationship with her by putting safety measures in place, and then breached its duty of protection to her by not complying with its own school safety plan.**

A strange man appeared in the gym during class. He struck the teacher and then left. The teacher sent a student to alert a security guard about the intruder, but the student came back to say he couldn't find a guard. The intruder returned unnoticed and hit the teacher from behind, knocking her unconscious. Her injuries included a fractured skull, a fractured rib and hemorrhaging around her left temple.

The teacher sued the city for personal injury, but the court granted the city summary judgment.

New York law almost always found the city immune to personal injury suits based on the operation of a school's security system. The only exception to this was if the injured party could prove a special relationship existed which created a duty of protection. This teacher couldn't establish the existence of a special relationship.

The teacher claimed the school assumed a special duty to protect her because it implemented safety measures, such as metal detectors, door locks, panic bars, video surveillance, patrols by school aides and safety agents, and security telephones in the classrooms. But the rule in New York was that police protection was owed to the community at large, not to specific individuals.

To claim the city owed her a heightened, individualized level of protection, the teacher would have to establish that someone with the authority to make promises on the city's behalf had created a special relationship with her by promising her that the city would keep her safe. The teacher admitted that all the safety training she had received at school by city employees was addressed to the group of teachers she was a part of, not to her personally.

The teacher also alleged the city breached its contract with her teachers' union by not implementing its safety plan properly, but it was already the rule in New York that teachers' union contracts didn't give teachers the right to sue the state for an alleged breach of its terms. *Daniels v. City of New York*, No. 04-CV-7612(CM), 2007 WL 2040581 (S.D.N.Y. 2007).

◆   A student at a high school with escalating violence and chronic security shortages **couldn't hold the school district responsible for injuries he suffered when he was attacked by another student because the district didn't create or increase the dangers he faced**.

A 10th-grader was punched in the eye by another student in a school stairwell. The other student was aiming at someone else, but that person ducked. The student who was struck suffered a fractured facial bone and traumatic hyphema of the eye. He spent six days in the hospital.

Violence at the high school had been steadily increasing over the previous four years. The principal described the school as "out of control" with fights, fires and other serious incidents. However, there was no surveillance camera in the stairwell, and no security guard was present to witness the attack. The school was short by four security officers on the day of the incident, and it had not been fully staffed with security in 83 of the 85 days before that day. The principal had complained about this to the district and, only days before the incident, had met with security officials to discuss the problem.

The student sued the school district, alleging it violated his Fourteenth Amendment right to bodily integrity and safety. The court granted the school district summary judgment. The student appealed to the Third U.S. Circuit Court of Appeals, but it affirmed judgment for the school district.

The student couldn't hold the school district responsible for his injury because the district didn't create the danger he faced. Because of the general atmosphere of violence at the school, it was foreseeable that any student might be attacked there by another student. While foreseeability was one element that had to be proven to hold the district responsible, the court also had to find the attack was a direct result of the district's actions. It did not make this finding.

To establish that the district created the danger that caused his injury, the student had to show:

- the harm was foreseeable, and its cause and effect were fairly direct
- a district employee was guilty of the kind of wrongdoing that "shocked the conscience" – not just indifference about student safety
- the district and the student had a special relationship; the student had to show he was not simply another member of the public, but someone who was particularly likely to be harmed, and
- a district employee used his or her authority to act in a way that created more danger to the student than the danger that would have existed if the employee hadn't acted at all.

The student did not make this showing.

He argued that the district should have been monitoring the stairwell where he was injured, but he couldn't show that such monitoring was necessary. Of the nearly 200 violent attacks preceding the one against him, only one took place in that stairwell.

The student also did not show that a surveillance camera monitoring the stairwell would have prevented the attack or that the lack of security staff increased the danger that he would be attacked. Even if the full security staff had been at school on the day of the incident, there was no guarantee that a guard would have been in the stairwell at the time of the attack. *Mohammed v. School Dist. of Philadelphia*, 196 Fed.Appx. 79 (3d Cir. 2006).

◆ The failure of school authorities to stop classmates from repeatedly attacking a student did not violate his constitutional rights because he couldn't hold them responsible for third-party violence. Therefore, **the student couldn't hold school authorities liable for not creating a school safety plan that trained staff to deal with student violence.**

A sixth-grade student was attacked by classmates over a period of two months. Although the attackers were suspended, the attacks continued – even after the victimized student filed juvenile criminal charges against the classmates. The classmates ultimately received 12 months of probation and community service. Then, one of the classmates and a gang of his friends assaulted the victim and his father at a town music festival. After this incident, the father transferred his son to a private school.

The student and his father sued the school board, the superintendent and the school principal, arguing their failure to stop the attacks deprived the student of his constitutional interests in a public education and in bodily integrity. They also claimed the school board made the violence worse by not developing adequate school safety plans and by not training school staff how to respond to violent students.

But the court found no constitutional violations. School authorities didn't deprive the student of his right to a public school education. Instead, they took steps intended to stop the attacks, and it was the student's voluntary decision to withdraw from the school. The student also failed to show that school authorities violated his right to bodily integrity because there was no special relationship between the victimized student and school authorities, and because school authorities did nothing to make the attacks worse.

The student was suing under 42 U.S.C. § 1983, so he could hold school authorities liable for damages caused by a failure to train only if this failure led to constitutional violations. As there were no constitutional violations here, the student couldn't make this claim.

The student also claimed the school authorities violated the Safe and Drug-Free Schools and Communities Act of 1994 by failing to adopt a safety plan to help control student violence, but this was not a law that gave individuals a right to sue. Instead, it was a federal grant program that provided money to states for anti-violence and anti-drug programs in schools. *Stevenson v. Martin County Board of Educ.*, 3 Fed.Appx. 25 (4th Cir. 2001).

◆ A teachers' union contract and an official circular creating a school security plan did not create a special relationship that enabled a teacher to hold the state responsible for injuries he suffered in an attack in a school hallway.

A teacher was assaulted and injured in the hall outside his classroom. He sued the school board, alleging his union contract and the state's official circular adopting and implementing a school security plan created a duty for the school to protect him.

Although a jury found in the teacher's favor, the trial court set the verdict aside, finding these documents didn't create a special relationship between school authorities and the teacher that meant he could hold them liable for not protecting him from third-party violence on school property. The teacher appealed, but the appellate court affirmed the decision. **The teacher failed to establish a special relationship and thus couldn't meet the narrow exception to the rule that the city couldn't be held responsible for a third party's violence.** *Krakower v. City of New York*, 217 A.D.2d 441 (N.Y. App. Div 1995).

◆ A teacher injured by an intruder on the playground he was monitoring couldn't sue the city for negligence concerning a broken gate that allowed the intruder's entry because the city had no special duty to ensure the teacher's safety.

The teacher was one of five who were assigned to supervise the playground during recess. The playground was surrounded by a high chain-link fence. The entrances were two iron gates, but one had come off its hinges and couldn't be locked. After the teacher was called over to break up a fight, he discovered one of the boys wasn't a student at the school. The teacher forcibly ejected the boy, but the boy returned with a baseball bat and swung it at the teacher, hitting and injuring his wrist.

The teacher sued the city, arguing it was negligent to allow the gate to remain broken and to provide inadequate playground security.

Although a jury returned a $20,000 verdict in the teacher's favor and the appellate court affirmed the judgment, a higher court reversed. **The teacher couldn't sue the city for negligence because there was no special duty on the city's part to ensure his safety and the city had no responsibility to protect him from third-party violence without one.** *Bonner v. City of New York*, 536 N.E.2d 1147 (N.Y. 1989).

2. Negligence

In the case below, an injured student failed to convince the court to find the school was negligent for not following its security plan.

◆ A student struck by an object that was impulsively thrown by another student could not hold the school district responsible for his injury. **Negligence could not be based on the fact that the school did not follow its own security plan** by having a hall monitor present when the incident occurred.

During lunch period at a high school, a student in the hallway picked up the U-shaped top of a broken metal locker padlock and impulsively threw it. It struck another student in the eye. The injured student sued the school district. The school district asked the court to dismiss the case, but the court refused. The school district appealed, and the appellate court did dismiss the case.

The school had a security plan that called for the provision of hall monitors, but there was no monitor in the hall on the day the student was injured. The lower court found the school was negligent because it failed to follow its own security plan by failing to ensure a monitor was in the hall when the incident occurred, but the appellate court disagreed. Although a decision in a different case had found that a school's deviation from its security plan could be a factor in determining whether the school had been negligent, this school's deviation from its security plan didn't count as a factor here. Unlike the school in the other decision, this school did not assign hall monitors in response to a legitimate threat of violence, but for general student supervision as required by state law. Also, given the spontaneous nature of the student's impulsive act, it wasn't likely a hall monitor could have prevented the injury. *Malik v. Greater Johnstown Enlarged School Dist.*, 669 N.Y.S.2d 729 (N.Y. App. Div. 1998).

3. Claims Based on State's Safety Plan Requirement

In 2007, Georgia courts heard three appeals involving the interplay between the state's requirement that schools have crisis management plans and lawsuits brought by students who were seriously injured at school. In two cases, the school was sued because it didn't have a plan in place. In the third, the school was sued, although it did have a plan in place. In each case, the court found the school was immune to the student's lawsuit.

◆ A student who was nearly raped at school couldn't sue the members of the school board for negligence based on the board's failure to implement a school safety plan at her school because the board had state immunity to this claim.

A female student was sexually molested at school by a male student who also tried to rape her. Despite a state law requiring schools to have safety plans, there was no such plan in place at her school.

The student brought a Title IX claim against the school board. She also sued the individual board members, alleging they were negligent for failing to implement a school safety plan. The board members objected to her lawsuit, arguing they couldn't be held negligent because they had no individual legal duty to create the safety plan.

In Georgia, state employees were immune to lawsuits alleging negligence only if the duty they allegedly failed to perform was discretionary rather than ministerial. Discretionary duties called for greater personal authority and judgment, whereas ministerial duties were more like those performed pursuant to orders.

Because the *Murphy v. Bajjani* case (reported below) had determined Georgia school boards and superintendents had a discretionary duty when it came to preparing school safety plans, this court agreed with the board members that the student could not sue them for negligence based on their failure to develop a school safety plan. As a result, the court invited the board members to ask the court to grant it summary judgment. *Snethen v. Board of Public Educ. for the City of Savannah*, No. 406CV259, 2007 WL 2345247 (S.D. Ga. 2007).

◆ The Georgia Supreme Court held that a student severely injured by another student at school couldn't sue school administrators or members of the school board for negligence based on their failure to create a school safety plan as required by state law. Georgia law granted them immunity to negligence claims unless they acted with actual malice or intent to cause injury – which they did not.

In June 2007, the Supreme Court of Georgia reversed a lower court's judgment in favor of a high school student who was seriously injured at school by another student. The lower court determined the individuals sued by the student – including his principal, vice principal and members of the school board – were responsible for the student's injuries because the school hadn't created a school safety plan as required by Georgia state law. The law called for schools to devise a plan to respond to the following potential emergencies: natural disasters, hazardous material or radiological accidents, terrorism and violence.

The state supreme court reversed the judgment for the student and dismissed the case against the school defendants because it determined **these public employees had qualified immunity under the state's constitution with respect to safety plans.** This meant that they could not be sued for negligence unless they had acted maliciously or with intent to injure.

This decision hinged on which kind of duty the safety-plan law created: ministerial or discretionary. The court determined that drafting safety plans was a discretionary act (an exercise of educated, personal judgment) as opposed to a ministerial act (something more akin to following established procedures). Ministerial acts weren't covered by qualified immunity for negligence, but discretionary acts were.

The court dismissed the case against the school defendants because it found that creating a school safety plan was a discretionary act and the school defendants hadn't acted with actual malice or intent to cause injury. This meant they were immune to the student's claims. *Murphy v. Bajjani*, No. S06G1483, 2007 WL 1804380 (Ga. 2007).

◆ A county board of education, its individual members, the superintendent and **a school's principal and staff were entitled to official immunity because there was a valid safety plan in place at the school when a psychologically disturbed stranger gained unauthorized entry to it and attacked a 10-year-old with a hammer**.

Georgia law requires schools to create safety plans. This school provided evidence that it did have a safety plan in place before the intruder attacked the 10-year-old, but the child's parents argued that the plan wasn't valid because it had been developed by the Georgia Emergency Management Agency (GEMA) and other third parties instead of the school itself. But the Georgia Court of Appeals found that the law specifically sanctioned input from approved third parties and that it required GEMA to provide public schools training and technical assistance, which included safe school planning and model school safety plans.

This case pre-dated the state's supreme court decision that settled the law by finding creation of a school safety plan was a discretionary duty instead of a ministerial duty. But it also held the duty was discretionary and therefore shielded school officials from negligence charges. *Leake v. Murphy*, 644 S.E.2d 328 (Ga. Ct. App. 2007).

4. Evacuating Students with Disabilities

◆ A student with a disability couldn't sue the school board for disability discrimination based on school personnel's failure to properly execute the emergency evacuation plan for children with disabilities.

A middle school student had a form of dwarfism that limited her strength and mobility. She operated a computer with voice recognition software so that she didn't have to type. She also had a motorized wheelchair and a full-time aide.

In 1996, her school was evacuated because of a bomb threat. For just over an hour, this student and another student with disabilities were left alone in the building under adult supervision. No bomb was discovered.

Her parents filed a complaint with the state department of education, alleging the school board discriminated against her based on her disability by not evacuating her from the building during the bomb threat. After mediation, the parents agreed to drop their complaint in exchange for the school board's agreement to adopt a new emergency preparedness plan for students with disabilities.

This plan called for sending students with disabilities to one of several "safe rooms" during school emergencies. Each safe room was assigned a responsible adult (plus an alternate) and was equipped with a special flag to alert emergency responders of their presence and also a cell phone. In case evacuation was necessary, the plan called for emergency personnel to rescue the students from the safe rooms.

The school instituted the plan based on advice from local fire and police officials and then explained it to staff and students. It also held a successful practice drill. But two months later, the school had an unscheduled fire drill and the student was left alone for two minutes until the student's math teacher – not assigned as a responsible adult for that room – stopped by to make sure the student was OK. The math teacher stayed with the student for the rest of the fire drill.

The student's parents sued the school board, alleging disability discrimination in violation of Section 504 of the Rehabilitation Act and Title II of the Americans with Disabilities Act based on the bomb-threat and fire-drill incidents.

The court granted the school board summary judgment. The parents appealed, but the Fourth U.S. Circuit Court of Appeals affirmed judgment for the school. The parents couldn't sue concerning the bomb-threat incident because the parents definitively resolved that dispute with the school board when they agreed to drop the complaint in return for institution of the new safety plan.

Based on only the fire-drill incident, the parents couldn't show the school board excluded the student from safe evacuation procedures during an emergency. The school had developed a plan, based on expert advice, specifically aimed at safely evacuating children with disabilities. It had equipped its safe rooms and run a successful drill. **Although the student was left alone for two minutes in a safe room, the imperfect execution of an otherwise reasonable evacuation plan did not constitute disability discrimination.** *Shirey v. City of Alexandria School Board*, 229 F.3d 1143 (4th Cir. 2000).

5. Cases Involving Staff

◆ A district's former security specialist couldn't claim the district violated his First Amendment rights by retaliating against him for raising concerns about its safety and security procedures. Because he didn't raise these concerns as a private citizen but instead raised them as a public employee to district officials and as part of his job, the speech wasn't constitutionally protected.

After the man worked as a high school security specialist for two-and-a-half years, the school's new principal relieved him of certain duties but also asked him to prepare a new school emergency plan. He did.

Over the next year, the specialist said he brought staff and student safety concerns to the principal's attention, but the principal wasn't responsive. The specialist also said he attended a meeting of the district's Safe and Drug Free School Advisory Council, where participants discussed the district's lack of coordination with law enforcement.

A few months later, the specialist gave the district's chief administrative officer (CAO) a binder containing a 13-page letter and 20 exhibits outlining his concerns about safety at the high school. The letter explained that the specialist was worried that he couldn't provide adequate security under current conditions. The CAO assured him he would not be fired for bringing these matters to his attention. The CAO and the superintendent asked him to write a protocol for a district-wide security position, which he did. Not long after, the specialist was reassigned to work primarily at a different school, returning to his original school only to perform bus duty at the end of the day.

Approximately six months later, his position and a gate security position were cut for budgetary reasons. The duties of these two positions were combined into a new position. Although the former specialist applied for this position, the district hired an applicant who had a college degree and could therefore also serve as a substitute teacher.

The former specialist sued the district, alleging it violated his First Amendment rights by firing and then not rehiring him in retaliation for raising safety concerns at the high school. But the court granted the district summary judgment.

Based on the Supreme Court decision *Garcetti v. Ceballos*, 126 S.Ct. 1951 (U.S. 2006), this court determined that **public employees do not have free speech rights in statements made concerning their official duties**. Here, the former specialist was not expressing his concerns as a citizen (to a newspaper or a legislator, for example) but as a district employee to district officials about his job. *Posey v. Lake Pend Oreille School Dist. No. 84*, 2007 WL 420256 (D. Idaho 2007).

◆ A teacher, who was arrested and prosecuted for making a phone call threatening to shoot staff and bomb the school, couldn't sue the district or police after she was acquitted because her arrest and prosecution were supported by probable cause.

The teacher had received two written warnings about her job performance, and students and parents had complained about her. The principal offered her the option of resigning, and she accepted. Eleven days later, the teacher had a physical fight at school with a female student and the principal told her to stay home on paid leave until he investigated. Two days later, someone identifying herself as the teacher called the school and told a secretary she was going to shoot everyone on the administrative staff and blow up the school.

After unsuccessfully trying to reach the teacher at home, the principal called a police officer assigned to a nearby school. The principal turned the investigation over to the officer before focusing on evacuating the school.

The secretary who had spoken to the caller told the officer she had recognized the voice as belonging to the teacher. The officer arrested the teacher for aggravated harassment.

The district issued a press release stating that "a female voice identifying herself as [… the teacher] threatened to blow up the school and shoot office staff. [… The principal] immediately notified the police and implemented the school security plan. The school was locked down and the case was turned over to the police."

The former teacher was acquitted. Among other parties, she then sued the district, the principal and the officer who arrested her, raising claims including libel, malicious prosecution, false arrest and a violation of her civil rights.

The court dismissed the former teacher's lawsuit. **Concerning the libel charge, the court found that the district's press release contained no false statements.** Although it identified her by name, the release stated only that someone claiming to be the former teacher had called the school and made threats. This accurately described what had happened. As for the other charges, the police had probable cause to arrest the former teacher based on the secretary's report of the call and her identification of the voice as belonging to the former teacher. *Rizzo v. Edison, Inc.*, 419 F.Supp.2d 338 (W.D.N.Y. 2005).

III. BEST PRACTICES FOR CRISIS MANAGEMENT PLANS

The real goal of school crisis management plans is nicely stated by the Model Emergency Plan for Schools posted at the National Incident Management System Web site, nimsonline.com: "The most important part of the school emergency plan is to account for all students, their safety and well being, and release them as soon as possible to their parent or designated guardian." The best practices for school crisis management plans are those that are geared toward keeping everyone at school safe and getting students safely back to their parents as soon as possible.

Much time, thought and effort in every state has gone into creating crisis management plans for schools, and the GAO's 2007 study of this planning found broad compliance with recommended practices, and only a few areas that still needed work. After going over some basic plan elements, this section will address those areas still needing work in more detail.

A. Basic Plan Elements

The U.S. Department of Education points out that there is no one-size-fits-all approach when it comes to crisis management plans. For one thing, each school has a unique school community with unique needs. For another, schools in different parts of the country are subject to different risks, and big-city schools face very different challenges than schools that are located in the same general area but in quieter, more rural regions. Finally, each state has different laws that its schools must follow. All of this means that for a crisis management plan to be effective to the maximum extent possible, it must be tailored to the school's specific needs.

Despite the need to take individual differences into account, there are some things that can be said of all plans. For example, each one has to comply with its state and local laws. Also, every crisis management plan should be considered a work in progress. As the Office of Safe and Drug-Free School's *Practical Information on Crisis Planning* states: "Good plans are never finished. They can always be updated based on experience, research, and changing vulnerabilities." The day-to-day realities at school are constantly changing. New students and staff join the community or leave it, shifting the established needs of the community. This can lead to necessary adjustments caused by different student disabilities having to be accommodated or new languages having to be taken into account to make effective communication with students and their parents possible. Also, lessons learned from a previous incident can mean that the plan should be tweaked to take advantage of real-life experience.

CHECKLIST – BASIC PLAN ELEMENTS

- The plan complies with state and local laws.
- The plan is periodically reviewed and updated as needed.
- The plan includes provisions relating to students with disabilities.
- The plan addresses potential language barriers.
- The plan is updated based on real-life experiences when appropriate.

B. Four Stages of Planning

The Office of Safe and Drug-Free School's *Practical Information on Crisis Planning* suggests that schools take these four stages into account when setting up their plans:
- Mitigation and Prevention

- Preparedness
- Response
- Recovery

1. Mitigation and Prevention

Mitigation and Prevention is the preliminary planning stage when plans intended to reduce or eliminate harm before an incident occurs are formulated. Successful mitigation and prevention depend on accurate risk assessment, which is the crucial first step, already discussed previously in this chapter.

2. Preparedness

Preparedness is also based on risk assessment, but this is where things move past preliminary planning and the plan's protocols are established.

One important preparedness step is to **assign crisis duties to personnel**. A good place to start that initial determination is to find out who has first aid and CPR training – and who is willing to get it.

Preparedness is also the stage when **emergency supplies are gathered and stored**. There are several ways to approach the practical matter of gathering emergency supplies, but they all tend to fall under two categories: either the school gathers all the emergency supplies, or the school gathers some of the supplies while parents and students or some other party supplies the rest.

Under the model plan posted at nimsonline.com, for example, parents are instructed to pack up specified drinks and snacks and a few other items (a laminated copy of the student's emergency card, a reassuring message and photo from the family, pocket-sized tissues and a small book or game) in a gallon zip-lock bag placed inside a 50-gallon plastic snap-top container and then bring it to school for storage.

In addition to food and water, emergency supplies typically include first aid gear, radios and flashlights.

The preparedness stage is also when **parents are told where and how to get information about an ongoing incident**. The Office of Safe and Drug-Free Schools' *Practical Information on Crisis Planning* suggests that schools clearly let families know they should not call the school's direct line or come to the campus during an emergency. The calls could tie up desperately needed communication lines in and out of the school, and parents' cars could physically block ambulances, fire trucks and emergency personnel.

Possible alternative ways for parents to get information about an incident in progress include calling a pre-arranged phone number to reach a recorded message that will be updated as often as possible under the circumstances or by tuning in to the local TV or radio station that has agreed to broadcast this information in case of a serious emergency.

The preparedness stage is also when schools need to make specific plans relating to evacuation, lockdowns and sheltering-in-place.

Evacuation requires a pre-determined evacuation plan that specifies a few alternatives for both on-site assembly sites (to evacuate from) and off-campus assembly sites (to evacuate to). Specifying alternative sites is recommended because the first choices might be unreachable or unusable due to the emergency, making alternate choices for on-campus and off-campus sites necessary.

Schools generally expect to evacuate staff and students by using school buses, but the roads may be impassable or buses may be unavailable. Therefore, alternate ways to remove students from danger should be discussed.

The evacuation provisions in the model plan posted at nimsonline.com stress the importance of making sure students remain accounted for by:

- keeping classes together during the evacuation so that teachers can continue to keep track of their own students, and
- having teachers take roll both immediately before the evacuation and as soon as they arrive at the evacuation destination.

Keep in mind that authorities may ask that a school be evacuated during more severe crises. On September 11th, for example, Stuyvesant High School was near ground zero, but that was not why it was evacuated. Instead, the FBI wanted to use the school building as a command center.

Lockdowns are needed when the danger is outside the school and the best chance of keeping students safe is to secure them inside. The school's outside doors are locked, and students and teachers remain in classrooms. If possible, classroom doors are also locked and windows may need to be covered. An example of a sample notice to parents regarding a school lockdown drill is provided in chapter nine (Form II-2).

Sheltering-in-place is a response to the more specific danger of needing to minimize students' exposure to contaminants in the environment – a chemical accident, for example. Sheltering-in rooms should have as few windows as possible. Basic necessities, such as food, water and bedding, should be stored there in advance, along with emergency supplies, such as flashlights and radios, as well as first aid supplies and medicine.

For sheltering-in, the American Red Cross suggests an interior room with no windows that is located above the ground floor. This is because some dangerous chemicals are heavier than air. Even with precautions, heavy chemicals could seep into basement rooms. As an extra safety measure, people should be provided a wet cloth to keep over their noses and mouths.

The Red Cross also says all HVAC and fans should be turned off and all vents and cracks around doors should be sealed with duct tape. If only a room with windows is available, it should be covered with plastic and sealed over completely with duct tape. Checklists showing specific steps to take in the event of a gas leak or hazardous spill are provided on Form II-3 and Form II-4 in chapter nine.

One recommended practice is not only to keep emergency supplies such as food, water and first aid at school, but also to regularly replace or replenish them.

The universal food of choice for emergency supplies seems to be energy bars. The model plan posted online at the NIMS site includes two energy bars in its per-child emergency food kit, and it also includes prepackaged fruit cups, Jell-O cups, fruit roll-ups, unsalted crackers, two small cans of juice, and a pint plastic bottle of water. For an example of a crisis kit checklist, see Form II-5 in chapter nine.

3. Response

Response is the stage where a crisis occurs and the plan is followed.

Paraphrasing the first steps of the Office of Safe and Drug-Free Schools' Action Checklist, they suggest:

- determining if a crisis is really happening
- deciding what type of crisis it is, and
- choosing the best response.

As the word *response* suggests, this is the time to act – and to act as quickly as possible. The Office of Safe and Drug-Free Schools' guidance for responding to an actual crisis includes keeping hesitation to a minimum. *Practical Information on Crisis Planning* baldly tells administrators: "Respond within seconds."

One reason for planning so carefully in the first place is to make a fast response possible. If you already know what you're doing, you don't have to stop and think about it.

Speeding up response time is also one reason why the Office of Safe and Drug-Free Schools considers it so vital for schools to train with their plans' procedures – and include first responders, staff and students in this training if possible.

Apart from the fact that run-throughs can reveal unexpected problems – giving schools a chance to fix them – there's a lot of truth in the old saying: Practice makes perfect. People who drive everyday don't have to lose any time in figuring out which pedal makes the car go forward. And they're also much less likely to plow into the car behind them if they have to resort to trial and error and then get it wrong.

The goal for anyone who has to follow a school crisis plan is to achieve such a level of familiarity with it that following its procedures during an emergency is almost as automatic as driving.

That said, virtually every crisis presents situations no one could have imagined – and therefore no one could have planned for. But having the basics down makes it a lot likelier that staff can intelligently adapt these basics to cover unexpected events.

Sometimes the unexpected element is people's own reactions. No one knows what they'll be like under pressure until they actually experience it. Also, people are all different – and so are their responses to a crisis. Some people may find themselves cool-headed and decisive while others might have to fight the tendency to freeze while their minds go blank. Most people probably fall somewhere in between these two extremes, but training can help tilt the scale toward cool-headed decisiveness.

Another thing that can help with that is having easy-to-read-and-understand checklists on hand. Many plans call for them – and some call for them to be laminated to make them more durable and legible, since lamination means they can be wiped off.

Simple, straightforward checklists that contain not only basic action plans but also relevant contact information can help get frozen people up and going again and then on to the next step. Even if everyone stays calm, focused and moves quickly, it's a good idea to have simple reminders that can be easily scanned and followed. Examples of a crisis team member list and a list of emergency telephone numbers are provided in chapter nine on Form I-2 and Form II-6.

One mistake the Office of Safe and Drug-Free Schools believes many schools make during a crisis is waiting too long to call in emergency services and alert its own crisis team. The office's advice is to call for help and alert the team even if there's a chance the situation might be resolved by the time help arrives. If that turns out to be the case, that's actually a good thing. And if there's any risk of injury or loss of life or property, it's best to err on the side of safety.

The Department of Education also reminds schools that an important goal to aim for is the earliest possible safe release of students – and to keep it in mind that this might be possible even before the incident is actually over. A sample letter to send home after a crisis event is provided in chapter nine on Form II-7. Form II-8 is a sample initial announcement of a crisis event, and Form II-9 is a post-disaster parent information sheet.

4. Recovery

Recovery is the stage where schools work at getting things back to normal again so they can get back to their mission of educating students.

Experience has shown that there are several predictable recovery needs that many schools experience after an emergency is over. Because they're predictable, they can be planned for and addressed in the crisis plan. They include:

- helping students, families and staff cope with trauma
- repairing any physical damage to the facility
- addressing insurance requirements, and
- dealing with the media.

Perhaps the most predictable recovery need in the wake of a crisis at school is that students, families and school staff are likely to need help coping with the emotional fall-out that accompanies living through a disaster. One way to support staff is by utilizing a thank-you letter such as the one provided on Form II-10 in chapter nine.

One standard crisis-planning recommendation from the Department of Education is for schools to get advice from experts in whatever field is needed. When planning for coping with the after-effects of trauma, many schools have their own onsite experts because they have their own counselors. A school's counselors have the added advantage of already having a relationship with many of the people who might be needing help.

Schools that go off campus for emotional recovery advice can also use the advice-gathering process for another purpose: to determine if the expert might also be a good person to bring back after a crisis, not only for more specific advice given more precise circumstances but also to work with students or teachers to help them cope with the experience.

As a general rule, contemplating the recovery stage is a good time to make contact with the experts that can help the school bring about the actual recovery.

Another predictable recovery need concerns the brick and mortar of the school itself. Even apart from additional safety considerations – such as leaking roofs that could lead to slip-and-fall accidents or falling rubble that could cause injury – the physical damage left after a disaster can be a potent reminder. And one important psychological way to move beyond the crisis is to repair the physical damage.

On a practical level, it can also be a good idea to find out in advance exactly what kind of insurance requirements the school is likely to have to comply with in case it has to make claims on any policies. Knowing what kind of documentation and paperwork will be required might be an important thing to know before anything happens. For example, knowing that photos of damaged facilities will be required gives administrators the opportunity to make sure there are disposable cameras in the office, just in case.

Another predictable recovery-stage need is for a spokesperson or spokespeople to deal with the media. Many schools already have staff and established procedures in place for this.

Finally, for the recovery stage, the plan should call for debriefing sessions with school staff and emergency personnel to follow any actual crisis so that the school can incorporate the lessons learned from the incident into the plan.

C. Commonly Neglected Areas

The GAO's study of school planning and preparedness found that the overwhelming norm among schools was an emergency management plan that addressed multiple specific scenarios. It found virtually all these plans addressed bombs or bomb threats, school intruder or hostage situations, and the natural disasters likely for the locality. Those bases are pretty thoroughly covered in the majority of school crisis management plans. For a bomb threat report form, see Form II-11 in chapter nine. For specific steps key personnel should take in the event that an intruder gains unauthorized access, see Form II-12 in chapter nine.

The GAO also found that city-based school districts were more likely than rural school districts to plan crisis responses for terrorism (86% as opposed to 70%) and much more likely to plan for incidents involving radiation (60% to 29%), anthrax (57% to 26%) and pandemic flu (52% to 36%).

In addition to the findings relating to provisions addressing potential radiation, anthrax and pandemic events in crisis management plans, the GAO study also identified four areas in which many plans weren't following recommended practices.

The GAO's June 2007 study of emergency management at schools found that many school districts were not following these recommended practices:

- including procedures to ensure the safety of special needs students
- including a plan to continue teaching students in case the school closed due to a pandemic or other emergency
- conducting school drills and exercises, and
- training with first responders and community partners.

Because the GAO found schools already were largely well-prepared with respect to other areas of planning, this section will focus on the topics that many schools and districts may still need information in addressing.

1. Special Needs Students' Safety

Just as a good plan is tailored to address the crises a school is more likely to face, a good crisis management plan for students with disabilities is likely to take into account the special needs of known students with disabilities in the school's own student population.

The U.S. Department of Education recommends including the emergency procedures for special needs students in writing in the crisis management plan. However, the GAO found that 28% of school districts with plans had not included specific provisions for students with disabilities. Of those that had, the provisions were not in writing.

The GAO's report focused on the following recommended practices concerning special needs students:

- keeping track of where special needs students are located throughout the school day
- identifying the staff assigned to evacuate or shelter with these students, and
- providing any devices needed to transport them to evacuation areas.

Educators told the GAO that districts devise their own procedures for keeping special needs students safe in a crisis because disability groups don't agree on the best practices.

One reason for this might be that while all students are unique, students with disabilities tend to be the most unique of all. Some need motorized wheelchairs to cross a room, while others need specialized laptops to communicate. Still others – Down syndrome children, for example – have cognitive limitations that may require a teacher with real experience of what works with this particular student in order to get her on the evacuation bus or keep her from panicking during lockdown or sheltering-in. Special needs students often need extra help under normal circumstances, and this need for extra help can be greatly increased during a crisis. As the National Organization on Disability has said, perhaps the most effective tactic for special needs individuals to survive an emergency is to have strong relationships with other people.

Disabilities are categorized differently by different groups, but there are some special needs experiences that may be common enough to take account of for crisis management planning. For example:

- People who need wheelchairs, crutches or other mobility devices are going to need special help if an emergency disables elevators or leaves piles of rubble blocking paths – especially if a speedy exit is required.
- Individuals who are blind are likely to be badly disoriented by loud, overwhelming noises – like sirens. Extremely loud noises drown out the ambient sounds that normally give blind people cues about who and what is in their immediate environment and what is happening there.
- People with cognitive or developmental disabilities like ADHD, Down syndrome and Tourette's are likely to have trouble following instructions.

Other considerations when planning for special needs students and staff might include:

- Establishing a pre-set location to which special needs students can be escorted so they can be rescued.
- Consulting with emergency responders about their own protocols for dealing with special needs individuals, and adopting them if appropriate.
- Alerting emergency responders to the presence of any special needs students likely to need additional help, such as the mobility-impaired.
- Obtaining devices – such as specialized, light-weight chairs – to help evacuate students with severe mobility problems.
- Training staff to use any specialized devices, and assigning more people than are actually needed in order to operate them.
- Providing (or training) a sign-language interpreter if needed.
- Providing written instructions in Braille if needed.
- Making sheltering-in arrangements for service animals. Although pets aren't permitted in shelters, federal regulations allow service animals – although they can be excluded if they threaten others' lives or safety or if they become a nuisance. That said, anyone with known allergies to animals should be assigned to a different room.

- Storing pet foods, medicines, plastic bags and disposable gloves for service animals along with other emergency supplies and earmarking water for them.
- Storing backup devices of any vital special needs device.
- Storing spare or alternative power sources for the devices.
- Storing needed medicine along with emergency supplies.
- Providing cards special needs students can wear to alert first responders of their condition and the limitations it causes them. For example, a card for a person with a cognitive disability might state that this person has trouble understanding language, so patience and a simple vocabulary are needed.

A form that can be used to build a list of students and staff who require special assistance for evacuation can be found at Form II-13 in chapter nine. The American Academy of Pediatrics and the American College of Emergency Physicians have created a form designed to present a brief but accurate record of special needs students to help ensure they receive proper care during an emergency. It can be downloaded at www.aap.org/advocacy/blankform.pdf

2. Planning for a Pandemic

Another area of crisis planning that the GAO identified as neglected was planning for a pandemic flu event and how to continue to educate students in case of the extended school closure likely to accompany it.

Flu pandemics are caused by a highly contagious flu virus so new that people have built up little or no immunity to it. A virus-specific vaccine may not be available until six months after the virus is identified, and this lack of natural and vaccine-related immunity heightens the chance people will become seriously ill or die. This risk is already significant, as the regular seasonal flu strains kill approximately 36,000 Americans and send another 200,000 to the hospital. As a comparison, the 1918 pandemic killed 500,000 Americans – although the 1957-58 pandemic caused 70,000 fatalities and the 1968-69 pandemic only 34,000.

When it came to crisis management planning for pandemic flu, the GAO found only 52% of urban schools and 36% of rural schools had plans in place.

According to recommendations from the U.S. Department of Health and Human Services (HHS) and the Centers for Disease Control and Prevention (CDC), pandemic flu planning could include education campaigns to prevent spread of the virus by:

- frequent hand washing
- sneezing and coughing only into either a tissue which is then immediately disposed of, or against the upper arm if a tissue isn't available, and
- encouraging everyone in the school community to stay home at the first sign of illness.

The GAO advises schools to contact and work with local health authorities in anticipation of a pandemic. It identifies these procedures for educating students when the school is closed:

- electronic or human telephone trees to convey academic information
- Web-based instruction
- mailed lessons and assignments, and
- broadcasting of classes by local TV or radio stations.

The GAO determined that 56% of districts did not include any of these procedures in their crisis management plans. Alternative education plans are extremely important because experts can anticipate circumstances in which schools could be closed for longer than a year, although a more conservative estimate is that pandemic-related school closure could last from a few weeks up to three months.

Schools might have to be closed to protect public health by limiting the spread of the virus. Alternatively, there may be so few teachers available because of the flu that there aren't enough to supervise the students.

HHS and CDC have also developed a checklist to help school districts plan for pandemic influenza. It can be downloaded at http://www.pandemicflu.gov/plan/school/schoolchecklist.html.

3. Learning the Drill

Based on its survey of school districts, the GAO estimated that 27% of districts had never trained with first responders on implementing the school's crisis management plan and that approximately three-quarters of all districts were not training at least once a year with each of the following three resources: law enforcement, firefighters and emergency medical services.

The danger of not conducting this participatory training is that it can lead to confusion over who's doing what – and who's supposed to do what – during an actual event.

The Office of Safe and Drug-Free School's *Practical Information on Crisis Planning* recommends that schools develop relationships with the groups that will respond to actual school emergencies long before any occur.

Through such training, responders can learn basic and necessary information, such as how to get into the school, where to turn on (or off) utilities, and how to find their way around. It speeds up response – and may save lives – if, for example, medics who are told to come to the gym already know where the gym is.

For a sample list to be used to compile phone numbers of first responders and other emergency response personnel, see Form II-6 in chapter nine.

4. Training with First Responders/Community Partners

i. First Responders

It is important to keep in mind that law enforcement, firefighters and emergency medical services have their own protocols. By training with them, schools can learn whether all these protocols conflict or are otherwise counterproductive. Also, first responders have a level of training and experience that most school staffs lack. This is a valuable resource of which schools should take advantage.

Training with first responders can also clarify whether you're likely to have communication problems. FEMA suggests always using plain language to make sure everyone understands what is needed. It may be obvious to someone very familiar to the campus that "Ken-one" is short for No. 1 Kendall Street and means the auditorium, but it won't be obvious to Officer Rodriguez who just moved here from two states away.

Plain language is a good idea even when it comes to communicating effectively with staff inside the school. A first-time substitute teacher will have no idea that the "Code Purple" announcement over the intercom means she's supposed to lock her classroom door and tell students to lie flat on the floor.

Training with first responders can also help schools make sure in advance that their technology will work with emergency responders' equipment so that they can communicate in a crisis instead of failing to connect or even jamming each other's equipment so that no one can communicate with anyone. Eight of the 27 districts that the GAO interviewed in researching its 2007 study said that their one-way radios and other equipment didn't work with the first responders' equipment. School officials in Iowa told the GAO that their district had a special problem in that it shared a radio frequency with only some of the first responders, not all of them.

ii. Community Partners

While the police, the fire department and emergency medical services spring immediately to most school staffs' minds, not as many think of working with public health professionals and benefiting from the training and expertise they can provide. These community partners can be especially helpful in the event of a biological and radiation emergency.

In addition to other help, public health professionals can help schools include provisions relating to biological and radiation events in their school's crisis management plans by providing expert guidance on specific hazards as well as such information as when sheltering-in-place is called for and the needs of children who may have been outside when an event occurred.

Biological weapons ultimately make people very ill, but the initial symptoms can fall within the normal range of everyday complaints. Therefore, one of the greatest risks of a biological attack is that it will not be recognized as such until after there has been a significant loss of life. The more quickly a biological attack is recognized, the more casualties can be prevented by distributing the available vaccines and antidotes.

In the case of anthrax, for example, the initial signs of the gastrointestinal form of the disease look a lot like food poisoning. The preliminary symptoms of the inhalation form of anthrax could easily be mistaken for a cold or the flu. Symptoms could appear within a month after contact with the bacterium, but they can take longer than a month to appear. There is a vaccine to prevent the disease. Even after it is contracted, a 60-day course of antibiotics can sometimes provide a cure.

Schools can help reduce the lag time between seeing the symptoms and recognizing a biological attack – and thus save lives – by assigning a staff member to monitor diseases at school and look for patterns, and having other staff who:

- can distinguish between normal illnesses and anomalies caused by biological weapons
- keep in close touch with the public health department, and
- know how and where to report unusual symptoms.

In terms of crisis management planning for an actual incident, a supplement to the Report of the National Advisory Committee on Children and Terrorism suggests:

- training staff in Blood Borne Pathogen Standards
- training staff to use personal protective gear and respirators and conduct a decontamination
- having one accessible switch to perform an emergency shutdown of the HVAC system in order to keep anything airborne from spreading, and
- having a procedure in place to let parents know about the illness and the best way to treat it.

As with pandemics, a biological attack might require schools to close – with all that this implies – in order to avoid the spread of disease.

The CDC's Web site has an A-Z listing of bioterrorism agents posted at www.bt.cdc.gov/agent/agentlist.asp. This listing includes information about how the diseases are contracted, the symptoms, and if vaccines or cures are available.

With respect to radiation, ideally schools would be prepared to administer potassium iodide in case of radiation exposure within two hours of a "dirty bomb" explosion or a catastrophic incident at a nuclear plant. A radiation event could require either sheltering-in-place or an evacuation. Public health professionals can help schools to determine when each of these options is the most appropriate choice.

Schools want the best for their staff and students. That's exactly why the GAO found schools are already largely on top of the game when it comes to crisis planning.

But remember: It's always a work in progress. And anyone's game can always get even better.

CHAPTER THREE

Student Issues

I. BULLYING AND HAZING

A. School Violence

Students who are victimized by threats or bullying at school often seek legal recourse against a school district or school officials for their injuries. However, the law typically does not allow an entity such as a school district to be liable for the misconduct of a third person, such as a bullying or harassing student. Schools may be liable in personal injury cases for third-party misconduct if there is a pattern of negligence by the school district or staff members that shows a conscious disregard for safety.

Schools may be held liable for injuries which result from the failure to provide a reasonably safe environment. Courts have held that schools and staff members are not liable for injuries that are unforeseeable. Schools are not considered the "insurers of student safety."

◆ A Michigan teacher lined up most of her students in a hallway and led them to a computer class. She left five students in the classroom because they had not completed their work. A student took a pistol out of his desk, put bullets into it and shot a classmate to death. The teacher was in the hallway at the time. The classmate's parent claimed the student had been involved in several behavior incidents in the months before the shooting, including beating up other students and stabbing another student with a pencil. The parent sued the teacher, principal and school district in a federal district court, asserting a variety of civil rights violations claims. The court held for the district and school employees, and the parent appealed.

The U.S. Court of Appeals, Sixth Circuit, stated that **generally, a state's failure to protect an individual against violent acts by a private party is not a violation of the Due Process Clause.** Federal courts have recognized an exception to the general rule known as the "state-created danger" theory. Under it, there may be liability for a due process violation if the state takes some affirmative act that creates or increases the risk of a special danger to the victim, as distinguished from the public at large. **The teacher's act of leaving five students unsupervised in the classroom was not an "affirmative act" creating a specific risk to the classmate. She would have been in about the same degree of danger had the teacher remained.** The danger was the student's possession of the gun, not the teacher's positioning. A court or jury could not conclude the teacher knew the student would use a gun to kill another student if she left him unsupervised for a few minutes. He had never brought a weapon to school or threatened anyone before. The parent did not show the principal approved of any unconstitutional conduct by the teacher. **To hold the district liable for a civil rights violation, there had to be evidence of a district policy or custom of depriving persons of their constitutional rights.** There was no such evidence in this case. As the parent could not show the teacher violated her daughter's civil rights, the claims against the district and principal failed, and the court affirmed the judgment. *McQueen v. Beecher Community Schools*, 433 F.3d 460 (6th Cir. 2006).

◆ Philadelphia's Olney High School experienced increasing attacks on students and staff from 1999 to 2003. An Olney student was punched by an unknown attacker who was trying to hit someone else. On the day of the incident, the student took the only available stairs to his classroom. The intended victim ducked, and the attacker hit the student in the eye, severely injuring him. Neither the attacker nor the intended victim was ever identified. The student's mother sued the school district and school officials in a federal district court, asserting due process violations and willful misconduct. The court rejected the claims, including one alleging that school officials had created the danger leading to the injury.

On appeal, the U.S. Court of Appeals, Third Circuit, considered the mother's arguments that there were no surveillance cameras or security staff in the stairwell at the time of the attack. The school was short four security officers that day, and had been short of a full security staff on 83 of the previous 85 school days. The school's principal admitted "the building basically was out of control." The court stated that to impose liability under the Due Process Clause for creating a danger, **the harm must have been foreseeable and fairly direct. The entity must have acted with a degree of culpability that "shocks the conscience." There must be a "special relationship" between the victim and the state, and the authority must be used in a way that created the danger to the victim. The court held that the injury to the student was not foreseeable to the district. The atmosphere of violence at the school did not make it foreseeable that he would be attacked.** School officials had no knowledge that the student was in any more danger than anyone else at Olney High School. He was not an intended victim of the assault, and only one prior violent incident had taken place in the stairwell. The court found that additional surveillance or security might have helped apprehend the attacker, but it was speculation to say this would have prevented the attack. As the school did not place the student in a position of increased danger, there was no basis for a state-created danger claim. The court affirmed the judgment. *Mohammed v. School Dist. of Philadelphia*, 196 Fed.Appx. 79 (3d Cir. 2006).

◆ A New York student and a classmate fought in their school cafeteria about some money. The district suspended the classmate from school for a day, with a day of in-school suspension. The classmate had been disciplined six times in sixth and seventh grades, including suspensions for fighting, but this was his first discipline for grade eight. He was not involved in any prior cafeteria incidents and had no prior encounters with the student. The student sued the district and school officials in a federal district court, claiming they did nothing to protect him even though the classmate's record of fighting and discipline put the district on notice of his "propensity for violence." The court dismissed the federal claims, and the district moved for summary judgment on his state law claims.

In *Mirand v. City of New York*, 84 N.Y. 44, 637 N.E.2d 263 (N.Y. 1994), the state's highest court held a school is liable for student-on-student violence only if it had "specific, prior knowledge of the danger that caused the injury." **A student's acts must have been foreseeable by the district to impose liability. New York courts have held there is no school liability for injuries caused by sudden, impulsive acts that are not preceded by prior misconduct. If an assault occurs so suddenly that it could not be prevented by any amount of supervision, there is no school liability.** Prior unrelated incidents of student discipline do not put a school on notice of a specific threat of danger requiring supervision. **While New York courts hold schools have a duty to adequately supervise students, "this duty does not make schools insurers of the safety of their students, for they cannot be reasonably expected to continuously supervise and control all movements and activities of students."** The student had never seen the classmate before the incident. The classmate's disciplinary record did not put the district on notice of a possible attack on the student. As there was no specific threat to the student, and the district was not required to constantly supervise the classmate, it was not liable for negligence. *Smith v. Half Hollow Hills Cent. School Dist.*, 349 F.Supp.2d 521 (E.D.N.Y. 2004).

♦ An Illinois student was reluctant to go to school after being bullied, shoved and kicked. His mother complained to the school principal but did not identify the bullies. She later called a school social worker to obtain counseling for her son. The mother told the social worker the names of the bullies and said her son did not wish them to be revealed. The social worker agreed not to disclose their names but soon provided them to the principal. The principal then met with the bullies and revealed the student's name before assigning them to detention. The student claimed to suffer emotional distress from the disclosure of his name to the bullies. He transferred schools and filed a state court privacy rights violation action against the principal, social worker, school board and the rural special education cooperative that employed the social worker. The court held the social worker and cooperative were immune from suit under the Illinois Confidentiality Act, 740 ILCS § 110/11(ii). The principal and board had immunity under the state Tort Immunity Act, 745 ILCS § 10/2-201.

On appeal, the Appellate Court of Illinois stated the Confidentiality Act was implicated whenever a communication was made to a therapist. The social worker was protected under Section 11 of the act, which **permits a good-faith disclosure to protect a person against a clear, imminent risk of serious injury. The trial court correctly held the social worker had sole discretion to decide whether disclosing confidential information was necessary to protect the student.** He relayed this information to the principal in the belief there was a risk of further harm. **The principal's actions involved disciplinary matters and were policy determinations** under Section 2-201. **The principal's handling of bullying fell within the definition of "discretionary," as principals had broad discretion to handle these situations.** The principal and school board were immune from suit under Section 2-201. *Albers v. Breen*, 346 Ill.App.3d 799, 806 N.E.2d 667 (Ill. App. Ct. 2004).

♦ A California school opened its campus at 7:00 a.m., but trouble spots such as restrooms were unsupervised before 7:45 a.m. School administrators knew that one eighth-grade special education student was usually dropped off at 7:15 a.m. A classmate who also had disabilities teased and ridiculed the student daily before classes began. The student sometimes went to the office to escape this, and he complained to the staff. He was told to stay away from the classmate, even after he told the vice principal this did not work. The classmate twice isolated the student and sexually assaulted him. The district learned of the incidents and expelled the classmate, who was also arrested. The student was hospitalized with depression, and he attempted suicide. He filed a state court action against the school district and the classmate's family. A jury trial resulted in a verdict of over $2.5 million for the student, and the district appealed.

The Court of Appeal of California observed that **schools have a special relationship with students which imposes an affirmative duty on school districts to "take all reasonable steps to protect students."** The duty arose from the compulsory nature of education and a state constitutional declaration of each student's inalienable right to attend safe, secure and peaceful campuses. **School districts have a well-established duty to supervise students at all times while on school grounds and to enforce necessary rules and regulations for their protection. This duty included supervision during recess and before or after school.** The district was liable for injuries resulting from the failure of school staff to use ordinary care to protect students. The district unlocked its gates at 7:00 a.m. each day, but did not provide supervision until 7:45 a.m. **It could have simply precluded students from arriving early or kept them in particular areas of the school.** The district's claim to immunity failed because there was no exercise of discretion by the principal, and evidence that he knew of the classmate's violent behavior. The damage award was not excessive, and the court affirmed the judgment. *M.W. v. Panama Buena Union School Dist.*, 1 Cal. Rptr. 3d 673 (Cal. Ct. App. 2003).

◆ Three Louisiana students assaulted a classmate in their locker room after a PE class, causing serious injuries. The classmate sued the school board, the parents of the students and their insurers in a Louisiana court for personal injuries. A jury found the students were not at fault, and the court found the board 100% at fault. It held the coach caused the injuries by failing to supervise the students. According to the court, an atmosphere of roughhousing and lack of supervision invited the attack, and the board failed to conform to the required standard of care. On appeal, the state court of appeal apportioned 70% of the fault to the board and 30% to one of the students.

The state supreme court held **school boards have a duty of reasonable supervision over students. Boards are not insurers of student safety, and constant supervision of all students is not required. To hold a school board liable for negligence, it must be shown that a risk of unreasonable injury was foreseeable and could have been prevented with the required degree of supervision.** In this case, the attack happened suddenly and without warning. Because it was unforeseeable to the classmate himself, there was no way for the coach to foresee and prevent it. The trial court had erroneously imposed liability on the board independent of the students. As the incident could not have been prevented with a reasonable degree of supervision, the court reversed the judgment. *Wallmuth v. Rapides Parish School Board*, 813 So.2d 341 (La. 2002).

◆ A Louisiana high school student was harassed and threatened by three classmates after he came to the defense of a new student while on their school bus. He got off the bus at a stop where he believed that he would be safer than if he disembarked at his regular stop. However, he was followed by the three classmates. While attempting to intervene, the student was thrown to the ground and beaten by the three students. He suffered personal injuries including tremors, loss of memory and post-traumatic stress disorder. His mother sued the other students, their parents, the school board and school officials, including the bus driver, in a Louisiana trial court. The assaulting students, their parents and insurers were voluntarily dismissed. The court held the school board alone was liable for a general damage award of $75,000 for the student and $5,000 for his mother. It also awarded the student special damages.

The Court of Appeal of Louisiana held the trial court had erroneously failed to compare the fault of the parties in this case, as required by state law. **While the school board was responsible for the reasonable supervision of students, it was not the insurer of student safety. In a personal injury case involving negligent supervision, it is necessary to show an unreasonable risk of injury is foreseeable to the board that is known and preventable in the exercise of proper supervision.** Evidence indicated school administrators did not follow board policies regarding the prevention of fights among students despite receiving advance notice of a potential fight. The school disciplinarian failed to inform the bus driver about the harassment of the new student. The driver failed to note unauthorized bus riders and other problems on the bus. **The court held the board 20% at fault and each of the assaulting students 25% at fault for the injuries.** The student was 5% at fault for failing to report the strong possibility of a fight. *Frazer v. St. Tammany Parish School Board*, 774 So.2d 1227 (La. Ct. App. 2000).

◆   A Florida law school student allegedly threatened to blow up an office at the law school and frightened three students with intimidating behavior. A school counselor called him "the most volatile and frightening student she had encountered." The school dean issued the student an expulsion letter based on "serious threats" and "physically intimidating conduct." The student claimed he did not receive any notice of the charges and was not provided with a hearing. He sued the school and several of its officials in a federal district court for negligence, defamation and breach of contract.

The school and officials moved to dismiss the case for failure to state a claim upon which relief could be granted. The court agreed to dismiss the negligence claim. Under Florida law, a student may be suspended or expelled for breaching a university's code of conduct. Even if school officials were mistaken in issuing the notice, they were not liable unless they acted with malice. **As there was no finding of malice in this case, the negligence claim was dismissed. There could also be no liability for defamation. The dean's statements were privileged because they were based on the school's interest or duty to investigate and resolve the case.** The court held a contract existed between the student and school, which was governed by the terms of the student handbook. The law school's code of academic integrity specified that students would receive procedural protections before any expulsion decision. The court denied the school's motion to dismiss this claim, as it had apparently breached these contract terms. The court dismissed the remaining claims. *Jarzynka v. St. Thomas Univ. School of Law*, 310 F.Supp.2d 1256 (S.D. Fla. 2004).

B. Threats and Bullying

Student speech may implicate the First Amendment. However, threats of violence have never been considered "protected speech" that warrants First Amendment protection. Moreover, students do not enjoy the extensive speech rights protections available to adults in open society.

Even speech that is not a "threat" may be prohibited by school officials, if it could reasonably be interpreted as creating a threat of school disruption, or would infringe upon the rights of others. This rule comes from the U.S. Supreme Court's leading case on student speech rights, *Tinker v. Des Moines Independent Community School Dist.*, 393 U.S. 503 (1969), which remains one of the most frequently cited of all education cases.

◆   A Georgia art teacher asked a student to hand over a notebook she had passed to a classmate. The teacher read a passage from the notebook labeled "Dream." It described, in first person, an account of a student's feelings while taking a gun to school. The student's narrative expressed loathing her math teacher "with every bone in my body," then shooting him. She wrote of being chased by the police, then seeing a "bullet running at me." The narrative concluded "Then, the bell rings, I pick my head off my desk, shake my head and gather up my books off to my next class." The art teacher spoke with the school liaison officer and principal about the narrative. The officer believed it was "planning in disguise as a dream," and the student was removed from class the next day. At a meeting of school officials, the student and her parent, the student dismissed the narrative as a piece of creative fiction. The principal consulted with the student's math teacher, who expressed shock and stated that he felt threatened by the narrative. He stated he was uncomfortable with having the student in his class. The principal suspended the student for 10 days and recommended expelling her for threats of bodily harm, disregard of school rules and disrespectful conduct. After a hearing, the recommendation was upheld. However, the school board overturned the expulsion decision. The student did not appeal the board's decision to affirm the suspension and retain a record of it. She later sued the school board for an order declaring violation of her First Amendment rights, and clearing her records of the discipline. A federal district court disagreed and awarded pretrial judgment to the school board.

The student appealed to the U.S. Court of Appeals, Eleventh Circuit. The court stated its prior decisions held that "school officials must have the flexibility to control the tenor and contours of student speech within school walls or on school property, even if such speech does not result in a reasonable fear of immediate disruption." The court held that writing the narrative and sharing it with a classmate were reasonably likely to cause material and substantial disruption to school order. While First Amendment rights are not forfeited at the school door, those rights should not interfere with the professional judgment of school administrators. **In the climate of increasing school violence and government oversight, the court found the school had a compelling interest in acting quickly to prevent violence on school property.** The school board and officials did not violate the student's First Amendment rights. *Boim v. Fulton County School Dist.*, 494 F.3d 978 (11th Cir. 2007).

◆ A sixth-grade New York student wrote a violent story about a boy who is bullied at school, stabs a "mean kid" in the head, and later chops off the head of a girl who is having sex with another student. Some characters were named after actual classmates. The student had no prior disciplinary record at the time. The principal suspended him for five days and notified his parents of the suspension. A school psychiatrist conducted a number of psychological tests on the student without informing the parents. After a hearing, the principal imposed a 30-day suspension. The student sued the school district in a federal district court for federal constitutional violations, and for defamation.

The court held schools can prohibit speech that would substantially interfere with the work of the school or impinge upon the rights of others. Speech that constitutes a true threat of violence can be prohibited. It does not matter whether the speaker intends to carry out the threat. The student's speech and due process claims failed. Even though no notice of the harassment charge was provided, he received sufficient notice of the charges forming the basis of the hearing. A 30-day suspension was not excessive. The court dismissed a Fourth Amendment claim for unreasonable search and seizure. **The school was justified in conducting psychological tests on the student because it was reasonable to believe he was capable of violence.** He failed to show that he was defamed, as the principal's statements were truthful. *D.F. v. Board of Educ. of Syosset Cent. School Dist.*, 386 F.Supp.2d 119 (E.D.N.Y. 2005).

The U.S. Court of Appeals, Second Circuit, affirmed the judgment and the U.S. Supreme Court denied further review in 2007.

◆ An Indiana student told friends he was going to get his father's gun, "bring it to school, start with the seventh grade, and work his way up." The threat was made off school grounds, but school officials learned of it. The student admitted making a threat and admitted "what he had done was wrong and against school rules." The student's locker was searched, but no gun was found. Police officers did not find "an unlawful act" and did not file charges against him. The school suspended the student for 10 days for violating its student code of conduct, which adopted Section 20-8.15.7(a)(1) of the Indiana Code. The superintendent held a hearing and expelled the student for three months. The school board upheld the expulsion after a hearing, and a state court upheld the action.

On appeal, the Court of Appeals of Indiana explained that **Section 20-8.1-5.1-9 permits student discipline for unlawful activity on or off school grounds if it may reasonably be considered an interference with school purposes or an educational function**. Removal of a student is authorized if necessary to restore order or protect persons on school property. The court found it was not necessary for law officers to determine whether the student engaged in unlawful activity for school officials to expel him. The board had found his threat was an unlawful act of intimidation. *Sherrell v. Northern Community School Corp. of Tipton County*, 801 N.E.2d 693 (Ind. Ct. App. 2004).

◆ A South Carolina teacher claimed a student disrupted her classroom for over two hours. He also took a swing at the teacher before being escorted from the class. Officials filed a juvenile delinquency petition against him for violating S.C. Code Ann. Section 16-17-420 "by willingly, unlawfully, and unnecessarily interfering with and disturbing the students and teachers." The student sought to dismiss the petition, asserting Section 16-17-420 was unconstitutionally vague and overbroad in violation of the First Amendment to the U.S. Constitution. The court upheld the statute and committed the student to the custody of the juvenile justice department for 90 days, with one year of probation. The student appealed to the state supreme court. He argued the statute was overly broad because it punished a substantial amount of protected speech and was so vague that persons of common intelligence would have to guess at its meaning.

The court noted that Section 16-17-420 was appropriately analyzed under cases involving statutes that targeted conduct which was termed "disruptive" to schools. Most analogous was *McAlpine v. Reese*, 390 F.Supp. 136 (E.D. Mich 1970) which upheld a similar Michigan ordinance prohibiting any noise, disturbance or improper diversion in schools. The Michigan ordinance applied to the type of conduct that could not be tolerated in any ordered society. **The South Carolina court held Section 16-17-420 did not prohibit any speech that was protected by the First Amendment. By its terms, the statute did not apply to protected speech or broadly regulate conduct. "Instead, Section 16-17-420 criminalizes conduct that 'disturbs' or 'interferes' with schools, or is 'obnoxious.'" Section 16-17-420 was limited and was not a substantial threat to free speech. It dealt specifically with school disturbances, not public forums.** The state had a legitimate interest in maintaining the integrity of its education system by preserving classroom discipline. The court found any conduct interfering with the state's legitimate objectives could be prohibited. Section 16-17-420 drew "the very same constitutional line drawn by *Tinker*" and was not unconstitutionally overbroad. The court vacated the lower court's ruling on vagueness for lack of standing. *In re Amir X.S.*, 371 S.C. 380, 639 S.E.2d 144 (S.C. 2006).

◆ A Pennsylvania sixth-grader had no disciplinary record and was described as a good student. She was excused from class and went to the lavatory. There, she found a note on a toilet that read: "A bomb will go off in the school tomorrow." The student notified her teacher about the note. The teacher called the school principal, who in turn called police. Two officers interviewed the student without anyone else present. After extensive questioning, the student admitted she had written the note as "a joke." The student was immediately suspended for violating the district's policy against terroristic threats. The school board held a hearing at which it credited a police officer's testimony. It did not find testimony by the student's father credible and voted for expulsion.

The student sued the school district in a state court. It held the board's decision was not supported by substantial evidence, because it was not shown that she intentionally communicated a threat or placed the note in the lavatory. The school district appealed to the Commonwealth Court of Pennsylvania, which held there was no need for direct evidence that the student put the note in the lavatory. **Circumstantial evidence was sufficient to establish that she communicated a threat. The court found the state can meet its burden of proof in criminal cases with circumstantial evidence.** Courts may not substitute their judgment for that of a school board. As the evidence was sufficient to support expulsion, the court reinstated it. *A.B. v. Slippery Rock Area School Dist.*, 906 A.2d 674 (Pa. Commw. Ct. 2006).

◆ A Pennsylvania student wrote and recorded four "rap songs" at his home that were thought to represent threats against three classmates. He mentioned classmates in two recordings. Some content was uploaded onto a Web site. One CD track was titled "Murder, He Wrote." Although the expression took place at home and none of the CDs were brought on school grounds, the school board voted to expel the student and ban him from school grounds. The student sought a federal court order preventing the expulsion and the ban from school property.

The court found no evidence of a "true threat" to the classmates. The rap genre used rhymes, metaphors and "violent imagery," but the court found no actual violence was intended. **There was no evidence that the student directly communicated a message to classmates. The "songs" were either published on the internet or sold in the community. The classmates themselves did not indicate they felt threatened.** The school district did not perform its own investigation before acting. According to the court, there was no evidence that copies of the CDs were sold or distributed in school. As there was no evidence of any school disruption due to the student's expression, he was entitled to a preliminary order preventing expulsion. *Latour v. Riverside Beaver School Dist.*, No. Civ.A. 05-1076, 2005 WL 2106562 (W.D. Pa. 2005).

◆ A Louisiana student drew a sketch of his high school being soaked with gasoline and threatened by a missile launcher, helicopter and armed figures. The sketch included obscenities and racial epithets, and it showed a brick being thrown at the principal. The sketch pad was put in a closet for two years. The student's brother found the pad and drew a picture on it. He brought the pad to school, and a classmate noticed the student's old sketch. He told a school bus driver "look, they're going to blow up EAHS." The driver confiscated the pad and gave it to the principal. School officials questioned the student and searched him after he admitted he drew the sketch. They found a box cutter, notebooks referring to death, drugs, sex and gang symbols, as well as a fake ID. The principal recommended expulsion. Before the hearing, the student's mother signed a waiver form agreeing to enroll the student in an alternative school. After returning to the high school the next year, the student sued the school board in a federal district court. The court held the sketch was not entitled to First Amendment protection, because it was a "true threat" under standards set by the U.S. Supreme Court.

The court found no Fourth Amendment violation in the search, and no due process violation concerning the waiver of a hearing. The family appealed to the U.S. Court of Appeals, Fifth Circuit. It held the sketch was not speech on school grounds. **The fact that the student's brother unwittingly took the sketch to his school did not make it campus-related speech. The district court improperly found the sketch was a "true threat" with no First Amendment protection.** The school lacked authority to discipline the student for its accidental appearance on campus. Despite the First Amendment violation, the court found the line between fully protected "off-campus speech" and less protected "on-campus speech" was unclear. The principal was entitled to qualified immunity, as he had acted reasonably. The court upheld the judgment on the Fourth Amendment and due process claims. The search was appropriate under the circumstances. The mother knowingly waived a hearing so her son could gain the alternative school placement. The student admitted his responsibility for the sketch and his ownership of the box cutter. The district court had correctly awarded summary judgment to the school board and officials. *Porter v. Ascension Parish School Board*, 393 F.3d 608 (5th Cir. 2004).

◆ Two Ohio eighth-grade students with criminal records watched television coverage of the Columbine incident together. One of them called a classmate and told her that they planned to bring a gun or a bomb to school. The student told her he would "kill the preps" first and she would be "one of the first to go." Two days later at school, one of the students wrote a similar threat to another classmate. The classmates told a school guidance counselor, and a vice principal obtained their written statements. After attempting to reach the first student's mother, the vice principal contacted the student's probation officer and showed him the classmates' statements. The probation officer inquired about their credibility and the vice principal verified he believed them. Both students were placed in a detention facility and then appeared in juvenile court. A prosecutor eventually dropped their cases. The first student's mother received no suspension notice, but kept him home from school for over a week to shield him from any backlash by peers. The assistant superintendent told the second student's parent there would be no expulsion unless he was convicted.

The parents sued school and law enforcement officials in a federal district court, which held for the officials. The parents appealed to the Sixth Circuit. The court noted the probation officer investigated the classmates' statements before he acted. The vice principal met with the first student, who confirmed he knew about the note and admitted talking about Columbine. **The court found the probation officer and his supervisor had probable cause to believe the students made threats of aggravated menacing.** The Due Process Clause does not impose formalities on short-term school discipline. **Oral or written notice of the charges and an opportunity for the student to explain his or her side of the story usually satisfies due process.** Neither student was even suspended. The first student's mother admitted she made the choice to keep him home. The second student's mother was advised that suspension papers would not be prepared unless her son was found guilty of the juvenile charges. Both students received all the process they were due, and the court affirmed the judgment on their due process claims. Their state law claims for false arrest and false imprisonment failed because there was probable cause to detain them. *Williams v. Cambridge Board of Educ.*, 370 F.3d 630 (6th Cir. 2004).

◆ An Illinois sixth-grade student earned good grades and had no disciplinary record until he brought CDs to school containing a "song" titled "Gonna Kill Mrs. Cox's Baby." A classmate played the CD twice in the school's computer lab. The school suspended the student and scheduled an expulsion hearing. At the hearing, a police officer testified the student was not dangerous and did not intend to harm the teacher. Many witnesses testified about the student's good character. The principal recommended expelling him for the remaining 50 days of the school year. The school board voted in favor of the recommendation. The student petitioned a state court for a temporary restraining order reinstating him to school. The court held for the student, finding he did not cause any disruption at school and that "the disruption resulted from the investigation."

On appeal, the state appellate court explained **school officials were in a better position than judges to decide what to do with disobedient students**. The court rejected the trial court's findings. The school administration could not turn a blind eye to a CD stating a teacher's baby would be killed. It was not unreasonable to suspend the student for 50 days for a threat that was "gross disobedience" or "misconduct" under state law. School policy prohibited threats or joking about violent acts that might be reasonably interpreted as a threat or plan to engage in violence. The student clearly committed a violation of school rules. **Threats of violence in school were not permitted whether they were serious or not.** A threat like this one was not subject to an immediate determination about whether a student intended to carry it out. The court found the board had reasonably imposed the 50-day expulsion. State law permitted expulsions of up to two calendar years, and the student would be allowed to return for seventh grade. School officials have wide discretion in their disciplinary actions. As the trial court abused its discretion, the appellate court reversed and vacated its decision. *Wilson ex rel. Geiger v. Hinsdale Elementary School Dist. 181*, 349 Ill.App.3d 243, 810 N.E.2d 637 (Ill. App. Ct. 2004).

◆ New Jersey school officials grew concerned about three incidents involving threats by young students to use firearms. The principal visited each class to discuss firearms threats. She wrote letters to parents asking them to discuss the situation with their children. Five days after the principal addressed students and sent home the letter, a student said he was playing cops and robbers with his friends when he said "I'm going to shoot you." However, a teacher reported other students were upset and took the student and three others to the office. The principal suspended them for four days. She was unable to contact the student's parents, but sent them a letter explaining the suspension. The student's father sued the school board, principal and district superintendent in a federal district court for constitutional rights violations. The court held for the board and administrators on immunity grounds. The father appealed to the U.S. Court of Appeals, Third Circuit.

The court explained that "**a school's authority to control student speech in an elementary school is undoubtedly greater than in a high school setting.**" **Officials need not provide students the same latitude afforded to adult speakers and do not have to tolerate student speech that is inconsistent with the school's basic educational mission.** The student did not establish a First Amendment violation. The principal acted within her discretion by determining threats of violence and simulated firearms use were unacceptable. The court dismissed the student's attempt to "ratchet up" his playground speech to the level of a political statement. Unlike *Tinker v. Des Moines Independent Community School Dist.* (this chapter) there was no political speech here. The prohibition on threats of violence and firearms was a legitimate decision related to reasonable pedagogical concerns and was not a First Amendment violation. The school officials were entitled to immunity as they could reasonably believe they were acting within their authority. The student's claims of due process and equal protection violations had no merit, and the court affirmed the judgment. *S.G., as Guardian of A.G. v. Sayreville Board of Educ.*, 333 F.3d 417 (3d Cir. 2003).

C. Hazing

Hazing was traditionally seen at higher education institutions, but some incidents have occurred in secondary schools in recent years. The liability standard in hazing cases is similar to that used in bullying cases. The plaintiff in a hazing case must show that the school was aware of the hazing before liability may be imposed on the school. The official in the following case invoked a speech rights argument in his defense.

◆ A New York school athletic director (AD) complained to the school board and district superintendent that the high school football coach improperly supervised students and encouraged them to use a dangerous muscle enhancer. A parent of one team member wrote to the school board president that she heard stories of severe misconduct in the locker room, including shoving a bottle up a student's rectum. During a subsequent school investigation, a 14-year-old freshman football player told the AD that some teammates had rubbed their genitals in his face, a form of hazing called "tea-bagging." The district changed its supervision protocols in football locker rooms. It also sought involvement by the state police and advised parents that unspecified sexual harassment and/or hazing had been discovered. The AD sent the superintendent a letter repeating his criticisms of the football coach. He further expressed concern about the district's handling of the tea-bagging investigation. A number of students and teachers were arrested, and the entire high school football coaching staff was suspended. The school board met in an executive session and reached "informal consensus" to abolish the AD position from the district budget. He called a press conference, where he stated that the decision to abolish his position was in retribution for his criticism of the coach and the district's investigation. After being demoted to a social studies teaching position at a lower salary, the AD sued the board and administrators in a federal district court for retaliation. The court held for the board, finding no causal connection between the AD's speech and the elimination of his position.

On appeal, the U.S. Court of Appeals, Second Circuit, stated **"the First Amendment protects any matter of political, social or other concern to the community."** The AD's speech arose from an incident of obvious public concern – the sexual assault of a student on school property. The fact that the letter was private did not make its content a purely private grievance. Having a personal stake in the speech did not destroy any public concern the speech contained. The court held a reasonable jury could reject the board's argument that the AD's position would have been eliminated even if not for his protected speech. *Cioffi v. Averill Park Cent. School Dist. Board of Educ.*, 444 F.3d 158 (2d Cir. 2006).

◆ An Ohio student claimed two older students invited him to a "jazz band meeting" early in a school year. He followed them into a lavatory, where he was punched and kicked by a group of students. The student said he received numerous bruises and neck and back injuries and was threatened with more beatings. He sued the board and school officials in a state court, asserting the school board and administration knew of and tolerated a "Freshman Beating Day." The court held for the board and administrators, and the student appealed.

State law authorized civil actions against student organizations, schools and school employees, if the school knew or should have known of hazing and made no reasonable attempt to prevent it. The Court of Appeals of Ohio held "student organization" meant a specific organization, not an entire student body. The "jazz band meeting" reference did not make the beating an initiation into a student organization. "Initiation" implied voluntary membership and consent by the victim to be hazed. The student did not agree to be beaten and would probably not have entered the lavatory had he known it was planned. **The court held that even if the school officials were aware of and tolerated "Freshman Friday," the beating did not constitute "hazing" under state law.** It affirmed the judgment for the board and officials. *Duitch v. Canton City Schools*, 157 Ohio App.3d 80, 809 N.E.2d 62 (Ohio Ct. App. 2004).

◆ A University of Pittsburgh student applied to the Beta Epsilon chapter of the Kappa Alpha Psi fraternity after Kappa lifted a restriction on inducting new members that had been imposed when a Kappa pledge died in Missouri. The student attended a fraternity gathering and was paddled more than 200 times by four fraternity brothers. He went to the hospital the next day and remained there for three weeks with renal failure, seizures and hypertension. He later sued Kappa, the local chapter, the chapter advisor and a number of others for negligence.

A Pennsylvania appellate court found that even though Kappa owed a duty of care to the student, he failed to show that it breached that duty. For example, he failed to show that the two-year moratorium on new members was merely a symbolic gesture and not a sincere attempt to curb hazing. However, **he was allowed to proceed with his lawsuit against the chapter advisor.** The evidence indicated that the chapter advisor failed to discuss hazing with local chapter members and did not advise them to read the executive orders that imposed sanctions for hazing. *Kenner v. Kappa Alpha Psi Fraternity*, 808 A.2d 178 (Pa. Super. Ct. 2002).

◆ The Texas A&M Corps of Cadets is a voluntary student military training organization consisting of approximately 2,000 students (about 5% of the student population). Members of the Corps live together, drill together, stand for inspections and physically train on a daily basis. A freshman student enrolled as a member of the Corps and joined a precision rifle drill team. **During "hell week," he was allegedly subjected to numerous hazing incidents by the drill team advisors, including having his head taped like a mummy, and endured several beatings.** He also was allegedly beaten after the drill team lost a competition to another school. He never reported the incidents to school authorities, but his parents informed them that hazing was occurring. Near the end of his first year, the student went to a "hound interview" where he was beaten and forced to cut himself with a knife. He and his parents then met with the Commandant of the Corps, who took them to the university police to file criminal charges. All the drill team advisors were then expelled or suspended for hazing. The student sued a number of Corps officials under 42 U.S.C. § 1983 and Texas' hazing statute, alleging the officials' failure to supervise Corps activities showed deliberate indifference to his constitutional rights.

The U.S. District Court for the Southern District of Texas held that **the actions of the Corps officials in educating students about the illegality of hazing were reasonable**. They disseminated brochures and other materials to explain what hazing was and how to prevent it. They met with students and their parents to discuss hazing and to encourage parents to report it if they saw evidence of it, and they reasonably believed that their efforts were sufficient to prevent constitutional violations. **As a result, the court found that the officials were entitled to qualified immunity from suit.** On appeal, the Fifth Circuit Court of Appeals affirmed the grant of immunity to the officials. The student failed to show that the officials were deliberately indifferent to his constitutional rights. *Alton v. Hopgood*, 168 F.3d 196 (5th Cir. 1999).

◆ A student who attended Cornell University allegedly enduring beatings, torture, psychological coercion, and embarrassment, while pledging a fraternity. He sued Cornell for negligent supervision, premises liability and breach of an implied contract to protect him. The U.S. District Court for the Northern District of New York dismissed the action, finding that there was no special relationship between the university and the student, and that the university published information about the dangers of hazing and its prohibition on campus. **Further, the university did not have sufficient reason to believe that hazing activities were going on; and once it became aware of the hazing, it took disciplinary action against the perpetrators.** Finally, the court could find no evidence of any specific promises by the university that could be deemed part of an implied contract. The university was not liable for the hazing of the student. *Lloyd v. Alpha Phi Alpha Fraternity*, 1999 U.S. Dist. LEXIS 906 (N.D.N.Y. 1/26/99).

◆ A 17-year-old New York college freshman was invited to pledge a fraternity and died after consuming excessive amounts of alcohol during a hazing ritual. His parents sued several members of the fraternity for negligence and also asserted claims under two New York statutes. The fraternity members sought to have two of the causes of action against them dismissed, and the case reached the Supreme Court, Appellate Division. The court held the fraternity members were not entitled to dismissal. **The parents alleged their son's intoxication was not entirely voluntary and that careless acts by the fraternity members went beyond the mere furnishing of intoxicants.** The action against the fraternity members could proceed. *Oja v. Grand Chapter of Theta Chi Fraternity*, 684 N.Y.S.2d 344 (N.Y. App. Div. 1999).

◆ A five-year veteran of the Navy enrolled in the Military College of Vermont of Norwich University under a Navy Reserve Officer Training

Corps scholarship. He lasted for only 16 days, during which he was subjected to, and observed, repeated instances of hazing by upperclassmen. After withdrawing from school, he sued the university for assault and battery, infliction of emotional distress and negligence, asserting that it was vicariously liable for the actions of the upperclassmen. A jury returned a verdict in the student's favor, awarding him almost $500,000 in compensatory damages and $1.75 million in punitive damages. The Supreme Court of Vermont affirmed the compensatory damage award against the university, but reversed the award of punitive damages, finding no evidence of malice on the university's part. Here, **the university had charged the upperclassmen with "indoctrinating and orienting" the student**. As a result, this was not a simple case of student-on-student hazing for which the university could not be held liable. Because the upperclassmen were acting as agents of the university, it breached its duty of care toward the student. The court also found that the nearly $500,000 in compensatory damages awarded by the jury was not clearly erroneous. *Brueckner v. Norwich Univ.*, 730 A.2d 1086 (Vt. 1999).

II. NON-STUDENT THREATS AND VIOLENCE

A. Student to Teacher

◆ A New Jersey teacher was supervising an assembly in a school auditorium when a student bolted from his seat and charged another student. The teacher was knocked down from behind and injured. She sued the school district and officials in the state court system for negligence, carelessness and other unreasonable conduct. The teacher stated the district should be liable for damages due to the student's history of behavioral problems and inadequate discipline. She claimed school administrators should not have allowed him to remain in the regular student body. A state trial court awarded judgment to the school district and officials, and the teacher appealed. **The Superior Court of New Jersey, Appellate Division, stated workers' compensation is an employee's sole remedy against an employer for on-the-job injuries, except where the employer commits an "intentional wrong."**

The student had a "troubled past," including juvenile delinquency adjudications based on assault and resisting arrest. The school had suspended him and placed him in an alternative school. The student's most serious incident was "trashing" a school bus, and most of his disciplinary incidents involved skipping detention assigned to him on Saturdays. A board-certified psychiatrist had evaluated the student several months before the incident, concluding he was not a threat to peers and could return to school. The court noted testimony by school officials that no student had been expelled from the school for many years. None of these incidents involved physical violence. **The court found "student fights cannot be said to be so totally unexpected or unusual as to allow an** injured teacher to recover outside the Workers' Compensation scheme." Teachers were involved in "a multitude of activities involving students that go far beyond the teaching curriculum." They acted as advisors, counselors, hall, bus and cafeteria monitors, and as disciplinarians. The court held the legislature intended to immunize teacher injuries performing their various "multifunctional roles" under the Workers Compensation scheme. The trial court had properly recognized teachers are often called upon to supervise teachers in non-teaching settings. The court found the injury was not intentional and affirmed the dismissal of the lawsuit. *Kibler v. Roxbury Board of Educ.*, 392 N.J. Super. 45, 919 A.2d 878 (N.J. Super. 2007).

◆ A California student pushed students and made sexual innuendos to girls as a third-grader. His parents rejected placement in a program for those with emotional/behavioral problems. As a fourth-grader, the student hit or pinched others, punched two students and was suspended two or three times. The parents again rejected any special placement, as they did not want their son "labeled." The student told classmates "he wanted to put a bullet in the head of his teacher," the teacher's wife and baby. In fifth grade, the student was suspended for defiant and obscene acts and hitting others. A psychologist stated the student was a "significant risk for expulsion" and might be a danger to self and others. He recommended a more self-contained environment. The student made a journal entry about his fifth grade teacher stating "I hate her .... I can make her dead. I can beat the heck out of her. I can make her cry for a thousand years." A meeting was held to discuss a "Crossroads program," and the mother consented to the placement. The student reportedly tried to choke his mother at the meeting, and she changed her mind. The parents finally provided the school with medical information they had previously withheld. The records indicated the student met eligibility criteria for an emotionally disturbed special education classification. The student was out of school for weeks. When he returned, the psychologist recommended placing him in a program for emotionally disturbed students. The mother again insisted he remain in a regular classroom. On a day when the student had knocked down a classmate on the playground, the teacher accompanied him to the school bus. The student charged into her and knocked her down on the school bus.

The teacher filed a workers' compensation claim and received total benefits of over $91,000. She sought additional workers' compensation, alleging serious and willful misconduct. The state Workers' Compensation Appeals Board awarded the teacher an additional $45,785, representing one-half the total benefits previously paid. On appeal, the Court of Appeal of California explained that the amount of compensation for an injured employee is increased by one-half if the employer engages in serious and willful misconduct. **A finding of serious and willful misconduct must be based on evidence of failure to act for employee safety, despite knowledge that failure would probably result in injury. The court held**

the school district did not deliberately or consciously fail to take action for the teacher's safety. School staff had been trying to place the student in a behavior-based placement since third grade. The parents had repeatedly refused their consent to this placement. The school district had finally overcome the parents' reluctance to release his medical and behavioral information and found him eligible for an emotionally disturbed program, put him on a daily contract and suspended and counseled him several times. As the district did not deliberately or consciously fail to act for the teacher's safety, the court annulled the award of additional benefits. *Elk Grove Unified. School Dist. v. Workers' Compensation Appeals Board*, No. C052945, 2007 WL 1169336 (Cal. Ct. App. 4/20/07).

B. Parent Misconduct

◆ Under Louisiana law, parents are legally accountable for the acts of their children. An 11-year-old student with impulsivity and aggression problems pointed a toy gun at a teaching assistant (TA). The TA did not know the gun was a toy and claimed to be emotionally and mentally traumatized. The TA received workers' compensation benefits for psychological injuries. In an effort to recover what was paid to her in workers' compensation benefits, the school board sued the student's mother in a state court. The board claimed the student was negligent and argued the mother was personally liable for his actions.

The court held for the mother, and the board appealed. The Court of Appeal of Louisiana stated that **Louisiana courts have held the parents of minor children liable for harm caused by a child's conduct under Civil Code Article 2318, even where a parent is not personally negligent**. The student could be deemed negligent only if a court found he violated the applicable standard of care. The court affirmed the judgment, finding that given his maturity level, lack of awareness of risks and his inclination to be impulsive and aggressive, he did not breach the standard of care. Because the student was not negligent, his mother could not be held liable for his actions. *Lafayette Parish School Board v. Cormier*, 901 So. 2d 1197 (La. Ct. App. 2005).

◆ A Tennessee father of two children sought to divorce his wife. She obtained a temporary restraining order splitting custody of the children. A school policy allowed students to leave with their parents, with the principal's approval. The date and time of student departure and return was to be recorded with the reason for leaving school. The father became upset when he came to school and learned his mother-in-law had taken the children to their mother. The mother told staff not to release the children to their father, but a staff member said that would require a court order. The next day, the father came to school for both children. The reasons he gave for signing them out were "keeping promise by mother" for the daughter and "pay back" for the son. The son's teacher read the reasons after he left and notified the principal. However, the father had already left with both children. Police arrived at his house to find it ablaze. The father brandished a knife and the police shot him to death. The children's bodies were found inside. The mother sued the school board in a state court for negligence.

The court held for the board, and the mother appealed. The state court of appeals held **schools, teachers and school administrators have a duty to exercise ordinary care for student safety**. The board was not liable for negligently violating its own sign-out policy. There was no evidence that staff knew of a dispute until the mother called the day before the murders. The trial court correctly held a **school has no legal duty to follow the instruction of one parent not to release a child to the other parent without a court order to this effect**. The court affirmed judgment on a claim based on the father's violent nature. However, **failure to read his reasons for signing out the children was evidence of breach of the duty to exercise ordinary care for the children's safety. The court rejected the board's claim that it had no legal duty to examine a parent's reason for signing out a child.** The reasons the father wrote for signing out the children might cause a reasonable person to suspect he intended harm. The state Governmental Tort Liability Act did not protect the board, since the decision to release the children involved no planning. The case was reversed and remanded for further consideration. *Haney v. Bradley County Board of Educ.*, 160 S.W.3d 886 (Tenn. Ct. App. 2004).

◆   An Ohio student with autism and pervasive disability disorder exhibited violent, disruptive behavior in kindergarten and first grade. His second grade individualized education program (IEP) placed him in regular classes with a full-time aide. Early in the year, the IEP team met and modified the student's IEP to include pull-out services and a behavior plan to address his increasingly violent and disruptive behavior. Days after the meeting, the student disrupted his class during a math test, flew into a rage and repeatedly struck his teacher. She took him to the hallway and restrained him, but when she released him, he kicked her in the face and neck. The teacher sued the student's parents and the school district in a state court for negligent and intentional conduct. The court found nothing in the student's behavioral history indicated he would cause injuries of the kind alleged by the teacher. It held for the parents and the school district, and the teacher appealed.

The Court of Appeals of Ohio held that parents may be held liable for the wrongful conduct of their children when the injury is a foreseeable consequence of their negligence. Ohio courts have recognized that **parents may be held liable for failing to exercise reasonable control over a child, despite knowledge that injury to another person is a probable consequence**. The student frequently hit and kicked students, teachers and aides, lashing out when frustrated in his classes or when touched or bumped by classmates. The case was complicated by special education law purposes and procedures. Merely advocating for the placement of the student in regular education settings could not make the parents liable.

While they were IEP team members, the placement decision was not theirs alone. However, there was evidence that the parents' "aggressive participation and pressure at the IEP meetings was a major factor in the IEP team's final decision." The court reversed the judgment for the parents, but held the trial court had correctly found the district was entitled to sovereign immunity under the state code. The judgment for the district was affirmed. *Coolidge v. Riegle*, No. 5-02-59, 2004-Ohio-347, 2004 WL 170319 (Ohio Ct. App. 2004).

◆ A Minnesota student's parent was accused of yelling at two teachers when he came to school to ask why his son was not enrolled in computer classes. The school principal wrote him a letter responding to his questions, directing him to control his anger, refrain from yelling at her staff and to sign in at the school office when he visited campus. The parent responded with a threatening letter to the principal. Later in the school year, he came to school and became angry when he learned that a class in which he was attempting to enroll his son was unavailable. The parent threatened to return to the school "with witnesses" and left the building. The principal called 911 as a precaution, but the parent did not return to the school. The school district petitioned a state court for an anti-harassment restraining order. The court issued a temporary order and after a hearing, it held that the letter and yelling incidents constituted harassment. The court issued a permanent restraining order against the parent, and he appealed.

The Minnesota Court of Appeals found sufficient evidence to support a finding of harassment under the harassment restraining order statute. The statutory term "harassment" included a single incident of physical or sexual assault, or repeated incidents of intrusive or unwanted acts, words or gestures that had a substantial adverse effect on the safety, security or privacy of another. **It was unnecessary to show the harassing conduct is obscene or vulgar.** The parent had yelled at staff members and wrote a threatening letter to the principal. Based on this evidence, the trial court did not abuse its discretion in permanently restraining him from harassing school staff. The court affirmed the judgment. *Independent School Dist. No. 381 v. Olson*, No. C9-00-888, 2001 WL 32807 (Minn. Ct. App. 2001).

◆ An Illinois mother had sole custody of her two children, but her divorce decree specified the children's father had joint, equal access rights to school records. The parents were required to cooperate to ensure authorities sent them dual notices of their children's school progress and activities. The father criticized a school principal at public meetings, complained that nothing was done when his son was bullied, and claimed the school did not provide him notices, records, correspondence and other documents sent to custodial parents. He wrote letters to the principal about these matters, then stated the principal excluded him from the playground when he sought to observe his son during recess, and turned him down as a volunteer playground monitor. The father sued the principal and school district in a federal district court for constitutional and state law violations. The court dismissed the case, and he appealed.

The U.S. Court of Appeals, Seventh Circuit, noted the difficulty for schools to accommodate demands by divorced parents. **School officials could not know a parent's rights until they consulted the divorce decree, but did not have to be dragged into fights between divorced parents over their children.** The father's rights concerning his children's records were no greater than the school's interest in keeping as free as possible from divorce matters. **The only constitutional right concerning the education of one's child was the right to choose the child's school. The court held this was not a right to participate in the school's management. Schools also have a valid interest in limiting a parent's presence on campus.** The court rejected the father's claim to a constitutional right to participate in his children's education in the degree he sought. However, he should receive a chance to show that the principal had deliberately treated him differently than custodial parents, and had violated his speech rights. While most of the father's criticisms of administrators were "personal," he also alleged being critical of them in public meetings and questioned their inadequate responses to bullying. The district and the principal prevailed on the father's due process claims, but the equal protection and speech rights claims were remanded to the district court for further consideration. *Crowley v. McKinney*, 400 F.3d 965 (7th Cir. 2005).

◆   A Texas parent yelled at his son's first-grade teacher and followed her into a parking lot. He spanked his son and a classmate while they walked in a school hallway, and he used profanity when speaking to administrators. The school restricted him from classrooms and instructed him to schedule a formal conference with the principal if he wanted to speak to teachers. When the parent ignored these directives, the school banned him from campus, and twice called the police to have him removed from school property. The parent picketed in front of the school and confronted a teacher during a class field trip, shouting and swearing in front of students. He sued the district in a federal district court, claiming a constitutional right to be on school grounds, and alleging speech violations and infliction of emotional distress by the district.

A federal magistrate judge found **no court has ever construed the Due Process Clause as creating a parental right of access to school facilities. Courts have "consistently upheld the authority of school officials to control activities on school property."** The magistrate judge held **this included the authority to bar parents from campus when necessary to maintain order**. There was an escalating pattern of threatening, abusive and disruptive conduct by the parent toward the school faculty and administration, defeating his due process claim. **Under *Connick v. Myers*, 461 U.S. 138 (1983), speech is only protected by the Constitution if it addresses a "matter of public concern."** The parent's speech claim was based on private communications about his own children, and did not involve the public concern. There was no evidence that the school was motivated by retaliation. It banned him from campus as a result of his threatening, abusive and disruptive behavior. The magistrate judge recommended that the court award summary judgment to the district on all the parent's claims. *Rogers v. Duncanville Independent School Dist.*, No. 3-04-CV-0365-D, 2005 WL 770712 (N.D. Tex. 2005).

The district court reviewed the magistrate judge's findings and recommendations, found them correct and adopted them. It awarded summary judgment to the district. *Rogers v. Duncanville Independent School Dist.*, No. 3:04CV0365D, 2005 WL 991287 (N.D. Tex. 2005).

◆ The non-custodial parent of a Virginia high school student complained repeatedly to school employees that his son was not selected for the varsity basketball team. The student's mother had previously requested notice from the school so that she could be present for discussions involving her children. The school principal notified the father that such meetings had to be scheduled in advance to accommodate the mother's request, and that he should otherwise limit his presence on school property to public events. The father asserted that these limitations violated his constitutional rights. The superintendent sent him a letter barring him from school property due to continuing inappropriate behavior toward school officials, staff, and board members. The father sued the district in a federal district court for constitutional rights violations. The case was dismissed, and he appealed to the U.S. Court of Appeals, Fourth Circuit.

The court held "school officials have the authority and responsibility for assuring that parents and third parties conduct themselves appropriately while on school property." While the specific contours of this authority and responsibility were defined by state law, **"officials should never be intimidated into compromising the safety of those who utilize school property."** In this case, the school district gave the father ample opportunity to complain about the conduct of school board members and officials before the superintendent's letter. **The superintendent found the father's conduct was a threat and appropriately requested that he not enter school property.** The right to communicate is not limitless, and the letter banning the father from school property did not implicate any constitutional rights. The court held the claims against the superintendent for money damages were frivolous. *Lovern v. Edwards*, 190 F.3d 648 (4th Cir. 1999).

III. STALKING AND HARASSMENT

A. Gender

1. Harassment

Sexual harassment has been recognized by the courts as a form of sex discrimination. Title IX of the Education Amendments of 1972 prohibits sex discrimination by recipients of federal funding. In *Davis v. Monroe County Board of Educ.*, below, the Supreme Court held schools could be liable under Title IX for student-on-student harassment. To prevail, students must show (1) sexual harassment by peers; (2) deliberate indifference by school officials with actual knowledge of the harassment; and (3) harassment so severe, pervasive and objectively offensive it deprived the student of access to educational opportunities. A teacher's knowledge of peer harassment is sufficient to create "actual knowledge" that may trigger district liability.

◆   A Georgia fifth-grader complained to her teacher of sexual harassment by a male student. The teacher did not immediately notify the principal about it. **Although the harasser was eventually charged with sexual battery, school officials took no action against him.** The student sued the school board in a federal district court for Title IX violations. The court dismissed the case and the student appealed to the U.S. Court of Appeals, Eleventh Circuit. The court reversed the judgment but granted the board's petition for rehearing. On rehearing, the court observed that if it adopted the student's argument, a school board must immediately isolate an alleged harasser to avoid a Title IX lawsuit. It affirmed the dismissal of the student's claims and she appealed.

The U.S. Supreme Court reversed the judgment, holding **school districts may be held liable under Title IX for deliberate indifference to known acts of peer sexual harassment, where the school's response is clearly unreasonable under the circumstances**. A recipient of federal funds may be liable for student-on-student sexual harassment where the funding recipient is deliberately indifferent to known sexual harassment and the harasser is under the recipient's disciplinary authority. To create Title IX liability, the harassment must be so severe, pervasive and objectively offensive that it deprives the victim of access to educational opportunities or benefits. The Court held the harassment alleged by the student was sufficiently severe enough to avoid pretrial dismissal. It reversed and remanded the case. *Davis v. Monroe County Board of Educ.*, 526 U.S. 629, 119 S.Ct. 1661, 143 L.Ed.2d 839 (1999).

◆   A Pennsylvania general education student claimed her school did nothing to address repeated sexual harassment by a disabled classmate for over four years. The classmate's individualized education program (IEP) had a behavior plan for grade seven, but no mention was made of his harassing behavior toward the student and no services were provided to address it. The student continued to report unwanted attention from the classmate over the next four years, such as notes, drawings, and offers to be her boyfriend. In grade eleven, she reported the classmate began to stalk her, but the IEP team removed his behavior plan and recommended no discipline. In their senior year, the classmate found the student alone in a school weight room and prevented her from leaving for half an hour. School administrators met with the student's family and a state trooper. Criminal charges were not filed because the trooper found the classmate "was too low functioning to understand the nature of the offenses." The school district advised staff that the classmate was to have no contact with the student, and a behavior plan was placed in his IEP. The student's mother had worked for 26 years as a vision specialist for an education agency that served the school district. She asked to address the district's board, but the superintendent told her to write a letter instead. The mother wrote a letter reviewing the situation and asking the board to take steps to prepare and train district administrators and staff on handling students with noncompliant behavior. Her complaint to the state department of education was dismissed.

The district superintendent asked the education agency's director to reassign the mother. She filed an unsuccessful grievance to challenge the transfer, then sued the school district, education agency, superintendent and others in a federal district court. **The court held liability for sexual harassment exists under Title IX if a school official with control over a harasser had actual knowledge of sexual harassment, but was deliberately indifferent to it.** The student and her mother had reported the classmate's conduct to teachers, guidance counselors and vice principals, who should have informed the principal. Officials with control over school discipline had actual knowledge of the harassment, beginning in grade eight. While a "district is not required to purge its schools of actionable peer harassment," officials must "respond to known peer harassment in a manner that is not clearly unreasonable." The district's response was unreasonable. It removed a behavior plan from the classmate's IEP, and he had no behavior plan for much of his high school career. The court denied a motion to dismiss the student's Title IX claim. The mother's claims were not dismissed either, as she raised issues of public concern about school safety and sexual harassment. Public agencies cannot retaliate against employees based on their speech. *Jones v. Indiana Area School Dist.*, 397 F.Supp.2d 628 (W.D. Pa. 2005).

◆ A Michigan student claimed a classmate raped her in a school lavatory during school hours. She sued the district, its board and two administrators in a federal district court for violations of state and federal law. The student claimed the principal and an assistant principal knew the classmate was sexually active, warranting liability for the district. The court awarded summary judgment to the district, finding no evidence that the district knew of sexual harassment by the classmate prior to the rape. The court declined jurisdiction over the state law claims, and the student appealed to the U.S. Court of Appeals, Sixth Circuit.

The court noted the Supreme Court recognized a private cause of action under Title IX for peer sexual harassment in *Davis v. Monroe County Board of Educ.* The *Davis* standard imposes liability on a district for harassment so severe, pervasive and objectively offensive it deprives the victim of educational benefits. The court noted **the district could be found to have subjected the student to harassment by the classmate only if it acted with "deliberate indifference to known acts of student-on-student harassment." The student could not meet this standard, as there was no evidence the district knew of even one incident of student-on-student harassment before the reported rape.** Evidence that the principal knew students engaged in sexual activity on campus was irrelevant. Harassment claims involve only "unwelcome" sexual advances. As there was no evidence of any student-on-student sexual harassment prior to the reported rape, the student could not show the district "subjected" her to sexual harassment. The court affirmed the judgment for the district. *Winzer v. School Dist. for City of Pontiac*, 105 Fed.Appx. 679 (6th Cir. 2004).

◆   An Illinois kindergartner reported a male classmate jumped on her back during a recess period near the start of the school year. He continued to exhibit inappropriate behavior, including repeatedly unzipping his pants. The school assigned the classmate to detention and sent him to the school psychologist's office. Several female students were also sent to the psychologist, and they reported the classmate had been jumping on them and kissing them during recess. Later in the year, the kindergartner's mother informed the school that the kindergartner had experienced nightmares, bedwetting and a growing fear of school. The principal suspended the classmate for two days and reassigned him to a new classroom, lunch and recess period. However, the classmate and kindergartner were later returned to the same lunch and recess periods, and the mother alleged he continued to bother her. A counselor diagnosed the kindergartner as having acute stress disorder and separation anxiety, and she received therapy. The district granted the parents' request to transfer her to a different school for first grade, and they sued the district for sexual harassment under Title IX. A federal district court awarded the district summary judgment.

The parents appealed to the Seventh Circuit, which applied the *Davis* deliberate indifference standard. While common sense weighed against a finding that kindergartners could engage in sexual harassment, the case could be decided without answering that question. As noted in Davis, **young students are still learning how to act appropriately, and they "regularly interact in a manner that would be unacceptable among adults."** For this reason, **"simple acts of teasing and name calling among children" do not create Title IX liability**. The kindergartner was unable to report conduct other than "vague and unspecific" allegations that the classmate "bothered her by doing nasty stuff." This did not provide the court with necessary details to evaluate its severity and pervasiveness. There was evidence kindergartners were unaware of the sexual nature of the conduct. The kindergartner was not denied access to an education, as neither her grades nor her attendance suffered. The court affirmed the judgment, because the district's response to the harassment was not clearly unreasonable and did not amount to deliberate indifference. *Gabrielle M. v. Park Forest-Chicago Heights School Dist. 163*, 315 F.3d 817 (7th Cir. 2003).

◆   Two female second-graders claimed a boy repeatedly chased, touched and grabbed them and often made sexual remarks and gestures. This conduct continued for several months, but the girls did not communicate the sexual nature of it, telling the teacher that the boy was "annoying," "gross," "nasty" or "disgusting." While staff members observed the boy's behavior and disciplined him for it, no adult saw him engage in overtly sexual behavior. Near the end of the school year, a third girl began attending the school and promptly complained to her teacher that the boy had told her to "suck his dick." The third girl's mother contacted the school principal and teacher and was told that the school was working with the boy's parents to resolve his problems. After meeting with the third girl's mother, the principal suspended the boy for one week, followed by an in-school suspension. The principal instructed the teacher to keep the boy away from the third girl. When the girls' attorney notified the principal that the boy's misconduct was continuing, the school suspended him for the rest of the school year. The families sued the school board in a federal district court, asserting Title IX violations. The court awarded summary judgment to the board, and the parents appealed to the Eleventh Circuit.

The court stated **whether conduct amounts to harassment depends on the circumstances, expectations and relationships of the people involved. This includes consideration of the ages of the harasser and victims. Damages are not available for "simple acts of teasing and mere name-calling"** among children even when comments target differences in gender. Although the conduct alleged by the first two girls persisted for months and was sexually explicit and vulgar, it was not so severe, pervasive or offensive that it denied them access to their education. They suffered no physical exclusion from school facilities. While the third girl's complaints were more explicit, the school responded to them and was not deliberately indifferent. **To create liability, discrimination must be more widespread than a single instance of peer harassment.** The effects of the harassment must touch the whole of an educational program or activity. **As the girls were not denied access to their educational programs or activities and did not suffer any decline in grades or participation, the board could not be held liable for harassment.** *Hawkins v. Sarasota County School Board*, 322 F.3d 1279 (11th Cir. 2003).

◆   A Mississippi high school teacher with no history of sexually harassing students began a sexually inappropriate relationship with a student, though both he and the student denied that sexual intercourse ever occurred. A rumor circulated about the relationship, but the principal detected no sign of it. He confronted the teacher, who vehemently denied there was any inappropriate relationship. However, the truth eventually came out in some discarded love letters and some impassioned emails. The student's family sued the school district for negligent hiring and retention, among other claims. A court ruled for the school district, and the Court of Appeals of Mississippi affirmed.

The court held the school district did not have either actual or constructive notice of the inappropriate relationship between the student and teacher, as required to establish a claim for negligent hiring or retention. The teacher had no prior history of wrongdoing, and many of his contacts with the student were under the guise of innocence, such as his tutoring of the student and her babysitting of his child. *Doe v. Pontotoc County School Dist.*, 2007 WL 1412999 (Miss. Ct. App. 5/15/07).

◆   A Texas State University student was leaving a campus library one night at around 11:00 p.m. when an unknown person sexually assaulted her at knifepoint. She said the attacker dragged her under a dark stairwell of a campus building. The student sued Texas State and others, in a state district court, alleging it was negligent. She asserted the security on campus was inadequate because Texas State employees had "negligently implemented the campus safety policies." Texas State also was negligent, the student said, in its use or misuse of the lighting in the area where she was attacked and its use of security boxes on campus. The student contended she got hurt because Texas State did not use ordinary care to keep the campus safe, properly lit, and free from criminal trespassers. Furthermore, she said, the university failed to inspect the property for dangerous conditions or to warn the student of any such defect. The district court granted a motion to dismiss and the student appealed.

The Court of Appeals of Texas explained that under the Texas Tort Claims Act, state entities can waive governmental immunity only under limited circumstances. Section 101.021(2) of the Act provides a state governmental unit is liable for personal injury if, as a private person, it would be liable according to Texas law. **The student failed to establish immunity was waived because she did not show a connection between the alleged defect and her injuries. The court found the actions of the student's attacker, not the allegedly defective lights, were what caused her to be harmed**. It rejected the student's argument that governmental immunity was waived. As the negligent implementation of a security policy does not waive governmental immunity, the judgment was affirmed. *Dimas v. Texas State Univ. System*, No. 14-05-00664-CV, 2006 WL 2345960 (Tex. Ct. App. 8/15/06).

◆ An Indiana student alleged an ex-boyfriend and some of his friends, both male and female, began calling her names such as "bitch, slut and whore" at school. Although school administrators spoke with the perpetrators on several occasions, the student alleged their efforts were insufficient, as the abusive language continued. When the student accused a female student of hitting her car with a purse, the police were summoned. The student transferred to another school and sued the district in a federal district court for Title IX violations.

The court explained that Title IX requires a showing of sexual harassment by peers that is so severe, pervasive and objectively offensive that it undermines the educational experience by denying equal access to education. To become actionable, **the harassment must be based on sex, rather than a personal reason such as a failed romantic relationship.** Although the terms used by the perpetrators had some sexual connotations, this was not necessarily proof of discrimination. The name-calling started as the result of the break-up, and **the slurs were based on personal hostility to the student, not sexual desire or gender bias. The Supreme Court cautioned in** *Davis* **that Title IX damages are not available for simple name-calling and teasing.** The court entered judgment for the district. *Benjamin v. Metropolitan School Dist.*, No. IP 00-0891-C-T/K, 2002 WL 977661 (S.D. Ind. 2002).

◆ In 1998, the U.S. Supreme Court examined the liability of school districts for sexual harassment of students by teachers and other staff under Title IX. The case has become one of the most important legal precedents for courts attempting to analyze school liability based on harassment of students by staff members. The case involved a Texas student who had a sexual relationship with a teacher. The Court rejected the liability standard advocated by the student and by the U.S. government, which resembled *respondeat superior* liability under Title VII. Title IX contains an administrative enforcement mechanism that assumes actual notice has been provided to officials prior to the imposition of enforcement remedies.

An award of damages would be inappropriate in a Title IX case unless an official with the authority to address the discrimination failed to act despite actual knowledge of it, in a manner amounting to deliberate indifference to discrimination. Here, there was insufficient evidence that a school official should have known about the relationship to impose Title IX liability. Accordingly, the district could not be held liable for the teacher's misconduct. *Gebser v. Lago Vista Independent School Dist.*, 524 U.S. 274, 118 S.Ct. 1989, 141 L.Ed.2d 277 (1998).

2. Stalking

◆ A Connecticut university student contacted a female student in a chat room. He made several attempts to date her, but she rejected his advances. Despite the rejections, the student continued to pursue her, appearing uninvited at her dormitory room and presenting her with gifts. The student then sent an e-mail to a professor expressing an "excessive interest" in the female classmate. The professor was disturbed by the e-mail, and reported the student to a community standards specialist at the university. After interviewing the student, the classmate and the professor, the specialist instructed the student he was to have no further contact with the classmate. About a month later, the student offered to pay the classmate's friend to spy on her. A disciplinary hearing was held by the university, after which an administrative hearing officer concluded the student had stalked the classmate. The officer suspended the student from the university for a period of 15 months. The suspension barred the student from taking part in any student activities or earning any academic credits. The student filed an unsuccessful internal appeal, then sued the university in state court requesting reinstatement as a full-time student.

The court denied the student's request. He would be entitled to the requested injunction only if he could show the suspension proceeding failed to meet due process requirements. The student failed to make this showing. **He could not prove a violation of any substantive due process right, because there is no fundamental right to attend college. Nor was there any violation of the student's procedural due process rights. He received notice of the charges against him, and neither the form nor content of the notice prejudiced his ability to defend the charges.** Because the student failed to show he was denied due process with respect to the university's procedures, the court denied his request for a preliminary injunction. *Danso v. Univ. of Connecticut*, No. CV4006110, 2007 WL 344347 (Conn. Super. Ct. 1/17/07).

◆ A Western Kentucky University student died three days after she was assaulted, raped and set on fire in her dormitory room. Two men who were not residents of the dorm were later charged in the case. The student's estate filed negligence claims in a state court against the university, a foundation that operated the dormitory, and university officials. The court dismissed the case, and the state court of appeals affirmed the decision to dismiss the claims against the university and the officials. However it reversed the decision to dismiss the claims filed against the foundation. The parties appealed to the Supreme Court of Kentucky.

The supreme court explained that governmental immunity extends to state agencies that perform governmental functions, but does not extend to agencies which are not created to perform a governmental function. Officials of state agencies can also be entitled to immunity if the agency itself is immune to suit. Applying these principles, the court held the university was immune to the claims raised. It rejected the argument that the university's operation of the dorm was a proprietary rather than a discretionary function. **The university operated the dorm as part of its statutory duty to provide college instruction. As such, its operation of the dorm was not proprietary, and it was entitled to immunity. Because the claims against the university were barred by immunity, the claims**

against the officials in their official capacities were also barred. The foundation was entitled to immunity because it acted as an alter ego of the university and derived immunity status through it. The decision to grant immunity to the university and officials was affirmed, and its decision to deny immunity to the foundation was reversed. *Autry v. Western Kentucky Univ.*, No. 2005-SC-0451-DG, 2007 WL 1158547 (Ky. 4/19/07).

◆ A Pennsylvania university student was accused of bizarre behavior by several female students who feared he might harm them. They complained to the university that he graphically described how he would kill people. After two hearings, the university found the student guilty of threatening the safety of others and suspended him for the rest of the school year. When he reapplied for admission, the university denied his application and permanently expelled him.

The student appealed the denial of his application in a letter that was splattered with blood. He then sued the university in a federal district court. **The court found no basis for the lawsuit. The university committed no constitutional violation by disciplining him.** The student argued that the university treated his case differently from the way it handled a claim against a student stalker. The court found that at the very most, the university may have treated the student more harshly than the student stalker. However, that was not enough to prove the university violated his constitutional rights. The court granted the university's motion for dismissal. *Hubler v. Widener Univ.*, No. Civ.A. 05-01785-JF, Civ.A. 05-01920-JF, 2006 WL 437542 (E.D. Pa. 2/22/06).

◆ A New York college student was assaulted at knifepoint in her dorm room. At the time of the attack, the college had a security policy that required all outer doors to its residential halls be locked 24 hours a day. An exception was that during office hours, a "breezeway" entrance remained open to allow students to enter from the open quadrangle created by the four other student dorms. The policy also required those visiting a dorm to register with personnel stationed at resident hall lobby desks. Despite the policies, students held and even propped open doors to the resident halls so people could enter without registering. The student sued the college in a federal district court, alleging it was negligent. The court dismissed the complaint and the student appealed.

The U.S. Court of Appeals, Second Circuit, disagreed with the district court's conclusion that the attack was unforeseeable because of the low history of on-campus crime. In each of the previous five years, there had been significant events and a security reporting firm reported there were other assaults on campus that were not documented. **A jury could readily have found the college administration had been alerted to the presence of more crime than it publicly reported.** The district court's analysis of foreseeability was flawed, because it assumed that only actual prior crimes could put the college on notice of the risk of future crimes. The security firm had repeatedly raised security concerns with the college. **While the attack was foreseeable, the district court reasonably found that the student did not establish a causal connection between negligence by the college and the attack**. Because the attacker was never caught or identified, she did not prove he was a resident of the dorm. While New York law did not require the student to identify her assailant, she had to provide some evidence that he was an intruder. As she failed to do so, the judgment for the college was affirmed. *Williams v. Utica College of Syracuse Univ.*, 2006 WL 1755295 (2d Cir. 6/28/06).

◆ A Massachusetts high school student sodomized a six-year-old and was charged with various felonies. His school principal obtained a police report describing the student's description of the incident as "a joke." The principal suspended the student, finding he posed a threat to the safety, security and welfare of students at the high school. School officials notified the student's parents by letter of the disciplinary action, and they appealed to the superintendent of schools. After a hearing, the superintendent upheld the suspension and the parents sought a preliminary order from a state superior court. The court denied the request for preliminary relief but later reversed the suspension, finding the superintendent's action was an abuse of discretion. According to the court, Massachusetts General Laws Chapter 71, § 37H 1/2 requires more than criminal charges alone to justify a student suspension. On appeal, the Massachusetts Supreme Judicial Court observed that Section 37H 1/2 authorizes the suspension of students who have been charged with felonies. School principals or headmasters must provide students with written notice and a hearing before any suspension takes effect. As the trial court had found, a felony charge against a student is an insufficient basis for suspension. **There must be a finding that the student's continued presence in school would have a substantial detrimental effect** on the general welfare of the school.

   The superintendent's decision was within his discretion because it was fully supported by the evidence. The principal was permitted to draw inferences from the nature of the crime and the student's lack of remorse. **Given the seriousness of the charges, the principal reasonably concluded there was a danger the student would attempt similar behavior at school. The principal met the procedural requirements of Section 37H 1/2.** As the superintendent acted within his discretion by suspending the student, the court reversed and remanded the case. *Doe v. Superintendent of Schools of Stoughton*, 437 Mass. 1, 767 N.E.2d 1054 (Mass. 2002).

◆ A stockbroker who occasionally used the library at Oregon State University (OSU) was appropriately excluded from campus after OSU officials issued exclusion notices for stalking two students. The stockbroker was an OSU alumnus who used the library and attended public events on campus. An OSU student obtained a temporary protective stalking order against him in 1993, prohibiting any contact with her and excluding him from named OSU premises, including the fifth and sixth floor of the library. However, the order did not ban him from campus. In 1995, OSU security services published a policy providing for written trespass warnings to non-students as a way to protect students, staff and faculty. The stockbroker was arrested in the OSU library shortly thereafter, based on continuing complaints against him and the 1993 stalking order. The arresting campus security employee served the stockbroker with an exclusion notice purporting to ban him from the entire campus. OSU's campus security manager later sent the stockbroker a second exclusion notice because another OSU student had filed a complaint about the stockbroker. The complaining student obtained a temporary stalking protective order from a state court, and law enforcement officers cooperated with OSU security services by distributing a safety alert flier depicting the stockbroker.

OSU's security manager later denied the stockbroker's requests to return to campus for three specific events. State police cited him for criminal trespass in violation of the exclusion order, and he sued the security manager and others in a federal court asserting civil rights violations. The court dismissed the case and the stockbroker appealed. The Ninth Circuit noted that "[w]hile the OSU campus may be open to the public, it does not follow that the University must allow all members of the public onto its premises regardless of their conduct." Even without rules and regulations explicitly allowing officials to exclude persons for conduct, it was reasonable to infer this authority from OSU's exclusion policy. **The U.S. Supreme Court has recognized that educational administrators need flexibility to carry out their educational missions. Any individual right to use the campus had to be balanced against the university's right to protect its students. OSU acted reasonably in temporarily excluding the stockbroker from its campus**, and he was not entitled to due process protections. The court affirmed the judgment for OSU officials. *Souders v. Lucero*, 196 F.3d 1040 (9th Cir. 1999).

B. Sexual Orientation

In *Romer v. Evans*, 517 U.S. 620 (1996), the U.S. Supreme Court held that sexual orientation discrimination violates the Establishment Clause. In *Oncale v. Sundowner Offshore Services, Inc.*, 523 U.S. 75 (1998), the Court held same-sex harassment may violate Title VII of the Civil Rights Act of 1964. Many state human rights act establish sexual orientation as a protected class of persons. Most courts apply the analytical framework described in *Davis v. Monroe County Board of Educ.*, this chapter, to cases involving sexual orientation. However, the Supreme Court of New Jersey recently rejected the *Davis* standard as too lenient in the following case decided under the state law against discrimination.

◆ A New Jersey student claimed that classmates repeatedly and severely taunted him with homosexual epithets beginning in grade four. The student reported that peer harassment escalated when he entered middle school. The student's mother reported two incidents, but the school's assistant principal did not punish or reprimand the perpetrators. During the student's eighth-grade year, his mother claimed a school guidance counselor simply urged her son to "toughen up and turn the other cheek." At the time, he was experiencing daily harassment, including mock sexual molestations. The school principal later agreed to let the student leave classes to report problems directly to him. The school began to discipline perpetrators. Verbal abuse persisted, but to a lesser degree. When the student entered high school, the harassment resurfaced. To avoid derision on school buses, he decided to walk home from school. The student reported being followed by others as he walked home. He was punched in the face and knocked down by another student. The other student was suspended for 10 days and pled guilty to assault charges. A second student was also suspended for 10 days after a similar incident. The student never returned to the high school, and his mother placed him in another school. The mother filed a complaint with the state Division on Civil Rights for peer harassment due to perceived sexual orientation. The student won $50,000 in emotional distress damages, and his mother won $10,000 for emotional distress. The school district was fined $10,000 and ordered to pay the family's attorneys' fees. A state appellate division court affirmed the award for the student, but reversed the award for his mother. Appeal reached the Supreme Court of New Jersey.

The supreme court stated that the New Jersey law against discrimination (LAD) was the nation's first state anti-discrimination law. Its goal was "nothing less than the eradication of the cancer of discrimination." For this reason, **the court recognized a cause of action against school districts for student-on-student harassment based on perceived sexual orientation**. Recognition of this cause of action addressed the significant problem of harassment, intimidation and bullying by students. A safe and civil education environment was required for learning. The court held LAD liability would be imposed for peer harassment only if a school district failed to reasonably address harassment, where it knew or should have known about it. Schools are not expected to shelter students from all peer harassment. The court distinguished isolated insults and taunts from the kind of severe, pervasive discrimination that created school liability. **Harassment must create an intimidating, hostile or offensive school environment, and the district must fail to reasonably address it in order to create liability.** Failing to take action sends the harassed person the message that harassment is acceptable and supports the harasser. The court rejected the "deliberate indifference" standard from federal Title IX cases. The case was remanded to further supplement the record and let the parties argue the case under the new LAD standard. *L.W. v. Toms River Regional Schools Board of Educ.*, 189 N.J. 381, 915 A.2d 535 (N.J. 2007).

◆ An Iowa student claimed he endured years of severe harassment at school due to a perception that he was homosexual. He stated school administrators failed to provide a safe environment after dozens of incidents of vandalization and physical assault. The student said the school resource officer advised him to either ignore a harassing classmate or confront him. When the student confronted the classmate, the two got into a fight. The school suspended both students, and they were arrested for disorderly conduct. The student sued the district and several school and police officials in a federal district court for civil rights violations. He claimed he was unable to return to school during his senior year since he did not feel safe there. The court considered the student's motion for a preliminary order to prevent school officials from suspending him.

The court upheld the school's anti-fighting policy as content and viewpoint neutral. The school had a strong interest in maintaining order to promote its learning environment, and the anti-fighting policy helped promote this interest. There was no evidence that the district interfered with the student's expression. **To prevail on his Title IX claim, the student had to show the district intentionally failed to intervene to stop the harassment. The district could not be held liable for "negligent" failure to stop harassment.** The court held the student showed a likelihood of success on his Title IX claim by alleging repeated harassment resulting in a hostile environment that forced him to leave school. He also claimed administrators knew of the harassment but were deliberately indifferent to it. Despite the student's strong showing on his Title IX claim, he was not entitled to a preliminary order preventing his suspension. *Doe v. Perry Community School Dist.*, 316 F.Supp.2d 809 (S.D. Iowa 2004).

◆ A group of California students who were or were perceived by peers to be gay, lesbian or bisexual claimed harassment by classmates over a seven-year period. The students stated school officials took little or no action to protect them and sued the school district, its board and several school administrators in a federal district court. The court held the administrators were not entitled to qualified immunity for the claims. The officials appealed to the Ninth Circuit, which ordered the district court to reconsider the case. On remand, the district court held the students presented evidence of official failure to remedy peer harassment and that this failure was based on sexual orientation. As the students' right to be free from sexual orientation discrimination was clearly established, the officials were not entitled to immunity. The officials appealed again to the Ninth Circuit, which stated the general rule that officials enjoy qualified immunity in a Section 1983 action if their conduct does not violate clearly established statutory or constitutional rights of which a reasonable person would know.

To establish an equal protection violation, the students had to show intentional discrimination. The students were members of an "identifiable class" under the Equal Protection Clause because they asserted unequal treatment on the basis of sexual orientation. The court found evidence of years of harassment during which school administrators failed to enforce policies to protect the students. **There was evidence administrators were**

motivated by intentional discrimination or acted with deliberate indifference despite many complaints. The court explained "deliberate indifference" is found if school administrators are clearly unreasonable in response to harassment complaints. The students presented sufficient evidence of deliberate indifference to avoid summary judgment. This included failure to respond or inadequate response to at least two assault incidents, as well as repeated verbal harassment and pornography given to the students or placed in lockers. The district court had properly denied immunity to the administrators. *Flores v. Morgan Hill Unified School Dist.*, 324 F.3d 1130 (9th Cir. 2003).

◆ A lesbian student was allowed to proceed with discrimination claims against California school administrators who barred her from taking a physical education class based on her sexual orientation. The student told a friend she was lesbian after their physical education class. The next day, she was barred from attending the class and sent to the school principal's office. No school official met with the student or her mother to discuss the situation, and she continued to sit in the principal's office during school hours for the next week and a half, apparently as "discipline." The student sued the school district and officials in a federal district court.

The court denied the school officials' motion for summary judgment based on Eleventh Amendment immunity. The student was not barred from seeking damages against them in their individual and personal capacities, including punitive damages. The court stated **the U.S. Supreme Court held in *Romer v. Evans*, 517 U.S. 620 (1996) that arbitrary sexual orientation discrimination violates the Establishment Clause**. The court explained that several cases have held sexual orientation discrimination gives rise to an equal protection claim. The student made out an adequate showing of a constitutional rights deprivation. The officials could not immunize themselves from liability simply because there was no other Ninth Circuit case with nearly identical facts. The court also denied their claim to state tort law immunity, as immunity applied only to "basic policy decisions." *Massey v. Banning Unified School Dist.*, 256 F.Supp.2d 1090 (C.D. Cal. 2003).

C. Race

Title VI of the Civil Rights Act of 1964 prohibits race discrimination in any program that receives federal funds. Title VI is based on the principles of the Equal Protection Clause, and many discrimination complaints allege violations of Title VI, the Equal Protection Clause, and analogous state law provisions. Courts require proof of intentional discrimination in Title VI cases. School officials may be held liable for violating Title VI if they are deliberately indifferent to clearly established student rights. This occurs where a pattern or practice of civil rights violations is attributable to policy-making employees. As in other harassment cases, the courts frequently analyze race-based student-to-student harassment under the liability standard described in *Davis v. Monroe County Board of Educ.*

◆   An Oklahoma school district maintained a "fight policy" subjecting second-time offenders to expulsion for a semester. After the district expelled two African-American students for violating the fight policy, they alleged white students were not expelled despite similar conduct. They claimed the principal tolerated racial slurs and epithets by white students and allowed swastikas and the letters "KKK" to be inscribed in desks and placed in the lockers or notebooks of African-American students. The students sued the district in a federal district court for violating Title VI. The court awarded summary judgment to the district, and the students appealed to the Tenth Circuit.

   The court noted that the U.S. Supreme Court has not allowed a private right of action under Title VI to remedy non-intentional discrimination arising from neutral policies with an unintentional discriminatory effect. Since the students could not disprove the school's legitimate reasons for discipline, summary judgment was appropriate on the intentional discrimination claim. The court examined the students' hostile educational environment claims, which arose from events occurring before the fight leading to their discipline. They were entitled to an opportunity to prove their assertions of the principal's inaction in the face of a racist environment. The court held **school administrators could be liable under Title VI for remaining "deliberately indifferent" to known acts of student-on-student harassment."** The hostile race environment claim was remanded to the district court, with instructions to apply the standard of liability for peer sexual harassment claims from *Davis v. Monroe County Board of Educ.*, 526 U.S. 629 (1999). The district court was to determine if the harassment was so severe, pervasive and objectively offensive that it deprived the victims of access to educational benefits or opportunities. **The court held school administrators "are not simply bystanders in the school. They are the leaders of the educational environment."** *Bryant v. Independent School Dist. No. I-38, Garvin County, Oklahoma*, 334 F.3d 928 (10th Cir. 2003).

◆   Two Delaware students, one African-American, the other white, fought each other until a teacher stepped between them. The teacher reported the African-American student hit her as she tried to separate them. The school principal spoke to the African-American student immediately after the fight and asked him to write down his version of the incident. In this written description, the student admitted hitting the teacher. The principal suspended him for five days for "assaulting" the teacher, while suspending the white student for three days for "fighting" under separate provisions of the student code. The district's alternative placement committee assigned the African-American student to an alternative program for the rest of the school year. The district reported the incident to the police and after a family court trial, the African-American student was adjudicated delinquent for assault and disorderly conduct. Although he returned to his middle school for grade eight, his mother filed a complaint against the district with federal officials. An investigation determined the African-American student was disciplined more severely than his classmate due to his conduct, not his race. The student's mother sued the district in a federal district court for violations of Title VI, the Due Process Clause and state law.

The court observed that **private claims under Title VI must allege intentional discrimination**. To prove a facially neutral policy was intentionally discriminatory, a party had to show it was adopted because of its adverse effect on an identifiable group. As the school code of conduct did not discriminate against any identifiable group or minority, the district was entitled to summary judgment on the Title VI claim. There was no merit to the due process claim because the student received notice of the charges against him and an opportunity to present his side of the story. The principal spoke to the student immediately after the fight and asked him for his written version of the facts. The student code clearly defined "assault" and specified a five-day suspension as discipline for this offense. There was no evidence that criminal charges were brought to embarrass, humiliate or inflict severe emotional distress upon the student. As the principal reported the incident pursuant to state law, the district was entitled to summary judgment. *Harris-Thomas v. Christina School Dist.*, No. Civ.A. 02-253-KAJ, 2003 WL 22999541 (D. Del. 2003).

D. Disability

Harassment based on disability represents a growing body of discrimination cases filed against public school systems. In the following case, the U.S. Court of Appeals, Second Circuit, based school district liability for peer-based disability discrimination on the Individuals with Disabilities Education Act (IDEA), a federal law conferring specific rights on disabled persons. However, the courts have also begun to apply the liability standard from *Davis v. Monroe County Board of Educ.*, this chapter, to peer harassment cases based on disability.

◆ A Connecticut student was under five feet tall and weighed only 75 pounds in ninth grade. He had attention deficit hyperactivity disorder (ADHD). The student claimed that school employees knew of widespread harassment and bullying by classmates, but did nothing about it. The student withdrew from school, and his family sued the school board in a federal district court. The complaint included claims under the Individuals with Disabilities Education Act (IDEA). The family also alleged conspiracy to deprive the student of his due process and equal protection rights, and negligence. According to the student, the employees "condoned, permitted and/or acquiesced in" the mistreatment. He asserted the board failed to adequately train and supervise its employees in the necessary techniques and procedures for handling students with disabilities. The court dismissed the case, and the family appealed.

The U.S. Court of Appeals, Second Circuit, held the Due Process Clause of the Fourteenth Amendment to the U.S. Constitution creates no affirmative rights to government protection. **The court found the failure of school employees to respond to harassment and bullying conduct did not rise to the level of conduct so brutal and offensive as to create school liability**. The student did not even allege the deprivation of an interest that was protected by the Due Process Clause. He only stated he was deprived of his ability to enjoy the friendships he had established at school and the activities he enjoyed there before being forced to transfer. The district court had properly dismissed the student's equal protection claim. Nowhere did he allege that school employees treated him differently because of his size or his ADHD. The court noted that the IDEA does not provide for monetary damage awards. However, the Second Circuit has recognized monetary claims based on IDEA violations under 42 U.S.C. Section 1983. **The district court would have to reconsider the student's monetary damage claim based on his assertion that he was denied a free appropriate public education under the IDEA**. The state law negligence claims were also reinstated, but the district court could dismiss them if it also dismissed the federal claims. *Smith v. Guilford Board of Educ.*, 226 Fed.Appx. 58 (2d Cir. 2007).

◆ A Wisconsin student had a congenital development disorder characterized by abnormalities of the skull and teeth, and short stature. He had a hump on his back and was very sensitive to pain. His mother claimed his physical disabilities resulted in verbal attacks and mockery by other students. At her insistence, the student was included in a shop class with about 40 students. He claimed that two boys threw pieces of wood at him. Both students accused of throwing wood were suspended. The student suffered injuries and had to stay out of school for several weeks. To assure his safe return, his mother met with the special education director. The director promised that the student could leave classes early to avoid others in hallways. He said staff would watch carefully over the student in class and that the two attackers would not be in any of his classes. During an individualized education program (IEP) meeting, school employees assured the mother that the student would be safe upon his return. However, the IEP did not specify any protective measures and the only discussion of safety centered on accommodations to perform woodwork safely. The shop teacher attended the meeting, and said the student should not be assigned to his class because of the lack of a special education aide. The student returned to school and a third student threw safety glasses at him, causing a concussion and cracked teeth. The shop teacher made a disciplinary referral and the third student was suspended from school for three days. The student had to have his cracked teeth pulled. The mother sued the board and shop teacher on her son's behalf in a federal district court, asserting the board and teacher violated the Equal Protection and Due Process Clauses by failing to protect him from other students. The court first noted that an equal protection claimant must demonstrate intentional discrimination by a government entity in order to prevail. No evidence suggested the shop teacher did not stop the attacks based on the student's disability.

The Due Process Clause does not protect individuals from the actions of third persons, like the other students in this case. The student's mother had insisted upon the wood shop placement, undercutting her claim that the teacher or the school board placed her son in a position of danger. The teacher and board had no constitutional duty to protect the student from other students. Claims under the Rehabilitation Act and Americans with Disabilities Act also failed. **The court held that liability under these federal laws requires conduct that systemically denies the victim equal access to education**. The state law claims also failed, as Wisconsin law affords immunity to school boards and employees for their discretionary acts. *Werth v. Board of Directors of the Public Schools of City of Milwaukee*, No. 472 F.Supp.2d 1113 (E.D. Wis. 2007).

◆ A Wyoming school district expelled three students for marijuana violations. One was enrolled in special education programs and continued receiving the educational services described in his individualized education program. The others were adjudicated delinquent in juvenile court proceedings. The court held the Wyoming Constitution imposed a duty on the school district to provide the students a free appropriate education during their expulsion periods. The school district and the Wyoming School Boards Association intervened in the case and asked the Supreme Court of Wyoming to rule on the constitutional question. **The court held that while education is a fundamental right under the Wyoming Constitution, the state interest in student safety and welfare was compelling enough to temporarily interfere with this right.** The court noted with approval *Fowler v. Williamson*, 39 N.C. App. 715, 251 S.E.2d 889 (N.C. Ct. App. 1979), a North Carolina case recognizing that educational services are contingent upon appropriate conduct.

The school district in this case had offered students an education system that conformed to its constitutional obligation to provide an equal opportunity for a quality education. **Reasonable suspension rules did not deny the right to an education; they only denied students an opportunity to misbehave.** The court held the students could be temporarily denied educational services if their conduct threatened the safety and welfare of others and interfered with the district's obligation to provide equal opportunities to all its students. State law limited expulsions to one year. After this term expired, students could return to school and receive educational services until the age of 21. School districts were in the best position to judge student actions in view of the circumstances and to issue appropriate punishment. **The school district was not required to provide lawfully expelled students with an alternate education under** the circumstances of this case. **The court rejected the claim that the expulsions violated the non-disabled students' equal protection rights. Special education students must receive services under the Individuals with Disabilities Education Act (IDEA), even after discipline is imposed.** The IDEA's history demonstrated a compelling interest in treating disabled students differently than non-disabled students. *In re R.M.*, 102 P.3d 868 (Wyo. 2004).

◆   A Minnesota student was suspended pending an expulsion hearing after he was accused of sexually assaulting a female classmate. The student weighed 210 pounds and was active in football, wrestling and track. The classmate was five feet tall, weighed 93 pounds and had a mild form of cerebral palsy. The expulsion hearing was delayed for four months. When a hearing was finally held, the district failed to employ an independent hearing examiner. The school board voted to expel the student for sexual assault, based on evidence that his semen was found at the scene of the incident. The student appealed to the state education commissioner, who affirmed the expulsion decision.

The student appealed to the Minnesota Court of Appeals, which found no error in the findings of the board and commissioner. **The student was twice the size of the classmate and capable of controlling the circumstances. He failed to show he was prejudiced by the delay in his expulsion hearing or by the board's failure to timely disclose certain evidence. The provision of an audio tape and transcript of the hearing afforded him with procedural due process.** The dual roles played by the district's attorney as prosecutor and decision maker did not violate the state Pupil Fair Dismissal Act, which allows school boards to make their own findings in expulsion proceedings. The court affirmed the expulsion decision. *In re Expulsion of G.H.*, No. C1-00-2201, 2001 WL 799972 (Minn. Ct. App. 2001).

IV. USE OF TECHNOLOGY

A. Internet and Cyberbullying

In 2007, legislatures in the states of Arkansas, Illinois, New Jersey, Minnesota, Oregon and Washington, and enacted new legislation addressing "cyberbullying" and other forms of peer harassment through electronic means. The Washington law requires each school district to establish, by August 2008, a model policy prohibiting harassment, intimidation and bullying via electronic means on school grounds.

Electronic communication does not have any more or less protection under the First Amendment than expression via other media. A complicating factor for schools is that internet communications occurring off school grounds may not be subject to school discipline, unless there is some link between the off-campus conduct and some on-campus disruption.

The U.S. Supreme Court First Amendment landmark *Tinker v. Des Moines Independent Community School Dist.*, 393 U.S. 503 (1969), has been applied to Internet cases by the lower courts, and has been interpreted as allowing schools to prohibit off-campus student expression that materially and substantially interferes with school operations.

◆ A Pennsylvania high school student posted a parody of his principal on MySpace.com, using his grandmother's computer during non-school hours. The parody stated the principal was "too drunk to remember" his birth date and included a photo of the principal from the school Web site. Most of the school's students learned of the parody, and so many of them tried to access it at school that the system was closed to student use for several days. Several computer classes were cancelled as a result. The school held an informal hearing and found the student violated its disciplinary code by causing disruption, harassing the principal, and using obscene and vulgar language. He violated the school computer-use policy by using the principal's picture without authorization. The student was suspended for 10 days, assigned to an alternative school, and banned from his graduation ceremony and other school events. The student and his parents sued the school district in a federal district court, asserting the punishment violated his speech rights.

The court found considerable evidence that the Web parody disrupted day-to-day school operations. In addition to a computer system shut-down, the district technology coordinator and a co-principal spent at least 25% of their time during the week dealing with the disruption. **The student violated the school's computer policy by misappropriating the principal's picture.** The court found he substantially disrupted school operations and interfered with the rights of others. This conduct, along with his violation of school rules, provided a sufficient legal basis for the district's actions. The court held the student did not meet the standard for preliminary relief and denied his motion. *Layshock v. Hermitage School Dist.*, No. 412 F.Supp.2d 502 (W.D. Pa. 2006).

◆ The court later considered the case summarized above under a more fully developed record. The case was controlled by *Tinker v. Des Moines Community School Dist.*, 393 U.S. 503 (1969), which established the rule that **undifferentiated fear of disturbance, or disagreement with a speaker, is not enough for officials to limit student speech rights**. Other decisions have held that schools may not punish students for out-of-school speech. The U.S. Supreme Court's recent decision in *Morse v. Frederick*, 127 S.Ct. 2618 (U.S. 2007), indicated the complexity of this area, with the nine Justices issuing five separate opinions. The court held that **"the mere fact that the internet may be accessed at school does not authorize school officials to become censors of the world-wide web."** While officials may control student conduct within the scope of school activities, their reach was not unlimited. **The Pennsylvania Public School Code established a "temporal" test of school authority, permitting schools to**

enforce rules against students "during such time as they are under the supervision of the board of school directors and teachers." To discipline a student for off-campus speech, there must be an appropriate link between the communication and the school. There was no evidence in this case that the student had engaged in any lewd or profane speech while he was in school. According to the court, the school district did not show substantial disruption of the school. The district was unable to connect disruption to the student's conduct, as three other profiles of the principal could be seen on Myspace.com during the same time frame. As the district did not show any risk of substantial disruption in the future, it had violated the First Amendment. The court held a trial was necessary to determine the student's compensatory damages. However, the principal and other school officials were entitled to qualified immunity from any liability. First Amendment rights in the area of off-campus speech are not clearly established. The court concluded that the school district's policies on student responsibilities, abusive actions and bullying were not unconstitutional. *Layshock v. Hermitage School Dist.*, 496 F.Supp.2d 587 (W.D. Pa. 2007).

◆   New York parents enrolled their son in a public school as a non-resident student. The principal later suspended the student based on information that he had threatened others on a Web site. The parents sought a state court order to prevent the expulsion, asserting he did not create the Web site entries and claiming the district violated New York Education Law Section 3214 by removing him from school without proper notice or a hearing. They agreed to dismiss the case and the district agreed to end the suspension and to expunge all related records under a written agreement.

The parents attempted to reenroll their son in a district high school, but the district superintendent informed them he was not in good standing in the district based on the website threats. The parents filed another state court action against the district, arguing the superintendent's action was barred by their agreement. The court dismissed the case because they did not first appeal to the state education commissioner. On appeal, the New York Supreme Court, Appellate Division, held the agreement was binding. **The superintendent had based his decision at least partly on material he was foreclosed from considering by the terms of the agreement**. The interpretation of a contract did not involve educational expertise and was best resolved by a court. For this reason, the parents did not have to exhaust their administrative remedies by applying to the commissioner. **The court held the parents were entitled to have the superintendent determine if their son remained a student in good standing in the district.** He could not consider any records that the district had agreed to expunge. *Connolly v. Rye School Dist.*, 817 N.Y.S.2d 663 (N.Y. Ct. App. 2006).

◆   A Pennsylvania middle school student used a home computer to create a Web site called "Teacher Sux." The site included derogatory, profane, offensive and threatening comments about his algebra teacher and principal. One page showed an image of the teacher morphing into Adolf Hitler and a diagram of her with her head cut off and blood dripping from her neck. The site sought contributions "for a hitman" to kill the teacher and directed 136 profanities at her. It also accused the principal of having an extramarital affair with another administrator. Classmates accessed the site at school, and a teacher reported it to the principal. The student voluntarily took down the site. The algebra teacher was so upset by the Web site that she had to take a full year's leave of absence, requiring the district to employ substitutes. The school board eventually voted to expel the student. The student challenged the decision in a state court as a violation of his speech rights. The court affirmed the expulsion order, and the Commonwealth Court of Pennsylvania also upheld it. The student appealed to the Pennsylvania Supreme Court, which held the site did not represent a "true threat," and so was not beyond all First Amendment protection.

The inaction of district officials for several months after they learned of the site confirmed they did not consider it a true threat. **Speech that would otherwise enjoy constitutional protection may be subject to restriction and punishment if it materially disrupts the school environment. Officials may determine what speech is inappropriate in school.** While use of the Internet complicated the analysis of school-imposed speech restrictions, there was a sufficient connection between the site and the campus to consider the student's speech as occurring on campus. The disruption created by the site was substantial, and it harmed the entire school community. **As the site created disorder and significantly and adversely affected the school, the court affirmed the expulsion.** *J.S. v. Bethlehem Area School Dist.,* 807 A.2d 847 (Pa. 2002).

◆ A Michigan student created "Satan's Web Page," which included a list of people he wished would die and statements encouraging murder. The student admitted contributing to the site, and the district held an expulsion hearing. The expulsion was based on three school conduct code violations. The parents withdrew the student from school but then sought his re-enrollment. The district conducted a hearing pursuant to its "discipline hearing protocol" instead of the procedures described in its code of conduct. During the proceeding, the administrator who presided over the hearing apologized to the student's counsel and the recommendation for expulsion was withdrawn. The district notified the parents more than one month later that the student could re-enroll in the district, but they refused to do so.

The family sued the district in a federal district court. The court found the evidence did not establish any misconduct occurred at school. Even had this been the case, **the district could punish the student for his speech only if it substantially interfered with the school or infringed on the rights of other students. There was no evidence that the web page caused interference or disruption at school.** Naming other students on the site was not a true threat, as no reasonable person would interpret this as an intent to harm or kill anyone. The student was entitled to summary judgment on his speech and free expression claims. The district violated the student's due process rights by suspending him indefinitely. Use of the discipline hearing protocol denied him an opportunity to cross-examine witnesses or call district employees as witnesses. The student was entitled to code of conduct hearing protections, regardless of whether he was enrolled as a student in the district. The court awarded pre-trial judgment to the district. *Mahaffey v. Aldrich*, 236 F.Supp.2d 779 (E.D. Mich. 2002).

◆ An Ohio student made a Web site at home identifying three classmates as "losers." A teacher reported the site, and the district's technology specialist determined the student had viewed it at school. The district expelled the student for 80 days, but allowed him to stay in school if he did not further violate the student code. He sued the district and officials in a federal district court. The court noted the district had initially disciplined the student for the site's content, but now argued the discipline was for accessing the site at school. While the site was crude and juvenile, it contained no obscenity. As there was evidence that school officials were attempting to discipline the student for the site's content, the district and officials were not entitled to summary judgment. **The court held the school conduct code might be overbroad, as it had the potential to cover constitutionally protected speech.**

The code's prohibition on defiance and disrespect covered some speech that deserved constitutional protection. It was impermissibly vague because it did not inform students of what behavior could lead to discipline. The district and officials were entitled to summary judgment on the claim they had attempted to shut down the site to suppress the student's speech rights. The court denied summary judgment to the district on his speech rights claims under the Ohio Constitution and denied a motion for immunity by the superintendent and principal. *Coy v. Board of Educ. of North Canton City Schools*, 205 F.Supp.2d 791 (N.D. Ohio 2002).

B. Cell Phones and Other Electronic Communication

In the few cases dealing with student suspensions for possession of cell phones on campus, the courts have held for the school districts. Tennessee school officials did not violate a student's rights by issuing her a one-day, in-school suspension and confiscating her cell phone. However, one court has held that accessing a student's cell phone directory, voice mail and text messages amounted to a search or seizure under the Fourth Amendment.

◆ A Tennessee instructor seized an eighth-grade student's cell phone when it began to ring in her classroom. The school board's code of conduct prohibited students from having cell phones and other communication devices on school property during school hours. The code required that violations were to be reported to the principal. The cell phone or device would then be confiscated and returned to the student's parents after 30 days. The code of conduct imposed a one-day, in-school suspension for first offenses. The student's parent went to the school to retrieve the phone, but the principal refused to return it. The vice-principal then completed the disciplinary referral, indicating that the student was to serve one day of in-school suspension and that the phone would be returned after 30 days. Because she did not come to school that day, she did not learn of the suspension until the next day, when she was required to serve her day of in-school suspension in the school office. The parents did not learn of the in-school suspension until the student brought home the disciplinary referral. The father sued the school board, principal and vice-principal in a federal district court for constitutional rights violations. The court dismissed the father's due process claim regarding retention of the cell phone, but refused to dismiss the student's due process claim arising from the suspension.

The school board appealed to the U.S. Court of Appeals, Sixth Circuit, which reviewed *Goss v. Lopez*, 419 U.S. 565 (1975). In *Goss*, the Supreme Court held an Ohio school district that sought to discipline students had to provide notice of the charges, an explanation of the evidence against them, and an opportunity for them to state their side of the story. Like the students in *Goss*, the student in this case had a legitimate property interest in her education based on Tennessee's free education system. The court held an in-school suspension could, but did not necessarily, deprive a student of educational opportunities in the same way an out-of-school suspension would. However, the in-school suspension in this case did not resemble the out-of-school suspensions in *Goss*. The student was allowed to do her school work, and her attendance was recorded in the same manner as if she had attended regular classes. Accordingly, **the in-school suspension was not a due process violation based on her property interest in a public education**. The court found no due process violation based on the student's liberty interest in her good reputation. No other court has held that an in-school suspension would trigger such a constitutional interest. As a one-day in-school suspension did not deprive the student of any constitutionally-protected interest, the court reversed the lower court's judgment. *Laney v. Farley*, No. 06-6000, 2007 WL 2416177 (6th Cir. 8/28/07).

♦   A New York City School District rule forbade students from bringing cell phones into public schools without authorization. However, the rule permitted school principals to authorize cell phone possession by students in particular cases. Eight parents of New York City students sued the city board of education and other officials in the state court system. They sought a declaration that the cell phone ban violated their constitutional rights. The court found that any enforcement system focusing on the use, rather than possession, of cell phones would require teachers to observe and enforce the ban. Teachers would become involved in confronting students and punishment decisions. For that reason, the board had a rational basis to predict that the ban would lead to less distraction and disturbance. The involvement of teachers in enforcing the cell phone ban would take time from their teaching mission and increase the perception of teachers as adversaries to students. **The court held it was not inappropriate to conclude that a cell phone use ban would be more disruptive than a ban on cell phone possession**. There was an additional rational basis for upholding the cell phone rules based on the changing nature of cell phone technology. In any event, the cell phone rules were not absolute. Each principal could address specific situations by allowing students to carry cell phones when there was a special need for it. **Phone possession could be authorized when this would not be disruptive, such as at after-school activities on school grounds, including athletic events**.

The cell phone rules permitted principals to consider factors such as a student's need to communicate with parents. They could consider a student's willingness to have limited use cell phones, ability or maturity to abide by rules, and the availability of other phones. The parents raised constitutional claims based on their asserted right to be able to communicate with their children between home and school. **The court refused to recognize a "constitutional right to bear cell phones." The rule did not forbid communication among family members, it only forbade one mode of communication**. Schools had a right to maintain their own views of discipline in a reasonable and constitutional manner. The state constitution created no greater due process rights than its federal counterpart, and the court entered judgment for the school board. *Price v. New York City Board of Educ.*, 837 N.Y.S.2d 507 (New York County Supreme Court 2007).

◆ A New York eighth-grade English teacher told his class that threats would not be tolerated by the school. A student in the class then sent his friends instant messages with a small, crude icon depicting a pistol firing a bullet at a person's head, with dots representing blood. Beneath the drawing were the words "Kill Mr. VanderMolen," who was the English teacher. The student used his parents' computer software and did not send the instant message icon to the teacher or any other school official. However, a classmate told the English teacher about the use of the icon. The report was forwarded to school officials and the police, and the student admitted making the icon. The school suspended the student for five days, and the English teacher was permitted to stop teaching the class. A police investigator determined the icon was a joke and that the student was not a threat to any person. The pending criminal case was closed, and a psychological evaluation indicated he had no violent intent. The superintendent's hearing yielded a different result, finding the icon was found to be a threat and not a joke. The hearing officer found the student violated school rules and disrupted school operations by requiring staff time for interviewing students during class time, and causing his English teacher to be replaced. The hearing officer found the student's intent was irrelevant under state education law standards. She held the icon threatened the health, safety and welfare of others and disrupted the school environment. The student was suspended for a year, during which the district provided him with alternative education. His parents sued the school district in a federal district court for speech rights and state law violations and retaliation. The court found the icon was reasonably understood to be a "true threat" that was not protected by the First Amendment. The federal claims were all dismissed, and the court refused to accept the state law claims.

The parents appealed to the U.S. Court of Appeals, Second Circuit. The court held that even if the speech in this case was "opinion" within the meaning of *Tinker v. Des Moines Community School Dist.*, 393 U.S. 503 (1969), it "crosses the boundary of protected speech." **The court held the student's icon posed a reasonably foreseeable risk that it would come to the attention of school authorities, and would materially and substantially disrupt school work and discipline. Because of the risk of disruption caused by the icon, the student enjoyed no protection under** ***Tinker***. The fact that he created it off school property did not insulate him from school discipline. Off-campus conduct can create a foreseeable risk of substantial disruption in school. The potentially threatening content of the icon was reasonably foreseeable because it had been distributed to at least 15 persons, including classmates, over a three-week period. Once known to the teacher and other school officials, the icon would foreseeably create a risk of substantial disruption in the school environment. The court held school discipline was permitted in this case, regardless of whether the student intended the icon to be communicated to school authorities. The student was not being disciplined for conduct that was "merely offensive" or in conflict with the views of the school. The First Amendment claims against the school board and superintendent were properly dismissed, and the state law claims remained available for review by the state court system. *Wisniewski v. Board of Educ. of Weedsport Cent. School Dist.*, 494 F.3d 34 (2d Cir. 2007).

◆ A Pennsylvania student had his cell phone on, in violation of a school policy. A teacher confiscated the phone and stated that while she was in possession of it, a text message appeared on its screen from another student requesting marijuana. The teacher and an assistant principal then called nine students listed in the cell phone's directory to see if their phones were turned on in violation of school policy. They accessed the student's text messages and voice mail and used the cell phone's instant messaging feature. The student stated the district superintendent later told the press that the student was a drug user or peddler. The student and his parents sued the teacher, assistant principal, superintendent and school district for violations of state and federal law. A federal district court held the student and his parents had no standing to assert a claim under the Pennsylvania Wiretapping and Electronic Surveillance Control Act. A claim under that section could only be advanced by a caller, not by a recipient. The cell phone directory and call log were not "communications" as defined by the act. **The court held the superintendent could not assert absolute** immunity for the student's invasion of privacy, defamation and slander claims based on his statements to the press. This was because the family claimed he knew his statements were false at the time he made them. In further proceedings, the family would receive an opportunity to show the superintendent acted outside his authority. The teacher and assistant principal also had no immunity on the invasion of privacy claims.

The court agreed with the family that accessing the phone directory, voice mail and text messages, and use of the phone to call persons who were listed in the directory amounted to a search or seizure under the Fourth Amendment. While school officials are not held to the warrant and probable cause standard of the Fourth Amendment, they must have some reasonable grounds for a search or seizure at school. **The court found no basis for the "search," as it was not done to find evidence of wrongdoing by the student, but instead to obtain evidence of possible misconduct by others.** The student could pursue his Fourth Amendment claim in further court proceedings, but could not seek compensatory or punitive damages from the district under the Pennsylvania Constitution. However, the punitive damage claims against the teacher, assistant principal and superintendent would be considered in future court activity. The state law negligence claims also deserved further consideration. *Klump v. Nazareth Area School Dist.*, 425 F.Supp.2d 622 (E.D. Pa. 2006).

◆ A Delaware student used his cell phone at a school assembly, in violation of the school code of conduct. He refused to surrender his phone to a staff member, and the principal asked him four times to hand it over. The principal told the student he would have to come with him to the office. The student still refused to move, and the principal tried to escort him from the assembly by the elbow. The student struggled, pushed the principal and stepped on his foot. After being removed from the assembly, he continued to use his cell phone. The student remained disruptive in the school office and told the principal "you can't touch me," and "just wait till I call my mom. She'll sue you." He also threatened other students and teachers. The police arrived at the school and took the student into custody. The school board expelled the student for the rest of the school year and assigned him to an alternative school. The state board of education affirmed the action, and the student appealed to a state superior court.

The court held the state board could overturn a local board decision only if it was contrary to state law or state regulations, was not supported by substantial evidence, or was arbitrary and capricious. **The court found sufficient evidence that the student had pushed the principal and stepped on his foot. The student had intentionally and offensively touched the principal in violation of the school code. Expulsion with referral to an alternative program was not disproportionate to the misconduct.** The court affirmed the decision, as it was supported by substantial evidence. *Jordan v. Smyrna School Dist. Board of Educ.*, No. 05A-02-004, 2006 WL 1149149 (Del. Super. Ct. 2006).

V. TRANSPORTATION

This section discusses potential liabilities schools may face in the event of a transportation-related incident. For steps key personnel should take in the event of a bus accident, see Form III-1 in chapter nine. For a sample parent letter to be sent in the event of a bus accident, see Form III-2 in chapter nine.

◆ A nine-year-old New Jersey student was dismissed from school on an early-dismissal day, walked off school grounds without an adult, and was struck by a car a few blocks from school over two hours later. The accident paralyzed him from the neck down. The school district had a four-page policy memorandum titled "Pupil Safety" that addressed a wide range of student safety topics, including supervision of students at dismissal time. The memorandum stated that "[t]he chief school administrator shall seek the cooperation of parents/guardians to prevent any children [from] being unsupervised on school property during lunch hour and during morning arrival and afternoon dismissal times." The memorandum did not, however, outline how dismissal supervision would be administered by the schools. Instead, the school adhered to a practice that all school personnel supervise dismissal. On a typical school day, the school's 500 students were dismissed at 2:50 p.m. Teachers escorted the students from their classrooms to designated exits at the sounding of the school bell, and the teachers remained at their designated duty stations to ensure that the children left the school premises. According to the school principal, all school personnel – including teachers, teachers' aides, and security personnel – supervised dismissal to ensure that the children left school before the adults. The principal personally supervised early-dismissal days to "make sure that there were no children whose parents did not pick them up and they were still outside." The student and his family sued, alleging that the school district and principal breached their duty of reasonable supervision with respect to his dismissal from school. They also claimed they did not have advance notice of the early-dismissal day.

A state court granted the defendants' motion for summary judgment, finding that their duty of care did not apply to an accident that occurred hours after the student's dismissal and blocks from his school. The Appellate Division reversed, holding that schools have a duty of reasonable care to supervise children at dismissal, and remanded the matter for a trial to determine whether that duty was breached here. **The Supreme Court of New Jersey held that because a school's duty to exercise reasonable care for the children in its custody is integral to state's public education system, the duty does not summarily disappear when the school bell rings. Accordingly, schools in New Jersey must exercise a duty of reasonable care for supervising students' safety at dismissal.** The duty requires school districts to create a reasonable dismissal supervision policy, provide suitable notice to parents of that policy, and effectively comply with the policy and subsequent and appropriate parental requests concerning dismissal. The court substantially affirmed the decision of the Appellate Division and remanded the matter to the trial court for further proceedings consistent with its opinion. *Jerkins v. Anderson*, 191 N.J. 285, 922 A.2d 1279 (N.J. 2007).

◆ A New York elementary student alleged a school bus driver sexually molested her several times on her bus. Only one other student was on the bus when the incidents occurred. At the end of the school year, the other student told her father about the molestations, and the driver was charged with sexual abuse. The student sued the school district and officials in a state trial court for negligent hiring, retention and supervision of the driver, and for negligent supervision of the student. The court granted the district's motion for summary judgment on all claims except the one for negligently supervising the student.

The student appealed to a state appellate division court, which noted **New York courts have held school districts have a duty to adequately supervise students in their care, and may be held liable for foreseeable injuries proximately related to inadequate supervision.** Courts must compare a school's level of supervision and protection to what "a parent of ordinary prudence would observe in comparable circumstances." The district presented evidence that the bus driver had no prior criminal history and that no one had accused him of acting improperly in 27 years of prior work. The district had no reason to know he had a propensity to commit sexual misconduct. The court held for the school district on the student's claim for negligent supervision. *Doe v. Rohan*, 17 A.D.3d 509, 793 N.Y.S.2d 170 (N.Y. App. Div. 2005).

◆ Two emotionally disturbed North Carolina students rode a public school bus to a program for violent students. A bus attendant overheard them speak about committing robbery and murder with a gun one of them had at home. The attendant reported their conversation to the bus driver, but neither employee informed school officials, the school board or the police department. A week later, the students and two other youths stopped cars at an intersection between 7:00 and 8:15 p.m. A student shot a driver in the head and severely injured her. The students and their accomplices pleaded guilty to assault charges in criminal court proceedings. The victim sued city and county education officials in a state court for personal injuries. The court awarded summary judgment to the county board, and the victim appealed. The Court of Appeals of North Carolina held there might be a connection between the failure to report the conversation and the victim's injuries. It reversed and remanded the case to the trial court.

On appeal, the Supreme Court of North Carolina stated school personnel who overheard students planning criminal conduct had a moral and civic obligation to report this information. However, this did not create a legal duty which could afford a legal remedy for the victim. **The court**

held no legal duty exists unless an injury "was foreseeable and avoidable through due care." The school board could not be held liable for actions by students unless it had some "special relationship" with them. The victim was attempting to hold the board liable for the actions of students who were outside its control at 8:15 p.m. and not on school property. The appeals court had improperly held the board liable for failing to control them, and the judgment was reversed. *Stein v. Asheville City Board of Educ.*, 626 S.E.3d 263 (N.C. 2005).

◆ A Texas special education teacher worked at a public school for students with severe behavioral problems, emotional disturbance and learning disabilities. He agreed to drive a bus for special education students, and he soon began to document frequent and serious behavioral incidents on his bus routes. The teacher unsuccessfully sought the district's permission to use a monitor to supervise students. A student sprayed the teacher with a fire extinguisher while he was driving a bus. Although the teacher was able to bring the bus to a safe stop, he suffered permanent injuries that rendered him unable to teach or drive a bus. The teacher sued the district in a federal district court for knowingly creating a dangerous environment on the bus and acting with deliberate indifference to his safety. He claimed the district created a risk of foreseeable injury by segregating students with behavior problems into one school and transportation population. The court entered judgment for the district.

The teacher appealed to the Fifth Circuit, which declined to adopt the teacher's arguments for imposing liability on the district. With limited exceptions, **the Due Process Clause of the Fourteenth Amendment does not require the government to protect citizens from private parties**. Even if the teacher had a viable claim under this theory, he failed to show the district increased any danger he faced. The conduct of students created the dangers on the bus, and the fire extinguisher attack might have occurred regardless of whether a monitor was in place. The court upheld the district court's finding that **the school district did not create or increase the danger** to the teacher and that the district officials were not deliberately indifferent to known dangers. *McKinney v. Irving Independent School Dist.*, 309 F.3d 308 (5th Cir. 2002).

◆ A Washington school bus driver dropped off a student past her usual stop, but closer to her home and on the same side of the street as her house. After the bus pulled away, the student started walking across the street to get her mail and was severely injured when struck by another vehicle. She sued the school district and bus driver in a Washington trial court for negligence. The court held for the district and driver, and the student appealed. The state court of appeals held the accident was not caused by the drop off location. An expert had testified that any point between where the student was dropped off and her driveway would have been safe, since it was on the same side of the street as her house and even closer than the usual stop. The court noted the only proof the student offered to show the drop off point was dangerous was the accident itself. The driver did not violate a legal duty toward the student. **State rules governing school bus drivers required drivers to take reasonable action to assure a student crosses a road safely, but only if the student must cross the road.** The student did not need to cross the street to get home, and the driver was unaware that she intended to cross it. As the driver was not negligent, the court affirmed the judgment. *Claar v. Auburn School Dist. No. 408*, 125 Wash.App. 1048 (Wash. Ct. App. 1 2005).

VI. STUDENT SAFETY

◆   A Georgia student was severely beaten by a classmate after they left a classroom. The school principal and vice principal found the student unconscious and bleeding profusely in the hallway. According to the student's parents, nobody called 911 until 40 minutes after the student was found, even though he was vomiting blood and in serious condition. They claimed he was placed in an intensive care unit for traumatic brain injury due to the lack of immediate treatment. The parents filed a negligence action against the school district in a state court. They asserted the school knew of the classmate's extensive history of violence and that a teacher ignored his threats against the student. The court awarded judgment to the school district and the parents appealed. The state court of appeals found the district's school safety plan did not address the security issues mandated by OCGA § 20-2-1185. The court reversed the judgment on this issue and also held the negligence claims against the principal, assistant principal and school nurse should have been presented to a jury. State law claims based on failure to comply with statutory reporting requirements and failure to immediately obtain medical care for the student had been improperly dismissed, and the court reversed and remanded the case.

The school district appealed to the Supreme Court of Georgia, which noted **a Georgia state constitutional provision requires schools to prepare safety plans to address violence in schools, respond effectively to incidents at school, and to provide a safe environment.** Under state law, public officials and employees may be held personally liable only for ministerial acts that are negligently performed, and for those acts performed with malice or intent to injure. The court found the court of appeals had incorrectly held that the acts of the school officials in this case were "ministerial." **Safety plans must address preparedness for natural disasters, hazardous material or radiological accidents, acts of violence, and acts of terrorism.** The court held the statutory mandate to create a school safety plan called for the exercise of a discretionary duty, in other words, "the exercise of personal deliberation and judgment, which in turn entails examining the facts, reaching reasoned conclusions and acting on them in a way not specifically directed." **The constitutional provision**

requiring the creation of school safety plans did not create a civil cause of action for damages for failure to make timely reports. This defeated the negligence claims. The court held neither the Eighth Amendment nor the Due Process Clause of the Fourteenth Amendment can serve as the basis for a ministerial duty on the part of school employees to provide medical care to a student. The complaint did not allege actual malice by the school officials in a manner sufficient to overcome pre-trial judgment. As the duty to provide a school safety plan was discretionary, the court held the school officials were entitled to immunity. *Murphy v. Bajjani*, 282 Ga. 197, 647 S.E.2d 54 (Ga. 2007).

◆   A security guard at a Minnesota college noticed a car driving on a sidewalk near campus. He followed the car and local police were called. When the car finally stopped some 20 minutes later, the guard and local police officers approached the car. The driver did not respond when instructed to put his hands where they could be seen. He then attempted to get away, putting the car in reverse and ramming the guard's security vehicle before accelerating toward two police officers, who were on foot. The driver was shot 14 times and later pronounced dead at the scene. The college security guard did not fire any shots. All of the officers who fired weapons later said they did so because they feared for their lives or the lives of their fellow officers. The driver's widow alleged that her husband had bipolar disorder. She sued the police department, officers, security guard and college in a federal district court for violating his constitutional right to be free from unreasonable searches and seizures. The widow also claimed the police violated the Americans with Disabilities Act (ADA) by failing to train officers how to approach people with mental illness.

The case reached the U.S. Court of Appeals, Eighth Circuit, which rejected the constitutional claim against the police. **The use of deadly force was justified, because the officers had probable cause to believe the driver posed a threat of serious bodily harm.** He failed to obey an officer's instructions and then accelerated down the alley directly toward other officers. The court held constitutional claims against private actors, such as the college and security guard in this case, were viable "only if they are willing participants in a joint action with public servants acting under color of state law." **In this case, the security guard did nothing more than follow the suspect into the alley. His level of involvement was not sufficient to subject him or the college to liability for any alleged constitutional violation.** The court rejected the widow's ADA claim that the shooting could have been avoided if the officers had been trained how to approach people with mental illness. It was the suspect's threatening behavior and not a lack of training that caused the shooting. *Sanders v. City of Minneapolis*, 474 F.3d 523 (8th Cir. 2007).

◆   The U.S. Supreme Court will not review a case filed by a Boston University alumnus who claimed campus police illegally arrested him on a public street near the university. The police took the action in response to a complaint by a student who had an abuse prevention order against the alumnus requiring him to stay at least 30 yards away from her. A Massachusetts appeals court held the campus police officer who made the arrest was appointed as a special state police officer, with the same powers to make arrests as regular police have for any criminal offense committed on or near university property. **The officer had probable cause to make the arrest, and his authority extended to the areas surrounding the campus.** *Young v. Boston Univ.*, No. 05-10813, 2006 WL 3391248 (U.S. cert. denied 10/2/06).

CHAPTER FOUR

Campus Law Enforcement

I. SEARCH AND SEIZURE

A. The Fourth Amendment Standard

The Fourth Amendment to the U.S. Constitution protects individuals from unreasonable searches and seizures. The Fourth Amendment states: the right of the people to be secure in their persons, houses, papers and effects, against unreasonable searches and seizures, shall not be violated, and no Warrants shall issue, but upon probable cause, supported by Oath or affirmation, and particularly describing the place to be searched, and the persons or things to be searched.

Underlying all search and seizure cases in the criminal context is the "exclusionary rule," which allows a suspect to exclude from consideration any evidence that is seized in violation of the Fourth Amendment. Since unlawfully seized evidence is considered "the fruit of a poisonous tree," it is excluded from evidence in a criminal or juvenile case and may result in dismissal of the case. These considerations are not always present in school searches, where student discipline, not criminal prosecution, is the potential sanction, and school safety is the primary consideration.

School searches are deemed "administrative searches" as they do not result in criminal prosecution and loss of liberty. The "special need" beyond law enforcement that justifies relieving school administrators from the burden of obtaining warrants is the need to protect student safety.

B. *New Jersey v. T.L.O.*

The Fourth Amendment's warrant and probable cause standard does not typically apply to school officials who search students suspected of violating a law or school rules. Instead, the courts apply a "reasonableness" standard, by which the legality of a school search depends upon its reasonableness under all the circumstances. The test was established by the U.S. Supreme Court in *New Jersey v. T.L.O.*, below.

◆ A teacher at a New Jersey high school found two girls smoking in a school lavatory in violation of school rules. She brought them to the assistant vice principal's office, where one of the girls admitted to smoking in the lavatory. However, the other girl denied even being a smoker. The assistant vice principal then asked the latter girl to come to his private office, where he opened her purse and found a pack of cigarettes. As he reached for them, he noticed rolling papers and decided to thoroughly search the entire purse. He found marijuana, a pipe, empty plastic bags, a substantial number of one dollar bills and a list of "people who owe me money." The matter was then turned over to the police. A juvenile court hearing was held, and the girl was adjudicated delinquent. She appealed the juvenile court's determination, contending that her constitutional rights had been violated by the search of her purse. She argued that the evidence against her should have been excluded from the juvenile court proceeding.

The U.S. Supreme Court held that the search did not violate the Fourth Amendment's prohibition on unreasonable searches and seizures. Stated the Court: "The legality of a search of a student should depend simply on the reasonableness, under all the circumstances, of the search." Two considerations are relevant in determining the reasonableness of a search. First, **the search must be justified initially by reasonable suspicion of a violation**. Second, **the scope and conduct of the search must be reasonably related to the circumstances which gave rise to the search, and school officials must take into account the student's age, sex and the nature of the offense**. The Court upheld the search of the student in this case because the initial search for cigarettes was supported by reasonable suspicion. The discovery of rolling papers then justified the further searching of the purse, since such papers are commonly used to roll marijuana cigarettes. The Court affirmed the delinquency adjudication, ruling the "reasonableness" standard was met by school officials in these circumstances and the evidence was properly obtained. *New Jersey v. T.L.O.*, 469 U.S. 325, 105 S.Ct. 733, 83 L.Ed.2d 720 (1985).

Note the two-part analysis employed by the Supreme Court in *T.L.O.*: 1) A search by school officials need only be reasonable at its inception and 2) its scope may not exceed what is necessary under the circumstances.

For example, a teacher who smells marijuana odor wafting from a student would be reasonable in believing that there was some rules violation, satisfying the first requirement that the search be "reasonable at its inception. After the student is sent to the assistant principal's office, an administrator or school liaison officer then asks the student if he has marijuana in his possession and pats-down his pockets. This kind of search is regarded as "not intrusive" and satisfies the second part by "not exceeding what is necessary under the circumstances. By contrast, a highly intrusive "strip search" would go beyond what was necessary in this case and would be unreasonable.

C. Recent Search and Seizure Cases

School searches go best when police and school officials do not transpose their roles. As the next case indicates, campus searches may result in dismissal of juvenile charges if educators and police act outside their professional roles. The Supreme Court of New Hampshire gave a rare bit of legal advice to educators by cautioning them not to assume responsibilities beyond the scope of their administrative duties when working with police.

◆ A New Hampshire school resource officer was assigned to work at a high school by a municipal police department. He remained under the department's control and supervision and was assigned to investigate crime at the school. Soon after being assigned to the school, the officer instructed administrators to investigate "less serious matters," including drug possession, and refer only those involving weapons or a threat to school safety to the officer. If the officer felt he lacked probable cause for an arrest, he would deem the case a "school issue" and let administrators handle it. A science teacher observed a student passing tinfoil to a classmate and reported it to the resource officer. The officer referred the student to an assistant principal as a "school administrative issue." The assistant principal and another administrator questioned the student and asked if they could search him. The student agreed to be searched and they discovered tinfoil that the student admitted "might be LSD." The administrators contacted the resource officer and returned the case to him. A state trial court granted the student's motion to suppress evidence found by the administrators, finding that they had acted as agents of the police and were bound to provide him with procedural safeguards afforded to criminal suspects.

The state appealed to the Supreme Court of New Hampshire, which found that there was an agreement between the officer and administrators that the officer would inform school officials of suspicious behavior for which he lacked probable cause to investigate. **Warrantless searches or seizures are presumed to be illegal and evidence acquired by an agent of the police must be reviewed by the same constitutional standard that governs the police. This prevents the government from circumventing a suspect's rights.** The court held that school officials are responsible for school administration and discipline and must regularly conduct inquiries concerning both violations of school rules and violations of the law. Their duties do not include law enforcement and they should not be charged with knowing the intricacies of criminal law. However, school officials may take on the mantle of criminal investigators if they assume police duties. This is exactly what occurred in this case. **The court cautioned school administrators to "be vigilant not to assume responsibilities beyond the scope of their administrative duties" when establishing working relationships with police**. Because an agency relationship existed between the police and school officials, the court affirmed the trial court order granting the student's motion to suppress the evidence. *State of New Hampshire v. Heirtzler*, 789 A.2d 634 (N.H. 2002).

◆   An African-American library patron was using a computer in a library at the New Jersey Institute of Technology. An assistant librarian called the security department to report him for suspected theft of a stapler from the library's front desk. The patron agreed to a request by the police officers to answer their questions in the lobby area. He then agreed to permit them to search his bag. After they did not find the stapler, the patron left the building. The patron later sued the officers, institute and library staff in a federal district court for constitutional rights violations. He claimed the officers and staff falsely accused him of stealing computer software rather than a stapler and subjected him to an unreasonable search and seizure. The patron alleged a variety of other claims, including conspiracy to deprive him of his rights. The court awarded summary judgment to the institute and staff.

On appeal, the U.S. Court of Appeals, Third Circuit, noted that to prevail on a federal civil rights claims under 42 U.S.C. § 1983, the patron had to identify specific constitutional rights that were infringed, then show the institute had a policy or custom of depriving him of constitutional rights. While he admitted consenting to the questioning and the search of his bag, he claimed the consent was invalid because one officer failed to inform him that he had a right to refuse the search. The court found there was no such requirement and held the patron's consent was valid. Evidence indicated the investigation lasted seven minutes, took place in public, and was not threatening or intimidating. No jury could have found a Fourth Amendment violation. **None of the patron's allegations supported a finding that he was "seized." The U.S. Supreme Court has held a seizure does not occur every time police officers approach someone to ask a few questions.** The court found the patron obviously did not feel coerced or threatened into remaining in the library or responding to questions. After the brief search of his bag, he walked out of the library. **In any event, the court held the brief stop of the patron was based on reasonable suspicion, because it was based on information from the assistant librarian.** *Only v. Cyr*, 205 Fed.Appx. 947 (3d Cir. 2006).

◆   The U.S. Court of Appeals, Third Circuit, rejected an action by New Jersey parents who claimed they were wrongfully escorted from a school campus by a sheriff's deputy. **There was no evidence of physical force by the deputy, so no "seizure" occurred to support a constitutional claim. The school board did not violate the parents' rights by "illegally** banning" them from school property. **There is no due process right for parents to enter school property.** Even if the No Child Left Behind Act created a private cause of action as the parents claimed, they did not substantiate such a claim by alleging the board did not meet state education standards for five years. The superintendent had immunity, and the remaining claims had no merit. *Cole v. Montague Board of Educ.*, 145 Fed.Appx. 760 (3d Cir. 2005).

◆   An Alabama teacher customarily left her room unlocked when her class was at lunch. Her makeup bag was missing when the class returned from lunch one day. As usual, she had left the door open. The bag was valued at $450 and she had $12 inside it. The principal told students to empty their book bags and purses, and to take off their shoes and socks. Although the principal found the makeup bag in a trash can, he told students he would take them to the lavatory and search them. He took boys to the lavatory individually. The principal told them to drop their pants to their ankles and to raise up their shirts. One student was told to "wiggle his boxers to see if anything fell out." The principal patted down at least one student who had pulled up his pants. The counselor took the girls to the lavatory individually or in groups of two. She asked most of the girls to drop their pants to their ankles and pull up their shirts. A few were told to pull up their bras and one was told to shake her bra out. The counselor did not touch students or tell them to fully remove any clothing articles. One girl stated she wanted to call her parents, but permission was denied.

Parents of several students sued the school board, principal, assistant principal, and counselor in a federal district court. The court noted that the school district had a handbook stating the board's policy for searches. The policy allowed officials to search purses or pockets and pat down individual students if they had reasonable grounds for believing the search of a particular student would produce evidence of a rules violation. The policy stated officials should avoid frequent and unnecessary group searches where individualized suspicion was lacking. School officials were to call the police and parents if a more intrusive search was required. The policy forbade strip searching. The parents settled their claims against the school board. The court considered a pretrial judgment motion by the principal, assistant principal and counselor. **The court found the officials did not have individualized suspicion that any of the students took the makeup bag. Had the search been limited to student book bags, purses, pockets, socks and shoes, the court stated that there would have been no constitutional violation.** The classroom searches which did not involve the touching of students were justified, based on the school's "important interest in promoting order and discipline." They did not violate the Fourth Amendment, as they were not overly intrusive under the circumstances. The principal, assistant principal and counselor had no suspicion that any particular student had taken the makeup bag and money. **A strip search for the possible theft of $12 was unreasonable in scope.** The court held the strip searches were intrusive and violated the district's own policy, which instructed officials to contact the police. **As the search was beyond the school officials' authority under its own policy, the court held they were not entitled to qualified immunity from the Fourth Amendment violation claims.** Because the students alleged intentional harm caused by officials acting beyond their authority, the principal, assistant principal and counselor had no immunity from state law claims. *H.Y. v. Russell County Board of Educ.*, 490 F.Supp.2d 1174 (M.D. Ala. 2007).

◆ University of Rochester security guards chased down a man and took him to a room where he was searched for weapons. A metal scanner registered positive on one of his pockets. A guard removed three baggies filled with white powder from the pocket. When asked what the substance was, the man replied, "crack." A police officer field-tested the substance, determining that it was cocaine. The man was arrested for possession of a controlled substance. He sought to suppress the evidence, claiming the security officers had no reasonable basis to take him into custody or search him. He also claimed that any incriminating statements or identification of him had to be excluded from evidence because he did not receive any notice of statements or identification.

A New York court noted that the man would be entitled to relief only if he was detained and searched by state actors. **The private security guards employed by the university did not have to follow the same rules as city police officers. They did not work for the state and therefore were not required to comply with the Fourth Amendment.** As for the incriminating statements and the identification issues, the man was entitled to have that evidence precluded as to the police because he did not receive the notice he should have received under New York law. However, the statements he made to a private security guard were not precluded. The man was entitled to a hearing to determine whether these statements were made voluntarily. *People v. Capers*, 14 Misc. 3d 121 (N.Y. City Ct. 2007).

◆ A Pennsylvania assistant principal detained a student for nearly four hours while investigating a classmate's claim that the student touched her in a sexual manner without her consent in a class. The student denied unwanted touching. He instead claimed the incident was consensual and named some witnesses. The assistant principal told the student to remain in a conference room while he interviewed the witnesses. The student remained there and did school work for several hours. The student was allowed to leave for lunch and get a drink of water, but otherwise remained in the room from 10:15 a.m. until 2:00 p.m. The school principal suspended him for four days for inappropriate conduct. The student sued the school district, board and administrators in a federal district court for due process, equal protection and Fourth Amendment violations. The court held for the district, and he appealed to the U.S. Court of Appeals, Third Circuit. The court held confinement in a conference room was a "seizure" under the

Fourth Amendment. The student was not free to go for nearly four hours.

The court explained that public school searches are governed by the "reasonableness standard" of *New Jersey v. T.L.O.* **What is reasonable depends on the context of the search. In school cases, the courts balance the need for a search against the personal invasion that the search entails.** The court noted the detention was to investigate the incident, and to determine appropriate punishment. **In light of the serious nature of the charge, it was reasonable for the school to detain the student.** The court rejected his due process claim, as the assistant principal had allowed him to present his side of the story before discipline was administered. He claimed the district denied him equal protection by disciplining him and ignoring his evidence that any sexual misconduct was consensual. However, the student had admitted misconduct, while the classmate did not. The court held the student and classmate were not similarly situated, defeating his equal protection claim. The judgment was affirmed. *Shuman v. Penn Manor School Dist.*, 422 F.3d 141 (3d Cir. 2005).

◆ An Illinois high school dean suspected a student of marijuana possession after he saw her younger sister smoking marijuana inside her car. He searched the car and found several marijuana cigarettes there. The dean removed the student from class for further searching and questioning. The student refused the dean's request to search her personal property or face a one-week suspension. Her request for a hearing before the board was denied. The student and her father sued the dean and school district in a federal district court for violating her state and federal constitutional rights.

The court held the Fifth Amendment does not apply to school discipline. Consent to be searched is not a "self-incriminating statement" and does not amount to an interrogation. The student incorrectly argued the dean needed probable cause to search her. The court held school officials do not require probable cause to search a student suspected of violating rules. **A school search is permissible if it is both justified at its inception and reasonably related in scope to the circumstances that initially justified searching a student.** The court found reasonable grounds for a search and dismissed the Fourth Amendment claim. The student's remaining claim based on the alleged violation of her due process rights was also without merit. **A school suspension of 10 days or less only requires that a student receive oral or written notice of the charges and an opportunity to explain his or her conduct.** In most suspension cases of 10 days or less, due process is satisfied by an informal discussion between the student and disciplinarian within minutes of the misconduct. As this requirement was met, the student did not state a valid due process violation claim. She was not entitled to a hearing before the board, and the court dismissed the case. *Maimonis v. Urbanski*, No. 04 C 1557, 2004 WL 1557657 (N.D. Ill. 2004).

◆ A Texas assistant principal saw a student in a school hallway and asked him why he was not in class. The student gave evasive answers, lied about the location of his class and said he needed to go to his locker to get class materials. The two eventually went to the student's class. The student dropped his backpack under a table by another student upon arriving. The teacher told the assistant principal that no materials were required for that day's class. The assistant principal believed the teacher's information, coupled with the student's behavior, indicated he was hiding contraband. The assistant principal took the student into a library office and asked to search the backpack. The two argued, and the principal alleged the student eventually gave him permission to search the backpack. The search revealed marijuana. A school liaison officer asked the student to empty his pockets and found cocaine there. The student was arrested and charged with possession of cocaine. In juvenile court proceedings, the student claimed the cocaine evidence was unlawfully seized and moved for a suppression order. The court denied the motion and placed him on community supervision.

The student appealed to the Court of Appeals of Texas, which reviewed *New Jersey v. T.L.O.*, in which the Supreme Court held school officials do not need probable cause when searching students. Student searches need only be reasonable under all the circumstances and will be upheld if they are reasonable at the inception and reasonably related to the circumstances giving rise to the search. **A student search is "justified at its inception" when reasonable grounds exist that a search will reveal evidence of a violation of the law or school rules.** The assistant principal was justified in approaching the student because he was late for class, in violation of school policy and possibly state truancy law. His evasiveness and insistence on going to his locker for supplies he did not need created a reasonable basis to suspect he was concealing contraband. As the search was justified at its inception and reasonably related to the circumstances giving rise to it, the court held the search of the backpack was proper, and the cocaine evidence could be used in the juvenile court prosecution. *Briseno v. State of Texas*, No. 05-02-01630-CR, 2003 WL 22020800 (Tex. Ct. App. 2003).

◆ A California high school security aide and counselor entered a classroom to investigate incidents of defacing school property. They told students they were looking for markers and instructed them to take their belongings from pockets and backpacks and put them on their desks. As they walked around the room searching for markers, they observed a lighter on a student's desk. They detected the odor of marijuana and brought him to the principal's office, where they asked him to empty his pockets. The employees observed a baggie in the student's jacket and after the principal ordered the security aide to conduct a pat-down search, the student admitted that it contained marijuana. The state initiated juvenile court proceedings against the student. The court denied his motion to suppress the marijuana and declared him a ward of the state. **The state court of appeal observed that *New Jersey v. T.L.O.* relieved schools of the warrant and "probable cause" requirements of the Fourth Amendment. School officials need only act reasonably under all the circumstances when searching**

students. The state supreme court has required "articulable facts supporting reasonable suspicion" of a rules violation in order to justify a student search. However, individual suspicion is not an absolute prerequisite for "reasonableness," which is determined by balancing the need to search against the invasion of privacy that the search entails.

In this case, the search was justified at its inception because of reported markings in the classroom. There were "articulable facts" to support an objectively reasonable suspicion that someone was marking school property. The scope of the search was not excessively intrusive, as students were initially told only to place their possessions on their desks. As the government interest in education outweighed the minimal intrusiveness of the search, and the search was based on reports that someone was marking school property, the court affirmed the decision. *In re Johnny F.*, No. B149430, 2002 WL 397046 (Cal. Ct. App. 2002).

◆ A California high school security officer observed a student in an area that was off limits to students. When she approached him, she noticed that he "fixed his pocket very nervously" and became "very paranoid and nervous." After the student entered a classroom, **the officer and a colleague summoned him to the hallway and performed a pat-down search that yielded a knife with a locking blade.** The state commenced judicial proceedings against the student and placed him on probation, declaring him a ward of the court. On appeal, the Supreme Court of California explained that schools may perform their primary duty of educating students by enacting disciplinary rules and regulations and enforcing them through police or security officers. The school environment calls for immediate, effective action, and school officials are allowed to exercise the same degree of physical control over students as parents are privileged to exercise.

While at school, students may be stopped, told to remain in or leave a classroom, sent to the office and held after school. They are deprived of liberty from the moment they enter school, and detention by a school official for questioning does not increase the limitations already in effect simply by being in school. **Although individualized suspicion is usually required to perform a search or seizure, special needs exist in the school environment that relax this requirement.** The governmental interest at stake is of the highest order, since school personnel need to send students in and out of classrooms, set schedules, send them to offices and question them in hallways. Detentions of minor students on school grounds did not violate the Constitution, so long as they were not arbitrary, capricious or for the purposes of harassment. Since the student in this case did not allege that the officer acted arbitrarily, capriciously or in a harassing manner, the court affirmed the judgment. *In re Randy G.*, 26 Cal. 4th 556, 110 Cal. Rptr. 2d 516, 28 P. 3d 239 (Cal. 2001).

◆ A Massachusetts school administrator saw three students in a parking lot when they should have been in class. One student's mother did not come to school to discuss the incident as requested. When the student came to the office, **school administrators and a school police officer searched him and found a small bag of marijuana** concealed in his socks. A juvenile court denied his motion to suppress the marijuana evidence and found him delinquent. On appeal, the Supreme Judicial Court of Massachusetts stated the general rule that school searches need only to be reasonable under all the circumstances. **The court explained that reasonable suspicion is not a hunch or "unparticularized suspicion," but instead requires common-sense conclusions about human behavior.** In this case, there was evidence that the student had recently been truant and failed to bring his mother to a meeting to discuss it. School officials had no evidence he possessed contraband or had violated a law or school rule.

The court rejected the argument that the search was appropriate because of the student's truancy. School searches should be limited to occasions when administrators have reasonable grounds to believe a search would yield evidence of a violation of law or school rules. **A violation of school rules alone would not provide reasonable grounds for a search unless the specific facts of the violation created a reasonable suspicion of wrongdoing.** As the administrators had no information of an individualized nature that he might possess contraband, their search had been unreasonable at its inception. The court vacated the juvenile court order. *Comwlth. of Massachusetts v. Damian D.*, 752 N.E. 2d 679 (Mass. 2001).

◆ A New Jersey teacher observed a high school student was acting strangely and had a flushed face, red eyes and dilated pupils. The school nurse determined that the student "looked high," and a school security guard searched the student's locker and book bag. After he found two kinds of pills in the locker, the school principal suspended the student and advised her father that she would have to complete a physical examination before she could return to school. A blood test performed on the student was negative for drugs and alcohol. The school promptly readmitted her and she sued the principal, school board and other officials in a federal district court for civil rights violations. The court awarded summary judgment to the officials, and the family appealed to the U.S. Court of Appeals, Third Circuit.

The court held **the testing was supported by reasonable suspicion that the student was under the influence of illegal substances**. The actions against the teacher and school nurse were properly dismissed, as their observations were not excessively intrusive, given the student's age, sex and the nature of the suspected violation. The possession of pills was a violation of school policy, and **the principal acted reasonably in requiring the student to undergo testing before returning to school. Requiring the student to submit to testing in a medical clinic was reasonable** under the circumstances, and summary judgment for the school officials was appropriate. The court rejected the student's assertion that school officials violated her privacy rights by inadvertently disclosing the results of the drug tests to other students. It found no connection between the injury she claimed and the nurse's inadvertent release of the test results. Because there was no link between the release of information about the negative test results by the nurse, the court affirmed the district court's judgment. *Hedges v. Musco*, 204 F.3d 109 (3d Cir. 2000).

D. Police Participation and *Miranda* Warnings

When police take a student into custody for questioning, the student must be advised of his or her Fifth and Sixth Amendment rights. Otherwise, any statement may not be used in juvenile or criminal proceedings under the exclusionary rule. The constitutional rights advisory includes the right to remain silent, to know that any statement can be used against the student in court, and the right to have an attorney present. This is known as a "*Miranda* warning." The courts have disagreed on what standard to apply to questioning done by school police. The Supreme Court of Pennsylvania has held school police officers are to be considered the same as municipal police on this issue. However, courts in Texas, Rhode Island, New Jersey, Massachusetts, Florida and California have held school officials need not issue *Miranda* warnings when questioning students about rules violations.

◆ Massachusetts' highest court reversed a juvenile court order suppressing evidence that had been obtained by a school resource officer. Although the officer did not read the student his *Miranda* warning in the presence of a parent, the public safety of 890 students outweighed any individual right to the warning. A Boston middle school administrator saw the student showing a clear plastic bag containing over 50 bullets to other students. The school resource officer was called, and he confiscated the bullets. The student was instructed to go directly to the main school office. The resource officer noted the student appeared out of breath and sweaty when he arrived in the office. However, a pat-down search yielded no further evidence. The officer then read the student his *Miranda* warnings and asked him to disclose the location of his gun. The student responded that he did not have a gun. The student's mother and grandmother arrived at school, and the officer continued questioning the student without informing the adults of his *Miranda* rights. The school held an expulsion hearing on the same day. After the hearing, the student led the officer to the gun, which he had hidden in a yard in the adjoining residential area. In the subsequent juvenile delinquency proceeding, the judge found the resource officer had unlawfully failed to provide the student *Miranda* warnings in the presence of an interested adult, as required by state law.

The state court of appeals reversed the judgment, and the student appealed to the Supreme Judicial Court of Massachusetts. The court noted that the juvenile court judge had refused to apply the "limited public safety exception" to *Miranda* established by the U.S. Supreme Court in *New York v. Quarles*, 467 U.S. 649 (1984). The court noted that the student was only 13 years old. **Under state law, *Miranda* warnings must generally precede police questioning whenever a person is deprived of freedom in any**

significant way. **Juvenile suspects under 14 may not waive their**
Miranda **rights in the absence of an interested adult, such as a parent.**
The court held the resource officer was faced with an emergency situation
that required him to protect 890 students at the middle school, as well as
area residents. **Under the circumstances, he reasonably concluded there**
was an immediate need to question the student. The student's
possession of 50 bullets was enough to support the inference that a gun
was in close proximity. The court found this was valid reason to invoke the
public safety exception to *Miranda*. Accordingly, the juvenile court order in
the student's favor was reversed. *Comwlth v. Dillon D.*, 448 Mass. 793, 863
N.E.2d 1287 (Mass. 2007).

◆ A Minnesota student left his backpack in a school locker room, where
it was discovered by a custodian. After finding that the bag contained a BB
gun, the custodian took the bag to the assistant principal's office with a note.
The next morning, the assistant principal found the bag on his chair with the
note and called a school liaison officer assigned to the district. The officer
examined the backpack and weapon and identified the owner, then
summoned the student to the office. The officer and assistant principal
interviewed the student for an hour without telling him that he was free to
leave or to talk to his parents or an attorney. The officer did not tell the
student whether he was under arrest or in custody. The student denied that
he had a gun and later testified that he was scared when the officer pulled
the gun out of the backpack. State officials commenced a juvenile
delinquency petition against the student for a gross misdemeanor charge.

The court denied the student's motion to suppress his admission in the
school office, concluding he was not in custody when interrogated and that
his statements were voluntary. The court adjudicated the student delinquent
but stayed the delinquency adjudication, and the student appealed to the
Court of Appeals of Minnesota. The student argued that the district court
was required to suppress his admissions while being questioned in the
school office because the interrogation was a custodial one conducted
without *Miranda* warnings. The court noted that *Miranda* warnings must be
given in order to safeguard the Fifth Amendment privilege against self-
incrimination of an accused. This warning includes notice that the accused
has the right to remain silent, that anything said may be used as evidence in
court, and they are entitled to the presence of an attorney. According to the
court, juveniles are entitled to receive *Miranda* warnings. The warnings are
required when a law enforcement officer initiates questioning after a person
has been taken into custody, or has otherwise been deprived of freedom in
any significant way. The student in this case was told that he had no choice
but to answer the questions. While the student was not told that he was under
arrest or that he was free to leave, the presence and participation of a
uniformed officer suggested a formal arrest. The student was repeatedly
asked whether he had something inappropriate in his backpack. He was then
told he would have to deal with law enforcement and asked questions that

were reasonably likely to elicit criminally incriminating responses. Even though school officials had the right to reasonably inquire about the student's conduct on school grounds, *Miranda* warnings were required in this case. The court reversed and remanded the case, holding that **where police interrogate a student in custody in a manner likely to elicit criminally incriminating responses, the student must be afforded Fifth Amendment protection.** *In re Welfare of G.S.P*, 610 N.W.2d 651 (Minn. Ct. App. 2000).

II. DRUGS, WEAPONS AND ALCOHOL

A. Weapons Possession

◆ Delaware police and a university security officer searched a student's dormitory room after the student had been arrested off campus by police for possessing marijuana and a handgun. When the university discovered the items in the student's dormitory room, it charged him with possession of illegal drugs, possession of drug paraphernalia and possession of a weapon and ammunition. It notified the student of his right to request a hearing, which the student exercised. The student was also told he had a right to be represented at the hearing by a student, faculty member or staff member. He was further informed that he could have witnesses testify on his behalf and could ask that his accuser be present at the hearing. The panel upheld the charge relating to the ammunition based on the student's admission that he possessed the bullet. The administrative process also resulted in a finding against the student on charges relating to the marijuana that was found in his dormitory room. As a result of these findings, the university informed the student that he was being expelled. His appeal was denied, and he sued the university and officials in a federal district court for violating his due process rights. The court awarded judgment to the university on the student's claim that the decision to expel him constituted cruel and unusual punishment. The Eighth Amendment prohibits cruel and unusual punishment, but it applies only to criminal convictions.

The Eighth Amendment does not apply to school disciplinary cases. The court rejected the student's claim of racial discrimination under the Civil Rights Act of 1964. **He did not show the university was a place of public accommodation, and presented absolutely no evidence that the decision to expel him was racially motivated. Instead, the evidence showed the student was expelled because he admitted to possessing the ammunition and was responsible for the marijuana found in his dormitory room.** Finally, the court rejected the student's claim that the defendants violated his due process rights. The university was not required to allow the student to appeal its decision to expel him, and the procedures it used satisfied due process requirements. Nor did the expulsion decision violate any of the student's protected liberty interests. The decision was rationally related to the legitimate purpose of fostering a safe and drug-free campus. *Marsh v. Delaware State Univ.*, No. CIVA 05-00087 JJF, 2007 WL 521812 (D. Del. 2/15/07).

◆   A New York school board suspended a student for possessing a handgun off campus after learning he had talked about the gun while in the school cafeteria. The police decided to lock the school down, and the guns were found off school grounds. The student was suspended for the rest of the school year. The state education commissioner affirmed the suspension, but a New York court held the hearing officer denied the student a fair hearing and vacated the discipline. The student sued the board and hearing officer in a federal district court for civil rights violations. The court dismissed the student's due process claim, since he already had received notice and a hearing to consider his suspension. This was all the process to which he was entitled under state law. The state court had vacated the discipline, curing any procedural defects. The court held that talking with students about handguns was a material and substantial disruption of the educational process. The suspension did not violate the student's substantive due process rights. **The court agreed with the board that public school students may be disciplined for conduct off school grounds. It was within the board's discretion to punish conduct "outside the school situation, so long as there exists a nexus between the behavior and the school."**

Misconduct occurring off campus could adversely affect the educational process or endanger students. However, a lockdown incident, occurring three months after the student's gun possession, was not "definitive proof" that his speech and actions were a "substantial disruption." The court refused to dismiss the student's speech rights claim. He raised a valid equal protection claim by asserting the other students implicated in the conversation were only suspended for three weeks, while he was suspended for the rest of the school year. The court refused to dismiss the equal protection claims against the board and hearing officer, and held they were not entitled to qualified immunity. *Cohn v. New Paltz Cent. School Dist.*, 363 F.Supp.2d 421 (N.D.N.Y. 2005). The Second Circuit affirmed the decision in a brief memorandum. *Cohn v. New Paltz Cent. School Dist.*, 171 Fed.Appx. 877 (2d Cir. 2006).

◆   A Kentucky high school received a bomb threat. The administration contacted a private company under contract with the district to provide canine detection services. The search revealed no explosives, but a dog alerted to a car parked in the school parking lot that was identified as belonging to a student. The principal called the student from his class but did not accompany him to the parking lot, despite a board policy requiring principals or their designees to be present when any student search was conducted. A dog handler said "he could handle the situation," but advised the principal to send somebody to the parking lot as soon as possible. The handler went with the student to the car and found marijuana inside it. A school liaison officer and an assistant principal promptly arrived, and the student was suspended pending an expulsion hearing. The board voted to expel the student, and a state court affirmed the decision.

The student appealed to the Court of Appeals of Kentucky. It held **the board could expel students for bringing drugs to school, but its policy mandated that the school principal or designee be present during any student search. Because the evidence for the expulsion was obtained in violation of the board's own policy, the decision to expel the student was arbitrarily based on incompetent evidence. The board had to comply with its own policy.** The principal knew of the search and declined to accompany the dog handler. The presence of the dog handler did not satisfy the board's requirement, as this would have made the board's express policy superfluous. The court held the evidence used against the student was incompetent and inadmissible. Since it was the only evidence upon which the board had relied, the expulsion decision was clearly erroneous. The court reversed the decision as arbitrary. *M.K.J. v. Bourbon County Board of Educ.*, No.2003-CA-0003520MN, 2004 WL 1948461 (Ky. Ct. App. 2004).

B. Possession of Drugs and Alcohol

◆ A Florida student reported feeling dizzy at school and lost consciousness in a lavatory. He then told a school monitor he did not feel well. The monitor escorted the student to a school office. The assistant principal later said the student was quiet, subdued, and a little pale. The assistant principal ordered the student to empty out his pockets and bookbag. After noticing he had removed a plastic baggie that appeared to contain marijuana from his pocket, she called the police. The contents of the bag tested positive for marijuana. The student was arrested and charged with marijuana possession. A Florida county court denied his motion to suppress the evidence and adjudicated him delinquent.

The student appealed to a Florida District Court of Appeal, arguing the search was illegal because the assistant principal lacked reasonable suspicion of any criminal activity. The court explained that **school officials must have reasonable grounds to suspect that a search will result in evidence that the student has violated the law or school rules**. The court held "the State is obligated to elicit specific and articulable facts that, when taken together with the rational inferences from those facts, reasonably warrant the intrusion." The court found no such facts were present in this case. The search was premised entirely upon the student's lavatory incident and his appearance. The court held the student's pale or quiet appearance alone was "entirely consistent with non-criminal behavior such as illness."

In a 2002 case, the court had found no reasonable suspicion to search a student simply because he had bloodshot eyes and "was not himself." Similarly, the court found in a 2003 case that there was no reasonable basis to search a student whose speech was slurred and who was "not acting right." The court reversed the adjudication of delinquency. *C.G. v. State of Florida*, 941 So.2d 503 (Fla. Dist. Ct. App. 2007).

♦   At the end of a school day, an Atlanta high school resource officer was instructed by another officer to stop a car that had circled the school "with some possible students in it." When the officer tried to stop the car, the front seat passenger tried to jump out. The passenger removed marijuana from his pocket when the officer approached him. The officer handcuffed all four of the occupants and had them sit on the ground. The school's assistant principal arrived and instructed the officer to search the other students for marijuana. A search of one student revealed car keys and $500. The student denied driving to school that day, but a staff member pointed out the student's car on school property. The officer and assistant principal searched the student's car together and found a handgun. A K-9 unit arrived and found 15 bags of marijuana in the car. The Fulton County Superior Court granted the student's motion to exclude evidence seized from his car. The search "bore no relation to the stated reason for the stop." It was based on the discovery of a key and some money, and upon rumors and suspicions. Such actions were "whimsical, tyrannical and unreasonable" under *State v. Young*, 234 Ga. 488, 216 S.E.2d 586 (Ga. 1975).

On appeal, the Court of Appeal of Georgia noted that searches by school officials are subject only to the most minimal restraints necessary. The state supreme court had given great leeway to school officials in *Young*, but distinguished between searches conducted solely by school officials and those involving police. *Young* was inapplicable if a school official directed a search by the police. **The court held a police resource officer should be considered a law enforcement officer and not a school official.** The student's first contact with the police came when the car was stopped with no input from any school official. *Young* clearly did not apply, and the search was governed by traditional Fourth Amendment principles. The court rejected the state's assertion that the stop was valid on the basis of a suspected truancy violation. Mere suspicion that students might be in the car did not lead to an articulable suspicion of any criminal activity. As the police lacked any probable cause to stop the car, and the student's consent to search his car was a product of an illegality, the court upheld his motion to suppress the evidence. *State v. Scott*, 630 S.E.2d 563 (Ga. Ct. App. 2006).

♦   The U.S. Supreme Court declined to review an order allowing the state of Indiana to use as evidence a firearm seized by school officials in a drug dog sweep search to support firearms possession charges against a student. The Supreme Court of Indiana determined school officials who conducted the search should not be held to the "probable cause" standard to which police are held. The officials decided when and where the search was to be conducted, and there was no evidence that police directed them. As school officials could conduct the search without a warrant, the state supreme court held the firearm they seized could be used as evidence in the proceeding against the student. *Myers v. Indiana*, No. 05-1202, 126 S.Ct. 2295 (U.S. cert. denied 5/22/06).

◆ A North Carolina school district's conduct code imposed long-term suspensions or expulsions on students for drug offenses. It allowed first-time offenders to avoid long-term suspension if they agreed to enroll in approved drug education programs. The high school handbook permitted the principal to modify disciplinary action, if parents agreed. Teachers discovered two bags of cocaine in a student's possession. An assistant principal suspended him for 10 days and recommended suspending him for the rest of the school year. The student signed an agreement to enroll in an approved drug education program, but the district superintendent recommended suspending him for the rest of the school year. The school board then voted to accept the recommendation. The student and his parents appealed, and a state trial court reversed the decision.

The board appealed to the Court of Appeals of North Carolina. The case did not reach the court until over a year after completion of the school year at issue. The court held the case was now moot and review was inappropriate. **State law allowed suspensions "in excess of 10 school days but not exceeding the time remaining in the school year." Even if the court were to reverse the decision, the board could not "re-suspend" the student.** As the case was moot, the court did not review whether the evidence supported the suspension. *J.S.W. v. Lee County Board of Educ.*, 604 S.E.2d 336 (N.C. Ct. App. 2004).

◆ A New Mexico school security guard noticed a car parked in a faculty lot without a required permit. He contacted a law enforcement agency to check its registration and then observed a knife in plain view between the passenger seat and console. The guard called the student who had driven the car from his class and had him open the car. He found a sheathed hunting knife, handgun, ammunition and drug paraphernalia. The student claimed he did not know the items were in the car, which belonged to his brother. He was then suspended pending a hearing. A hearing officer held the student should be suspended for a year. The school board upheld the decision, and the student sued the board in a federal district court for civil rights violations. He added claims against school and law enforcement officers for violating his due process rights. **The court found the board could not suspend a student who unknowingly brought drugs or weapons to school.** It granted the student a preliminary injunction that allowed him to return to school and graduate. The board appealed.

The U.S. Court of Appeals, Tenth Circuit, held the appeal was moot because the student had graduated. The district court then partially dismissed the student's civil rights claims. The board appealed again to the Tenth Circuit, which held **a school suspension decision is to be upheld unless it is arbitrary, lacking a rational basis or shocking to the conscience**. The board did not suspend the student for "unknowingly" bringing a knife to school. Instead, it found he should have known he was in possession of a knife, since it was in plain view to persons standing outside the car. The board also found the student should have known he was responsible for the vehicle and its contents after driving the car to school. The court found the board had a legitimate interest in maintaining a safe school environment. **It was not unreasonable for it to conclude the possession of weapons on school property threatened this interest, and there was a rational basis for the one-year suspension.** The decision was not arbitrary or shocking to the conscience, and there was no substantive due process violation. The court reversed and remanded the district court decision, finding the board was entitled to qualified immunity. *Butler v. Rio Rancho Public Schools Board of Educ.*, 341 F.3d 1197 (10th Cir. 2003).

◆ **A Pennsylvania court held a school district had no power to expel an honor student for using drugs on a school playground after school hours, when no school activity was taking place.** A trial court properly found the student was not under school supervision at the time of the incident and had exceeded its statutory powers by expelling him. The school board had voluntarily reinstated the student to school prior to the trial court decision, and the court's order required it to expunge the expulsion from his record. *D.O.F. v. Lewisburg Area School Dist.*, 868 A.2d 28 (Pa. Commw. Ct. 2004).

III. TRUANCY AND JUVENILE JUSTICE

◆ A St. Louis city ordinance makes parents responsible for truancy by their minor children. Parents who knowingly permit their children to miss school without excuse may be fined $25 for each day of school missed. A city municipal court judge directed a student to participate in therapy, attend school every day and refrain from using force against her parents. The family was ordered to cooperate with the court or face contempt charges. The parent alleged her daughter assaulted her. The judge held the daughter in contempt and encouraged the parent to file criminal charges against her. The mother filed charges but dropped them within a few days. The judge later ordered the parent to be incarcerated for several days until her next appearance. The parent claimed that while she was incarcerated, state social workers took custody of her grandson. The grandson, who was the truant daughter's child, was then adopted by a foster family. The parent sued the judge and the city in a federal district court for federal civil rights violations. The court awarded summary judgment to the city and held the judge was entitled to judicial immunity.

The parent appealed to the U.S. Court of Appeals, Eighth Circuit. **The court held a municipality may be held liable for federal civil rights violations only where an official with final policymaking responsibility makes a deliberate choice to violate constitutional rights.** Orders of municipal judges were subject to state court review, but the parent had failed to appeal within the state court system. Instead, she brought this action asserting the city and judge had violated federal constitutional rights. The court held the municipal judge's order was a judicial decision for which the city could not be held responsible. As the order incarcerating the parent was not a final policy decision of the type creating municipal liability, the court affirmed the judgment for the city. *Granda v. City of St. Louis*, 472 F.3d 565 (8th Cir. 2007).

◆   A New York Appellate Division court held the adjudication of a 16-year-old student as a child in need of supervision did not constitute a change in placement under the Individuals with Disabilities Education Act. A high school principal initiated a family court proceeding to determine the student was in need of supervision based on 16 unexcused absences from school during a two-month period. The student admitted the absences, and the family court ordered the school's committee on special education (CSE) to conduct an evaluation.

The CSE found the student was emotionally disturbed and had a disability. The student renewed his objection to the child protection proceeding, but the court rejected it, placing him on probation for a year. He appealed to the appellate division, which affirmed the family court order. It observed that not every petition for supervision of a child contemplated a change in educational placement. There was no change in placement in this case. **The family court had simply ordered the student to attend school and participate in his individualized education program.** The court affirmed the family court's order. *Erich D. v. New Milford Board of Educ.*, 767 N.Y.S.2d 488 (N.Y. App. Div. 2003).

◆   The Court of Appeals of Michigan upheld an order by a family court to exercise jurisdiction over a student with disabilities whose mother claimed she was home-schooling him. The court found evidence she was not even at home during most of the school day. The family court assumed jurisdiction over the student based on the mother's failure to ensure he would receive a proper education. It found the student had missed 111 out of the 134 days of the current school year. Nothing indicated the mother was ensuring his educational needs were being met. The mother appealed to the court of appeals, stating she had gone to great efforts to get the student to attend school. She also expressed disagreement with the school district's educational intervention. The court expressed sympathy with the challenge presented to a single parent with a full-time job who was attempting to raise a child with special needs. However, it was troubled by the mother's responses to school intervention.

The court noted the mother's reluctance to use negative consequences for improper conduct by the student. Although there might be clinical support for her approach, it had been clearly ineffective. Since the mother's methods did not succeed, it was appropriate for her to try something new. It appeared she had been resistant to the school's methods, and her response was contrary to the student's best interests. The court found the student's best interests would be better served by her full cooperation with the district.

It was not in the student's best interests to be home-schooled, especially where this required him to be unsupervised for most of the day. **The court found the mother's home-schooling plan "painfully neglectful" of his educational needs. Although this was not a severe case of educational neglect, it was proper for the trial court to assume jurisdiction over the student.** *Flint v. Manchester Public Schools*, No. 240251, 2003 WL 22244692 (Mich. Ct. App. 2003).

◆ Two Massachusetts children were not enrolled in school and lacked approved home schooling plans. The parents contended that school committee approval of their home schooling activities would conflict with their learner-led approach to education, and that the Constitution prohibited infringement on their privacy and family rights. The school committee initiated a state district court proceeding for the care and protection of the children. The court found the parents had failed over a two-year period to show the children's educational needs were being met, effectively preventing any evaluation of their educational level and instructional methods. The parents did not comply with a court order to file educational plans, resulting in adjudication of the children as in need of care and protection. The court transferred legal custody of the children to the social services department, although they remained in their parents' physical custody. The parents appealed.

The Appellate Court of Massachusetts noted that the trial court order had required the parents to submit a detailed home schooling plan to the school committee to allow assessment of the program and the children's progress. **This was a legitimate educational condition that a school committee could impose on a home school proposal without infringing on the constitutional rights of a family.** The U.S. Supreme Court has recognized a degree of parental autonomy to direct the education of children, but state laws effectively incorporated this requirement by allowing for flexibility in the evaluation of private instruction in homes and private schools. The parents had rejected accommodations proposed by the school committee, and the custody order was entered only after they had received a final opportunity to comply with the committee's requests. The court affirmed the order for temporary care and protection of the children. *In re Ivan*, 717 N.E.2d 1020 (Mass. App. Ct. 1999).

◆ An Alabama high school handbook required the referral of tardy students first into parent conferences, then for discipline or alternative programs. After a student's third unexcused absence in a semester, the handbook provided for referral to an "early warning program" conducted by the county juvenile court system. After a student's tenth tardy in one semester, the school principal reported her to the school truant officer. The principal did not refer her to the early warning program or contact her parents, as specified in the school handbook. The truant officer filed a child in need of supervision petition in the juvenile court. After a trial, the court adjudicated the student a child in need of supervision and placed her on probation for the rest of the school year. The student appealed to the Alabama Court of Civil Appeals.

The court reviewed testimony by the principal, who allowed the student to accumulate 10 tardies before notifying the truant officer and never sought an explanation from the student about the reasons for her tardiness. The principal stated he did not attempt to contact the student's father or provide an in-school conference as required by the school handbook. The student asserted the principal violated the Compulsory School Attendance Law and school policy by failing to investigate the causes of her tardiness before referring her to the truant officer. The student admitted being tardy on 10 occasions, but explained she had a medical condition that made it difficult for her to be on time to school. **The court found nothing in state law requiring the principal to investigate the causes of a student's tardiness.** The law stated parents will not be convicted if they can establish one of five defenses, including sickness or other "good cause or valid excuse." The principal did not violate the student's due process rights by failing to follow the student handbook's progressive discipline policies before submitting her name to the truant officer. The handbook placed a duty on students to provide a timely excuse for their absences. The student was unable to show the school selectively enforced the prosecution of truancy cases. The compulsory attendance law applied after a child reached the age of 16, when parents were no longer accountable for truancy by their children. The juvenile court petition correctly named the student as the subject of the proceeding, excluding her parents from it. The court affirmed the judgment. *S.H. v. State of Alabama*, 868 So.2d 1110 (Ala. Civ. App. 2003).

◆ An Ohio school policy required the school to provide parents with written notification of state compulsory education laws upon a student's third unexcused absence. After the fifth absence, the school was required to hold an informal conference with the parents, student and a probation officer, and upon the tenth absence, a formal hearing was mandated. **A student was absent without excuse approximately 20 days during a four-month period.** On some occasions, the parents explained, there was a medical problem. The school accepted these explanations until the parents applied to the county educational service center for permission to home-school the student. They did not tell the school about the pending home-school application, and the school did not send them any notices concerning truancy proceedings. The service center advised the school principal that the student's home school application was being denied, and the principal filed a complaint against the parents in an Ohio county court on charges of contributing to the delinquency of a minor.

The trial court conducted a jury trial and sentenced the parents to seven days in jail and fines of $250. They appealed to a state appeals court, which found that to uphold the conviction, the state was required to prove the student was actually delinquent or unruly. The definition of "unruly child" included one who was habitually truant. Reference to the school policy was a crucial factor in determining whether habitual truancy occurred. The state presented the school's policy on unexcused absences as contained in its parent/student handbook. It was required to show under local standards that the student was habitually truant, but it failed to make this showing. **Because truancy involved more than absenteeism, the state was required to show a lack of excuse or permission as established by school policy.** It was, therefore, required to show evidence that it sent the parents written notices that their daughter was absent without an excuse for three or more days. Without this proof, the state could not satisfy the essential element of habitual truancy. As the school was bound to follow its own policies and abide by them, the court reversed the judgment. *State v. Smrekar*, No. 99 CO 35, 2000 Ohio App. Lexis 5381, 2000 WL 1726518 (Ohio Ct. App. 2000).

◆   An 18-year-old West Virginia student missed five days of school without an excuse. He was warned that continued absences could result in criminal prosecution. **After continuing unexcused absences, the county prosecutor's office filed a criminal complaint against the student.** After he was convicted of violating a state compulsory attendance statute, he petitioned the Supreme Court of Appeals of West Virginia for review. The court observed that the compulsory attendance statute mandated school attendance for children between the ages of six and 16 and provided enforcement sanctions against parents, guardians or custodians, but not against individual students. **There was no possibility of liability under the statute for a non-attending student, regardless of age.** A different statute applied to cases involving students who were 18 or older, and school boards were allowed to suspend students for improper conduct. For students under the age of 18, the possibility of a delinquency adjudication also existed. The court granted the writ as requested. *State ex rel. Estes v. Egnor*, 443 S.E.2d 193 (W. Va. 1994).

IV. GANGS AND CAMPUS INTRUDERS

◆   Section 810.0975(2)(b), Florida Statutes, makes it unlawful for any person to enter a "school safety zone" without legitimate business or other authorization at the school during the period from one hour prior to the start of school until one hour after the conclusion of school. A Miami-area high school student was spotted walking away from the campus of a high school he did not attend at 7:25 a.m. on a school day. Police had warned him not to enter the school's safety zone on two prior occasions, and he was arrested. Prosecutors filed a delinquency petition against the student, and he was charged with trespass in a school safety zone and resisting an arrest.

The student moved to dismiss the petition, arguing the law

unconstitutionally restricted peaceful conduct and communication. The case reached the Florida District Court of Appeal, Third District, which observed that Section 810.975(2)(b) allowed those with proper authorization or legitimate business at a school to remain in a school zone. The student did not show that persons seeking to engage in constitutionally-protected speech or assemblies could not receive "authorization" to do so. He did not show that persons who had previously received notices barring them from school safety zones have First Amendment rights to return to a school safety zone to express themselves. **The court found the law clearly was to protect children, which is a compelling government interest.** As the law was not unconstitutional, the court affirmed the lower court order declaring the student a juvenile delinquent. *J.L.S. v. State,* 947 So.2d 641 (Fla. Ct. App. 2007). The Supreme Court of Florida let the decision stand, refusing to review the case in *J.L.S. v. State*, 958 So.2d 919 (Fla. 2007).

◆ Section 985.23(2)(a), Florida Statutes, allows courts to consider whether a juvenile is a member of a criminal street gang at the time of the commission of an offense when imposing a sentence in juvenile delinquency proceedings. At least two of eight statutory criteria must be proven in order to find a juvenile a "criminal street gang member." A student was charged with assaulting a law enforcement officer, resisting arrest and disruption of a school function. At his disposition hearing for juvenile delinquency, the state department of juvenile justice recommended probation. The state presented evidence that the student was a member of a gang called the "Weedside Boys." A school resource officer testified that the student was seen wearing homemade shirts and book bags identifying him as a gang member. The court adjudicated the student a delinquent, and deviated from the recommendation of probation by the department of juvenile justice. The court found the student was a criminal street gang member and placed him in a moderate-risk residential placement.

The student appealed to a Florida District Court of Appeal, which noted the resource officer's testimony that the student wore shirts and had a book bag decorated with gang symbols. However, there was no testimony that he frequented a particular street gang's area or associated with known criminal street gang members. Under the statute, it was necessary to establish that the student met at least one other criteria. **As there was no competent substantial evidence establishing the student met the definition of "criminal street gang member," the court held the trial court could not rely on alleged gang membership when imposing a sentence on him**. The case was reversed and remanded to the trial court. *R.C. v. State of Florida,* 948 So.2d 48 (Fla. Dist. Ct. App. 2007).

◆ A California school security employee saw three young men sitting on the front lawn of a high school during school hours. He estimated them to be between 16 and 18 years old. Because the employee did not recognize any of them as students, he called a police officer. The officer approached the intruders and asked them for identification. The minor produced an identification paper from another school. The officer decided to escort the three intruders to the office to verify their identities. For his own safety, he decided to pat them down. The officer discovered a knife with a locking blade on the minor and confiscated it. The minor was charged with unlawful possession of the knife on school property. He was placed on probation, but later tried. The Los Angeles County Superior Court denied the minor's motion to exclude the knife as evidence, and he admitted the violation. He then appealed, arguing that a pat-down search on school grounds can only be justified by a belief that the person is armed and dangerous.

The Court of Appeal of California noted the state constitution declares "the inalienable right" of students and staff "to attend campuses which are safe secure and peaceful." The special need for schools to maintain a safe and orderly learning environment required different search and seizure rules than those for the general public. Searches of students are justified if there is reasonable suspicion of a violation of a law, school rule or regulation. **Students may be detained without any particularized suspicion, so long as the detention is not arbitrary, capricious, or for the purpose of harassment.** The minor did not attend the school. He had a lesser right of privacy than students who were properly on school grounds. The officer had ample cause to believe the minor did not belong on campus and had to escort three persons to the school office by himself. The state's interest in preventing violence on a high school campus outweighed the minimal invasion to the minor's privacy rights. "The mere fact that he had no legitimate business on campus created a reasonable need to determine whether or not he posed a danger." As the pat-down search of the minor was proper, the court affirmed the judgment. *In re Jose Y.*, 141 Cal.App.4th 748, 46 Cal.Rptr.3d 268 (Cal. Ct. App. 2006).

◆ Horace Mann Middle School in Los Angeles adopted a uniform policy in response to being found one of California's lowest performing schools. The policy was expected to help students concentrate on schoolwork by reducing any distractions caused by clothing. It was further intended to allow easy identification of non-students who entered campus, help prevent students from leaving campus, and help protect students from gang-related incidents. The school reported significant improvements in attendance and test scores, and a big decrease in behavior problems after adopting the policy. The policy was voluntary and had a parental opt-out feature. One student's grandparent told staff she would not wear a uniform. She was the only one to opt out of the policy in 2003. The student claimed that administrators, security guards and other school staff confronted her several times when she appeared at school out of uniform. She was also barred from a Valentine's day dance, and denied permission to have her class picture taken because she was out of uniform. The student sued the school district and 10 school staff members in the state court system for a variety of civil rights violations, and for intentional infliction of emotional distress. The trial court granted the school district's motion to non-suit most of the student's civil rights and speech claims.

After a trial, the jury returned a verdict against the student on her emotional distress and battery claims. On appeal, the Court of Appeal of California explained that **conduct "is protected by the First Amendment if it 'is inherently expressive.'"** To be "expressive," the conduct must be "sufficiently communicative" by demonstrating "an intent to convey a particularized message" that is likely to be understood by viewers. The court held **"federal and California state cases have concluded that personal expression in clothing or hair style, without more, is not protected speech." The student's "generalized desire to express her middle-school individuality" was an "unfocused message of personal expression" that was unprotected.** The student did not claim she was forbidden to wear clothing imprinted with speech or political symbols, or clothes with "specific symbolic significance." As the trial court had properly non-suited the First Amendment, state Education Code and Equal Protection Clause claims, the court of appeal affirmed the judgment. *Land v. Los Angeles Unified School Dist.*, No. B189287, 2007 WL 1413227 (Cal. Ct. App. 5/15/07).

◆ An Illinois school disciplinary code defined "gang activity" as "prohibited student conduct." Gang activity included any act in furtherance of a gang, and use or possession of gang symbols, such as drawings, hand signs and attire. The code stated gangs and their activities substantially disrupted school by their very nature. A student was suspended three times for drawing gang-related symbols, including an inverted pitchfork and crowns with five points. Each time, the student was informed about the code prohibition on gang symbols and warned of its disciplinary implications. After the third incident, the superintendent notified the student's mother of a proposed expulsion, the date of a hearing, and the right of the student to counsel. A school resource officer testified at the hearing that the pitchfork and crowns were gang-related signs. She said drawing them could be dangerous if misconstrued as a sign of disrespect by another gang.

The school board voted to expel the student for the second half of the school year. His mother sued the board in a state court for constitutional violations. The board removed the case to a federal district court. **The court explained that "a school need not tolerate student speech that is inconsistent with the school's basic educational mission," under** *Hazelwood School Dist. v. Kuhlmeier*, **484 U.S. 260 (1988). To claim First Amendment protection, the student had to show he intended to convey a particular message that would be understood by those who viewed it. Although he claimed his drawings were "artistic expression," he did not claim he was attempting to convey any particular message.** The court rejected the student's argument that the student code did not sufficiently define "gang symbol." A common-sense interpretation showed the student code was specifically directed at gang affiliations that disrupted the educational process. School disciplinary rules did not have to be as detailed as criminal codes. The court rejected all of the student's First Amendment arguments, and his due process claim fared no better. The board provided him with notice of the charges against him and a hearing with a full opportunity to be heard. Finding no constitutional violations, the court upheld the expulsion. *Kelly v. Board of Educ. of McHenry Community High School Dist.*, No. 06 C 152, 2006 WL 2726231 (N.D. Ill. 2006).

◆ A Kentucky school-based decision-making council devised a student dress code for a school district through a parent/teacher subcommittee. The council adopted the subcommittee's recommended dress code based on the need to address the school's gang problem, promote student safety, prevent violence and disputes over clothing, and enable the identification of non-students and intruders on campus. The dress code limited the clothing available to students as well as the way it could be worn. It prohibited logos, shorts, cargo pants, jeans, the wearing of certain jewelry outside clothes, and other specified items.

A number of students who were disciplined for dress code violations sued the school board in a federal district court for First Amendment violations. The court held **school officials had an important and substantial interest in creating an appropriate learning environment by preventing the gang presence and limiting fights**. The regulation of student expression furthered an important government interest without suppressing free speech. The council and subcommittee believed the dress code would help reduce gang activity, ease tension among students who fought over attire and otherwise enhance student safety. The dress code addressed those issues in a manner that was unrelated to the expressive nature of student dress. The court held **school officials may control student speech or expression that is inconsistent with a school's educational mission**. The goal of maintaining a safe and focused educational atmosphere was viewpoint-neutral and did not offend the First Amendment. The board had struck a reasonable balance between the need to anticipate problems and the personal rights of students, and it was entitled to judgment. *Long v. Board of Educ. of Jefferson County, Kentucky*, 21 Fed.Appx. 252 (6th Cir. 2001).

◆ An Illinois school board's anti-gang rule specifically prohibited students from representing gang affiliation, recruiting others for gang membership, and threatening or intimidating others to further gang purposes. The board voted to expel six African-American students for two years because of their involvement in a fight. The board reviewed a videotape of the incident and found the students were members of rival street gangs. The videotape revealed that each of the students actively participated in the fight. After twice voting to expel each student for two years, the board met with an advocacy group led by the Reverend Jesse Jackson and representatives of the state governor. One student withdrew from school, but the board agreed to reduce the expulsions to one year and allow the others to immediately attend alternative education programs. Despite the board's concessions, the students sued the board in a federal district court for civil rights violations, alleging that the anti-gang provision violated the Due Process Clause of the U.S. Constitution.

The court awarded judgment to the board, and the students appealed to the Seventh Circuit, arguing the anti-gang rule was unconstitutionally vague due to its lack of clear definitions. According to the court, **the anti-gang rule clearly defined what conduct it prohibited and was not unconstitutionally vague. The rule did not involve speech rights**, and fighting by the students in support of their gang was clearly within its definitions. It was reasonable for school officials to see the fight as gang-like activity, and the rule was sufficiently definite to avoid a constitutional challenge. The court affirmed the judgment for the school board. *Fuller v. Decatur Public School Board of Educ., Dist. 61*, 251 F.3d 662 (7th Cir. 2001).

CHAPTER FIVE

Employment

I. HIRING PRACTICES

School employers, whether public or private, need to conduct reasonable background checks on potential employees to ensure that the employees are fit for their positions. An employer can be held liable when its failure to exercise ordinary care in hiring or retaining an employee creates a foreseeable risk of harm to a third person.

A claim for negligent hiring arises when, before the time the employee is hired, the employer knew or should have known that the employee was unfit for the position, yet hired the employee anyway.

In addition to a claim for negligent hiring, it also might be possible for a school board to be sued for negligent failure to hire, where the school board's failure to hire for a position results in injury to a third party. The failure to act where there is a duty to do so can result in as great a liability as improperly acting in the first place.

State laws and collective bargaining agreements determine what sort of background checks are required, as well as the limitations on what sort of information can be obtained. Also, state laws and bargaining agreements may define whether certain acquired information can be used to deny a position to an applicant.

◆ A New York student claimed that her high school hired a teacher as a substitute without performing adequate background checks. Before that, the teacher had engaged in pedophilic activities. Afterward, he began engaging in pedophilic behavior with the students at the high school, and began engaging in sexual relations with at least one minor student, videotaping the sex acts. He then aggressively pursued the student both in and out of school in an attempt to have sex with her. Eventually, **he "statutorily raped,** assaulted, molested, sodomized, and abused" her in his classroom after classes ended. Later, police raided the teacher's home and found more than 10,000 photographs of children and more than 500 video clips of children, including videos depicting infants as young as four years old being raped and sodomized. The minors sued the high school, alleging negligent hiring, negligent retention, negligent supervision, inadequate protection, and gross negligence.

The student brought a motion to compel the district to produce certain records, namely its employment records and personnel file on the teacher; the files or documents of the Special Commissioner of Investigation of the Department of Education; and any records relating to allegations by other students of incidents involving the teacher prior to her assault. The court ordered the records released for its inspection, but the school district only released a heavily redacted (blacked out) version of the records. The student appealed to the Supreme Court, Appellate Division, which found that the district's actions constituted a waiver of any objections to disclosure. **It ordered the district to comply with the order for disclosure.** *Anonymous v. High School for Environmental Studies*, 820 N.Y.S.2d 573 (N.Y. App. Div. 2006).

◆   An applicant for a teaching position at a Bureau of Indian Affairs (BIA) boarding school admitted on his employment application that he had been arrested and charged with violating an Oklahoma statute ("Outrage to Public Decency"), and that a valid bench warrant was outstanding on that charge. No investigation was ever made, and he was sent out to the boarding school as a teacher. He eventually kidnapped, assaulted, and raped several children who were enrolled at the BIA school. He committed these acts while off duty in his own quarters. He was convicted on 11 felony counts in connection with those acts and was sent to prison. Any investigation of his admissions on his employment application would have shown that he had been charged with acts of child molestation similar to those he committed at the BIA school.

Sixteen parents and eight children sued the federal government under the Federal Tort Claims Act (FTCA) for damages caused by the government's negligence, which resulted in the molestation of the children. The case reached the Ninth Circuit, where **the government conceded that failing to investigate was negligent, that hiring the teacher was negligent, and that permitting the teacher to continue in his job after his conduct gave notice to his supervisors that he was molesting children was negligent**. The question for the court was whether sovereign immunity insulated the government from liability where its own negligence was the proximate cause of the injury. **The court held that the assault and battery exception to FTCA liability** did not apply to insulate the government from liability because of evidence that the government was negligent in hiring and continuing to employ the teacher despite indications of a predilection toward sexual abuse. *Bennett v. U.S.*, 803 F.2d 1502 (9th Cir. 1986).

◆ A freshman at a public school academy chartered by Central Michigan University claimed that the dean of students sexually assaulted her in an abandoned and unlit stairwell on school grounds and during school hours. She sued the school for negligence, vicarious liability, negligent hiring and violation of the Michigan Constitution. A state court granted pretrial judgment to the school, holding that the school was entitled to governmental immunity and that the dean's conduct was outside the scope of his employment. Therefore, the school was not vicariously liable.

The court of appeals affirmed. Here, the school procured a criminal background check of the dean before hiring him, which revealed that he had been arrested on one occasion for felony insurance fraud. However, he did not have any criminal convictions. More importantly, **the criminal background check did not reveal that he had ever been arrested for, or convicted of, criminal sexual conduct**. Because the student did not provide documentary evidence to support the conclusion that school officials were aware or should have been aware that the dean might sexually assault a student, the dean's **conduct was not foreseeable and the ruling in the school's favor was proper**. *Wilson v. Detroit School of Industrial Arts*, 2006 WL 1237033 (Mich. Ct. App. 5/9/06).

◆ The Portland Public School District proposed terminating its existing custodial workforce and contracting for custodial services. The custodians' union sought a declaratory ruling from the Employment Relations Board that the district's proposal violated the Custodians' Civil Service Law (CCSL) and, therefore, was a prohibited subject of bargaining. The board concluded that the CCSL did not prohibit the district from contracting for its custodial services. The union appealed that decision, and the court of appeals concluded that the district could contract for custodial services notwithstanding the provisions of the CCSL.

The union appealed to the Supreme Court of Oregon, arguing that in accordance with the text of the CCSL, the district had to employ custodians consistently with the merit system set out in that law. It asserted that, in enacting the CCSL the legislature intended to ensure the protection of children. It cited a portion of the statute:

"The civil service board may require an applicant for a custodial position to furnish evidence satisfactory to the board of good character, mental and physical health, and such other evidence as it may deem necessary to establish the applicant's fitness, including any information concerning a criminal conviction for a crime involving the possession, use, sale or distribution of a controlled substance, sexual misconduct … theft or a crime of violence. The board shall not approve the employment of any applicant unless the board is satisfied that the applicant poses no danger to school children."

The supreme court noted that not all custodial positions are part of the classified civil service. Exceptions exist for positions where workers either work less than eight hours per day, work less than 12 months a year, or receive an hourly pay rate. Still, even though such positions are not part of the classified civil service, the civil service board nevertheless maintains a degree of authority over who will fill them. Applicants for custodial positions in general, not just those subject to the classified civil service, are subject to the civil service board's scrutiny during the hiring process.

The legislative intent behind the CCSL was clear. **It prohibits the civil service board from approving any applicant's employment unless the board satisfies itself, from its review of the applicant's fitness, that the applicant poses no danger to the school children in the district's care.** The beneficiaries of that requirement are the district school board and the public, especially parents and students. The district's proposed interpretation of the statute would thwart that legislative intent because it would authorize the district to contract with custodians who have never established, to the satisfaction of the civil service board, that they are fit for service and pose no danger to school children. That approach simply would eliminate the assurance of the safety of school children that the law was designed to secure. The school district was required to employ custodians pursuant to the terms of the CCSL. *Walter v. Scherzinger*, 339 Or. 408, 121 P.3d 644 (Or. 2005).

II. POST-HIRING ISSUES

Liability for negligent supervision or retention occurs after employment begins, where the employer knows or should have known of an employee's unfitness and fails to take further action such as investigating the employee to determine potential unfitness, discharging the employee or reassignment.

Public entities generally can be held liable for the negligent acts or omissions of their employees acting within the scope of their employment except where either the employee or the public entity is immunized from liability by statute.

Where an employee is exercising discretion with respect to school safety and is not acting in bad faith, maliciously or with a conscious indifference to the rights of others, the employee probably will be entitled to immunity from suit.

A. Immunity

◆ An Ohio student attacked another student after gym class. The victim's parents sued the school district, claiming it knew of the attacker's history of assaulting students, yet did not take the necessary precautions to protect other students from him. **A trial court held that the district was immune, noting that it did not act with malice, in bad faith or recklessly.** It also found that **the teacher's supervision at the time of the attack was not even negligent**. The Ohio Court of Appeals affirmed. Although the student aggressor was disruptive at times, there were no indications that he was terrorizing other students. The fact that he had been in a juvenile detention center several times was not enough to put the school on notice that he was likely to attack another student. *Aratari v. Leetonia Exempt Village School Dist.*, 2007 WL 969402 (Ohio Ct. App. 3/26/07).

◆ The Georgia Constitution provides: "Every public school shall prepare a school safety plan to help curb the growing incidence of violence in schools, to respond effectively to such incidents, and to provide a safe learning environment for Georgia's children, teachers, and other school personnel. Such plan shall also address preparedness for natural disasters, hazardous material or radiological accidents, acts of violence, and acts of terrorism. School safety plans of public schools shall be prepared with input from students enrolled in that school, parents or legal guardians of such students, teachers ... , community leaders, ... other school employees and school district employees, and local law enforcement, fire service, public safety, and emergency management agencies. ..."

It also provides that "[s]chool safety plans prepared by public schools shall address security issues in school safety zones...". In a case involving student-on-student violence, the Georgia Supreme Court held that **the mandatory action called for by the constitution involved a discretionary duty rather than a ministerial duty, allowing for immunity on the part of school officials**. Further, the delay in obtaining medical care did not result in liability for the school officials because the law does not create a civil cause of action for damages in favor of the victim or anyone else for the purported failure to report timely.

Also, neither the Eighth Amendment nor the Due Process Clause of the Fourteenth Amendment can serve as the basis for a ministerial duty on the part of school employees to provide medical care to a student. Because there was no express statutory duty imposed on school employees to provide medical care to students, there existed no ministerial duty to provide medical care. And since the duty was discretionary, the school officials were entitled to immunity. *Murphy v. Bajjani*, 647 S.E.2d 54 (Ga. 2007).

◆ On the last day of the school year for an Alabama elementary school, various teachers and coaches were called into the guidance counselor's office and asked to sit in the chair facing the guidance counselor's desk. As each teacher sat in the chair, the chair slowly reclined in the back, causing the back portion of the seat to sink down and the front part to slant upward. As each teacher sat in this "sinking" chair, the guidance counselor and the other teachers present would laugh. The teachers would then summon to the guidance counselor's office another staff member, on whom they could play the practical joke.

A coach who was summoned to the office and instructed to sit in the chair did so, at which point the chair reclined under her. She reinjured her back, upon which she had undergone several surgical procedures. She sued the principal (one of the first people duped by the "sinking chair"), the guidance counselor and others for negligence, wantonness, conspiracy, and failure to warn. A trial court granted judgment as a matter of law for the defendants, and the coach appealed.

The Court of Civil Appeals of Alabama noted that **the principal had testified that she was responsible for safety on the school** campus and premises. The county school policy provided:

"[T]he principal shall be immediately responsible for the condition of the school plant and shall provide direct supervision to the custodial maintenance personnel assigned to his[her] building. The principal will ... [i]nspect the school plant periodically for conditions that might endanger the health and safety of students and or employees. Fire, accident and health hazards should be remedied or reported immediately.... [Principals should] [i]nitiate through the Maintenance supervisor, when necessary, prompt correction of safety related deficiencies in the school plant or grounds."

The principal testified that she had familiarized herself with the school's safety guidelines and had, in the past, reported hazardous or worn-out equipment to the county school system. The court noted that the policy was broadly phrased and was drafted in general terms designed to advise the principal of his or her responsibility for the overall safe condition of the school plant. Here, the principal knew of the condition of the chair, because she had sat in it earlier on the date of the accident, and it had slowly reclined under her weight. She testified that she never viewed the chair as a safety problem. She left shortly after the joke was played on her and was absent from the school when the guidance counselor asked the coach to sit in the chair.

The court determined that **the principal was exercising her judgment regarding school safety and concluded that she was entitled to state-agent immunity on the coach's claims of negligence and wantonness**. It stated that it might have reached a different result if, instead of the broadly stated, general safety policy, the principal had instead been responsible for following a detailed rule or checklist and had failed in this responsibility. In addition, the principal would not have been entitled to state-agent immunity if there had been any evidence of willful, malicious, or fraudulent behavior, evidence of bad faith, or evidence of actions beyond her authority or done under a mistaken interpretation of the law. There also was no evidence of a conspiracy, nor did the other teachers present have a duty to warn the coach about the sinking chair. The only person with potential liability to the coach was the guidance counselor, who brought the chair to school. *Bayles v. Marriott*, 816 So.2d 38 (Ala. Civ. App. 2001).

B. Complying with Safety Policies

◆ Michigan amended its education laws in 2006 to require the department of information technology to work with the department of education and the department of state police to develop and implement an automated program that does a comparison of the education department's list of registered educational personnel with the conviction information received by the department of state police. Unless otherwise prohibited by law, this comparison must include convictions contained in a nonpublic record. If a comparison discloses that a person on the education department's list of registered educational personnel has been convicted of a crime, the department must notify the superintendent or chief administrator, and the board or governing body of the school district, intermediate school district, public school academy, or nonpublic school in which the person is employed of that conviction. The law makes the same requirement for individuals holding a teaching certificate or state board approval.

It was expected that the comparison would result in some "false hits" because some data fields, such as Social Security numbers, might match. However, state officials assumed that final confirmation would take place at the school district level, so that any false convictions would not result in adverse action. A number of education employees sued state officials, alleging that they were falsely accused of having criminal convictions. They asserted defamation claims as well as infliction of emotional distress. The Michigan Court of Appeals ruled that **the state officials were entitled to immunity because they were acting within the scope of their authority in attempting to comply with the school safety legislation**. *Frohriep v. Flanagan*, 2007 WL 1375888 (Mich. Ct. App. 5/10/07).

◆ A North Carolina sixth-grade student was robbed and assaulted by two classmates on the second day of school. For the next month the student was bullied by one of his previous assailants, who punched him in the head during an art class. When he asked the teacher for help, she refused to get involved. He tried to go to the principal's office but was followed by his attacker and another student. They beat him up in the hallway and assaulted another teacher who tried to stop them. Other students finally rescued him, and his attackers were suspended. However, the principal did not report the assaults to the authorities.

The student continued to receive threats from his attacker's friends and eventually transferred to a private school. He then sued the school board and various officials under 42 U.S.C. § 1983, alleging that the defendants violated his liberty interest in bodily integrity and his property interest in a public education when they allowed his classmates to physically assault him at school over a period of several weeks. He also alleged a violation of the Safe and Drug-Free Schools and Communities Act as well as constitutional and common law claims under North Carolina law. A federal court dismissed the lawsuit and the Fourth Circuit Court of Appeals affirmed. Here, the school did not expel or even constructively expel the student. Rather, his father voluntarily transferred him to a private school. Also, the attackers were private individuals, not school officials. And the school officials did not have a special relationship with the student triggering the protections of the Due Process Clause.

Although school officials here may have been irresponsible and ineffective in not heeding the warnings that the student was helpless at the hands of bullies, they did not commit a constitutional violation. Nor did they act with deliberate indifference. Since the school officials did not violate the student's constitutional rights, **the school board could not be held liable for failing to develop an adequate school safety plan.** Finally, **the student had no private right of action under the Safe and Drug-Free Schools and Communities Act.** *Stevenson v. Martin County Board of Educ.,* 3 Fed.Appx. 25 (4th Cir. 2001).

◆   A nine-year-old New Jersey student was dismissed from school on an early-dismissal day, walked off school grounds without an adult, and was struck by a car a few blocks from school over two hours later. The accident paralyzed him from the neck down.

The school district had a four-page policy memorandum titled "Pupil Safety" that addressed a wide range of student safety topics, including supervision of students at dismissal time. The memorandum stated that "[t]he chief school administrator shall seek the cooperation of parents/guardians to prevent any children [from] being unsupervised on school property during lunch hour and during morning arrival and afternoon dismissal times." The memorandum did not, however, outline how dismissal supervision would be administered by the schools.

Instead, the school adhered to a practice that all school personnel supervise dismissal. On a typical school day, the school's 500 students were dismissed at 2:50 p.m. Teachers escorted the students from their classrooms to designated exits at the sounding of the school bell, and the teachers remained at their designated duty stations to ensure that the children left the school premises. According to the school principal, all school personnel – including teachers, teachers' aides, and security personnel – supervised dismissal to ensure that the children left school before the adults. The principal personally supervised early-dismissal days to "make sure that there were no children whose parents did not pick them up and they were still outside."

The student and his family sued, alleging that the school district and principal breached their duty of reasonable supervision with respect to his dismissal from school. They also claimed they did not have advance notice of the early-dismissal day. A state court granted the defendants' motion for summary judgment, finding that their duty of care did not apply to an accident that occurred hours after the student's dismissal and blocks from his school. The Appellate Division reversed, holding that schools have a duty of reasonable care to supervise children at dismissal, and remanded the matter for a trial to determine whether that duty was breached here.

The Supreme Court of New Jersey held that because a school's duty to exercise reasonable care for the children in its custody is integral to state's public education system, the duty does not summarily disappear when the school bell rings. Accordingly, schools in New Jersey must exercise a duty of reasonable care for supervising students' safety at dismissal. **The duty requires school districts to create a reasonable dismissal supervision policy, provide suitable notice to parents of that policy, and effectively comply with the policy and subsequent and appropriate parental**

requests concerning dismissal. The court substantially affirmed the decision of the Appellate Division and remanded the matter to the trial court for further proceedings consistent with its opinion. *Jerkins v. Anderson*, 191 N.J. 285, 922 A.2d 1279 (N.J. 2007).

C. Fitness for Duty

◆   A Mississippi high school teacher with no history of sexually harassing students began a sexually inappropriate relationship with a student, though both he and the student denied that sexual intercourse ever occurred. A rumor circulated about the relationship, but the principal detected no sign of it. He confronted the teacher, who vehemently denied there was any inappropriate relationship. However, the truth eventually came out in some discarded love letters and some impassioned e-mails. The student's family sued the school district for negligent hiring and retention, among other claims. A court ruled for the school district, and the Court of Appeals of Mississippi affirmed. Here, **the school district did not have either actual or constructive notice of the inappropriate relationship between the student and teacher, as required to establish a claim for negligent hiring or retention.** The teacher had no prior history of wrongdoing, and many of his contacts with the student were under the guise of innocence, such as his tutoring of the student and her babysitting of his child. *Doe v. Pontotoc County School Dist.*, 2007 WL 1412999 (Miss. Ct. App. 5/15/07).

◆   A tenured high school teacher in New York received several unsatisfactory evaluations and claimed that he was also denied certain benefits and opportunities. He sought an accommodation for dust and pollen allergies, which the school claimed it provided; he asserted that its efforts were insufficient. He then sent letters to the assistant principal, calling her "Mein Fuhrer," and referring to her as a "snooperviser." He also referred to himself as "an indentured subject of her sick experiment." Fearing he represented a threat to the safety of staff and students, the school reassigned him to administrative work at another high school and required a psychological evaluation. Pending the results, his photograph was given to school safety officers and custodial staff who worked in his old high school building during evenings and weekends to ensure that he would not enter the building.

He was determined to be fit for duty and was returned to the classroom without any loss of pay or benefits. He then sued for discrimination under state and federal law. A federal court granted pretrial judgment to the defendants, finding no issue of fact that could resolve itself in his favor. Here, the school provided an accommodation that met the requirements listed in the Board of Education Accommodation. He merely found them unsatisfactory. Further, **the reassignment was a temporary measure taken to ensure the safety of students and staff, and he was transferred back to a teaching position once the evaluation found him fit for duty.** *Krinsky v. Abrams*, 2007 WL 1541369 (E.D.N.Y. 5/25/07).

III. SCHOOL SECURITY OFFICERS

At schools in many states, school security officers are an integral component of an overall plan to maintain safety. Schools must ensure that these officers possess all required qualifications and/or certifications.

In Virginia, for example, state law requires that all school security officers are certified via a program administered by the state's department of criminal justice services. Training requirements for school security officers are established by regulation.

New school security officers in Virginia must complete the certification course, which is a 32-hour course, within 60 days from their date of hire. School security officers also are provided with opportunities to supplement their training. The state's department of criminal justice services also offers a course that school security officers can take to become certified school security officer instructors. Individuals who successfully complete this course can provide training to other school security officers. The state also has an online database of school security officers.

The certification program includes renewal requirements. Specifically, school security officers must complete 16 hours of in-service training during each two-year period after initial certification.

IV. EMPLOYEE PREPAREDNESS AND RESPONSE

Coordinating employee responsibilities with respect to crisis prevention and response is critical. One way to aid in forming an effective team among school employees is to conduct a staff skills inventory that matches individual employees with particular areas of experience and/or expertise. For a form that can be used to conduct such a skills inventory, see Form I-1 in chapter nine.

The federal Department of Education has compiled the following general checklists to assist in crisis prevention and response.

CHECKLIST: MITIGATION AND PREVENTION

- Connect with community emergency responders to identify local hazards.
- Review the last safety audit to examine school buildings and grounds.
- Determine who is responsible for overseeing violence prevention strategies in your school.
- Encourage staff to provide input and feedback during the crisis planning process.
- Review incident data.
- Determine major problems in your school with regard to student crime and violence.
- Assess how the school addresses these problems.

- Conduct an assessment to determine how these problems – as well as others – may impact your vulnerability to certain crises.

CHECKLIST: PREPAREDNESS

- Determine what crisis plans exist in the district, school, and community.
- Identify all stakeholders involved in crisis planning.
- Develop procedures for communicating with staff, students, families, and the media.
- Establish procedures to account for students during a crisis.
- Gather information about the school facility, such as maps and the location of utility shutoffs.
- Identify the necessary equipment that needs to be assembled to assist staff in a crisis.

CHECKLIST: RESPONSE

- Determine if a crisis is occurring.
- Identify the type of crisis that is occurring and determine the appropriate response.
- Activate the incident management system.
- Ascertain whether an evacuation, reverse evacuation, lockdown, or shelter-in-place needs to be implemented.
- Maintain communication among all relevant staff at officially designated locations.
- Establish what information needs to be communicated to staff, students, families, and the community.
- Monitor how emergency first aid is being administered to the injured.
- Decide if more equipment and supplies are needed.

CHECKLIST: RECOVERY

- Strive to return to learning as quickly as possible.
- Restore the physical plant, as well as the school community.
- Monitor how staff are assessing students for the emotional impact of the crisis.
- Identify what follow-up interventions are available to students, staff, and first responders.
- Conduct debriefings with staff and first responders.
- Assess curricular activities that address the crisis.
- Allocate appropriate time for recovery.
- Plan how anniversaries of events will be commemorated.
- Capture "lessons learned" and incorporate them into revisions and trainings.

CHAPTER SIX

Extracurricular Activities

I. AFTER-SCHOOL PROGRAMS

Schools can no longer throw open their doors so that neighborhood children can use their facilities after the school day ends. Nor can they rely on minimal supervision for after-school programs. Threats to security and student safety mean they must now devise plans for how to safely engage students after the school day ends.

Some well-recognized means of decreasing risk are:
- reducing the number of open doors
- concentrating after-school activities in limited areas
- assigning trained personnel to supervise activities rather than relying on custodians

- developing emergency/crisis preparedness training, and
- if contracting with an outside entity to run a program, building into the contract security requirements that must be followed.

A. Negligent Supervision

◆ A New Jersey school board, in conjunction with the county, provided an after-school program for homeless and at-risk students. The county devised the after-school program, provided the teachers, presented the activities and supervised the children. The county was also the direct recipient of the funds provided by the grant to underwrite the cost of the program. Although the school board did not directly fund the program, its cooperation was an indispensable component of the county's ability to obtain the grant. An 11-year-old student who attended the program was seriously injured by a 15-year-old juvenile while leaving the program but still on the school's playground. A teacher gave him permission to walk home even though his mother had made clear that the student's older brother was going to be picking him up after the program. He sued the school board to recover for his injuries. A state court granted pretrial judgment to the school board, and the student appealed to the Superior Court of New Jersey, Appellate Division.

The appellate court noted that a jury could find an apparent agency relationship between the school board and the county such that the school board could be held liable. Without the direct participation by the school board, funding for the program would not have been possible. Thus, **a rational fact-finder could find that the county and the school board were involved in an apparent agency relationship to bring about this after-care program** for both homeless children and "at risk" students. The principal and school personnel were involved in choosing the children who could participate in the program, and the parental authorization had to be returned to the principal. Accordingly, there was a jury question as to whether the county's agents were negligent in releasing the student despite the mother's instructions, and whether that negligence was a cause of the student's injuries. A trial was required. *Muniz v. Belleville Board of Educ.*, 2003 WL 21962246 (N.J. Super. Ct. App. Div. 7/17/03).

◆ A Connecticut elementary student participated in an after-school program run by the town of New Milford. While hanging on a basketball rim installed seven feet above the ground, he fell onto the concrete surface below and sustained injuries. He sued the town and the employees who had been supervising the program for negligence. After examining the "imminent harm" exception to discretionary act immunity, the Superior Court of Connecticut ruled in favor of the town. The imminent harm exception test requires three things: (1) an imminent harm; (2) an identifiable victim; and (3) a public official to whom it is apparent that his or her conduct is likely to subject that victim to that harm. Here, the supervisors testified that no one else had ever been hurt after dropping from the rim. Nor was hanging on the rim a prohibited activity. **Since there was no apparent risk of injury to the student, the town and employees were entitled to immunity.** *Zaborowski v. Town of New Milford*, 2007 WL 1413911 (Conn. Super. Ct. 4/24/07).

◆ The parents of a child injured on a school playground sued St. Christopher-Ottilie and the Center For Family Life In Sunset Park, which together provided an after-school program, alleging negligent supervision. The child was injured when he slipped and fell while engaged in normal play on a "monkey-bars" apparatus in a schoolyard during an after-school program operated by the two defendants. Two supervisors employed by the defendants were approximately 15 feet away from the child when they saw him fall. At least one other supervisor was within the same complex of playground equipment, and two additional adult volunteers were assigned to supervise the group of 25 to 30 children of which the child was a member. The case reached the New York Supreme Court, Appellate Division, which noted that the child was not engaged in any rough or inappropriate play prior to the accident and that **the defendants were not on notice of any horseplay or defective condition so as to warrant closer supervision or intervention.** Accordingly, the degree of supervision afforded by the defendants was reasonable and adequate under the circumstances, and the child's injury was not proximately caused by a lack of supervision. The lawsuit was dismissed. *Berdecia v. City of New York*, 289 A.D.2d 354, 735 N.Y.S.2d 554 (N.Y. App. Div. 2001).

B. Duty to Protect Students

◆ A California school opened its campus at 7:00 a.m., but trouble spots, such as restrooms, were unsupervised before 7:45 a.m. School administrators knew that one eighth-grade special education student was usually dropped off at 7:15 a.m. A classmate who also had disabilities teased and ridiculed the student daily before classes began. The student sometimes went to the office to escape this, and he complained to the staff. He was told to stay away from the classmate, even after he told the vice principal this did not work. The classmate twice isolated the student and sexually assaulted him. The district learned of the incidents and expelled the classmate, who was also arrested. The student was hospitalized with depression, and he attempted suicide. He filed a state court action against the school district and the classmate's family. A jury trial resulted in a verdict of over $2.5 million for the student, and the district appealed.

The Court of Appeal of California observed that **schools have a special relationship with students, which imposes an affirmative duty on school districts to "take all reasonable steps to protect students."** The duty arose from the compulsory nature of education and a state constitutional declaration of each student's inalienable right to attend safe, secure, and peaceful campuses. **School districts have a well-established duty to**

supervise students at all times while on school grounds and to enforce necessary rules and regulations for their protection. This duty included supervision during recess and before or after school. The district was liable for injuries resulting from the failure of school staff to use ordinary care to protect students. The district unlocked its gates at 7:00 a.m. each day, but did not provide supervision until 7:45 a.m. **It could have simply precluded students from arriving early or kept them in particular areas of the school.** The district's claim to immunity failed because there was no exercise of discretion by the principal, and evidence that he knew of the classmate's violent behavior. The damage award was not excessive, and the court affirmed the judgment. *M.W. v. Panama Buena Union School Dist.*, 1 Cal. Rptr. 3d 673 (Cal. Ct. App. 2003).

◆ The family of a New York student brought a lawsuit against the board of education, seeking to recover damages for injuries the student allegedly sustained when, upon being pushed by a schoolmate, he fell down a staircase at a public school during an after-school program run by the YMCA of Greater New York. There was no handrail on the right side of the staircase where the student was walking. The supreme court denied the board's motion for pretrial judgment and the Supreme Court, Appellate Division, affirmed.

The testimony of the student at a hearing and at his deposition demonstrated that he tried to grab the handrail on the opposite side of the stairs to stop his fall, but could not reach it. The unchallenged statement of the family's expert **engineer demonstrated that the absence of a handrail on the right side of the staircase was a violation of the applicable building code.** Thus, there were triable issues of fact as to whether the absence of the handrail was a proximate cause of the student's injuries and whether the fact that he was pushed by a fellow student severed any nexus (connection) between the city's alleged negligence in the design of the staircase and his injuries. The case required a trial. *Ocasio v. Board of Educ. of City of New York*, 35 A.D.3d 825, 827 N.Y.S.2d 265 (N.Y. App. Div. 2006).

II. FIELD TRIPS AND OFF-CAMPUS ACTIVITIES

Field trips provide a dual challenge to schools. First, they must ensure the safety of their students off school grounds, in settings where outside influences are not as easily controllable. Second, they must ensure the safety of the general public from reasonably foreseeable acts of violence or horseplay by students. This latter concern, while slight for many schools (especially elementary schools), can be a real problem for others.

Increased supervision presents the single easiest solution, especially the usage of parent volunteers to assist with oversight. But this also presents a problem: how to verify that parent volunteers are not a threat. Background checks are the best insurance policy against threats to students. Some schools charge parents to conduct background checks; others impose a fee for all students for field trips, a part of which can be used to conduct the background checks. For a sample field trip permission slip, see Form VI-3 in chapter nine. A sample questionnaire for chaperones can be found at Form VI-1, and a sample of chaperone guidelines can be found at Form VI-2 in chapter nine.

A. Negligent Supervision

1. Duty of Care

◆ Approximately 200 eighth-grade students from a middle school in Texas went on a field trip to an athletic club, where the activities included swimming. School district employees attended the event to supervise the students. The school district opted not to hire lifeguards for the event. Sometime during the day, an eighth-grader drowned in the swimming pool. His family sued the district and various employees under 42 U.S.C. § 1983, claiming the district employees violated their son's constitutional substantive due process rights to life, liberty, and bodily integrity. The district employees sought pretrial judgment, asserting that they were entitled to immunity for their actions. The trial court disagreed, and the employees appealed to the Texas Court of Appeals.

The employees argued that they were entitled to qualified immunity from the family's claims, absent a showing of a violation of clearly established constitutional law. The court noted that government officials performing discretionary functions are protected from civil liability under the doctrine of qualified immunity if their conduct violates no "clearly established statutory or constitutional rights of which a reasonable person would have known."

The claims here included allegations that the school district employees committed constitutional violations because they failed to properly supervise and/or discipline the student on the field trip. The court held that the school district employees were acting within the scope of their discretionary authority at the time of the incident. Further, **there was no special relationship to create a constitutional duty on the part of the employees to safeguard the student against potential harm during the field trip**. The employees should have been granted pretrial judgment. The appellate court reversed the lower court's decision. *Leo v. Trevino*, No. 13-05-516-CV, 2006 WL 1550839 (Tex. Ct. App. 6/8/06).

◆ An Arkansas student attended a band competition in Atlanta with his school band. He became ill after arriving and missed the entire competition while remaining in his hotel room. Shortly after the student returned home, his mother took him to a medical center. However, he suffered a cardiac arrest and died the next day. The death was attributed to undiagnosed diabetes. The mother sued the school district and officials in a federal district court for negligence and deliberate indifference to her son's medical needs. The court dismissed her federal constitutional claims. It held federal jurisdiction should be rejected in cases that involved common law torts incidentally involving action by a government employee. The mother appealed to the U.S. Court of Appeals, Eighth Circuit. The court echoed the district court's opinion, noting **"the Due Process Clause of the Fourteenth Amendment is not a 'font of tort law.'"** Neither the text nor the history of the clause indicated state entities must guarantee minimal safety and security to individuals. **The Due Process Clause generally does not confer affirmative rights to government aid, even if this may be necessary to secure individual life, liberty or property interests.**

A state assumes a constitutional duty to protect an individual's safety only when it has restrained the individual's liberty through incarceration, institutionalization or some other form of restraint that renders the individual incapable of self-care. The district court had correctly dismissed the due process claim against the school district, because there was no district policy of violating student constitutional rights. There was also no evidence that the band director had restrained the student's ability to care for himself. **School officials have no duty to care for students who participate in voluntary school-related activities such as school band trips.** There was no claim that the student could not leave the band activity at any time, and his family was not prevented from arranging for him to leave Atlanta. The court found no evidence that the student's "voluntary participation evolved into an involuntary commitment" during the trip. While a tort remedy might still be available in the state courts, the judgment for the school district on the mother's federal claims was affirmed. *Lee v. Pine Bluff School Dist.*, 472 F.3d 1026 (8th Cir. 2007).

2. Harmful Acts of Others

◆   A student on a field trip to the National Zoo in Washington claimed that he was assaulted, kicked, and beaten by five male students, who were also on a school field trip from their school: a private, non-profit school chartered under District of Columbia law for at-risk youths. **He alleged that at the time of attack, the students were unsupervised.** He also alleged that he suffered a concussion and injuries to multiple areas of his body. He sued the school, alleging negligent supervision. The school sought to dismiss the case, arguing that it owed the victimized student no duty to provide a constant watch over its students during a school field trip in order to prevent an unforeseeable act of violence. The injured student argued that the school did owe him a duty of care and cited to the Restatement of Torts (2d) § 319:

> One who takes charge of a third person whom he knows or should
> know to be likely to cause bodily harm to others if not controlled is
> under a duty to exercise reasonable care to control the third person
> to prevent him from doing such harm.

The court permitted the injured student to maintain his negligence claim on the ground that the school had a duty to make reasonable efforts to protect members of the public from its students during the field trip. **A**

school's duty to supervise its students to guard against foreseeable harm does not disappear on field trips. So if the injured student could show that the school should have known his attackers had a propensity for violence, the school could be liable. *Thomas v. City Lights School*, 124 F.Supp.2d 707 (D.D.C. 2000).

◆ A New York student's sixth-grade class, along with five other fifth- and sixth-grade classes, attended a drug awareness fair at a park near their school. Sponsored by the board of education and the police department, the fair permitted students to walk through the park on their own and participate in program activities that interested them. Seven teachers and four or five aides supervised the group. A student received permission to get lunch at a nearby pizzeria, but she did not return from lunch by the time her teacher decided to return to school. The teacher looked for her, but did not inform any teachers or police officers providing security at the fair that he could not locate her. The student had left the park to walk home after she failed to find her classmates. On the way home, she was raped by a junior high school student and his friend. She sued the board of education for her injuries.

A jury ruled in her favor and awarded her $2,250,000 in damages, but the Supreme Court, Appellate Division, reversed. The case then reached the Court of Appeals, New York's highest court, which held that a rational jury could have determined, as the jury in this case did, that the foreseeable result of the danger created by the school's alleged lack of supervision was an injury such as occurred here. A fact finder could have reasonably concluded that the very purpose of the school supervision was to shield vulnerable schoolchildren from such acts of violence. The jury permissibly determined that **the rape was the foreseeable result of a danger created by the school's failure to adequately supervise the student.** Thus, the board was liable for the student's injuries. The case was returned to the appellate division court for further proceedings. *Bell v. Board of Educ. of the City of New York*, 687 N.E.2d 1325, (N.Y. 1997).

◆ A 16-year-old boy was shot and killed by another teen who had escaped 60 days earlier from a residential facility for troubled youth in the District of Columbia. The boy's mother sued the District, the Administrator of the D.C. Youth Services Administration (YSA), and the company that contracted with the YSA to run the facility. She claimed that the defendants knew the teen had absconded on two prior occasions and negligently failed to supervise him accordingly – a failure that caused her son's untimely death. A federal court ruled for the defendants, noting that **at the time of the shooting, the teen was far beyond the facility's custodial control**. Further, **the facility did not know of the teen's dangerous propensities**. Juveniles who are determined to pose a public danger are not assigned to group homes like the facility here. Thus, the defendants could not be held liable for the shooting of the boy. *Johnson v. District of Columbia*, 2006 WL 2521241 (D.D.C. 8/30/06).

◆   A Washington high school sponsored a "Workday" event, in which community members donated $15 for three hours of student work to raise funds for a student association. A student's mother agreed to let her daughter split and stack firewood with a classmate's father. She learned on the day of the event that the classmate's father planned to have the students split logs with a hydraulic log splitter. The mother cautioned the student, but apparently did not turn in a parental permission slip to perform the work. While the students were operating the log splitter, they were distracted by a car, and the student lost three fingers.

The student sued the school district and classmate's father in a state court for negligence. The court found the student's mother had consented to the activity and awarded judgment to the school district. The student appealed. The Court of Appeals of Washington stated **the general rule that schools have a duty to protect students from reasonably foreseeable harm. School districts are not insurers of student safety, but are liable for foreseeable wrongful acts of third parties.** Harm is foreseeable if the risk was known or should have been known in the exercise of reasonable care. Liability may result if a school supervises and exercises control over extracurricular activities. **Students are under the control and protection of their schools, and are unable to protect themselves. This supervisory duty extends to off-campus activities under district supervision.** As the student was in the district's custody, it owed her a duty of reasonable care. A jury could have found the district should have taken appropriate steps to find out what was planned for each Workday location and identify any obvious safety problems. The court held the student had presented enough evidence to receive a jury trial to decide whether her mother's consent superseded the district's duty. The court reversed and remanded the case for a trial. *Travis v. Bohannon*, 115 P.3d 342 (Wash. Ct. App. 2005).

B. School Policies – Permission

◆   A group of Ohio students attended a school-sponsored student exchange program in Germany. Before the trip, a teacher explained to students that they would stay with a "host family" for two weeks. They would have some supervised field trips, but would spend a great deal of time with host families without any direct supervision by school staff or the host school. While in Germany, a number of students consumed alcoholic beverages at biergartens with their "host parents." They were of legal drinking age in Germany and believed they were permitted to drink without supervision. Upon returning home, the school suspended the students for three to five days for violating student code prohibitions on consuming or possessing alcohol while in the school's control and custody. The students asked for a hearing before the school board, arguing the teacher had "verbally created an exception to the school's code of conduct regarding the consumption of alcohol." Students and parents understood the exception as allowing the parents and host parents to determine whether students could drink alcohol. The board overturned the suspensions but required the students to perform community service.

An Ohio trial court vacated the discipline, and the board appealed to the Court of Appeals of Ohio. **The court stated Ohio Rev. Code § 3313.661 gives school districts and boards the authority to devise codes of conduct, adopt a policy for suspension, expulsion, removal and permanent exclusion of students, and to specify the types of misconduct resulting in discipline.** There was undisputed evidence that the teacher had "engrafted an exception on the disciplinary code's provisions concerning alcohol consumption." Only the teacher and another employee had testified that the "exception" required direct supervision of host parents for any student drinking. The exception was not written. The students and parents had all stated their understanding of the policy allowed parents and host parents to determine the circumstances for alcohol consumption by students. The court upheld the trial court's decision to vacate any discipline. *Brosch v. Mariemont City School Dist. Board of Educ.*, No. C-050283, 2006 WL 250947 (Ohio Ct. App. 2006).

◆ Minnesota students attending an auto shop class were bused to a body shop for class instruction. En route, the teacher observed a student holding a knife that was passed to him from a classmate. When the bus arrived at the body shop, the teacher called a school coordinator to report the knife. The coordinator and principal decided each student should be searched, and the principal called a school liaison officer. Before the search began, the classmate voluntarily handed over the knife. The liaison officer found a collapsible baton in the student's pocket, and he was charged with violating a state law prohibiting possession of a dangerous weapon on school property. The district brought an expulsion proceeding against the student for violating its ban on weapons and look-alikes. The student pursued civil rights claims against the liaison officer and his municipality in a state court. Municipal officials removed the case to a federal district court, where they obtained summary judgment.

The student appealed to the Eighth Circuit, which recited the general rule that school and municipal officers are entitled to qualified immunity when their conduct does not violate clearly established federal statutory or constitutional rights of which a reasonable officer would have knowledge. While law officers are normally required to have probable cause of wrongdoing to support a search or seizure of persons or property, the more lenient standard of "reasonable suspicion" applies to searches and seizures in the context of public schools. There is a special need to ensure safety in schools, and officials may conduct a search that is "justified at its inception" and reasonable in scope. The court held **the *New Jersey v. T.L.O.* standard applies to law enforcement officers who conduct student searches away from traditional school grounds**. School administrators initiated the search, and one of them played a substantial role in it. **The fact that the search took place off school grounds did not call for imposing the stricter probable cause standard.** The liaison officer's conduct was reasonable, as he did not know whether other students might also have weapons. He had reasonable grounds to believe that the student possessed a knife and was not required to use the least intrusive means of performing a search. As the search was justified and reasonable in scope, the officer was entitled to immunity and the court affirmed the judgment. *Shade v. City of Farmington, Minnesota*, 309 F.3d 1054 (8th Cir. 2002).

♦ A teacher employed by the Kansas State School for the Deaf (KSSD) asked an assistant football coach to recruit players to help him improve property he owned. The project involved moving discarded railroad ties that weighed 150 pounds. The school's head teacher turned down a written request for a field trip to the property, but later signed the request form. Two students and the assistant football coach accompanied the teacher to the property. When the teacher left to prepare lunch, one of the students was struck and killed by a train. KSSD's board ruled the teacher's conduct did not reflect high standards of professional conduct, especially for the safety needs of deaf students. A KSSD investigation committee adopted a motion terminating the teacher's employment for jeopardizing the health and safety of students, failing to exercise appropriate professional judgment, failing to comply with school policies, and failing to conduct himself "in a manner reflecting positively on the school." However, a KSSD hearing committee held for the teacher, finding the board did not prove he displayed a lack of professional judgment.

The board appealed to a Kansas district court, which reversed the hearing committee's decision. The teacher appealed to the Kansas Supreme Court, which held the KSSD operated under laws similar to those applying to all Kansas teachers. It was appropriate to evaluate the case under the numerous decisions of state courts regarding the discharge of tenured teachers. **The court upheld the hearing committee's finding that no school policy or student safety regulations applied to the case. The board showed no evidence of a loss of confidence in the teacher**, as the testimony of members of the deaf community was "all to the contrary." While the teacher did not inform parents about the nature of the field trip, this was the head teacher's duty. There was evidence that the practice of taking railroad ties from railroad property was common and not inappropriate. The court refused to reweigh the evidence or substitute its judgment for that of the committee. As the board did not show substantial evidence supporting discharge, and the committee did not act fraudulently, arbitrarily or capriciously, the court reversed the judgment. *Kansas State Board of Educ. v. Marsh*, 50 P.3d 9 (Kan. 2002).

III. ATHLETIC EVENTS

Student-athletes assume the risks incidental to sports participation and, absent a showing of gross negligence or intentional conduct by a coach, league or school, may not recover damages for their injuries.

A. Participants

1. Duty of Care

State laws require a showing that the school or its staff acted recklessly or intentionally to overcome the defense of governmental immunity.

◆ A California community college student played on a visiting baseball team in a preseason game against a host college. The host team's pitcher hit him in the head with a pitch, cracking his batting helmet. The student claimed he was intentionally hit in retaliation for a pitch thrown by his teammate at a batter from the host team in the previous inning. After being hit, the student staggered, felt dizzy, and was in pain. His manager told him to go to first base. The student did so, but complained to his first-base coach, who told him to stay in the game. Soon after that, the student was told to sit on the bench. He claimed no one tended to his injuries. The student sued the host college in a state superior court for breaching its duty of care by failing to supervise or control its pitcher and failing to provide umpires or medical care. The court dismissed the case, but the state court of appeal reversed the judgment. The Supreme Court of California agreed to review the case. It held Section 831.7 of the California Government Code did not extend to injuries suffered during supervised school sports.

Section 831.7 was intended to be a premises liability provision for public entities. The court found no intent by the legislature to limit a public entity's liability for supervision of sporting activities. **When an athletic participant is injured, the court must determine the required duty of care and whether the student has assumed the risk of injury. In sports, the doctrine of assumption of risk precludes any liability for injuries deemed "inherent in a sport." Previous court decisions established that athletic participants have a duty not to act recklessly or outside the bounds of the sport. Coaches and instructors have a duty not to increase the risks inherent in sports participation.** The court found no reason intercollegiate athletics would be harmed by extending a limited duty to a host school not to increase the risk of participation to visiting players and necessary co-participants. The college did not fail to adequately supervise and control the pitcher. Being hit by a pitch is an inherent risk of baseball. Colleges are not liable for the actions of their student-athletes during competition. The failure to provide umpires did not increase risks inherent in the game. The student's own coaches, not the host college, had the responsibility to remove him from the game for medical attention. The court reversed the judgment. *Avila v. Citrus Community College Dist.*, 38 Cal.4th 148, 41 Cal.Rptr. 299, 131 P.3d 383 (Cal. 2006).

◆ A Louisiana freshman football player injured his back in a weight training session. His physician diagnosed him with a lumbar strain and dehydrated disc, and gave him a medical excuse excluding him from football for one week with instructions for "no weightlifting, squats or power cleans." The coaching staff interpreted the weightlifting limitation to be for only one week, and a coach instructed the student to do a particular lift. He did the lift and suffered severe back pain. The student was diagnosed with a disc protrusion and a herniated disc. He lost interest in school, failed classes and transferred to an alternative school. The student sued the school board for personal injury. A state trial court awarded him less than $7,500 for medical expenses, but awarded him $275,500 for pain and suffering, future medical expenses and loss of enjoyment of life.

The school board appealed to a Louisiana Circuit Court of Appeal, which reviewed testimony that the student continued to experience severe back pain and often could not sleep. **The evidence supported the trial court's finding that he had been severely injured and would experience recurring pain that would limit his daily activities indefinitely.** The trial court did not commit error in awarding the student damages for pain and suffering. The court affirmed the damage award for loss of enjoyment of life, based on evidence that the student lost the opportunity to play varsity baseball and football. There was further evidence he suffered depression and emotional anguish. *Day v. Ouachita Parish School Board*, 823 So.2d 1039 (La. Ct. App. 2002).

◆ A Maryland high school junior was the first female football player in her county's history. She participated in weightlifting, strength-training exercises and contact drills. In the first scrimmage with another team, the student was tackled while carrying the football and suffered multiple internal injuries. Three years later, the student and her mother sued the school board, claiming it had a duty to warn them of the risk of serious, disabling and catastrophic injuries.

A Maryland trial court granted the board's motion for summary judgment, finding no such duty to warn of the risk of varsity football participation. The student and her mother appealed to the Court of Special Appeals of Maryland. There they argued the lower court had erroneously held the board had no duty to warn of catastrophic risks and that the student had assumed the risk of injury by participating. **The court found no case from any jurisdiction holding that a school board had a duty to warn varsity high school football players that severe injuries might result. The dangers of varsity football participation were self-evident, and there was no duty to warn of such an obvious danger.** The court affirmed the order for summary judgment. *Hammond v. Board of Educ. of Carroll County*, 639 A.2d 223 (Md. Ct. Spec. App. 1994).

2. Governmental Immunity

The doctrine of governmental immunity (sometimes called discretionary or official immunity) precludes school or individual liability when employees are performing "discretionary duties" within the scope of their employment. By contrast, employees performing "ministerial duties" are unprotected by immunity, as are those who do not act in the scope of their employment.

◆   An Ohio student injured his forehead and wrist during a pole vault at a high school track meet. He landed on improper padding near the landing pad. The padding was later identified as in violation of National Federation of State High School Associations rules. The student sued the school district, coach and other officials in the state court system for negligence. The court awarded summary judgment to the district and school officials. The student appealed to the Court of Appeals of Ohio, which held the trial court had improperly granted immunity under the state recreational user statute. The student was not a "recreational user." The statute relied on by the trial court applied to defects in state-owned lands or buildings, not to negligence from the setting up of equipment for a track meet. The trial court also committed error by finding the student had assumed the risk of injury by inherent dangers in pole vaulting. He did not assume the risk of being provided inadequate safety equipment for pole vaulting. **The court held the sponsor of a sporting event has a duty not to increase the risk of harm over and above any inherent risks of the sport.**

While the Ohio Political Subdivision Tort Liability Act generally grants immunity to government entities, an exception applies when an injury was caused by employee negligence occurring on school grounds in connection with a governmental function. **The court rejected the district's claim to immunity, as there was no discretionary, policy-making, planning or enforcement activity in this case.** The Tort Liability Act protects employees unless they act with a malicious purpose, in bad faith, or in a wanton or reckless manner. **The track coach was entitled to immunity, because there was no evidence he acted with malice, bad faith or reckless or wanton conduct.** The court affirmed the judgment in the coach's favor, but held the action could proceed against the school district. *Henney v. Shelby City School Dist.*, No. 2005 CA 0064, 2006 WL 747475 (Ohio Ct. App. 2006).

◆   A Maine high school wrestling team ran timed drills in school hallways as part of its warm-up routine. A wrestler was seriously injured after being bumped into a window by a teammate during a drill. The school had no policy prohibiting athletic training in school hallways at the time. The student sued the school district in a state court for personal injury, asserting officials negligently allowed the team to competitively race through the hallways. The court held the district and officials were protected by discretionary immunity. The student appealed to the Maine Supreme Judicial Court, which stated that **governmental entities are generally entitled to absolute immunity from suit for any tort action for damages**. One of four state law exceptions to this rule imposes liability on government entities for the negligent operation of a public building.

The court held that allowing relay races in the school hallway was not the "operation of a public building." The focus of this case was the manner in which the team was required to run through the halls, not the operation of a high school building. To impose liability under the "public building" exception to immunity, the claim must implicate the physical structure of the building. Decisions such as wrestling team rules focused on the supervision of students, not the maintenance or operation of the building. **Since the failure to prohibit racing in the halls was not related to the operation of a public building, the district and officials were protected by discretionary immunity.** *Lightfoot v. School Administrative Dist. No. 35*, 816 A.2d 63 (Me. 2003).

◆ A Kansas school football team held its first practice on an August day when the temperature reached 83 degrees by 8:00 a.m. Players practiced from then until 12:50 p.m. with a 45-minute break at 10:15 and five-minute water breaks every 20 minutes. The team then began circuit conditioning. Players spent four minutes at various stations, then rested for two minutes before rotating to another. A student reported feeling ill after completing the first two stations. An assistant coach instructed him to drink some water, which he did. He asked to sit out further drills and was told again to get water. As the team left practice, the student collapsed and was taken to a hospital, where he died the next day. His estate sued the school district and head coach for negligence. A state court granted the estate's motion to prevent the district and coach from relying on the "recreational use" exception to the Kansas Tort Claims Act (KTCA), which precludes liability for injury claims arising from the use of any public property used for recreational purposes, except in cases of gross and wanton negligence.

The district and coach appealed to the state supreme court, which observed the trial court did not take into account the KTCA's legitimate purpose to encourage construction of public recreational facilities. The court found a rational basis for distinguishing between injuries occurring on public recreational property and those occurring elsewhere. The trial court committed error by refusing to apply the discretionary function exception to the KTCA. **The discretionary function exception protects government entities and employees from claims based on the exercise of discretion or the failure to exercise it.** The recreational use exception eliminated any liability for ordinary negligence and barred all the claims. The court reversed and remanded the case for a determination of whether the district or coach acted with gross or wanton negligence. *Barrett v. Unified School Dist. No. 259*, 32 P.3d 1156 (Kan. 2001).

3. Assumption of Risk and Waiver

Many courts have determined that when a participant has assumed the risks of playing sports, a school district should not be held liable for injuries. One way to guard against liability is through the use of releases. Cases involving parental releases are uncommon, but the Supreme Judicial Court of Massachusetts upheld the use of one in *Sharon v. City of Newton,* below.

◆ A Massachusetts school district required a signed parental release for all students seeking to participate in extracurricular activities. For four years, the father of a high school cheerleader signed a release form before each season. During her fourth year, she was injured during a practice. When the cheerleader reached age 18, she sued the city in a state superior court for negligence and negligent hiring, and retention of the cheerleading coach. The court awarded summary judgment to the city on the basis of the parental release, agreeing that **the father had forever released the city from any and all actions and claims.**

The cheerleader appealed to the Massachusetts Supreme Judicial Court, asserting the release was invalid. The court held the trial court properly allowed the city to amend its answer by asserting release. **Enforcement of a parental release was consistent with Massachusetts law and public policy.** There was undisputed evidence that the father read and understood the release before signing it, and that the form was not misleading, since it required two signatures and clearly ensured parental permission was granted. It was not contrary to public policy to require parents to sign releases as a condition for student participation in extracurricular activities. The father had signed the release because he wanted the student to benefit from cheerleading. The court found that to hold the release unenforceable would expose public schools to financial costs and risks that would lead to the reduction of extracurricular activities. *Sharon v. City of Newton*, 437 Mass. 99, 769 N.E.2d 738 (Mass. 2002).

♦ **Indiana parents received a new trial in a lawsuit based on the death of their son from heatstroke after a school football practice. The release forms they signed did not specifically waive claims based on negligence.** The student, who weighed over 250 pounds, had "dry heaves" early in a morning practice session. He stopped his activity for a minute, then told two coaches he felt better. The student ate lunch during a team rest period, and kept it down. He spent time lying on the locker room floor. The head coach asked the student how he felt, and the student again said he was okay. Near the end of the afternoon session, the student told a coach he did not feel well. The coach told him to get water, but he soon collapsed. The coaches took him to the locker room and placed him in a cool shower. The student lost consciousness, and the coaches called for an ambulance. He died at a hospital the following day.

The student's parents sued the school district in a state court for negligence. After a trial, a jury returned a verdict for the school district. The parents appealed to the Court of Appeals of Indiana, which held they did not submit sufficient evidence to find the district negligent as a matter of law. **The head coach had responded to hot weather by shortening parts of the schedule and adding more frequent water breaks. The coaching staff emphasized the importance of drinking fluids, and several of them checked on the student.** Coaches had no indication that the student was ill until he collapsed. They responded to his collapse and called 911. The trial court did not improperly allow the case to go before a jury. **The court noted the release forms signed by the parents and students did not refer to** "negligence." It held that in order to negate a legal duty of care and avoid any finding of negligence, a participant must have "actual knowledge and appreciation of the specific risk involved and voluntarily acceptance of that risk." The court agreed with the parents that as the release forms did not contain the word "negligence," the district was not effectively released from negligence claims. The trial court should have granted the parents' request for a jury instruction stating they had not released the district from negligence. As their proposal correctly stated the law, the court reversed and remanded the case for a new trial at which their jury instruction was to be used. *Stowers v. Clinton Cent. School Corp.*, 855 N.E.2d 739 (Ind. Ct. App. 2006).

◆   A New York student participated on his high school wrestling team and was instructed before a match to wrestle an opponent in the next higher weight class. The student agreed to do so and was injured when the opponent hit his jaw during a take-down maneuver. The student voluntarily continued participating in the match after a medical time-out. He later filed a personal injury lawsuit against the school district in a New York trial court, which denied the district's dismissal motion. On appeal, the New York Supreme Court, Appellate Division, stated that **the student had assumed the risk of incurring a blow to the jaw and that the injury was reasonably foreseeable in a wrestling match.** There was evidence that the size of the opponent had not caused the injury and that the student was aware of the risks involved in wrestling. **The district's duty of care was limited to protecting the student from unassumed, concealed or unreasonable risks.** The trial court judgment was reversed. *Edelson v. Uniondale Union Free School Dist.*, 631 N.Y.S.2d 391 (N.Y. App. Div. 1995).

B. Spectators, Employees and Parents

◆   A West Virginia spectator slipped and fell on ice and snow on school grounds while going to a high school basketball game. On the day of the injury, the superintendent of schools cancelled all classes in county schools because of a major snow storm. But, the high school principal and athletic director decided not to cancel the basketball game. The spectator sued the board in the state court system, arguing it was negligent to hold the basketball game on a day when the entire school system was closed.

The school board claimed immunity under the state Governmental Tort Claims and Insurance Reform Act. Provisions of the Act create immunity from claims resulting from snow or ice conditions or from temporary or natural conditions on any public way, "unless the condition is affirmatively caused by the negligent act of a political subdivision." The court denied the board's motion to dismiss the case, and the board appealed. The Supreme Court of Appeals of West Virginia, the state's highest court, agreed with the school board that the language of the act was plain. **A political subdivision was not immune from suit if it acted to place snow or ice on a public way.** There were several ways this could happen. An employee might move snow from a roadway onto the sidewalk, or cause ice to form by letting water leak on a sidewalk during cold weather. **The court rejected the spectator's argument that the decision to hold the basketball game was an affirmative act that was not immunized. While the act of holding the game may have encouraged her to venture out into the snow, it did not cause the conditions at the school.** The Tort Claims and Insurance Reform Act provided immunity for losses or claims resulting from snow or ice on public ways caused by the weather. As there was no merit to the spectator's arguments, the court reversed the decision of the lower court. *Porter v. Grant County Board of Educ.*, 633 S.E.2d 38 (W.Va. 2006).

◆ A spectator at a high school football game in New York was stabbed during a fight that occurred on school grounds following the game. The spectator sued the school district and school officials in a New York trial court. The court held for the spectator, and the school appealed to a New York appellate division court. The spectator claimed the school was negligent when it failed to properly supervise the crowd. The court disagreed, holding **the district could not be found negligent because it did not have a duty to supervise non-student spectators at the game**. The court reversed the judgment and held for the district. *Jerideau v. Huntingdon Union Free School Dist.*, 21 A.D.3d 992, 801 N.Y.S.2d 394 (N.Y. App. Div. 2005).

IV. OTHER SCHOOL ACTIVITIES

Courts have held schools liable for injuries during school events that resulted from the failure to provide a reasonably safe environment, failure to warn participants of known hazards (or to remove known dangers), failure to properly instruct participants in the activity, and failure to provide supervision adequate for the type of activity and the ages of the participants.

A. Physical Education Class Accidents

1. Duty of Care

Courts have held that schools and staff members are not liable for injuries that are unforeseeable. It has long been recognized that schools are not the insurers of student safety. The fact that each student is not personally supervised at all times does not itself constitute grounds for liability.

◆ **The Court of Appeals of Ohio agreed with a school board that the death of a student who had a history of mild asthma was unforeseeable.** The student was a 14-year-old eighth-grader. During a gym class, he obtained his teacher's permission to retrieve his prescription inhaler from his locker. Minutes later, another teacher found the student unconscious and not breathing on the locker room floor. Despite the administration of medical treatment, he died. The school board maintained a policy requiring parents or guardians to bring prescription medications to the school office. Students were not allowed to bring medicine to school themselves, but the school principal let students carry inhalers once they were at school. The student's estate sued the school board in the state court system for wrongful death. The case went before a jury in two phases – one on the question of liability for negligence, the other on the question of damages. The jury found for the school board, and the estate appealed.

The court of appeals found the trial court did not have to exclude evidence of procedures used by the parents in the event of an asthma attack. These facts were not prejudicial to the estate and were relevant in establishing the standard of care for the school board. The trial court did not commit error by failing to instruct the jury that the school board could be held liable if it found the student's possession of prescription medication at school violated school policy. This would have misinterpreted the policy, which did not prevent students from possessing prescriptions at school. State rules of civil procedure allowed courts to separate issues of liability and damages, and they were more inclined to do this in emotionally charged cases, such as this one. The trial court allowed a physician to testify that the death of a student previously recognized as having only "mild asthma" was "one in a million." **According to the physician, not even medical professionals could have foreseen the death.** The court rejected the estate's additional arguments and affirmed the judgment for the school board. *Spencer v. Lakeview School Dist.*, No. 2005-T-0083, 2006 WL 1816452 (Ohio Ct. App. 2006).

◆ A California school district was not liable for injuries to a student who was hit by a golf club swung by a classmate in their physical education class. The golf class teacher was relatively new. His only golf training was an hour-and-a-half seminar. During the sixth day of golf class, the teacher showed students how to do a full golf swing. Before students could try the full swings, he advised them of certain safety precautions. The teacher's practice was to whistle commands and signal when to hit balls and when to rotate positions. According to the student, the class was disorganized and the instructions confusing. She claimed at times students had to decide when to hit and when to change positions. A classmate who was in front of the student swung her club and hit the student in the mouth. According to the student, the teacher did not give a whistle command for the classmate to hit the ball. She sued the school district in a state superior court for negligence. The court applied the standard of care announced by the Supreme Court of California for cases involving dangerous conditions or conduct considered integral to a sport (see *Kahn v. East Side Union High School Dist.*, 31 Cal.4th 990 (2003)). The *Kahn* standard is an exception to the usual standard of care in negligence cases, which generally creates liability for failure to use due care. The court found the district did not breach the limited duty described in *Kahn* and awarded summary judgment to the district.

The student appealed to a California District Court of Appeal. The court found the policies in *Kahn* did not apply to a seventh-grade golf class. **The state supreme court has applied the "prudent person" standard of care to decide liability in cases of students injured during school hours. This simply required persons to avoid injuring others by using due care.** Applying the prudent person standard in this case would not deter vigorous athletic participation. *Kahn* was inapplicable because being hit by a golf club is not an inherent risk in the sport. As the superior court should have applied the prudent person standard of care, the court reversed the judgment. *Hemady v. Long Beach Unified School Dist.*, 143 Cal.App.4th 566, 49 Cal. Rptr.3d 464 (Cal. Ct. App. 2006). The Supreme Court of California denied review in this case in 2007.

◆   A 16-year-old Louisiana student who weighed 327 pounds collapsed and began having seizures during a physical education class. The class was conducted by a substitute art teacher in a gym that was not air-conditioned. The temperature was at least 90 degrees. The student collapsed after playing basketball for 20 minutes and died at a hospital. The substitute teacher had played in the game instead of monitoring students. The student's parent sued the board and its insurer in a state court for wrongful death, and the court awarded her $500,000.

The Court of Appeal of Louisiana found no error in trial court findings that the board breached its duty to exercise reasonable care and supervision. The lower court was also entitled to hear the testimony of a physical education professor and allow medical testimony as reliable. The court held **teachers have a duty to exercise reasonable care and supervision over students in their custody, and to avoid exposing them to an unreasonable risk of injury. As physical education classes may involve dangerous activities, due care must be used in them to minimize the risk of student injury.** *James v. Jackson*, 898 So.2d 596 (La. Ct. App. 2005). The state supreme court denied the board's appeal. *James v. Jackson*, 902 So.2d 1005 (La. 2005).

◆   A New York student was playing football in a physical education class when a classmate threw a football tee that hit her in the eye. A state trial court denied the school district's motion for summary judgment, and the district appealed. A state appellate division court held school districts have a duty to adequately supervise and instruct students, and are liable for foreseeable injuries proximately caused by their negligence. **However, school districts are not insurers of student safety and will not be held liable for every spontaneous, thoughtless or careless act by which one student injures another. The degree of care required is what a reasonably prudent parent would exercise under similar circumstances.** The court found the teacher had not instructed students on how to properly handle the tee and never told them not to throw it. The evidence differed as to whether the students had previously thrown the tee or seen the teacher throw it. **In affirming the judgment for the student, the court held a trial court must determine if the injury causing conduct was reasonably foreseeable and preventable.** *Oakes v. Massena Cent. School Dist.*, 19 A.D.3d 981, 797 N.Y.S.2d 640 (N.Y. App. Div. 2005).

◆   Three Louisiana students assaulted a classmate in their locker room after a physical education class, causing serious injuries. The classmate sued the school board, the parents of the students and their insurers in a Louisiana court for personal injuries. A jury found the students were not at fault, and the court found the board 100% at fault. It held the coach caused the injuries by failing to supervise the students. According to the court, an atmosphere of roughhousing and lack of supervision invited the attack, and the board failed to conform to the required standard of care. On appeal, the state court of appeal apportioned 70% of the fault to the board and 30% to one of the students.

The state supreme court held **school boards have a duty of reasonable supervision over students. Boards are not insurers of student safety, and constant supervision of all students is not required. To hold a school board liable for negligence, it must be shown that a risk of unreasonable injury was foreseeable and could have been prevented with the required degree of supervision.** In this case, the attack happened suddenly and without warning. Because it was unforeseeable to the classmate himself, there was no way for the coach to foresee and prevent it. The trial court had erroneously imposed liability on the board independent of the students. As the incident could not have been prevented with a reasonable degree of supervision, the court reversed the judgment. *Wallmuth v. Rapides Parish School Board*, 813 So.2d 341 (La. 2002).

◆   Arkansas parents claimed their son's school district did not administer his Ritalin prescription for five consecutive school days, despite knowledge that failure to do so placed him in jeopardy of physical and psychological injury. The student fell from a slide on school grounds and fractured his right wrist. The parents sued the district in the state court system for outrageous conduct causing injury. The court dismissed the case, and the parents appealed.

The state court of appeals held the parents could not prevail unless they showed the district intended to inflict emotional distress on the student. They were further required to demonstrate extreme and outrageous conduct by the district, and to prove its conduct caused emotional distress so severe that no reasonable person could endure it. **The court found no evidence of knowledge by the district that failure to administer the student's medication would result in emotional distress.** The parents did not show his suffering was so great that no reasonable person could be expected to endure it. The court affirmed the judgment for the district. *Foote v. Pine Bluff School Dist.*, No. CA 02-806, 2003 WL 1827282 (Ark. Ct. App. 2003).

2. Governmental Immunity

◆ A Wisconsin student gashed his knee while diving after a volleyball in his freshman physical education class. He collided with the sharp metal edge of a volleyball net stand and had to undergo surgery. His family sued the school district in a state court for negligence, alleging other students had previously been injured when coming into contact with the net stand. The court held the district was entitled to state law immunity. The family appealed to the state court of appeals, arguing the district was liable under the "known danger" exception to the immunity rule, in view of the previous injuries involving the same equipment.

The court explained that immunity will not apply in a negligence case if it involves a ministerial duty and is the result of a known and compelling danger. The known danger exception applied when a public officer's duty to act was absolute, certain and imperative. The court held the net stand was not so hazardous that the district was required to take some protective measure for students. As the danger was not so compelling that action was necessary, the known danger exception to immunity did not apply. The court affirmed the judgment for the school district. *Schilling v. Sheboygan Area School Dist.*, 705 N.W.2d 906 (Wis. Ct. App. 2005).

◆ A Wisconsin physical education teacher divided a class into two groups to practice golf. One group practiced driving while the other group practiced chipping. The teacher instructed the drivers to stand in line while waiting to hit and not to swing their clubs in the waiting area. While she was working with the chippers, the drivers practiced about 40 to 50 feet away. A student in the drivers' group was hit in the face by a club swung by a classmate. He sued the district in a state circuit court for personal injuries, but the case was dismissed.

The state court of appeals held Wis. Stat. § 893.80(4) bars actions against government entities and employees for acts done in the exercise of legislative, judicial and similar functions. The law allowed liability for the negligent performance of ministerial duties. **Ministerial duties were "absolute, certain and imperative," leaving nothing for judgment or discretion.** The teacher had a ministerial duty to conduct and supervise her class in a particular manner. **Her decision to provide students with safety instructions was discretionary and did not subject the district to liability.** The court affirmed the judgment, finding the danger created by swinging golf clubs was not so obvious and predictable as to be a compelling or known danger. *Livingston v. Wausau Underwriters Insurance Co.*, 260 Wis.2d 602, 658 N.W.2d 88 (Wis. Ct. App. 2003), review denied, 266 Wis.2d 62, 671 N.W.2d 849 (Wis. 2003).

◆ An Alabama purchasing foreman drafted bid specifications and made recommendations to his school board on bids for movable bleachers for a high school. After the board contracted for the bleachers, the foreman's office issued purchase orders, and the bleachers were installed. A student was severely injured when the bleachers collapsed on him as he and a classmate tried to close them at their teacher's request. The student filed a state court action against the district and school officials, including the purchasing foreman, for negligent inspection and maintenance of the bleachers. The trial court entered summary judgment for all the officials except the foreman, and he appealed.

The Alabama Supreme Court considered the foreman's claim to state-agent immunity based on the discretionary nature of his activities. The student argued the foreman did not deserve immunity, as he was not engaged in discretionary functions. The court held the question of immunity was not properly addressed in the framework of discretionary or ministerial functions. Instead, it had devised an analysis based on categories of state-agent functions under which government employees are immune from liability in the exercise of judgment. One category was the negotiation of contracts, so the foreman was entitled to summary judgment for the claims that he had failed to properly evaluate bids for the bleachers and inspect them after installation. However, the court found **the act of passing along a maintenance brochure to other employees did not require judgment. The foreman was not entitled to state agent immunity** with respect to this claim, and the case was remanded for further proceedings. *Hudson v. C.F. Vigor High School*, 866 So.2d 1115 (Ala. 2003).

◆ Students in an Illinois physical education class had to run laps or rollerblade around a wooden gym floor. Rollerbladers paid a $7 fee to use rollerblades with "experimental" toe brakes, and they were not furnished with helmets, gloves or shin, elbow and knee guards. A student who chose to rollerblade fell and broke two bones in his right leg. He sued the school district in a state court for negligence and willful and wanton failure to provide safety equipment. The court held the district was entitled to immunity under Sections 2-201 and 3-108(a) of the state governmental tort immunity act, which affords immunity to government entities and their employees for failing to supervise students except in cases of willful and wanton misconduct. The state appellate court reversed the judgment, and the district appealed to the Supreme Court of Illinois.

The supreme court observed that the immunity act did not create duties for government entities, but accorded them certain immunities based on specific government functions. The district's failure to provide necessary equipment did not involve supervision. The tort immunity act shielded any decision by district employees that involved a determination of policy or the exercise of discretion. **"Policy decisions" were those requiring the balancing of competing interests so that a government entity had to make a "judgment call." The court agreed with the school district that its decision not to provide safety equipment was discretionary and thus entitled to immunity.** *Arteman v. Clinton Community Unit School Dist. No. 15*, 763 N.E.2d 756 (Ill. 2002).

V. TEACHER BEHAVIOR OUTSIDE OF SCHOOL

Although teachers have the freedom to do as they like off school grounds while not on duty, they cannot break the law or engage in behavior that could be construed as harmful to students.

A. Inappropriate Relations with Students

◆   A Maryland high school teacher gave a 14-year-old student who had a crush on him a ride home. On the way, he took her to his house to play pool and allegedly had consensual sexual intercourse with her. After he was convicted of child abuse and sexual offenses, he appealed. The Court of Special Appeals of Maryland ruled that consensual sexual intercourse could constitute child abuse under Maryland law. The court stated that because a parent impliedly consents to a teacher taking all reasonable measures to assure the safe return of his or her child from school, including personally driving that child home; because the teacher assumed that responsibility when he agreed to drive the child home; because the events leading up to this unfortunate occurrence were set in motion on school property; and because, at the time of the offense, there had been no temporal break in the teacher and student relationship that existed between the teacher and the victim, the court would upheld his conviction.

The Court of Appeals of Maryland affirmed. It rejected the teacher's argument that once he was with a student off school grounds, for a non-school related activity, the implied consent rationale was inapplicable and that once he was no longer acting as a teacher, he did not have a responsibility to supervise the student, so could not be convicted of child abuse.

It was uncontested that the act of sexual intercourse by an adult with a 14-year-old girl qualified as "abuse" under the statute. **Although the teacher was neither a parent nor household or family member of the victim, he had "responsibility for the supervision" of the victim at the time of the alleged misconduct.** The evidence was sufficient to support the conviction. *Anderson v. State*, 372 Md. 285, 812 A.2d 1016 (Md. 2002).

◆   A Michigan high school soccer coach addressed players with obscenities, engaged them in "flirtatious conversations," and made suggestive remarks. He called players and sent them e-mails at unusual hours. He told one student on the team that he had "a special interest" in a particular teammate. The student said that when she discouraged the coach from pursuing the teammate, he threatened the entire team with consequences. The assistant principal, principal and athletic director met with him to address complaints by parents about his late-evening communications. The administrators composed a memo prohibiting him from late calls and from e-mailing players unless he copied the assistant principal. The coach was prohibited from counseling players about personal matters, conducting activities off-campus without parents present, and from inappropriate relationships. The teammate later informed the student she had broken off her relationship with the coach. According to the student, the coach blamed her for this and threatened to "break her nose and take out her knees so she would never play soccer again." The coach then threatened suicide. Police arrived at his residence, recovered a pistol, and took him to a hospital.

The coach resigned and was prohibited from entering school property. The student transferred to a different school and sued the district, coach and school officials in a federal district court. The case reached the U.S. Court of Appeals, Sixth Circuit, which held **the state civil rights act required her to show she was subjected to unwelcome sexual advances, requests for sexual favors, or sexual conduct or communication. The coach's threats to harm the student did not involve any sexual communication. While the threats were an abuse of authority, they did not pertain to sex. The district court correctly applied Michigan law, which holds that verbal or physical conduct or communications that are not sexual in nature cannot be considered sexual harassment.** The court noted that liability can be imposed for creating hostile environment harassment only if there is reasonable notice and failure to take action by officials. The meeting with administrators and the subsequent memo were evidence of a prompt and reasonable response. The student's claims for retaliation, negligence, sexual harassment and discrimination under Title IX and other federal laws failed for many of the same reasons as her state law claims. The extent of the coach's misconduct did not become known until he resigned. The judgment for the district and officials was affirmed. *Henderson v. Walled Lake Consolidated Schools*, 469 F.3d 479 (6th Cir. 2006).

◆ A Georgia teacher socialized with a troubled student's family, befriending his mother and promising to "look after" both him and his sister. An assistant school superintendent received an anonymous e-mail during the school year, accusing the teacher of having inappropriate relationships with a list of students who had graduated or dropped out of school. She learned of a similar complaint against the teacher three years earlier, but the student involved in that incident vehemently denied anything inappropriate. The teacher denied both the report and the e-mail accusation. The assistant superintendent warned her, both orally and in writing, to avoid any appearance of impropriety with students and situations where she would be alone with male students. Vehicles owned by the teacher and the troubled student were later seen parked together in some woods. The superintendent promptly notified the school board and the police, and asked the state Professional Standards Commission (PSC) to investigate the incident. She told the school principal to monitor the two, prevent unnecessary contact between them and to report suspicious behavior to her. The teacher resigned and surrendered her teaching certificate after a substitute teacher discovered a note written by the student that threatened to expose their relationship if she did not comply with certain demands. The parents sued the district in a federal district court for Title IX and civil rights violations under 42 U.S.C. § 1983. The court awarded summary judgment to the district, and the parents appealed.

The U.S. Court of Appeals, Eleventh Circuit, reviewed *Gebser v. Lago Vista Independent School Dist.* **A district is not liable under *Gebser* unless a school official with authority to institute corrective measures has actual notice of misconduct, but is deliberately indifferent to it. "Deliberate indifference" was defined as an official decision by the school district not to remedy a violation.** The court held the parents could not demonstrate school officials acted with deliberate indifference at any time. They responded to each report of misconduct by investigating the charges and interviewing relevant persons. The officials consistently monitored the teacher and warned her about her interaction with students. They requested a PSC investigation after they received the first report specifically linking the teacher and student, monitored her and confronted her when the explicit note was discovered. In light of the many corrective measures taken by district officials, the court held they were not deliberately indifferent. **A district is not deliberately indifferent because the measures it takes are ultimately ineffective in stopping the harassment.** The court affirmed the judgment for the district. *Sauls v. Pierce County School Dist.*, 399 F.3d 1279 (11th Cir. 2005).

◆ New York twins claimed their history teacher sexually harassed them. One of them claimed the teacher confided to her about his personal life. According to one of the twins, a school psychologist dismissed her report about the teacher and implied the relationship between her and the teacher was a good one. The psychologist later dismissed reports by the twins' mother and one of the twins. The psychologist did not investigate or report the teacher's conduct, which included improper touching and the giving of gifts and cards. Many incidents occurred before the principal met with the teacher and told him he was to have no more contact with the twins than he would with any other student. The following summer, the teacher spoke with one of the twins several times on her cell phone and left her a romantic message. Their parents gave the recorded message to the principal. The school reassigned the teacher the next day and told him not to report to the high school until further notice. The twins sued the school district in a federal district court for sexual harassment in violation of Title IX. **The court held that even though the case did not involve allegations of an official policy of sex discrimination, there could be district liability for sexual harassment under Title IX. The twins only had to show "an official of the school district – who at a minimum has authority to institute corrective measures on the district's behalf – had actual notice of, and was deliberately indifferent to, the teacher's misconduct."** The court rejected the district's claim that the principal had no actual notice that the teacher was harassing the twins until he heard the phone message. It denied the district's motion for summary judgment. *Tesoriero v. Syosset Cent. School Dist.*, 382 F.Supp.2d 387 (E.D.N.Y. 2005).

◆   **The Court of Appeals of Florida held a high school teacher accused
of exchanging sexually explicit e-mails with students did not have to
turn over all his home computers for inspection by his school board for
use in his formal employment termination hearing.** The board suspended
the teacher for misconduct for exchanging e-mails and instant messages
with students that were sexually explicit and made derogatory comments
about staff members and school operations. An administrative law judge
issued an order allowing a board expert to inspect the hard drives of the
teacher's home computers to discover if they had relevant data for use
against him in a formal termination hearing.

The teacher appealed, arguing production of the home computer
records would violate his Fifth Amendment right against self-incrimination
and his privacy rights. He argued the production of "every byte, every word,
every sentence, every data fragment, and every document," including those
that were privileged, substantially invaded his privacy and that of his family.
The court noted that computers store bytes of information in an "electronic
filing cabinet." It agreed with the teacher that **the request for wholesale
access to his personal computers would expose confidential
communications and extraneous personal information such as banking
records**. There might also be privileged communications with his wife and
his attorney. The only Florida decision discussing the production of
electronic records in pretrial discovery held **a request to examine a
computer hard drive was permitted "in only limited or strictly
controlled circumstances," such as where a party was suspected of
trying to purge data. Other courts had permitted access to a computer
when there was evidence of intentional deletion of data.** There was no
evidence that the teacher was attempting to thwart the production of
evidence in this case. The court held the broad discovery request violated
the teacher's Fifth Amendment rights and his personal privacy, as well as
the privacy of his family. It reversed the administrative order allowing the
board to have unlimited access to the teacher's home computers. *Menke v.
Broward County School Board*, 916 So.2d 8 (Fla. Dist. Ct. App. 2005).

◆   A 14-year-old Illinois student gave birth to a child in 1986. Blood tests
indicated a 99.99% probability that the assistant principal of her junior high
school was the child's father. The school district dismissed him under
Section 24-12 of the Illinois School Code. Almost two years later, the
assistant principal was acquitted of aggravated criminal sexual assault. The
student's paternity action was closed shortly after the acquittal based on
"lack of activity." A hearing officer reversed the school board's action
dismissing the assistant principal in 1991, finding the district did not prove
he had sexual contact with the student. A state court affirmed the assistant
principal's reinstatement, as did the Appellate Court of Illinois. In 1997, the
paternity case was reopened and a court ordered him to submit to DNA
testing. Testing indicated a 99.9% probability that the assistant principal
was the child's father. In 1999, the court entered a judgment of paternity and

ordered him to pay child support. The state superintendent of education notified the assistant principal of an action to suspend his teaching and administrative certificates for immoral conduct. A hearing officer upheld the action under Section 21-23 of the state school code.

The case reached the Appellate Court of Illinois, which held the action to suspend the assistant principal's certificates was not barred by the district's effort to dismiss him years earlier. The Section 24-12 employment dismissal and Section 21-23 certificate suspension proceedings were distinct and were brought by entirely different entities. **The court held the assistant principal's acquittal from criminal charges did not prevent the state superintendent from suspending his certificates. The code required the superintendent to suspend a holder's certificate for conviction of specified sex or narcotics offenses.** While suspension proceedings were to be terminated if a criminal conviction was reversed, Section 21-23 said nothing about an acquittal. The court held the suspension action was not untimely, as it was commenced soon after the paternity judgment was issued. The 1998 DNA test results were "evidence of immorality" permitting suspension. *Hayes v. State Teacher Certification Board*, 359 Ill.App.3d 1153, 835 N.E.2d 146 (Ill. App. Ct. 2005). The Supreme Court of Illinois denied further appeal.

B. Drugs and Alcohol

◆ An Oregon teacher was dismissed by her school district for "immorality" and "neglect of duty" after a police search and ensuing events brought to light evidence that her husband had been using their jointly owned home to grow and make sales of marijuana and that the teacher was aware of the sales. The teacher appealed to the Fair Dismissal Appeals Board, which, by a two to one vote, reversed the dismissal and ordered her reinstated. The district sought review before the Oregon Court of Appeals.

The court of appeals noted that the teacher's job responsibilities included instruction and extracurricular participation in the district's anti-drug program. The district instituted that program in response to a significant student drug-use problem. Also, teachers took workshop training and were told that they had to serve as role models for students in the say-no-to-drugs campaign.

Here, **the teacher did essentially nothing to deter her husband's use of their home for illegal drug activities**. According to the appeals board, she "did not know what she should do about the situation and, in fact, took no action other than to obtain counseling and urge her husband to obtain counseling." She told a police officer who participated in the search of the home "that she was aware of her husband's dealing in marijuana and had been aware of it for over two years, that she didn't know what to do about his activities, that she had been concerned about the effect this might have on her job and that she was aware that he kept marijuana in the house for purposes of selling it." She told the officer that she didn't condone her husband's activities but that he did "his own thing" and she didn't get involved.

The teacher's workshop training gave clear notice that off-duty personal drug involvement was contrary to a teacher's role in connection with the anti-drug instructional program. **She had a duty to prevent her home from being used for marijuana sales regardless of how that act might upset her occasionally violent husband.** Here, the appeals board focused on the reasonableness of her inaction in the light of her family circumstances and concerns; however, the correct focus was on the propriety of her conduct in the light of her responsibilities to the district and her students. The court reversed and remanded the case to the appeals board for reconsideration. *Jefferson County School Dist. No. 509-J v. Fair Dismissal Appeals Board*, 102 Or. App. 83, 793 P.2d 888 (Or. Ct. App. 1990).

◆   A South Carolina teacher was arrested for possessing crack cocaine in 1988, but authorities dismissed his case. In 2000, the teacher was arrested "in his car in a well-known drug area" while his passenger attempted to buy crack. Charges against the teacher were dropped when the passenger pled guilty. After the 2000 incident, the teacher was placed on administrative leave, pending an investigation into the arrest and "similar behavior in the past." The superintendent advised him by letter his contract was being terminated under S.C. Code Ann. § 59-25-430. At the teacher's school board hearing, the superintendent said the termination was based solely on the teacher's unfitness. The superintendent later testified he did not consider negative publicity in making the decision. The board upheld the discharge based on substantial, compelling evidence justifying immediate employment termination and "evident unfitness as manifested by his conduct. Conduct which, after a reasonable time for improvement, 12 years, shows an evident failure to improve." A state circuit court held that being arrested but not convicted for two criminal charges was not substantial evidence of unfitness to teach. The court reversed the board's decision, and the board appealed. The state court of appeals reinstated the board action. It found substantial evidence of the teacher's unfitness to teach, based on the arrests, his dishonesty, the publicity surrounding the 2000 arrest, and the negative response it caused in the community.

The teacher petitioned the Supreme Court of South Carolina to review his case. **The court held the appeals court committed error by failing to confine its decision to the grounds stated in the order terminating his employment.** The appeals court scoured the record and made independent factual findings supporting the action. **The supreme court found two drug arrests, 12 years apart, neither resulting in charges, did not support a finding of unfitness to teach.** This was especially true when the district did not contend the teacher ever used, possessed or sold illegal drugs. The teacher was entitled to reinstatement with back pay and benefits from the date of his suspension. *Shell v. Richland County School Dist. One*, 362 S.C. 408, 608 S.E.2d 428 (S.C. 2005).

◆ About 48 hours after the adult son of a veteran Iowa teacher moved into her house, police officers executed a search warrant on the teacher's house. They found drugs and drug paraphernalia in five locations, including the teacher's bedroom. The district proposed terminating her teaching contract for reasons including drug possession, unprofessional conduct, poor role modeling and leadership, and failure to maintain a good reputation. The school board held a hearing and found that just cause existed to immediately terminate the teacher's employment contract. The teacher appealed to an administrative adjudicator, who found that the board's decision was not supported by the evidence.

A state trial court affirmed the decision, and the district appealed. The Court of Appeals of Iowa found "just cause" for teacher termination exists when the teacher has a significant and adverse effect on the high quality education of students. Just cause "relates to job performance, including leadership and role model effectiveness." **The board's findings did not show the teacher's conduct significantly and adversely affected her job performance. There was no evidence that she ever bought, sold or used marijuana** during her 15-year tenure in the district. The board found it likely she did not know that most of the evidence seized by police was in her house, since her son had returned there less than 48 hours before the search. Other items were kept as "mementos of her deceased husband" and as evidence of her son's marijuana use. The teacher presented evidence that she did not condone drug use and regularly instructed students to stay away from drugs. Since there was insufficient evidence of just cause to discharge the teacher, the judgment was affirmed. *Fielder v. Board of Directors of Carroll Community School Dist.*, 662 N.W.2d 371 (Iowa Ct. App. 2003).

◆ A Texas teacher checked out a district vehicle to drive to a soccer clinic. Before picking up a colleague who was going to the clinic, the teacher stopped at a dry cleaner and then a grocery store, where he purchased beer and other items. A witness reported seeing him leaving the store with beer and getting into the vehicle. The teacher admitted buying beer while using the vehicle when the school principal confronted him about it. He submitted his resignation after being formally reprimanded, but he later changed his mind and rescinded it. The superintendent recommended not renewing his contract, and the school board voted for non-renewal after a hearing. The state education commissioner affirmed the decision, finding substantial evidence that the teacher was "in the course and scope of his employment while he was in possession of alcohol."

A Texas district court affirmed the decision, and the teacher appealed to the state court of appeals, arguing he was on a personal side trip to run errands when he bought beer. The court held the commissioner's decision had to be affirmed unless it was arbitrary and capricious. **A court could not substitute its judgment for the commissioner's and could only review it to determine if it was supported by substantial evidence.** The teacher had admitted his error and stated buying beer "was a dumb thing to do." He also stated to the board he was acting within the scope of his duties to attend the soccer clinic. The teacher agreed it was reasonable to assume he was acting for the school when the school day began. As the commissioner's decision was supported by substantial evidence, the court affirmed it. *Simpson v. Alanis*, No. 08-03-00110-CV, 2004 WL 309297 (Tex. Ct. App. 2004).

C. Assault

◆   An Oregon teacher served a school district for 19 years with no disciplinary problems. Her husband left her, moved in with his girlfriend, and sought a divorce. The teacher drove to the girlfriend's house and had an argument with her husband. She attempted suicide by taking prescription medications, then rammed her vehicle into her husband's vehicle and damaged the house. The teacher voluntarily committed herself for psychiatric treatment. The incident was reported in local newspapers. Law officials charged the teacher with four crimes, three of which were dropped via plea bargain. She pleaded no contest to a criminal mischief charge, which provided for dismissal with no charges if she completed her term of probation. The school board voted to dismiss the teacher after a hearing, and she appealed to the Oregon Fair Dismissal Appeals Board (FDAB).

An FDAB hearing panel heard testimony from a psychologist who said the teacher's conduct was isolated and unlikely to reoccur. The board had previously let two teachers return to work after suicide attempts, and another had returned after entering into a diversion agreement for domestic violence charges. The FDAB panel found the dismissal had been "unreasonable" under ORS § 342.905. The board overreacted to an isolated incident and had to reinstate the teacher. The Court of Appeals of Oregon reversed the panel's decision, and the teacher appealed. **The Supreme Court of Oregon stated that contract teachers may be dismissed only for immorality or neglect of duty.** The FDAB was authorized to determine whether actions by school boards were "unreasonable" or "clearly an excessive remedy." **In the context of the statute, "unreasonable" meant "acting without rational or logical justification"** for an action. The FDAB panel failed to apply this interpretation, and its decision did not provide a rational connection between the facts and the conclusion. The court returned the case to the panel to address facts such as the suicide attempt, criminal conduct, and publicity, and apply them to the criteria of ORS § 342.905(6). The panel also had to interpret the term "clearly an excessive remedy," and apply it to the facts of the case. *Bergerson v. Salem-Keizer School Dist.*, 341 Or. 401, 144 P.3d 918 (Or. 2006).

◆   After a Pennsylvania teacher pled guilty to simple assault of his wife, the state education department filed a notice of charges and a motion for summary judgment with the state Professional Standards and Practices Commission to revoke his professional teaching certification. The notice informed the teacher that simple assault was a crime involving moral turpitude, requiring revocation. The teacher admitted the assault, but he contended he had pled guilty to avoid embarrassment to himself and his family. He asserted his actions were unrelated to moral turpitude but were the result of his wife's attempt to gain an advantage in divorce proceedings. The commission revoked the teacher's license without a hearing. It held the circumstances surrounding the guilty plea were irrelevant, since simple assault was within the state code's definition of "moral turpitude."

The teacher appealed to the Commonwealth Court of Pennsylvania, arguing the commission denied him due process by refusing to give him a hearing. The court held a teaching certificate is a property right entitled to due process protection. The court agreed with the teacher that **simple assault is not necessarily a crime involving moral turpitude. It found the state code and cases defining the term "crime of moral turpitude" required the assailant to have a "reprehensible state of mind." At minimum, a crime of moral turpitude required knowledge of private impropriety or the potential for social disruption.** Crimes involving dishonesty, such as fraud, theft by deception, and specific intent drug trafficking offenses were crimes of moral turpitude. By contrast, the statutory definition of "simple assault" included negligence. A person could lack a "reprehensible state of mind" when engaged in a fight or scuffle by mutual consent. While many forms of simple assault, including spousal battery, were abhorrent, a simple assault was not always a crime of moral turpitude. The court held the commission had erroneously revoked the teacher's certification without a hearing. There was a material issue of fact concerning whether the teacher's guilty plea was for a crime of moral turpitude, and the court reversed and remanded the judgment. *Bowalick v. Comwlth. of Pennsylvania*, 840 A.2d 519 (Pa. Commw. Ct. 2004).

CHAPTER SEVEN

Health Issues

I. ALLERGIES

A. Food Allergies

All foods have the potential to cause an allergic reaction, and sometimes even a very small amount is all that is needed. Seven foods – peanuts, tree nuts, milk, egg, soy, wheat and fish – account for the vast majority of all food allergies. Of these, peanuts, tree nuts, eggs and milk most commonly cause problems for children, and the majority of severe and fatal reactions involve allergic reactions to peanuts and tree nuts. Food allergies can be managed, but they are not curable.

The prevalence of food allergies is growing. Between 1997 and 2002, the presence of food allergies increased by 55%, and about 11 million Americans are currently afflicted.

Allergies are diseases that cause the immune systems of affected individuals to overreact to substances known as allergens. In people with food allergies, the immune system identifies a specific protein in a food as a potentially harmful substance. The immune system responds to the perceived threat by producing an allergic antibody to the food. This response triggers the release of what are known as chemical mediators, such as histamine. The release of the mediators can cause inflammatory reactions in the skin, the respiratory system, the gastrointestinal system, and the cardiovascular system. A potentially life-threatening condition called anaphylaxis occurs when these inflammatory reactions occur in more than one of these systems. Common symptoms of anaphylaxis include hives, vomiting, itching, swelling, coughing, dizziness, and difficulty swallowing.

Children with food allergies present difficult challenges for school administrators and parents. Once a student is identified as having a food allergy, steps must be taken to ensure that the student can totally avoid the food while at school. Families, schools and students all bear responsibilities in effectively managing food allergies.

- It is the family's responsibility to notify the school of the existence of the student's food allergies and to work with the school to develop an effective management plan. It is also the responsibility of the family to teach the child to self-manage the food allergy to the maximum extent possible and to provide any required medications.
- **Schools** should develop teams, consisting of the student's teacher, the school's principal, the school's nurse, food service personnel and other key personnel to work with the student and the family to develop an effective management plan. It is advisable to adopt and enforce a policy barring eating on school buses, except to accommodate legitimate special needs. Schools would also benefit by providing training and education to staff regarding food allergies and practicing emergency drill responses to food allergy reactions.
- The **student** should be instructed not to exchange any food with others and not to eat anything with unknown ingredients. In

addition, the student should be instructed to notify an adult at once in the event he ingests something he believes might cause an allergic reaction.

For an example of a letter to parents explaining that a child in the class has a food allergy, see Form VII-1 in chapter nine. For a sample letter informing substitute teachers that a child in the class has a food allergy, see Form VII-2 in chapter nine.

◆ Residents of New York enrolled their child in a New Jersey nonprofit school that catered to developmentally atypical children. The child had severe food allergies and was accompanied by a private nurse at all times. He was instructed to eat only food that was supplied by his parents. The child died, allegedly after he was exposed to substances at the school and suffered an allergic reaction. The parents sued the school in a New York court, seeking monetary damages for personal injuries and wrongful death. The parents claimed that the school failed to exercise reasonable care of the child while the child was under its direction and control. The school filed a motion for summary judgment, arguing that it was immune from liability under a New Jersey statute that generally barred claims for damages against nonprofit corporations. The parents opposed the motion on the grounds that New York law did not recognize the principle of charitable immunity. The court held that the New Jersey law of charitable immunity did not apply because it offended the public policy of New York. The parents showed that sufficient contacts existed between them, the injury and New York, and they also showed that **application of the New Jersey charitable immunity statute would violate a "fundamental principle of justice."** The parents lived in New York, and the child's tuition at the New Jersey school was paid by the New York City Board of Education. Further, New York had an interest in protecting its citizens from "unfair and anachronistic foreign statutes," and the state of New York had first rejected the concept of charitable immunity nearly 50 years earlier. The school's motion for summary judgment was denied. *Begley v. City of New York*, 836 N.Y.S.2d 496 (N.Y. Sup. Ct. 2007).

◆ A child broke out in splotches and hives while at a day care facility. Following the incident, the child's doctor determined the child was allergic to peanuts and peanut derivatives. The child then suffered a second allergic reaction at the day care facility, after which the facility refused to provide further day care services to her. The child's mother then sued the facility under the Americans with Disabilities Act (ADA) and state law, claiming discrimination on the basis of disability. A district court granted summary judgment in favor of the day care facility, and the parent appealed. The appeals court upheld the district court's determination on the basis that the child did not have a "disability" as that term is defined in the ADA. Although the child's allergy was a physical impairment, it did not substantially limit her ability to eat or breathe. **The child's doctor stated** that the child's allergy impacted her life only "a little bit," and the record did not show she was restricted from eating any other kind of food. Nor did the parent show that the child was disabled under the ADA because she had a record of a disability or was regarded by the school as disabled. Finally, the court rejected the state-law claim because the child was not disabled under the state law. *Land v. Baptist Medical Center*, 164 F.3d 423 (8th Cir. 1999).

◆ A student with an allergy to peanuts went on a field trip with his elementary school class. The district's food staff, the boy's teacher, two school nurses and several parent volunteers all were aware that the child was allergic to peanuts. Nonetheless, the child was given a snack lunch that included peanut-based foods. The child reported feeling sick after he ate a peanut-based cookie. Trip chaperones did not want to curtail the activities of the other children on the trip, so they placed the student on the school bus to wait. His condition worsened, and he later died after being taken to a hospital by car. After the student's parents entered into a settlement agreement with the school district regarding the incident, a newspaper sought the release under a public disclosure act of an investigator's notes, an investigator's hand-drawn map, conference notes by counsel for the district, and counsel's report to an insurer. A trial court ruled that the records were not subject to disclosure because they were attorney work product and attorney-client privileged material. The newspaper appealed. The appealed court affirmed the determination that the records were not subject to disclosure. **The documents were attorney work product and were further protected by attorney-client privilege.** The public disclosure act's provisions relating to open government did not outweigh the countervailing interest in insulating confidential pretrial communications from public inspection. Finally, the district did not waive its privilege to keep the information private when it made selected disclosures of information to the public and the student's family. The trial court's decision was affirmed. *Soter v. Cowles Publishing Co.*, 130 P.3d 840 (Wash. Ct. App. 2006).

B. Other Allergies

◆ A nine-year-old student was allergic to horse dander. The student's parents claimed that the school's assistant principal admitted that a new substitute teacher had not received training regarding the use of an Epi-pen. The parents also alleged that school authorities suggested that the parents should transport the student to school. In addition, they claimed school authorities failed to respond to questions regarding teacher training relating to the student's condition. **The parents sought a preliminary injunction to bar school personnel and students from bringing horses or tack onto the school campus.** They also sought to require the school board to comply with an Individual Accommodation Plan that had been developed for the student. The court determined that the parents were not entitled to the requested injunction because they did not show they were likely to succeed on the merits of their claims under 42 U.S.C. § 1983 and Section 504 of the Rehabilitation Act. In addition, the parents did not show that the failure to grant the injunction would be likely to cause an irreparable injury. The parents had the option of keeping the child home or away from horses at school, and to provide alternative transportation. The request for an injunction was denied. *Smith v. Tangipahoa Parish School Board*, No. Civ.A. 05-6648, 2006 WL 16291 (E.D. La. 2006).

◆ A high school student with a hearing impairment asked for permission to bring his service dog with him to school. At the time, the school was already providing other disability-related accommodations, including sign-language interpreter services for most classes, an FM transmitter, a student note taker, and extra test-taking time. The school denied the student's request, claiming that it already was accommodating the student's disability-related needs and that the dog would disrupt the school environment. The student and his parents sued the school district under the Americans with Disabilities Act, the Rehabilitation Act and state law, challenging the district's refusal to allow the dog in school. The student and his parents filed a motion for a preliminary injunction that would force the school district to allow the student to enter school facilities with the dog. The court determined that the school provided the student with reasonable accommodations. It denied the motion because the balance of hardships tipped in favor of the school district and school officials. **Although the dog would benefit the student, the school would be forced to endure hardships because two of the student's teachers and other students were allergic to dogs.** In addition, the dog would need to be confined to a particular area during gym class, and the student's schedule would need to be changed. The request for an injunction was denied. *Cave v. East Meadow Union Free School Dist.*, 480 F.Supp.2d 610 (E.D.N.Y. 2007).

◆ The parents of an eighth-grade student with multiple chemical sensitivities protested a school board's plan to use pesticides on the playing fields at school district schools. The board approved the plan, and the parents asked the student's gym teacher to keep her inside while fields were sprayed. The student was assigned to begin ninth grade at a high school that was located across the street from a working farm. During the summer before the student's ninth-grade year, the student's parents asked the school district for a Section 504 Service Agreement that would permit the student to fulfill her gym requirement at a location away from the school. In addition, **they asked that the school not be sprayed with pesticides, and they asked for a transfer to a school that was located in a more urban area**. The school proposed a service agreement that excused the student from participating in outdoor physical education activities and offered a transfer to the urban high school. The parents objected to the proposed agreement for several reasons. Among other things, they wanted to substitute gym class with dance, and they stated there was no guarantee that balls used indoors had no pesticides on them. After the school proposed modified agreements, the parents withdrew their request for a service agreement but continued to seek accommodations for the student. The school district then submitted the matter for a due process hearing, and the hearing officer found the district had offered a reasonable agreement. The school district then informed the parents that the service agreement would be implemented and denied a request for a transfer to the other high school because a valid agreement was in place. The parents withdrew the student from school and sued the district and others under the Rehabilitation Act, the Americans with Disabilities Act, and 42 U.S.C. § 1983. **They claimed that the district's attempt to enter into a service agreement was an abuse of process and violated their due process rights.** The court granted the defendants' motion for summary judgment. There was no evidence that the district used process in any way not intended as proper use when it sought a due process hearing. In addition, the abuse of process claim was time-barred. The court also rejected the claim that the parents' civil rights were violated because they were forced into a Section 504 service agreement. To prove that the plan violated their due process rights, the parents were required to show actions on the part of the school district that "shocked the conscience." They failed to do so. The parents also failed to show that the district retaliated against them for exercising their First Amendment rights by intensifying the use of pesticides, forcing them into a service agreement or stigmatizing the student as disabled, and that claim was also time-barred. Finally, the court rejected claims of emotional distress and conspiracy. *Sutton v. West Chester Area School Dist.*, No. Civ.A. 03-3061, 2004 WL 999144 (E.D. Pa. 2004).

◆ The parent of an 11-year-old sixth-grade student with an allergy to scents demanded that school officials provide the student a scent-free environment. In response to the demand, the school implemented a voluntary scent-free classroom for the student. The parent spoke to the student's teachers, classmates and their parents regarding the student's condition, and the teachers and classmates voluntarily refrained from wearing scents. However, the student was exposed to scents at school on three occasions. On one occasion, a school administrator who was wearing a scent left the student's classroom. On a second occasion, a substitute teacher wore a fragrance. The student was sent to the library. The student was also sent to the library on a third occasion when a classmate wore cologne. The parent continued to request a mandatory scent-free environment, but the school refused to provide one. School officials said a mandatory scent-free environment policy would be impossible to enforce and would conflict with the rights of other students and teachers. When the student's physician informed school officials that the student required a scent-free classroom, the school informed the parent that the student would no longer be allowed to attend because it could not provide a scent-free environment. **The parent then sued the school, claiming that it** discriminated against the student on the basis of disability in violation of the Rehabilitation Act. The parent filed a motion for injunctive relief. The court denied the motion and entered judgment for the school and other defendants. The school met its duty to provide the student with a minor adjustment when it provided a voluntary scent-free classroom. It would not be reasonable to require the school to enforce a mandatory scent-free policy. The student attended several different classrooms and also spent time in the school gymnasium and church, and it would be unduly burdensome to require the school to implement a mandatory scent-free policy. The court also found that the school was not required to provide a written contingency plan in the event the student was exposed to scents, and it rejected a claim of retaliation. *Hunt v. St. Peter School*, 963 F.Supp 843 (W.D. Mo. 1997).

II. DIABETES

A. Symptoms and Management

Diabetes is an incurable, chronic disease that is characterized by an inability to properly produce or use insulin, which is a hormone that converts food into energy. Lack of insulin causes blood glucose to rise to an abnormally high level, resulting in a condition called hyperglycemia. When this happens, the body may excrete blood glucose in the urine, causing it to lose its main fuel source.

There are two main types of diabetes. Individuals with Type 1 diabetes, which often afflicts school-age children, are unable to produce insulin and must receive insulin on a daily basis. Type 2 diabetes involves an inability to utilize insulin that the body produces. It can be controlled with insulin, oral medications or both.

Management of diabetes involves maintaining proper blood glucose control, a task which requires constant vigilance. Careful monitoring is imperative, and administration of insulin therapy is often required.

Controlling blood glucose levels is often a difficult balancing act. If not enough insulin is given, the individual's blood glucose level will rise to an unacceptable level. But administration of too much insulin can cause a dangerous condition called hypoglycemia, or low blood glucose. According to the U.S. Department of Health and Human Services, hypoglycemia presents a greater danger to school-age students than hyperglycemia. Some of the symptoms of hypoglycemia, as noted by the U.S. Department of Health and Human Services, include the following:

- Shakiness
- Sweating
- Hunger
- Pale appearance
- Blurred vision

- Sleepiness
- Dizziness
- Confusion
- Disorientation
- Lack of coordination
- Irritability or nervousness
- Change in personality
- Inability to concentrate
- Weakness
- Lethargy
- Changes in behavior

In severe cases, there may be an inability to swallow, seizure or convulsions, or unconsciousness.

Because it is a relatively common disease among school-age children, many, if not most, schools will have a student or students with diabetes enrolled. School personnel play a key role in helping students manage the condition. For a sample diabetes management plan, see Form VII-3 in chapter nine.

B. Legal Decisions

◆   A seven-year-old second-grader with diabetes attended a parochial school. The student had Type I diabetes, which required that her blood sugar level be tested each day before lunch and before she participated in a weekly gym class. The board of education provided a nurse but limited her visits to just two per month. The school's principal asked the board to provide additional nursing services, but the board denied the request. As a result, the student's parents retained private nursing services, at a cost of $400 per week, to perform glucose testing and administer insulin injections to the child at school. The parents then filed a court petition to compel the board to provide additional nursing services. The trial court granted the petition and directed the board to provide the child with additional nursing services at her school. The trial court also ordered the board to reimburse the parents for the costs they incurred in retaining a private nursing service. On review, the court held that a provision of the state's education law required school boards to provide non-public school students within their districts with "all of the health and welfare services" that were provided to public school students. Those services were to be provided in the same manner and to the same extent as they were to public school students. In this case, there was no question that the daily nursing services required by the student were "health and welfare services" under the state law. As a result, the state law required the board to provide the student with the nursing services that would be available if she attended public school in the district. **The board employed a full-time nurse at a public school located within the district just two blocks away from the student's school.** The board conceded that the student's needs would be met if she attended the public school. Therefore, the court affirmed the trial court's decision. However, it modified the judgment to allow the board to determine the precise manner and location where the services would be provided. *Richard K. v. Petrone*, 31 A.D.3d 181 (N.Y. App. Div. 2006).

◆ The mother of a second-grade student became dissatisfied with the way her daughter's school was handling her diabetes. The mother informed the school nurse that she wanted the nurse to give the student insulin shots whenever her blood sugar tested higher than a specified level. The nurse told the mother that written authorization from a physician was required, but the mother never provided the authorization. The nurse later asked the student what she ate at home every day. She also called the student's doctor to ask what she should do if the student's blood sugar level showed a shot was needed and she could not reach the mother. Then, an anonymous caller filed a complaint against the mother with a governmental department of job and family services for medically neglecting the child. The mother later sued the school district and others, alleging, among other things, that the district violated her right to privacy by asking the student what she ate at home and allegedly filing the anonymous complaint of alleged medical neglect. The court rejected the mother's privacy claim because **the mother did not present authority to support the proposition that the mother had a fundamental liberty interest in information relating to her management of her child's diabetes.** In addition, the mother failed to produce evidence showing that the district or any of the other defendants had ever revealed the student's medical records to anyone. *Jenkins v. Board of Educ.*, 463 F.Supp.2d 747 (S.D. Ohio 2006).

◆ The mother of a nine-year-old student with diabetes met with the student's school nurse at the start of the school year to discuss her daughter's diabetes-related needs. The mother provided the nurse, a teacher and the school principal with written materials describing her daughter's condition and the care she would need. She provided 12 copies of the materials so all of the student's teachers could be provided their own copy. Sometime after these materials were provided, the student asked a teacher for permission to leave a reading class to see the school nurse. The student informed the teacher that the student was having a hypoglycemic reaction. The teacher refused to allow the student to leave the class until 45 minutes later. By the time the student reached the nurse, the student was intermittently losing consciousness and could not inform the nurse that she needed medication. The student received no medical care for two hours and was eventually hospitalized for six days. The mother sued the school district, the nurse, the teacher and the principal under 42 U.S.C. § 1983 for alleged due process and equal protection violations. She also used Section 1983 as the basis for a claim under the Education of the Handicapped Act. **The court held that the mother did not state a Section 1983 claim against the school district because a single isolated incident did not prove the existence of an official policy or custom, as is required to establish a Section 1983 claim.**

The equal protection claim against the individual defendants failed because children asserting disability discrimination by a public educator must proceed under the Education for the Handicapped Act and cannot assert a separate equal protection violation. The court dismissed the due process claims against the individual defendants because available common law remedies were available against them. Finally, the court rejected the claim related to the Education for the Handicapped Act because violations of the act cannot be redressed via Section 1983. *DeFalco v. Deer Lake School Dist.*, 663 F.Supp. 1108 (W.D. Pa. 1987).

♦ A child with Type 1 diabetes was accepted for admission into a preschool program. The child's status as a diabetic was disclosed at the time of the initial interview. A month before the child was to start attending the preschool, his mother informed the preschool's owner that the child had been fitted with an insulin pump. The mother then met with two teachers at the preschool to explain how the pump operated. She claimed that she offered to come to the school to train the teachers how to use the pump. The mother claimed that the owner withdrew the child's acceptance on the day of the meeting. She sued the preschool and the owner under a state law against discrimination. A trial court found that the school was a place of public accommodation under the state law and that the claim was not preempted by the Individuals with Disabilities Education Act. However, it granted summary judgment in the school's favor on the basis that the law did not obligate the school to provide reasonable accommodations in connection with the child's care. Both sides appealed, and the appeals court affirmed in part and reversed in part. The appeals court affirmed the conclusions that the school was a place of public accommodation under the state law and that the claim was not preempted by the Individuals with Disabilities Education Act. **However, it held that the lower court erred when it concluded that the state law against discrimination did not obligate places of public accommodations to provide reasonable accommodations to individuals with disabilities.** Regulations implementing the statute indicated that the provision of reasonable accommodations was required, and the law was to be construed broadly. In addition, federal precedent under the Americans with Disabilities Act, which requires places of public accommodation to provide reasonable accommodations, was relevant. The court was unable to determine whether the school had breached its duty to provide a reasonable accommodation. Therefore, it remanded the case for further proceedings. *Ellison v. Creative Learning Center*, 893 A.2d 12 (N.J. Super. Ct. App. Div. 2006).

♦ A board of education posted a job opening for a classroom aide. State law defined the position as an aide who had completed a state-approved training program, held a high school diploma, or received a general educational development certificate. It did not include additional requirements. When the board posted the opening, it added the requirement that the successful candidate must be licensed as a practical nurse. The board added this requirement because the successful applicant would serve the needs of two diabetic students. Both students were considered "brittle" diabetics. One received insulin through an insulin pump, and the other received insulin injections. The board hired an individual who was licensed as a practical nurse. Two unsuccessful applicants, who were not licensed as practical nurses, filed grievances with a state grievance board. **They claimed that the board wrongfully expanded the statutory qualifications of the aide position by requiring the successful candidate to be licensed as a practical nurse.** The grievance board granted the grievances, finding that only a school nurse could administer the required care based on the students' specialized health needs. A lower court affirmed, and the board appealed. The appeals court held that the board of education permissibly added practical nurse licensure as a qualification for the position. It was within the discretion of the school board to hire an applicant who possessed the additional qualification of licensure as a practical nurse. The decision of the lower court was reversed. *Board of Educ. of the County of Randolph v. Scott*, 617 S.E.2d 478 (W. Va. 2005).

◆   The parents of a seventh-grade student with diabetes alleged that a school district and school officials violated the Individuals with Disabilities Education Act (IDEA) and Americans with Disabilities Act by failing to recognize that their daughter was a student with a disability and by failing to accommodate her condition. The parents claimed that the defendants denied the student extra time to complete assignments. They also alleged that they ridiculed her in front of other students based on her disability and displayed animosity toward her. The court ruled against the parents because they failed to exhaust administrative procedures and remedies under the IDEA. Exhaustion of administrative remedies is generally required before a party can proceed to court with an IDEA claim. Exhaustion is excused when it would be futile or fail to provide relief, or when an agency has adopted a policy or pursued a practice that violates the law. The parents argued that exhaustion was not required because the monetary relief they sought could not be granted at the administrative level. However, **a plaintiff seeking monetary damages must exhaust administrative remedies even though money damages may be unavailable under the IDEA or through the administrative process.** In this case, the plaintiffs alleged injuries that could be redressed, at least partially, via the IDEA's administrative procedures. Therefore, they were required to exhaust administrative remedies before filing a court claim. The court granted the defense motion for summary judgment. *Eads v. Unified School Dist. No. 289*, 184 F.Supp.2d 1122 (D. Kan. 2002).

◆   While a high school pep band was returning to school via bus following a basketball game, a student who was a pep band member asked the band instructor if the bus could stop so he could use a restroom. The student claimed the instructor failed to respond to his request. He also claimed that the instructor denied his request when he asked a second time and then ignored a third request. Other students began to tease the student, and the bus driver deliberately pumped the brakes to jar the bus and aid in the teasing of the student and other students who needed to use a restroom. The student then used a profanity while demanding that the instructor let him off the bus. Before he was able to get off, the student wet himself. The next day, the instructor told the student he would not be allowed to participate in the pep band for the next game and that he might be removed from the pep band. The student was given a one-day out-of-school suspension for using profanity on the bus, and the principal later ordered him to serve three days of detention. A short time later, the student was diagnosed as having diabetes and post-traumatic stress disorder (PTSD). His parents sued the instructor, the principal and the school district, claiming that they triggered or accelerated the student's development of diabetes and caused his PTSD. After the student's physician testified that the added stress created by the bus incident "could have" contributed to the student's development of diabetes, a trial court granted summary judgment against the parents on the ground that the harm to the student was not foreseeable. The parents appealed. **The appeals court affirmed the trial court's decision because the parents failed to present enough evidence of a causal connection between the actions of the defendants and the student's injuries.** The physician's testimony was admissible only if it was based on an opinion that it was more likely than not that the defendants' conduct caused the student's injuries. The physician's testimony that the stress of the bus incident could have caused the student's injuries did not meet this standard. Therefore, the parents failed to meet their duty to present expert testimony showing the requisite causal connection between the defendants' actions and the student's injuries. The trial court's decision was affirmed. *Hinkle v. Shepherd School Dist. # 37*, 93 P.3d 1239 (Mont. 2004).

♦   While on a school field trip, a fourth-grade student informed her teacher that she felt sick. The school was aware that the child had diabetes, and the teacher instructed the student to eat a piece of fruit. A blood sugar reading showed that the student's blood sugar level rose after she ate the fruit. On the way back from the trip, the student threatened other students on the bus with an instrument that contained a nail file, a bottle opener and a one-half-inch knife. The next day, the principal suspended the student for five days and recommended that she be expelled. A hearing examiner, who was not notified that the student had diabetes, recommended expulsion, and the school superintendent concurred with the recommendation. The student's parents appealed the decision to the board of education, arguing that the student's diabetes caused her actions. They supported the appeal with a letter from the student's endocrinologist, who said the student could engage in belligerent behavior when her blood sugar fell below a certain level. The board of education upheld the expulsion, finding that the student violated the school code of conduct by possessing an object that could be considered a weapon and by using the object to intimidate other students. **The board of education also determined that the parents failed to prove the student's behavior was caused by low blood sugar.** The parents sued the school district, claiming violations of the Individuals with Disabilities Education Act (IDEA), the Rehabilitation Act and state law. They also filed a claim of negligence. The district filed a motion to dismiss or alternatively for summary judgment. The court rejected the IDEA and Rehabilitation Act claims because the parents failed to exhaust administrative remedies with respect to those claims. In addition, the district was not required to consider the effect of the student's diabetes on her actions because she had not been identified as a student with a disability at the time of the bus incident. In addition, the board did not violate state law because its decision to expel the student was not arbitrary and capricious. Finally, the parents' negligence claim failed because they did not allege that an alleged breach of duty by the district caused them harm. The district's motion was granted. *Brown v. Metropolitan School Dist. of Lawrence Township*, 945 F.Supp. 1202 (S.D. Ind. 1996).

III. ASTHMA

A. Symptoms and Management

Asthma is a chronic inflammation of the airways. It can leave the students who suffer from it feeling tired, wheezing, suffering a persistent cough or even struggling to breathe.

Without asthma, our bodies do a very good job of filtering out things like smoke, dust and mold. They get stopped before they reach our lungs when they are trapped by phlegm, and they can be coughed or sneezed away.

In people with asthma, the bronchial airways become inflamed by an over-reaction to irritants. The airways swell or become blocked, making it difficult for air to reach the lungs. This over-reaction could have several causes, but the overwhelming number of children with asthma – as many as 80% – also suffer from allergies. Other causes include viruses and airborne irritants.

Of all the chronic conditions that can lead to missed school, asthma comes first. In 2005 alone, the Centers for Disease Control and Prevention (CDC) estimates 12.8 million school days were lost due to asthma.

Asthma is also number three on the list of things that send children to the hospital. In 2004, more than 640,000 children under age 15 visited emergency rooms because of their asthma. Students occasionally die from asthma attacks, and the condition is affecting more students than ever.

According to a 2006 report from the CDC, the percentage of children with asthma more than doubled between 1980 and 1995. Although the numbers seem to have stabilized since then, the percentage of children who have the condition remains at a historically high level. How high? About one in every 15 children has asthma.

Despite this sobering statistic, we are doing a good job of treating childhood asthma. We've clearly figured out what works. The CDC report, *The State of Childhood Asthma, United States, 1980 – 2005*, shows a direct correlation between the drop in death rates from juvenile asthma and increased medical treatment.

But while it's true that the number of hospitalizations and deaths have been falling, some populations remain especially at risk. Schools that teach inner-city children, especially African-Americans, face a special challenge when it comes to asthma – because that's the group that represents a disproportionate number of the children who die from asthma. Experts say many of these deaths were avoidable. They were apparently caused by under-medication.

Which brings us to the most basic point about your school and asthma: Asthma can't be cured, but it can be controlled. And there are many things schools can do to make this possible.

The American Lung Association defines controlling asthma as taking steps to reduce its frequency and severity to reduce its interference with asthmatics' everyday life. From your perspective, you not only want to keep all your students physically safe, but you also want to do everything you can to make sure they are learning. A student who is worrying if the chest-tightness she's feeling is the first sign of an attack, or a student who is finding it hard to breathe, is too distracted to pay attention in class or concentrate on homework.

One crucial step in controlling asthma is to eliminate the common triggers for asthma attacks.

In its publication *Asthma & Physical Activity in the School*, the National Heart, Lung and Blood Institute has identified the following triggers that commonly affect students:

- Exercise, especially in cold weather
- Upper respiratory infections, such as head colds or the flu
- Laughing or crying hard
- Allergens, such as mold, dust and animal dander, and
- Irritants, such as tobacco smoke, chemical fumes and chalk dust.

B. Controlling Asthma's Impact at School

There are many ways to make your school environment a place where asthmatics can breathe freely. These include:

- eliminating dust, dust mites and other allergens by keeping rugs, padded furniture, stuffed animals and cushions out of classrooms
- making sure classroom surfaces are kept clear so that janitors can wipe and mop them
- impressing on staff that using highly scented personal products – including laundry detergents and fabric softeners – could cause some students distress
- keeping animals out of school

- maintaining a smoke-free environment, and
- having the right air filters – and keeping them clean.

There also are things that staff should be on the alert for when it comes to students. For example:

- Persistent coughing. The American Lung Association has stated that coughing is the most common symptom of asthma. Coughing can be a sign that an asthmatic child may be in distress. Concerning children not diagnosed with asthma, it could be a sign that they should be evaluated for it.
- Children who experience lots of respiratory infections also should be evaluated.
- Since exercise can be a trigger, gym teachers and playground monitors need to be especially vigilant – particularly when the air is cold.
- Emotion also can play a role in the onset and severity of asthma attacks. Adults can help by staying calm, themselves.

In the CDC's *Strategies for Addressing Asthma Within a Coordinated School Health Program*, a six-part plan of attack is suggested:

1. **Establish management and support systems for asthma-friendly schools.** These include identifying asthmatic students, setting up effective home-school-health provider communication, and assigning a person to coordinate asthma-control efforts.
2. **Provide appropriate school health and mental health services for students with asthma.** For example: following students' own asthma action plans or a standard emergency protocol for students without individualized plans.
3. **Provide asthma education and awareness programs for students and school staff.** This could include teaching everyone asthma-control basics as well as providing quit-smoking support programs for staff.
4. **Provide a safe and healthy school environment to reduce asthma triggers.** In addition to strategies similar to those discussed above, the CDC encourages schools to use integrated pest management techniques.
5. **Provide safe, enjoyable physical education and activity opportunities for students with asthma.** Students should be encouraged to participate fully when well, but some asthmatics need preventative medication before participation. Immediate emergency access to medication also should be available.
6. **Coordinate school, family, and community efforts to better manage asthma symptoms and reduce school absences among students with asthma.** One thing schools can do is ask for parents' permission for the school health staff and the student's doctor to share health information. They also can get involved with asthma-control initiatives in the wider community.

Schools have been rising to the challenge to help control the impact of asthma on their students in other ways.

Some schools have obtained special equipment to make sure children can get necessary treatment at school. In the year 2000, more than a quarter of schools reported having a peak-flow meter, a handheld device that measures how well people can move air out of their lungs. Some schools – around 13% – reported having a nebulizer available for all students (as opposed to a parent-provided nebulizer for a specific child). A nebulizer is a device that turns asthma medication into a fine mist that can be breathed in to penetrate deeply into the lungs.

In addition to understanding asthma, reducing triggers, training staff and having the right equipment, the following cases illustrate that a quick and appropriate response to a student asthma attack is absolutely necessary.

C. Legal Decisions

◆   The mother of third-grader who died from an asthma attack at school could sue the deceased child's teacher for violating his right not to be deprived of life without due process of law. There was evidence the teacher's actions led to his death.

When the asthmatic student entered the third grade, his mother told the school he'd been treated in an emergency room at least 10 times and that not treating his symptoms immediately could put his life at risk.

The school developed an individualized education program that called for him to use his inhaler before exercise and when suffering symptoms; for his mother to be called promptly about any asthma-related incident; and for the school to perform CPR and call emergency services if he stopped breathing.

In late September, the student told his teacher he felt tired and was having trouble breathing. Instead of administering his inhaler, she told him to rest with his head on the desk while she went on teaching her class. Although there was a phone in the classroom, she didn't call for medical help or let the student call his mother.

After about 15 minutes, one of his classmates noticed the child wasn't breathing and had turned purple. His teacher sent a student to tell the office this. No school official tried to administer his inhaler or perform CPR, but someone did eventually call for emergency help. When the medics arrived, the student was still slumped at his desk and they weren't able to revive him.

The school called the student's mother approximately 30 minutes after the onset of his symptoms and didn't explain it was a crisis. She lived nearby and arrived within minutes, under the impression her son wasn't feeling well and needed to go home. Instead, she got there just as he was being put in an ambulance. He died in the hospital not long after.

The mother sued her son's teacher, alleging she had violated the student's Fourteenth Amendment right to due process, and the court allowed the suit to go forward.

Under the state-created danger doctrine, a public school teacher can have a constitutional duty to protect a student if the court finds that:

- the harm was foreseeable
- the student was a foreseeable victim of it
- the teacher's actions were bad enough to "shock the conscience," and
- the teacher used classroom authority in a way that created the danger or made it worse.

Here, **the mother demonstrated that the school understood her son could die if his symptoms weren't promptly and properly treated** – so the harm and victim were both foreseeable. In addition, the court stated that refusing to let an asthmatic child seek medical help qualifies as conscience-shocking. Finally, if the mother could show that the teacher refused to let her son call her for help, a Fourteenth Amendment violation could be shown. *Taylor v. Altoona Area School Dist*, 2007 WL 2461714 (W.D. Pa. 2006).

◆ An appellate court affirmed a verdict in favor of a school district in a wrongful death suit brought by the parents of a student with mild asthma, who was found dead in a locker room shortly after his gym teacher gave him permission to go there to use his inhaler.

During gym class, a 14-year-old with a history of mild asthma asked his gym teacher for permission to go get his prescription inhaler from the locker room. The teacher said he could. Between five and 15 minutes later, the teacher found the student lying on the locker room floor with the inhaler in hand. The boy wasn't breathing and was later pronounced dead.

The boy's parents sued the school district for wrongful death. **The main issue during the trial was whether the school had been negligent in not supervising the boy when he went to the locker room to retrieve his inhaler.** If the court had found it was foreseeable the student was likely to die without supervision while he retrieved and used his inhaler, it would have found the school negligent.

But the Ohio trial court did not find this lack of supervision was likely to lead to the student's death. First, the father testified it was normal at their home for the boy to go off by himself to get and use his inhaler without adult supervision. Second, the court heard expert testimony that the likelihood of this kind of death from only mild asthma was "one in a million." The parents appealed, but the appellate court affirmed the verdict for the school. *Spencer v. Lakeview School Dist.*, 2006 WL 1816452 (Ohio App. Ct. 2006).

◆ The New Mexico Supreme Court decided parents could sue a school district for wrongful death after a substitute gym teacher ignored an asthmatic student's request to stop exercising and then administrators responded inadequately to her ensuing asthma attack.

The student had suffered from asthma since age three. By the time she was 14, she had learned to recognize the early signs of an attack and take measures to ward it off.

The school knew she was asthmatic because the condition was listed on her individualized education program (IEP). Also, her parents had given the school permission to get her emergency medical help without contacting them first in case of an asthma attack.

The student's parents also had spoken with her gym teacher about the fact that exercise could trigger an attack. The gym teacher agreed to let the student rest instead of participate if she felt an attack coming on.

On the day the student asked to rest, there was a substitute teacher in charge of her gym class. The substitute was requiring more strenuous exercise than the class was used to, and the student began to have trouble breathing. Others noticed her face was red. After the substitute refused to let her rest, the student cried as she struggled to keep up with the class.

The student used her inhaler afterward but then collapsed at her desk just as her next class began. That teacher called the front office and then tried to administer the student's inhaler. A school secretary with some nursing training arrived, checked the student's vital signs and asked the office to call 911 – but the call wasn't made immediately. Instead, staff put the student in a wheelchair and wheeled her into the hall. As soon as a school police officer saw her there, he called 911. By that time, it was 15 minutes after the start of her asthma attack. When medical personnel finally arrived, the student had stopped breathing and couldn't be revived.

Her parents sued the school district for wrongful death, but both the trial court and the appeals court found their suit couldn't go forward because they decided it did not fall under any exception to the state law that school districts couldn't be sued for negligence. The parents appealed to the New Mexico Supreme Court. It reversed the lower courts' decision and allowed the parents' wrongful death suit to go forward.

One exception to the state's immunity law allowed school districts to be sued for negligence in operating or maintaining a building. The supreme court found this exception wasn't limited literally to a "building." Instead, the court stated that **the school's failure to follow its safety procedures for a special needs student was similar to failing to follow procedures for a fire drill.** The school did not follow its procedures because it ignored the student's IEP, did not administer CPR and did not call 911 immediately.

Another reason the court determined immunity wasn't proper here was because the school knew the student was asthmatic, but a school employee forced her to keep exercising in spite of her visible distress. This meant that the school actively participated in causing the student's asthma attack. *Upton v. Clovis Municipal School Dist.*, 141 P.3d 1259 (N.M. 2006).

◆ In the case of a school found responsible for a student's asthma-related death, an appellate court changed the trial court's apportioned blame – determining a school counselor, rather than the principal, was primarily responsible.

A high school senior was at a school event with her eighth-grade sister when the older girl began to have an asthma attack. The younger sister asked a security guard to call 911. Instead, he used his walkie-talkie to call the principal, who was at a different part of the campus. The principal told the guard to call the student's parents.

The walk to the office to do so aggravated the student's condition. When they got there, the guard and the sister were holding up the student. She was bent over and had a hand over her face. The student's school counselor was in the office. The sister told him to call 911 because the student was having an asthma attack. Instead, he told the sister to call her mother to ask if she would pay for the ambulance.

The sister had to wait for a phone and couldn't reach her mother.

Meanwhile, the student's condition deteriorated. The counselor fanned her and tried to help her use her medication and then tried taking her outside for fresh air. The sister joined them. When the student told her, "I'm not going to make it," her sister called 911. About 10 minutes later, the counselor called 911, too. Almost immediately, the student lost consciousness and the school called 911 again.

The ambulance arrived around 50 minutes after the onset of the asthma attack. The student was pronounced dead at the hospital.

The student's sister and mother sued the school board, principal and counselor for negligence. The case was tried before a jury. **The court determined that the failure to immediately call for emergency medical help was a cause-in-fact of the student's death. It apportioned the blame for this as: 50% to the principal, 30% to the counselor and 20% to the school board. It awarded the family well over $1 million in damages.** The school defendants appealed.

The appellate court affirmed the school's responsibility for the student's death, but reduced the damages by about $170,000 – leaving the award at just about $1 million.

The appellate court also determined that the counselor bore the largest portion of the blame. He – unlike the principal – was there to see the seriousness of the student's condition, but both of them could have prevented her death. The court decided the principal was 30% to blame because he should have followed up on the report from the security guard and made sure someone called 911. The court found the counselor bore 50% of the responsibility. His failure to respond reasonably to a student in obvious distress created an immediate and fatal risk to her. *Declouet v. Orleans Parish School Board*, 715 So.2d 69 (La. Ct. App. 1998).

IV. MRSA INFECTION

A. Background

Methicillin-resistant staphylococcus aureus, more commonly referred to as MRSA, is a type of staph bacteria that is resistant to certain antibiotics. MRSA infection has been identified in hospital patients since the 1960s, and the overwhelming majority of cases continue to be associated with health care. However, MRSA infection is now occurring with steadily increasing frequency in other community-based settings, including schools. Within the school setting, members of athletic teams are at a higher risk of contracting MRSA infection, especially if they participate in a contact sport such as wrestling or football. Despite the rise in incidence rates, MRSA infection is both preventable and treatable.

An October 2007 study released by the Centers for Disease Control and Prevention (CDC) reported the results of the agency's population-based surveillance for MRSA infection in nine geographic areas between July 2004 and December 2005. The study, which tracked nearly 9,000 cases, showed that MRSA infection affects particular populations disproportionately. Specifically, the study reported a significantly higher incidence rate among people age 65 or older. In addition, the incidence rate among African-Americans was about double the rate among others, and it was slightly higher among males.

The study also identified risk factors for MRSA infection. Among the most common were a history of hospitalization, a history of surgery, and long-term-care residence.

The CDC has identified the following five factors, which it refers to as the "5 C's," that increase the risk of the spread of MRSA infection:

- **Crowding**
- Frequent skin-to-skin **Contact**
- **Compromised** skin (i.e., cuts or abrasions)
- **Contaminated** items and surfaces, and
- Lack of **Cleanliness**.

B. Diagnosis and Treatment

MRSA infection occurs when staph bacteria, which sometimes are carried on the skin or in the nose of healthy people as well as in people who already are infected, enter a break in the skin of another person via skin-to-skin contact or a shared item such as a towel or piece of athletic equipment. The entry of the bacteria causes a skin infection that is characterized by symptoms such as pimples, rashes, boils, and impetigo. MRSA also can cause more serious infection, such as pneumonia and bloodstream infection. Symptoms of more serious infection include fever, swelling, headache and fatigue.

MRSA is definitively diagnosed via laboratory testing that specifically identifies the bacteria at the root of the infection. Laboratory testing helps health care professionals decide whether treatment with antibiotics will be required and, if so, which antibiotics to administer.

The specific course of treatment for MRSA infection varies depending on a number of factors, including the severity of the illness and the site of the infection. Treatment of MRSA infections typically includes keeping the infected area clean and dry. Infected individuals must also wash their hands after caring for the infected area and properly dispose of bandages.

Treatment also may involve drainage of pus and the administration of antibiotics. If more severe infections occur, such as pneumonia or bloodstream infections, additional measures must be taken. However, such complications are rare in healthy people who contract MRSA infections.

C. Prevention

1. Generally

There are many steps schools should take to prevent the occurrence of MRSA infection among students.

Perhaps the best way for schools to prevent MRSA infection is to encourage the practice of good hygiene. This involves frequent hand-washing with soap and water or use of an alcohol-based hand sanitizer. Encouraging good skin care is another way to prevent the spread of MRSA infection. Cuts, scrapes and other breaks in the skin must be kept clean and covered with a bandage, and contact with other people's bandages and wounds must be avoided. Students also should be instructed not to share personal items, such as towels, toothbrushes, razors or water bottles. Schools also should establish cleaning procedures for surfaces that regularly come into contact with people's skin, such as sinks, showers and toilets. These surfaces, which also include light switches, door handles, handrails, tables and desks, should be cleaned with a disinfectant on a routine basis. Access to sinks, soaps and clean towels should be ensured, and hand soaps should not be used. Gloves should be worn when handling dirty laundry or caring for wounds.

2. Athletic Programs

Because MRSA infection occurs more frequently in student-athletes than it does in other members of the student population, special additional steps should be taken with respect to school athletic programs. These include the following.

- Athletic equipment should be disinfected between uses.
- Laundering of uniforms, towels and other items should be done using hot water and detergent for washing and the hottest available setting for drying.
- Athletes should shower with a non-hand soap and water immediately following participation in contact sports and use a dry clean towel.
- Athletic equipment and towels should not be shared.
- Students must avoid contact with other students' wounds or any items that have been in contact with the wounds.
- Antibiotics and ointments should not be shared.
- Students should avoid common hot tubs or whirlpools, especially if they have a break in the skin.

- Students should not share water bottles.
- Cuts and scrapes must be kept clean and covered.

In addition, sports equipment and athletic areas should be cleaned at least weekly using a disinfectant. High-use equipment, such as wrestling mats, should be disinfected prior to each practice and several times a day during tournaments.

D. Response

1. Generally

In most cases, MRSA infection does not necessitate school closure. There are situations, such as the occurrence of an outbreak, where consultation with public health officials with respect to this issue would be appropriate. When a MRSA infection occurs, the school should disinfect surfaces that are likely to come into contact with infected areas of the skin that are not properly covered. MRSA can be removed from the school environment by cleaning facilities with disinfectants. The Environmental Protection Agency has compiled a 25-page list of cleaning products that are effective against MRSA. To view the list, go to http://epa.gov/oppad001/chemregindex.htm.

When a case of infection occurs, the school nurse and physician should decide whether students, parents and staff should be notified. The CDC advises that it usually is not necessary to inform the entire school community in the case of a single MRSA infection. A MRSA-infected student should not be barred from attending school unless exclusion is directed by a treating physician. Infected students should be instructed to cover the wound and clean their hands frequently. For a sample notice to parents regarding MRSA in general, see Form VII-4 in chapter nine.

2. Athletic Programs

Some additional specific measures can be taken when a student-athlete contracts a MRSA infection. It is not necessary to test all team members for MRSA infection whenever a single student-athlete contracts a MRSA infection. However, it is helpful to take these steps:
- Prohibit student-athletes with MRSA infections from using whirlpools or hot tubs.
- Regularly clean all sports equipment and athletic areas that might come in contact with the wound.
- Place coverings over tables used to provide treatment.
- If disposable items come in contact with the infected site, dispose of them separately.
- Stress the importance of washing hands frequently.
- Make sure the student-athlete keeps the infected area covered at all times.

- Instruct the student-athlete to shower and wash clothes regularly.
- Use gloves to treat broken skin and discard them before treating another student-athlete.

V. MENTAL HEALTH

A. Emotional Problems vs. Mental Illness

The World Health Organization's definition of mental health is: "a state of well-being in which every individual realizes his or her own potential, can cope with the normal stresses of life, can work productively and fruitfully, and is able to make a contribution to her or his community."

At your school, students in this state of well-being are able to concentrate in class and while doing their homework. They get along well with others and are an active member of your school community – whether that's singing in the choir, playing on the basketball team, painting scenery for the school play, or attending Chess Club meetings.

The opposite is likely to be true for students with mental health issues. They might be having trouble keeping up scholastically. They also might be talking back to teachers or getting into fights with other students. Or – if they're depressed – it may be hard to get any response from them at all. Students with mental health issues also are more likely to hurt themselves with a weapon or by self-medicating with drugs, cigarettes, alcohol and other substances.

While there is a big difference between transitory emotional problems and serious mental illness, students need help with both.

You might find it easier to relate to the problems caused by transitory emotional problems because you may have experienced them yourself. The capacity to cope with the big ups and downs of life increases with life experience – which is why young students need adult help. This help could be anything from referring the matter to the school's counseling office to deciding a formal evaluation or an outside referral is required.

Alternatively, the best help available for a student struggling with a life issue might be an informal heart-to-heart with someone trusted – maybe the student's coach or music teacher.

The Centers for Disease Control and Prevention (CDC) has posted two online brochures that provide this kind of basic emotional guidance for students at www.bt.cdc.gov/preparedness/mind. One brochure is aimed at junior high students, and the other is intended for students in senior high. Titled, *Maintain a Healthy State of Mind*, the advice was compiled with the intention of helping children cope with disaster. But it also is useful for dealing with other emotional challenges – such as losing a pet or a loved one, or coping with serious illness.

This guidance doesn't wave any magic wands – there are some things only time can heal. But in the meantime, it can help students to know they

are normal if they are reacting to a serious emotional blow with:
- shock, numbness and disbelief
- having a hard time thinking clearly
- having trouble focusing on school, friends and family
- eating too much or too little
- having trouble sleeping
- experiencing bad dreams and nightmares
- crying more
- acting moodier, and
- wanting to either be alone or be surrounded by people more than usual.

If the problems connected to helping students with difficult (but transitory) emotional problems can seem daunting, the problems posed by students with mental illness can feel paralyzing.

One thing that helps is that there are mechanisms in place to deal with these serious conditions in the procedures related to the Individuals with Disabilities Education Act, Section 504 of the Rehabilitation Act, and state laws that address the rights of students with disabilities.

Otherwise, the percentage of children with really significant problems is low. The Federal Interagency Forum on Child and Family Statistics' Key National Indicators of Well-Being 2007 put the percentage of children ages 4-17 with a serious problem with emotions, concentration, behavior, or getting along with others at less than 5%.

But we know from the research that some groups of students are more at risk than others. Boys are more likely to have significant emotional or behavioral problems than girls, and students between the ages 15 and 17 represent the age group that is most at risk.

We also know poverty has a markedly negative impact on students' mental and emotional well-being. Only 4% of children from well-off households were found to have serious mental health issues, but this percentage rose to 5% in homes where money was tight, and then up to 7% for children from families that were living below the poverty line.

Although most people associate student mental illness with school violence, the connection is not necessarily accurate. As pointed out in the June 2007 Report to the President on Issues Raised by the Virginia Tech Tragedy, most people who are violent do not have a mental illness. Similarly, most people who do have a mental illness are not violent.

And as the CDC's Choose Respect initiative makes clear, violence is less likely to be a symptom of mental illness than it is to be rooted in denigrating attitudes caused by ignorance or a lack of empathy. Choose Respect is aimed at 11- to 14-year-olds. Its mission is to challenge harmful beliefs that lead to dating violence and thus eliminate the health problems that go with it, such as:
- injuries that send 8% of boys and 9% of girls to the emergency room after dates

- binge drinking
- suicide attempts
- unwanted pregnancies
- STDs and HIV infections, and
- poor self-esteem.

More information about this initiative is available at www.chooserespect.org.

Another reason it is important to de-link mental illness from school violence is because mental illness already bears a significant stigma that discourages many students from seeking help.

B. Violent Students and Privacy Laws

While most people with mental illness aren't violent, the university student who committed the deadliest shooting in U.S. history was. The young man who killed 32 people at Virginia Tech in April 2006 suffered from an anxiety disorder called selective mutism as well as from depression.

In middle and high school, he received help under a special education plan. When his middle school teachers noticed he was writing about killing himself and other people in 1999 after the Columbine shootings, he was treated by a psychiatrist.

The fact that the student's university wasn't alerted to these red flags led the governor-appointed Virginia Tech Review Panel to conclude that the state's mental health laws were flawed. Complicating the issue, the panel also found there was widespread confusion among schools. Even when it came to students likely to harm themselves or others, schools weren't sure what information they could release to other schools without violating state and federal privacy laws. Similarly, the Report to the President on Issues Raised by the Virginia Tech Tragedy found that schools were so worried about violating student privacy – or being sued for doing so – that they were likely to share less information about serious potential problems than the law actually allowed.

It is important to be aware of the fact that some state laws and regulations have stricter privacy requirements for student records than the federal Family Educational Rights and Privacy Act (FERPA) and the privacy rule of the Health Insurance Portability and Accountability Act. That said, one result of the Report to the President was the creation of new guides to help schools and parents better understand FERPA's requirements. They are available at ed.gov/policy/gen/guid/fpco/ferpa/safeschools.

This FERPA guidance for elementary and secondary schools specifies that:
- Schools don't need permission in an emergency to release "education records" to parties like law enforcement, public health officials or medical personnel if the release will protect anyone's health or safety.
- School officials also don't need permission to pass along their

personal observations about a student to the proper authorities. For example, if a teacher overhears a student making a threat, she can report it to the police.

- The school's employees who serve as the school's "law enforcement unit" – responsible for calling the police when the school suspects a crime – might keep its own records, such as investigation logs. These are not "education records" subject to FERPA, so no permission is needed to disclose them. But the Department of Education suggests avoiding any confusion by keeping these documents separate from "education records."

- Tapes of students recorded by security cameras maintained by the "law enforcement unit" are also not "education records" subject to FERPA. Because of this, the Department of Education suggests schools that haven't designated a "law enforcement unit" should do so and assign the unit this responsibility.

- Schools have to notify parents every year about FERPA rights. In this notification, the school has to let parents know which office or school official serves as its "law enforcement unit." The Department of Education has suggested one way to go about this, which you can see if you turn to its Model Notification of Rights for Elementary and Secondary Schools, see Form VII-5 in chapter nine.

- In your notification to parents, you should list "law enforcement unit" personnel employed by the school as "school officials" with a "legitimate educational interest." This will mean they can access protected student records – but also that they are bound by the same FERPA restrictions as other school officials concerning "education records."

- You can send all "education records" to a transfer school or postsecondary institution a student plans to attend without parents' permission – so long as you have stated on your notification to parents that you make these disclosures to other schools. If you haven't stated this, you have to make a reasonable attempt to notify the parent of the disclosure (unless the parent asked you to send the records, of course). Also, if asked, you have to provide the parents a copy of the information you disclosed as well as provide them the opportunity for a hearing on the matter.

- Finally, although the responsibility for any judgment call remains yours, if you need guidance on questions such as whether you are in a situation that requires release of a record to safeguard health or safety, you can call the Department of Education's Family Compliance Office at (202) 260-3887 for help.

School shooters, like the Virginia Tech student whose attack prompted this FERPA guidance, have typically ended the rampage by killing themselves. Student suicides highlight the need for schools to help students with transitory emotional problems. Many students who consider suicide (or actually commit it) are suffering an "unbearable" problem that could be made bearable with the right kind of help from an adult. For suggestions about ways to deal with a student that you believe may be suicidal, see Form VII-6 in chapter nine.

If a student does commit suicide, this is likely to be deeply traumatic not only for the student's family, but for his or her school community. For suggestions about how to announce a student suicide to the school, see Form VII-7 in chapter nine.

Whether or not the cause was suicide, any time a student dies it is a significant event in the life of the school that needs to be dealt with appropriately and with respect. For suggestions about making an announcement to let students know a classmate has died, see Form VII-8 in chapter nine. For model letters to provide more details to students or their parents after such an event, see Form VII-9 and Form VII-10 in chapter nine.

When a student does commit suicide, grieving parents may try to make sense of the tragedy by blaming the school for things the school did or did not do to prevent it. But as you will see from the cases summarized below, only very rarely will a court agree with the parents that the school had a duty to prevent the suicide.

In one of these decisions, the judge pointed out: "Attempted suicide by school-age children is no slight matter; but it has no single cause and no infallible solution [. ...] Different schools will react differently, depending upon resources, available information, and the judgment of school and public health authorities, who may fear making a bad situation worse. Absent a showing that the school affirmatively caused a suicide, the primary responsibility for safeguarding children from this danger, as from most others, is that of their parents; and even they, with direct control and intimate knowledge, are often helpless," *Hasenfus v. LaJeunesse*, 175 F.3d 68 (1st Cir. 1999).

C. Legal Decisions

◆ A student's bereaved family failed to establish that a teacher's negative remarks to the student, which were echoed in his suicide note, were a substantial factor in causing his death because there was not reliable evidence the teacher actually made the remarks.

A 13-year-old eighth-grader boy struggled with his grades, and his family made it a rule that he could not go hunting if he didn't pass his classes.

When the boy got his fall mid-term grades, he saw he had failed every class except for gym. He complained to his science teacher that this meant he would not be able to go deer hunting.

The teacher said he told the boy he wouldn't be going anywhere – meaning he wouldn't be going hunting. But according to the family, another student later told them the teacher actually said, "Your life is going nowhere" and called the student one of the dumbest people he had ever taught. The family couldn't identify the student who told them this.

The next day, the boy shot himself after the rest of his family left the house. He left a note saying, "I relize my life is going noware fast so I decided that i don't need to live anymore".

A trustee acting on behalf of the boy's family brought a wrongful death suit against the school, arguing school staff had caused the boy's suicide. The court held **the school didn't have a legal duty to prevent the suicide because the school could not have foreseen it**. The trustee also argued the boy used the same words in his note that his science teacher allegedly spoke to him, which meant these spoken words were a substantial factor in causing the suicide. However, the evidence that the teacher actually said those words wasn't reliable. The trustee appealed, but the appellate court affirmed. *Jasperson v. Anoka-Hennepin Independent School Dist. No. 11*, 2007 WL 3153456 (Minn. Ct. App. 2007).

◆ The mother of a boy who committed suicide after his guidance counselor determined he was not suicidal could not hold the counselor or the school district responsible for his death.

A 16-year-old boy passed a note to his ex-girlfriend after he found out she was dating someone new. Alarmed by the line in his note that the news "almost made me want to go kill myself," she took the note to a counselor.

The boy's guidance counselor called him into her office. The counselor told him some of his friends were worried about him and asked if he was having girl trouble. He said he'd been upset about a girl two months ago but was no longer upset. Asked if he had plans to hurt himself or if he would ever do so, he said, "definitely not." The counselor also asked him "forward thinking" questions and was relieved to hear he had future plans. She asked if anything else was upsetting him and he said no.

Believing he was not at risk, the counselor did not contact the school psychologist or the boy's mother.

A few days later, the student returned to the counselor's office to ask if a blond girl gave her a note he had written. The counselor said she could not tell him that. The boy said he had thought she would say that and did not seem upset.

That night, the boy and his mother had an argument. Later that night, he hanged himself.

The deceased student's mother sued the district and the counselor, **arguing they violated his constitutional right not to be deprived of life without due process of law because the counselor did not prevent his death by reporting he was suicidal**.

Generally, public schools cannot be held responsible for acts of violence committed by non-school-personnel. But there is an exception to that rule if the school created the danger that harmed the student.

The mother could not succeed on the state-created danger claim because she could not show:

- it was foreseeable the student would kill himself if the counselor didn't report she had screened him for suicidal ideation

- the counselor's behavior was bad enough to shock the conscience
- the student was a member of a group likely to commit suicide because of this behavior, and
- the counselor used her authority in a way that put the student in danger or rendered him more vulnerable to danger than if she hadn't acted at all.

When the case reached the Third U.S. Circuit Court of Appeals, it found that no one – including the student's mother – had considered him suicidal. It also did not consider the language in the note to be a clear cry for help and found the counselor responded to the situation quickly and appropriately. *Sanford v. Stiles*, 456 F.3d 298 (3d Cir. 2006).

◆ An English teacher didn't violate a state duty to report a student was suicidal – even though the student killed himself six months after turning in an essay about overcoming suicidal tendencies – because the essay discussed past (not present) suicidal ideation.

For the student's junior-year high school English class, he wrote an essay in April called "My Most Difficult Decision." In it, he stated he had overcome the urge to kill himself and that the trigger for that urge was gone and he could enjoy life now. His teacher wrote him a note on the essay saying he was glad he was no longer suicidal, but to come talk to him if the urge to kill himself ever came back.

The student's family moved to another state for the student's senior year. That November, his mother told police the student was missing and she'd found a note in his room saying "I'm sorry," and he'd written "Goodbye" on his calendar for the day he'd disappeared. The family was also missing a rifle, but the student's mother told police she had no reason to believe he was suicidal.

Not long after, his body was found in the state from where his family had moved. The deceased student's family sued the school district and his former English teacher, arguing they had failed to comply with their state law duty to warn if a teacher had direct knowledge a student had suicidal tendencies. The case reached the state supreme court, which found **there was no violation of the duty to warn because a student's suicidal tendencies had to be present rather than past in order to trigger it – and the student's essay discussed overcoming an urge to kill himself in the past.** *Carrier v. Lake Pend Oreille School Dist. No. 84*, 134 P.3d 655 (Idaho 2006).

◆ The parents of a student who killed herself could not prove the school was responsible for their daughter's death by saying that her tears in response to being suspended showed that she was in extreme distress.

The school received a report that a female seventh-grader had cigarettes at school. The assistant principal searched her locker in her presence and found them. He told her she would be suspended for three days. The girl began to cry and continued to cry hard as she got her things from her last classroom. She kept crying in the assistant principal's office as he told her she had been a good student, had not been in a lot of trouble and was not in a lot of trouble now. Despite her tears, she was composed enough to ask him questions about how to get her homework assignments.

When the end-of-day bell rang, he asked if she wanted him to call her mother, but she said she'd take the bus. After she went home, the assistant principal left a message on her family's answering machine to tell them about the suspension. When the student got home, she hanged herself.

The girl's parents sued the district and several individuals, including the assistant principal. The parents alleged the assistant principal violated the student's constitutional right not to be deprived of life without due process of law by causing her severe emotional distress and by not stopping her from going home alone.

One exception to the rule that public schools cannot be held responsible for non-school-personnel's acts of violence is if the school created or increased the danger that harmed the student.

The student's parents argued this was the case here. They said suspending their daughter created or worsened the danger she would kill herself, and that her tears should have let the assistant principal know she was in extreme distress. They also said previous student suicides should have alerted the school to the risk. Because of this, they said the school had been required to protect her by providing counseling or by keeping her at school until her parents could pick her up.

But the trial court found the school hadn't created or worsened the risk that the student would kill herself and therefore the school had no duty to protect her. This decision in the school's favor was upheld on appeal. *Martin v. Shawano-Gresham School Dist.*, 295 F.3d 701 (7th Cir. 2002).

◆ A school did not have the responsibility to protect a student from committing suicide even though the student could be considered emotionally fragile and there had been a rash of suicides at the school in previous months.

A female student was raped when she was 13 years old and then had the trauma of testifying against her rapist in court. Less than a year later, the student was out on the school softball field with her gym class when several of her classmates began harassing her about the rape and her decision to testify. **The student became upset and started shouting obscenities at them and threatening to hurt them.** The gym teacher broke this up and told the student to go back to the locker room. There, the student tried to hang herself.

Classmates found her and called for emergency help. The student did not die, but she went into a coma. She ultimately emerged from the coma but was left with permanent impairments.

In the three months before this incident, seven students at that middle school had attempted suicide. Several of the attempts had happened at school or school events, and the student knew at least two of the students.

The student's parents sued the board of education and the gym teacher, alleging they had violated the student's right to substantive due process. The trial court dismissed the case. The parents appealed, but the First U.S. Circuit Court of Appeals affirmed the dismissal.

The parents argued that the school had a duty to protect the student because it knew she had suffered a rape the year before and that other students had attempted suicide. But this was not enough for the school to recognize her as part of an identifiable group of students at risk for committing suicide. Also, the gym teacher's actions were not bad enough to shock the conscience, which is another prerequisite to a finding of a constitutional violation. Instead, he only reprimanded a 14-year-old for misbehavior and sent her out of class. *Hasenfus v. LaJeunesse*, 175 F.3d 68 (1st Cir. 1999).

◆   A principal and school counselor could be sued under the state-created danger theory for the suicide of a special education student with known emotional problems. They had enraged him by suspending him and then drove him home and left him there alone despite knowing he previously had threatened suicide and had access to guns.

A 16-year-old special education student had been classified as learning disabled. He also had psychological and emotional problems, including depression and impulsivity.

A teacher reported the student for harassing an elementary student. When the principal reprimanded him for this, he responded by threatening the teacher who reported him. The principal immediately suspended him and told a school counselor to drive him home. She also called the police to report the suspension and tell them to detain the student if they saw him on school property.

The school counselor knew the student had access to guns at home and also saw the student was very angry. Earlier that year, the student had told a school aide he might be better off dead and had threatened to shoot himself. Contrary to school policy, the principal did not tell the counselor to make sure the student's parents were at home and bring the student back to school if they were not. The counselor knew he should speak to the parents about the student's suspension, but he simply dropped off the student and then drove away. **When the student's parents got home that day, they found their son had shot himself.**

The parents sued the principal and the counselor, arguing they violated the student's constitutional right to due process. The school defendants asked for summary judgment. The court refused, finding a trial was needed to determine if the school defendants' acts fell under the two exceptions to the general rule that public schools cannot be held responsible for non-school-personnel's acts of violence.

The school defendants appealed. The Tenth U.S. Circuit Court of Appeals upheld the need for a trial on the state-created danger claims against the principal and counselor, but found the claims based on the special relationship exception couldn't go forward.

To find the school had a duty to protect the student under the special relationship exception, the court had to find the school had restrained him in a way that left him unable to protect himself. This wasn't the case here, as the student killed himself after he left the counselor's car.

The state-created danger claims could proceed, however, because a trial was needed to determine if the principal and counselor increased the risk the student would kill himself because:

- he was a member of a limited and definable group: special education students who had threatened to commit suicide, and
- the principal and counselor suspended him – making him so distraught he threatened violence – then took him home and left him there alone, knowing he had access to guns.

Armijo v. Wagon Mound Public Schools, 159 F.3d 1253 (10th Cir. 1998).

VI. OBESITY

A. Introduction

The term "obesity" refers to when a person's body weight is much higher than is considered healthy for a person of that height.

Children whose weight is above what is deemed a healthy range have been shown to be at greater risk of developing – or suffering more – from certain diseases and other health problems. These include:

- diabetes
- asthma
- liver problems
- sleep apnea
- hypertension
- high blood pressure
- high cholesterol levels, and
- depression linked to self-esteem.

The more overweight a student is, the likelier he is to experience these problems. But encouragingly, losing the excess weight also means decreasing these health risks.

The typical way to screen children and adolescents for excess weight and obesity is the body mass index (BMI) method, a formula that assesses weight in relation to height. It is pretty accurate in determining whether a person is carrying an unhealthy amount of fat, although it is not scientifically accurate enough to be called a diagnostic measure. More information about BMI – plus charts – is available at www.cdc.gov/growthcharts.

One touted advantage of using BMI to determine whether one is overweight is that it is minimally invasive – which is important when dealing with a vulnerable population like children. But while asking for students' weights or having them get on a scale does not physically invade their bodies, it might trigger a big emotional reaction.

Schools might want to remember how touchy the subject of personal body weight is in this culture. For many students, whether or not they are actually overweight, their weight is deeply connected to a personal sense of shame and unworthiness. This attitude can exist (perhaps it especially exists) among students who actually should put on a few pounds – particularly if there is an eating disorder involved.

Because of the possibility of an overwhelming emotional reaction (which can be closely followed by hurtful teasing as other students pick up on it) some sensitivity on the school's part might be called for if personal body weight is discussed.

And it easily could be because, increasingly, schools are getting involved in health initiatives to combat the problem. This is because excess weight does pose such serious health problems and because more and more children are becoming overweight.

B. Incidence of Overweight Children

The number of overweight children has tripled since the 1970s, according to the Centers for Disease Control and Prevention (CDC). The percentage of overweight children jumped from between 5% and 6% to its current percentage of around 17% – or more than one obese child among every six.

The percentage leap is even greater in some individual groups. In the early 1970s, 4% of 6- to 11-year-olds were overweight. By the early 2000s, that percentage had more than quadrupled to 18%.

The Federal Interagency Forum on Child and Family Statistics also tracked the trend. Although its numbers are slightly different, it found that among children ages 6 to 17:

- 6% were overweight in 1976-1980
- 11% were overweight in 1988-1994, and
- 18% were overweight in 2003-2004.

As we already have seen, being overweight puts students at risk for other health problems. One disturbing trend reported by the CDC is that Type 2 diabetes – formerly called "adult onset diabetes," because that is typically when it started – has begun showing up in children and adolescents. When onset occurs this early, the complications that go with the disease (such as kidney failure and cardiovascular disease) also set in that much earlier.

Even when obesity is not linked to a serious illness, overweight children are missing more days of school, according to a study published in a 2007 issue of the journal *Obesity*. Among the 1,000 4th- and 5th-graders the study followed, the overweight children missed two days more of school a year than the average-weight students.

Another problem related to overweight students that virtually every school has to deal with is teasing and bullying. A 2004 study showed that overweight children are more likely to be bullied than normal-weight children. There is a huge social stigma attached to obesity in this country.

C. Changes by Schools

The most basic way to increase anyone's body weight is to give them more calories and have them exercise less. There has been some evidence that schools were adding to the increase in student obesity – but now there is evidence schools are turning that around.

The CDC identified two important things schools got wrong:

- having sugar-sweetened soft drinks in school vending machines. Because soda is high in calories but not very filling, children are likely to have it in addition to something else rather than in place of something else, and
- letting students off the hook when it came to daily gym classes. The percentage of schools that required daily PE for adolescents plummeted from 42% in 1991 to 28% in 2003.

However, the CDC's 2006 study of school health policies found that things at schools have been changing. It found schools have been:

- replacing soda with bottled water in vending machines. In 2000, only about 29% of schools offered bottled water. In 2006, the percentage was 46%, and
- requiring recess in elementary school – up from only 4% in 2000 to 12% in 2006.

The CDC also has announced a four-part plan intended to help schools fight student obesity. It suggests schools:

(1) establish a coordinated school health program that includes these eight components:
  - health education
  - physical education
  - counseling, psychological and social services
  - health services
  - nutrition services
  - healthy school environment
  - parent/community involvement
  - staff wellness

(2) establish a school health council to promote healthy eating and exercise
  - Since 2004, federal law has required all school districts participating in federally funded school meal programs to establish a local school wellness policy through a process that involves parents, students, school representatives, and the public. A school health council can meet that requirement.

(3) assess existing health programs and suggest improvements
  - To help with this, the CDC provides a self-assessment and planning tool at apps.nccd.cdc.gov/shi.

(4) improve the school's food and exercise policies
  - For example, schools can find ways to make cafeteria food both healthy and tasty and come up with ways to incorporate exercise into the school day.

The CDC has come up with tactics to make important changes in things schools can control, such as its curriculum and policies. But as we will see below, even when it comes to wider social problems that drive up the incidence of obesity – and over which schools obviously have no control – the Department of Agriculture offers help through the National School Lunch Program and the School Breakfast Program of which schools might want to take greater advantage – and encourage their students to do so as well.

D. Obesity and Poverty

Obesity is obviously related to how many calories go in and how many then get burned off. But there are other influences we do not typically think of that can significantly impact students' body weight, including their physical environments, their cultures, their personal attitudes, and whether their families are prosperous or struggling financially. There is a direct correlation between poverty and obesity.

Fresh fruits and vegetables cost a lot more than fast food – and are not nearly as filling. A speaker at the 2007 Childhood Obesity Conference in Oklahoma put it this way: A dollar only buys 200 nutritious calories, but you can get 800 calories of junk for the same price. Similarly, the original reason behind the South's tradition of delicious fried foods was that it was a way for the poor to make a limited amount of food go farther. Adding fat was a good way to add filling calories and feed more people.

Where children live can also have a huge impact on their weight. It is almost universally true that poor areas of towns are short on two health basics: stores that stock affordable fresh food, and safe outdoor places where children can exercise.

One reason why national obesity rates for children have tripled since the late 1970s might be the increase in poverty in recent years.

Catholic Charities, for example, reported in late 2007 that they had experienced a 60% rise in people receiving their food services between 2002 and 2006. These services include food banks, soup kitchens and congregate meals.

And a Department of Agriculture study released in November 2007 found that more than 35.5 million Americans – or 12% of the population, more than one in every nine people – reported having to go hungry in 2006 because they did not have enough money to meet their basic needs. Of these 35.5 million people, 12.6 million were children.

Schools cannot be expected to tackle the problem of poverty, but they can help to fight off its nutritional impact on their students by making sure children get PE classes and by increasing their participation in the U.S. Department of Agriculture's School Breakfast Program and National School Lunch Program.

One great thing about these programs is that they require schools to serve meals that are low in fat and provide a certain percentage of the Recommended Dietary Allowances of protein, Vitamin A, Vitamin C, iron, calcium and calories – one-third for school lunches and one-quarter for school breakfasts. Poor nutrition, which many very heavy children actually suffer from, has a negative impact on brain development and school performance.

Another advantage of school meal programs is that they are based on parental income, so they are either free or available at a greatly reduced price for children that really need them.

Due to the stigma that can be associated with poverty, the very students who most need a nutritious breakfast and lunch may be dissuaded from getting them at school.

To encourage participation, it can be helpful to explain to students how important good nutrition is.

Here are some pointers for you to use to convince them, courtesy of the National PTA's Web site:

- children who eat meals served by the school meal programs are getting more nutritious meals than children who do not, and
- children who eat these meals have also shown improved standardized test scores, attendance and class participation.

Not all overweight children are underprivileged. Some children are overweight due to an overabundance of food and video games. You can help children who are not facing poverty but are overweight to develop healthy habits, such as:

- eating less fat
- eating more fruits, vegetables, lean meats and whole grains
- reducing portion sizes, and
- increasing their physical activity.

You also can help keep them from getting discouraged by reminding them that losing weight takes time but that every healthy thing they do today – like eating an apple instead of a candy bar or taking the stairs instead of the elevator – will pay off tomorrow. Getting into healthy habits has a cumulative effect.

Also, as opposed to going on and off calorie-reduced diets, developing healthy habits will not only take the weight off in the first place but will help keep it off in the future.

CHAPTER EIGHT

Statutes and Regulations

The following federal statutes and regulations address school safety and security issues.

I. SAFE AND DRUG-FREE SCHOOLS AND COMMUNITIES ACT

20 USC § 7101 et seq.

SUBCHAPTER IV - 21ST CENTURY SCHOOLS

PART A - SAFE AND DRUG-FREE SCHOOLS AND COMMUNITIES
7101. Short title.
7102. Purpose.
7103. Authorization of appropriations.

SUBPART 1 - STATE GRANTS
7111. Reservations and allotments.
    (a) Reservations.
    (b) State allotments.
    (c) Limitation.
7112. Reservation of State funds for safe and drug-free schools.
    (a) State reservation for the chief executive officer of a State.
    (b) In State distribution.
    (c) State activities.
7113. State application.
    (a) In general.
    (b) Interim application.
    (c) Approval process.
7114. Local educational agency program.

SUBPART 3 - GUN POSSESSION

SUBPART 4 - GENERAL PROVISIONS

PART A - SAFE AND DRUG-FREE SCHOOLS AND COMMUNITIES

Sec. 7101. Short title

This part may be cited as the "Safe and Drug-Free Schools and Communities Act."

Sec. 7102. Purpose

The purpose of this part is to support programs that prevent violence in and around schools; that prevent the illegal use of alcohol, tobacco, and drugs; that involve parents and communities; and that are coordinated with related Federal, State, school, and community efforts and resources to foster a safe and drug-free learning environment that supports student academic achievement, through the provision of Federal assistance to -

(1) States for grants to local educational agencies and consortia of such agencies to establish, operate, and improve local programs of school drug and violence prevention and early intervention;

(2) States for grants to, and contracts with, community-based organizations and public and private entities for programs of drug and violence prevention and early intervention, including community-wide drug and violence prevention planning and organizing activities;

(3) States for development, training, technical assistance, and coordination activities; and

(4) public and private entities to provide technical assistance; conduct training, demonstrations, and evaluation; and to provide supplementary services and community-wide drug and violence prevention planning and organizing activities for the prevention of drug use and violence among students and youth.

Sec. 7103. Authorization of appropriations

There are authorized to be appropriated -

(1) $650,000,000 for fiscal year 2002, and such sums as may be necessary for each of the 5 succeeding fiscal years, for State grants under subpart 1 of this part; and

(2) such sums for fiscal year 2002, and for each of the 5 succeeding fiscal years, for national programs under subpart 2 of this part.

SUBPART 1 - STATE GRANTS

Sec. 7111. Reservations and allotments

(a) Reservations

(1) In general

From the amount made available under section 7103(1) of this title to carry out this subpart for each fiscal year, the Secretary -

(A) shall reserve 1 percent or $4,750,000 (whichever is greater) of such amount for grants to Guam, American Samoa, the United States Virgin Islands, and the Commonwealth of the Northern Mariana Islands, to be allotted in accordance with the Secretary's determination of their respective needs and to carry out programs described in this subpart;

(B) shall reserve 1 percent or $4,750,000 (whichever is greater) of such amount for the Secretary of the Interior to carry out programs described in this subpart for Indian youth; and

(C) shall reserve 0.2 percent of such amount for Native Hawaiians to be used under section 7117 of this title to carry out programs described in this subpart.

(2) Other reservations

From the amount made available under section 7103(2) of this title to carry out subpart 2 of this part for each fiscal year, the Secretary -

(A) may reserve not more than $2,000,000 for the national impact evaluation required by section 7132(a) of this title;

(B) notwithstanding section 3 of the No Child Left Behind Act of 2001, shall reserve an amount necessary to make continuation grants to grantees under the Safe Schools/Healthy Students initiative (under the same terms and conditions as provided for in the grants involved).

(b) State allotments

(1) In general

Except as provided in paragraph (2), the Secretary shall, for each fiscal year, allot among the States -

(A) one-half of the remainder not reserved under subsection (a) of this section according to the ratio between the school-aged population of each State and the school-aged population of all the States; and

(B) one-half of such remainder according to the ratio between the amount each State received under section 6334 of this title for the preceding year and the sum of such amounts received by all the States.

(2) Minimum

For any fiscal year, no State shall be allotted under this subsection an amount that is less than the greater of -

(A) one-half of 1 percent of the total amount allotted to all the States under this subsection; or

(B) the amount such State received for fiscal year 2001 under section 4111 as such section was in effect the day preceding January 8, 2002.

(3) Reallotment

(A) Reallotment for failure to apply

If any State does not apply for an allotment under this subpart for a fiscal year, the Secretary shall reallot the amount of the State's allotment to the remaining States in accordance with this section.

(B) Reallotment of unused funds

The Secretary may reallot any amount of any allotment to a State if the Secretary determines that the State will be unable to use such amount within 2 years of such allotment. Such reallotments shall be made on the same basis as allotments are made under paragraph (1).

(4) Definition

In this section the term "State" means each of the 50 States, the District of Columbia, and the Commonwealth of Puerto Rico.

(c) Limitation

Amounts appropriated under section 7103(2) of this title for a fiscal year may not be increased above the amounts appropriated under such section for the previous fiscal year unless the amount appropriated under section 7103(1) of this title for the fiscal year involved are at least 10 percent greater that (!2) the amounts appropriated under such section 7103(1) of this title for the previous fiscal year.

Sec. 7112. Reservation of State funds for safe and drug-free schools

(a) State reservation for the chief executive officer of a State

(1) In general

The chief executive officer of a State may reserve not more than 20 percent of the total amount allocated to a State under section 7111(b) of this title for each fiscal year to award competitive grants and contracts to local educational agencies, community-based organizations (including community anti-drug coalitions) other public entities and private organizations, and consortia thereof. Such grants and contracts shall be used to carry out the comprehensive State plan described in section 7113(a) of this title through programs or activities that complement and support activities of local educational agencies described in section 7115(b) of this title. Such officer shall award grants based on -

(A) the quality of the program or activity proposed; and

(B) how the program or activity meets the principles of effectiveness described in section 7115(a) of this title.

(2) Priority

In making such grants and contracts under this section, a chief executive officer shall give priority to programs and activities that prevent illegal drug use and violence for -

(A) children and youth who are not normally served by State educational agencies or local educational agencies; or

(B) populations that need special services or additional resources (such as youth in juvenile detention facilities, runaway or homeless children and youth, pregnant and parenting teenagers, and school dropouts).

(3) Special consideration

In awarding funds under paragraph (1), a chief executive officer shall give special consideration to grantees that pursue a comprehensive approach to drug and violence prevention that includes providing and incorporating mental health services related to drug and violence prevention in their program.

(4) Peer review

Grants or contracts awarded under this section shall be subject to a peer review process.

(5) Use of funds

Grants and contracts under this section shall be used to implement drug and violence prevention activities, including -

(A) activities that complement and support local educational agency activities under section 7115 of this title, including developing and implementing activities to prevent and reduce violence associated with prejudice and intolerance;

(B) dissemination of information about drug and violence prevention; and

(C) development and implementation of community-wide drug and violence prevention planning and organizing.

(6) Administrative costs

The chief executive officer of a State may use not more than 3 percent of the amount described in paragraph (1) for the administrative costs incurred in carrying out the duties of such officer under this section.

(b) In State distribution

(1) In general

A State educational agency shall distribute not less than 93 percent of the amount made available to the State under section 7111(b) of this title, less the amount reserved under subsection (a) of this section, to its local educational agencies.

(2) State administration costs

(A) In general

A State educational agency may use not more than 3 percent of the amount made available to the State under section 7111(b) of this title for each fiscal year less the amount reserved under subsection (a) of this section, for State educational agency administrative costs, including the implementation of the uniform management information and reporting system as provided for under subsection (c)(3) of this section.

(B) Additional amounts for the uniform management information system

In the case of fiscal year 2002, a State educational agency may, in addition to amounts provided for in subparagraph (A), use 1 percent of the amount made available to the State educational agency under section 7111(b) of this title for each fiscal year less the amount reserved under subsection (a) of this section, for implementation of the uniform management information and reporting system as provided for under subsection (c)(3) of this section.

(c) State activities

(1) In general

A State educational agency may use not more than 5 percent of the amount made available to the State under section 7111(b) of this title for each fiscal year less the amount reserved under subsection (a) of this section, for activities described in this subsection.

(2) Activities

A State educational agency shall use the amounts described in paragraph (1), either directly, or through grants and contracts, to plan, develop, and implement capacity building, technical assistance and training, evaluation, program improvement services, and coordination activities for local educational agencies, community-based organizations, and other public and private entities. Such uses -

(A) shall meet the principles of effectiveness described in section 7115(a) of this title;

(B) shall complement and support local uses of funds under section 7115(b) of this title;

(C) shall be in accordance with the purposes of this part; and

(D) may include, among others activities -

(i) identification, development, evaluation, and dissemination of drug and violence prevention strategies, programs, activities, and other information;

(ii) training, technical assistance, and demonstration projects to address violence that is associated with prejudice and intolerance; and

(iii) financial assistance to enhance drug and violence prevention resources available in areas that serve large numbers of low-income children, are sparsely populated, or have other special needs.

(3) Uniform management information and reporting system

(A) Information and statistics

A State shall establish a uniform management information and reporting system.

(B) Uses of funds

A State may use funds described in subparagraphs (A) and (B) of subsection (b)(2) of this section, either directly or through grants and contracts, to implement the uniform management information and reporting system described in subparagraph (A), for the collection of information on -

(i) truancy rates;

(ii) the frequency, seriousness, and incidence of violence and drug-related offenses resulting in suspensions and expulsions in elementary schools and secondary schools in the State;

(iii) the types of curricula, programs, and services provided by the chief executive officer, the State educational agency, local educational agencies, and other recipients of funds under this subpart; and

(iv) the incidence and prevalence, age of onset, perception of health risk, and perception of social disapproval of drug use and violence by youth in schools and communities.

(C) Compilation of statistics

In compiling the statistics required for the uniform management information and reporting system, the offenses described in subparagraph (B)(ii) shall be defined pursuant to the State's criminal code, but shall not identify victims of crimes or persons accused of crimes. The collected data shall include incident reports by school officials, anonymous student surveys, and anonymous teacher surveys.

(D) Reporting

The information described under subparagraph (B) shall be reported to the public and the data referenced in clauses (i) and (ii) of such subparagraph shall be reported to the State on a school-by-school basis.

(E) Limitation

Nothing in this subsection shall be construed to authorize the Secretary to require particular policies, procedures, or practices with respect to crimes committed on school property or school security.

Sec. 7113. State application

(a) In general

In order to receive an allotment under section 7111(b) of this title for any fiscal year, a State shall submit to the Secretary, at such time as the Secretary may require, an application that -

(1) contains a comprehensive plan for the use of funds by the State educational agency and the chief executive officer of the State to provide

safe, orderly, and drug-free schools and communities through programs and activities that complement and support activities of local educational agencies under section 7115(b) of this title, that comply with the principles of effectiveness under section 7115(a) of this title, and that otherwise are in accordance with the purpose of this part;

(2) describes how activities funded under this subpart will foster a safe and drug-free learning environment that supports academic achievement;

(3) provides an assurance that the application was developed in consultation and coordination with appropriate State officials and others, including the chief executive officer, the chief State school officer, the head of the State alcohol and drug abuse agency, the heads of the State health and mental health agencies, the head of the State criminal justice planning agency, the head of the State child welfare agency, the head of the State board of education, or their designees, and representatives of parents, students, and community-based organizations;

(4) describes how the State educational agency will coordinate such agency's activities under this subpart with the chief executive officer's drug and violence prevention programs under this subpart and with the prevention efforts of other State agencies and other programs, as appropriate, in accordance with (5) provides an assurance that funds reserved under section 7112(a) of this title will not duplicate the efforts of the State educational agency and local educational agencies with regard to the provision of school-based drug and violence prevention activities and that those funds will be used to serve populations not normally served by the State educational agencies and local educational agencies and populations that need special services, such as school dropouts, suspended and expelled students, youth in detention centers, runaway or homeless children and youth, and pregnant and parenting youth;

(6) provides an assurance that the State will cooperate with, and assist, the Secretary in conducting data collection as required by section 7132 of this title;

(7) provides an assurance that the local educational agencies in the State will comply with the provisions of section 7881 of this title pertaining to the participation of private school children and teachers in the programs and activities under this subpart;

(8) provides an assurance that funds under this subpart will be used to increase the level of State, local, and other non-Federal funds that would, in the absence of funds under this subpart, be made available for programs and activities authorized under this subpart, and in no case supplant such State, local, and other non-Federal funds;

(9) contains the results of a needs assessment conducted by the State for drug and violence prevention programs, which shall be based on ongoing State evaluation activities, including data on -

(A) the incidence and prevalence of illegal drug use and violence among youth in schools and communities, including the age of onset, the perception of health risks, and the perception of social disapproval among such youth;

(B) the prevalence of risk factors, including high or increasing rates of reported cases of child abuse or domestic violence;

(C) the prevalence of protective factors, buffers, or assets; and

(D) other variables in the school and community identified through scientifically based research;

(10) provides a statement of the State's performance measures for drug and violence prevention programs and activities to be funded under this subpart that will be focused on student behavior and attitudes, derived from the needs assessment described in paragraph (9), and be developed in consultation between the State and local officials, and that consist of -

(A) performance indicators for drug and violence prevention programs and activities; and

(B) levels of performance for each performance indicator;

(11) describes the procedures the State will use for assessing and publicly reporting progress toward meeting the performance measures described in paragraph (10);

(12) provides an assurance that the State application will be available for public review after submission of the application;

(13) describes the special outreach activities that will be carried out by the State educational agency and the chief executive officer of the State to maximize the participation of community-based organizations of demonstrated effectiveness that provide services such as mentoring programs in low-income communities;

(14) describes how funds will be used by the State educational agency and the chief executive officer of the State to support, develop, and implement community-wide comprehensive drug and violence prevention planning and organizing activities;

(15) describes how input from parents will be sought regarding the use of funds by the State educational agency and the chief executive officer of the State;

(16) describes how the State educational agency will review applications from local educational agencies, including how the agency will receive input from parents in such review;

(17) describes how the State educational agency will monitor the implementation of activities under this subpart, and provide technical assistance for local educational agencies, community-based organizations, other public entities, and private organizations;

(18) describes how the chief executive officer of the State will award funds under section 7112(a) of this title and implement a plan for monitoring the performance of, and providing technical assistance to, recipients of such funds; and

(19) includes any other information the Secretary may require.

(b) Interim application

(1) Authority

Notwithstanding any other provision of this section, a State may submit for fiscal year 2002 a 1-year interim application and plan for the use of funds under this subpart that is consistent with the requirements of this section and contains such information as the Secretary may specify in regulations.

(2) Purpose

The purpose of such interim application and plan shall be to afford the State the opportunity to fully develop and review such State's application and comprehensive plan otherwise required by this section.

(3) Exception

A State may not receive a grant under this subpart for a fiscal year after fiscal year 2002 unless the Secretary has approved such State's application and comprehensive plan as described in subsection (a) of this section.

(c) Approval process

(1) Deemed approval

An application submitted by a State pursuant to this section shall undergo peer review by the Secretary and shall be deemed to be approved by the Secretary unless the Secretary makes a written determination, prior to the expiration of the 120-day period beginning on the date on which the Secretary received the application, that the application is not in compliance with this subpart.

(2) Disapproval

The Secretary shall not finally disapprove the application, except after giving the State educational agency and the chief executive officer of the State notice and an opportunity for a hearing.

(3) Notification

If the Secretary finds that the application is not in compliance, in whole or in part, with this subpart, the Secretary shall -

(A) give the State educational agency and the chief executive officer of the State notice and an opportunity for a hearing; and

(B) notify the State educational agency and the chief executive officer of the State of the finding of noncompliance, and in such notification, shall -

(i) cite the specific provisions in the application that are not in compliance; and

(ii) request additional information, only as to the noncompliant provisions, needed to make the application compliant.

(4) Response

If the State educational agency and the chief executive officer of the State respond to the Secretary's notification described in paragraph (3)(B) during the 45-day period beginning on the date on which the agency received the notification, and resubmit the application with the requested information described in paragraph (3)(B)(ii), the Secretary shall approve or disapprove such application prior to the later of -

(A) the expiration of the 45-day period beginning on the date on which the application is resubmitted; or

(B) the expiration of the 120-day period described in paragraph (1).

(5) Failure to respond

If the State educational agency and the chief executive officer of the

State do not respond to the Secretary's notification described in paragraph (3)(B) during the 45-day period beginning on the date on which the agency received the notification, such application shall be deemed to be disapproved.

Sec. 7114. Local educational agency program

(a) In general

(1) Funds to local educational agencies

A State shall provide the amount made available to the State under this subpart, less the amounts reserved under section 7112 of this title to local educational agencies for drug and violence prevention and education programs and activities as follows:

(A) 60 percent of such amount based on the relative amount such agencies received under part A of subchapter I of this chapter for the preceding fiscal year.

(B) 40 percent of such amount based on the relative enrollments in public and private nonprofit elementary schools and secondary schools within the boundaries of such agencies.

(2) Administrative costs

Of the amount received under paragraph (1), a local educational agency may use not more than 2 percent for the administrative costs of carrying out its responsibilities under this subpart.

(3) Return of funds to State; reallocation

(A) Return

Except as provided in subparagraph (B), upon the expiration of the 1-year period beginning on the date on which a local educational agency receives its allocation under this subpart -

(i) such agency shall return to the State educational agency any funds from such allocation that remain unobligated; and

(ii) the State educational agency shall reallocate any such amount to local educational agencies that have submitted plans for using such amount for programs or activities on a timely basis.

(B) Carryover

In any fiscal year, a local educational agency, may retain for obligation in the succeeding fiscal year -

(i) an amount equal to not more than 25 percent of the allocation it received under this subpart for such fiscal year; or

(ii) upon a demonstration of good cause by such agency and approval by the State educational agency, an amount that exceeds 25 percent of such allocation.

(C) Reallocation

If a local educational agency chooses not to apply to receive the amount allocated to such agency under this subsection, or if such agency's application under subsection (d) of this section is disapproved by the State educational agency, the State educational agency shall reallocate such amount to one or more of its other local educational agencies.

(b) Eligibility

To be eligible to receive a subgrant under this subpart, a local educational agency desiring a subgrant shall submit an application to the State educational agency in accordance with subsection (d) of this section. Such an application shall be amended, as necessary, to reflect changes in the activities and programs of the local educational agency.

(c) Development

(1) Consultation

(A) In general

A local educational agency shall develop its application through timely and meaningful consultation with State and local government representatives, representatives of schools to be served (including private schools), teachers and other staff, parents, students, community-based organizations, and others with relevant and demonstrated expertise in drug and violence prevention activities (such as medical, mental health, and law enforcement professionals).

(B) Continued consultation

On an ongoing basis, the local educational agency shall consult with such representatives and organizations in order to seek advice regarding how best to coordinate such agency's activities under this subpart with other related strategies, programs, and activities being conducted in the community.

(2) Design and development

To ensure timely and meaningful consultation under paragraph (1), a local educational agency at the initial stages of design and development of a program or activity shall consult, in accordance with this subsection, with appropriate entities and persons on issues regarding the design and development of the program or activity, including efforts to meet the principles of effectiveness described in section 7115(a) of this title.

(d) Contents of applications

An application submitted by a local educational agency under this section shall contain -

(1) an assurance that the activities or programs to be funded comply with the principles of effectiveness described in section 7115(a) of this title and foster a safe and drug-free learning environment that supports academic achievement;

(2) a detailed explanation of the local educational agency's comprehensive plan for drug and violence prevention, including a description of -

(A) how the plan will be coordinated with programs under this chapter, and other Federal, State, and local programs for drug and violence prevention, in accordance with section 7846 of this title;

(B) the local educational agency's performance measures for drug and violence prevention programs and activities, that shall consist of -

(i) performance indicators for drug and violence prevention programs and activities; including -

(I) specific reductions in the prevalence of identified risk factors; and

(II) specific increases in the prevalence of protective factors, buffers, or assets if any have been identified; and

(ii) levels of performance for each performance indicator;

(C) how such agency will assess and publicly report progress toward attaining its performance measures;

(D) the drug and violence prevention activity or program to be funded, including how the activity or program will meet the principles of effectiveness described in section 7115(a) of this title, and the means of evaluating such activity or program; and

(E) how the services will be targeted to schools and students with the greatest need;

(3) a description for how the results of the evaluations of the effectiveness of the program will be used to refine, improve, and strengthen the program;

(4) an assurance that funds under this subpart will be used to increase the level of State, local, and other non-Federal funds that would, in the absence of funds under this subpart, be made available for programs and activities authorized under this subpart, and in no case supplant such State, local, and other non-Federal funds;

(5) a description of the mechanisms used to provide effective notice to the community of an intention to submit an application under this subpart;

(6) an assurance that drug and violence prevention programs supported under this subpart convey a clear and consistent message that acts of violence and the illegal use of drugs are wrong and harmful;

(7) an assurance that the applicant has, or the schools to be served have, a plan for keeping schools safe and drug-free that includes -

(A) appropriate and effective school discipline policies that prohibit disorderly conduct, the illegal possession of weapons, and the illegal use, possession, distribution, and sale of tobacco, alcohol, and other drugs by students;

(B) security procedures at school and while students are on the way to and from school;

(C) prevention activities that are designed to create and maintain safe, disciplined, and drug-free environments;

(D) a crisis management plan for responding to violent or traumatic incidents on school grounds; and

(E) a code of conduct policy for all students that clearly states the responsibilities of students, teachers, and administrators in maintaining a classroom environment that -

(i) allows a teacher to communicate effectively with all students in the class;

(ii) allows all students in the class to learn;

(iii) has consequences that are fair, and developmentally appropriate;

(iv) considers the student and the circumstances of the situation; and

(v) is enforced accordingly;

(8) an assurance that the application and any waiver request under section 7115(a)(3) of this title will be available for public review after submission of the application; and

(9) such other assurances, goals, and objectives identified through scientifically based research that the State may reasonably require in accordance with the purpose of this part.

(e) Review of application

(1) In general

In reviewing local applications under this section, a State educational agency shall use a peer review process or other methods of assuring the quality of such applications.

(2) Considerations

In determining whether to approve the application of a local educational agency under this section, a State educational agency shall consider the quality of application and the extent to which the application meets the principles of effectiveness described in section 7115(a) of this title.

(f) Approval process

(1) Deemed approval

An application submitted by a local educational agency pursuant to this section shall be deemed to be approved by the State educational agency unless the State educational agency makes a written determination, prior to the expiration of the 120-day period beginning on the date on which the State educational agency received the application, that the application is not in compliance with this subpart.

(2) Disapproval

The State educational agency shall not finally disapprove the application, except after giving the local educational agency notice and opportunity for a hearing.

(3) Notification

If the State educational agency finds that the application is not in compliance, in whole or in part, with this subpart, the State educational agency shall -

(A) give the local educational agency notice and an opportunity for a hearing; and

(B) notify the local educational agency of the finding of noncompliance, and in such notification, shall -

(i) cite the specific provisions in the application that are not in compliance; and

(ii) request additional information, only as to the noncompliant provisions, needed to make the application compliant.

(4) Response

If the local educational agency responds to the State educational agency's notification described in paragraph (3)(B) during the 45-day period beginning on the date on which the agency received the notification, and resubmits the application with the requested information described in paragraph (3)(B)(ii), the State educational agency shall approve or disapprove such application prior to the later of -

(A) the expiration of the 45-day period beginning on the date on which the application is resubmitted; or

(B) the expiration of the 120-day period described in paragraph (1).

(5) Failure to respond

If the local educational agency does not respond to the State educational agency's notification described in paragraph (3)(B) during the 45-day period beginning on the date on which the agency received the notification, such application shall be deemed to be disapproved.

Sec. 7115. Authorized activities

(a) Principles of effectiveness

(1) In general

For a program or activity developed pursuant to this subpart to meet the principles of effectiveness, such program or activity shall -

(A) be based on an assessment of objective data regarding the incidence of violence and illegal drug use in the elementary schools and secondary schools and communities to be served, including an objective analysis of the current conditions and consequences regarding violence and illegal drug use, including delinquency and serious discipline problems, among students who attend such schools (including private school students who participate in the drug and violence prevention program) that is based on ongoing local assessment or evaluation activities;

(B) be based on an established set of performance measures aimed at ensuring that the elementary schools and secondary schools and communities to be served by the program have a safe, orderly, and drug-free learning environment;

(C) be based on scientifically based research that provides evidence that the program to be used will reduce violence and illegal drug use;

(D) be based on an analysis of the data reasonably available at the time, of the prevalence of risk factors, including high or increasing rates of reported cases of child abuse and domestic violence; protective factors, buffers, assets; or other variables in schools and communities in the State identified through scientifically based research; and

(E) include meaningful and ongoing consultation with and input from parents in the development of the application and administration of the program or activity.

(2) Periodic evaluation

(A) Requirement

The program or activity shall undergo a periodic evaluation to assess its progress toward reducing violence and illegal drug use in schools to be served based on performance measures described in section 7114(d)(2)(B) of this title.

(B) Use of results

The results shall be used to refine, improve, and strengthen the program, and to refine the performance measures, and shall also be made available to the public upon request, with public notice of such availability provided.

(3) Waiver

A local educational agency may apply to the State for a waiver of the requirement of subsection (a)(1)(C) of this section to allow innovative activities or programs that demonstrate substantial likelihood of success.

(b) Local educational agency activities

(1) Program requirements

A local educational agency shall use funds made available under section 7114 of this title to develop, implement, and evaluate comprehensive programs and activities, which are coordinated with other school and community-based services and programs, that shall -

(A) foster a safe and drug-free learning environment that supports academic achievement;

(B) be consistent with the principles of effectiveness described in subsection (a)(1) of this section;

(C) be designed to -

(i) prevent or reduce violence; the use, possession and distribution of illegal drugs; and delinquency; and

(ii) create a well-disciplined environment conducive to learning, which includes consultation between teachers, principals, and other school personnel to identify early warning signs of drug use and violence and to provide behavioral interventions as part of classroom management efforts; and

(D) include activities to -

(i) promote the involvement of parents in the activity or program;

(ii) promote coordination with community groups and coalitions, and government agencies; and

(iii) distribute information about the local educational agency's needs, goals, and programs under this subpart.

(2) Authorized activities

Each local educational agency, or consortium of such agencies, that receives a subgrant under this subpart may use such funds to carry out activities that comply with the principles of effectiveness described in subsection (a) of this section, such as the following:

(A) Age appropriate and developmentally based activities that -

(i) address the consequences of violence and the illegal use of drugs, as appropriate;

(ii) promote a sense of individual responsibility;

(iii) teach students that most people do not illegally use drugs;

(iv) teach students to recognize social and peer pressure to use drugs illegally and the skills for resisting illegal drug use;

(v) teach students about the dangers of emerging drugs;

(vi) engage students in the learning process; and

(vii) incorporate activities in secondary schools that reinforce prevention activities implemented in elementary schools.

(B) Activities that involve families, community sectors (which may include appropriately trained seniors), and a variety of drug and violence prevention providers in setting clear expectations against violence and illegal use of drugs and appropriate consequences for violence and illegal use of drugs.

(C) Dissemination of drug and violence prevention information to schools and the community.

(D) Professional development and training for, and involvement of, school personnel, pupil services personnel, parents, and interested community members in prevention, education, early identification and intervention, mentoring, or rehabilitation referral, as related to drug and violence prevention.

(E) Drug and violence prevention activities that may include the following:

(i) Community-wide planning and organizing activities to reduce violence and illegal drug use, which may include gang activity prevention.

(ii) Acquiring and installing metal detectors, electronic locks, surveillance cameras, or other related equipment and technologies.

(iii) Reporting criminal offenses committed on school property.

(iv) Developing and implementing comprehensive school security plans or obtaining technical assistance concerning such plans, which may include obtaining a security assessment or assistance from the School Security and Technology Resource Center at the Sandia National Laboratory located in Albuquerque, New Mexico.

(v) Supporting safe zones of passage activities that ensure that students travel safely to and from school, which may include bicycle and pedestrian safety programs.

(vi) The hiring and mandatory training, based on scientific research, of school security personnel (including school resource officers) who interact with students in support of youth drug and violence prevention activities under this part that are implemented in the school.

(vii) Expanded and improved school-based mental health services related to illegal drug use and violence, including early identification of violence and illegal drug use, assessment, and direct or group counseling services provided to students, parents, families, and school personnel by qualified school-based mental health service providers.

(viii) Conflict resolution programs, including peer mediation programs that educate and train peer mediators and a designated faculty supervisor, and youth anti-crime and anti-drug councils and activities.

(ix) Alternative education programs or services for violent or drug abusing students that reduce the need for suspension or expulsion or that serve students who have been suspended or expelled from the regular educational settings, including programs or services to assist students to make continued progress toward meeting the State academic achievement standards and to reenter the regular education setting.

(x) Counseling, mentoring, referral services, and other student assistance practices and programs, including assistance provided by qualified school-based mental health services providers and the training of teachers by school-based mental health services providers in appropriate identification and intervention techniques for students at risk of violent behavior and illegal use of drugs.

(xi) Programs that encourage students to seek advice from, and to confide in, a trusted adult regarding concerns about violence and illegal drug use.

(xii) Drug and violence prevention activities designed to reduce truancy.

(xiii) Age-appropriate, developmentally-based violence prevention and education programs that address victimization associated with prejudice and intolerance, and that include activities designed to help students develop a sense of individual responsibility and respect for the rights of others, and to resolve conflicts without violence.

(xiv) Consistent with the fourth amendment to the Constitution of the United States, the testing of a student for illegal drug use or the inspecting of a student's locker for weapons or illegal drugs or drug paraphernalia, including at the request of or with the consent of a parent or legal guardian of the student, if the local educational agency elects to so test or inspect.

(xv) Emergency intervention services following traumatic crisis events, such as a shooting, major accident, or a drug-related incident that have disrupted the learning environment.

(xvi) Establishing or implementing a system for transferring suspension and expulsion records, consistent with section 1232g of this title, by a local educational agency to any public or private elementary school or secondary school.

(xvii) Developing and implementing character education programs, as a component of drug and violence prevention programs, that take into account the views of parents of the students for whom the program is intended and such students, such as a program described in subpart 3 of part D of subchapter V of this chapter.

(xviii) Establishing and maintaining a school safety hotline.

(xix) Community service, including community service performed by expelled students, and service-learning projects.

(xx) Conducting a nationwide background check of each local educational agency employee, regardless of when hired, and prospective employees for the purpose of determining whether the employee or prospective employee has been convicted of a crime that bears upon the employee's fitness -

(I) to be responsible for the safety or well-being of children;

(II) to serve in the particular capacity in which the employee or prospective employee is or will be employed; or

(III) to otherwise be employed by the local educational agency.

(xxi) Programs to train school personnel to identify warning signs of youth suicide and to create an action plan to help youth at risk of suicide.

(xxii) Programs that respond to the needs of students who are faced with domestic violence or child abuse.

(F) The evaluation of any of the activities authorized under this subsection and the collection of objective data used to assess program needs, program implementation, or program success in achieving program goals and objectives.

(c) Limitation

(1) In general

Except as provided in paragraph (2), not more than 40 percent of the funds available to a local educational agency under this subpart may be used to carry out the activities described in clauses (ii) through (vi) of subsection (b)(2)(E) of this section, of which not more than 50 percent of such amount may be used to carry out the activities described in clauses (ii) through (v) of such subsection.

(2) Exception

A local educational agency may use funds under this subpart for activities described in clauses (ii) through (v) of subsection (b)(2)(E) of this section only if funding for these activities is not received from other Federal agencies.

(d) Rule of construction

Nothing in this section shall be construed to prohibit the use of funds under this subpart by any local educational agency or school for the establishment or implementation of a school uniform policy if such policy is part of the overall comprehensive drug and violence prevention plan of the State involved and is supported by the State's needs assessment and other scientifically based research information.

Sec. 7116. Reporting

(a) State report

(1) In general

By December 1, 2003, and every 2 years thereafter, the chief executive officer of the State, in cooperation with the State educational agency, shall submit to the Secretary a report -

(A) on the implementation and outcomes of State programs under section 7112(a)(1) of this title and section 7112(c) of this title and local educational agency programs under section 7115(b) of this title, as well as an assessment of their effectiveness;

(B) on the State's progress toward attaining its performance measures for drug and violence prevention under section 7113(a)(10) of this title; and

(C) on the State's efforts to inform parents of, and include parents in, violence and drug prevention efforts.

(2) Special rule

The report required by this subsection shall be -

(A) in the form specified by the Secretary;

(B) based on the State's ongoing evaluation activities, and shall include data on the incidence and prevalence, age of onset, perception of health risk, and perception of social disapproval of drug use and violence by youth in schools and communities; and

(C) made readily available to the public.

(b) Local educational agency report

(1) In general

Each local educational agency receiving funds under this subpart shall submit to the State educational agency such information that the State requires to complete the State report required by subsection (a) of this section, including a description of how parents were informed of, and participated in, violence and drug prevention efforts.

(2) Availability

Information under paragraph (1) shall be made readily available to the public.

(3) Provision of documentation

Not later than January 1 of each year that a State is required to report under subsection (a) of this section, the Secretary shall provide to the State educational agency all of the necessary documentation required for compliance with this section.

Sec. 7117. Programs for Native Hawaiians

(a) General authority

From the funds made available pursuant to section 7111(a)(1)(C) of this title to carry out this section, the Secretary shall make grants to or enter into cooperative agreements or contracts with organizations primarily serving and representing Native Hawaiians for the benefit of Native Hawaiians to plan, conduct, and administer programs, or portions thereof, that are authorized by and consistent with the provisions of this subpart.

(b) Definition of Native Hawaiian

For the purposes of this section, the term "Native Hawaiian" means any individual any of whose ancestors were natives, prior to 1778, of the area which now comprises the State of Hawaii.

SUBPART 2 - NATIONAL PROGRAMS

Sec. 7131. Federal activities

(a) Program authorized

From funds made available to carry out this subpart under section 7103(2) of this title, the Secretary, in consultation with the Secretary of Health and Human Services, the Director of the Office of National Drug

Control Policy, and the Attorney General, shall carry out programs to prevent the illegal use of drugs and violence among, and promote safety and discipline for, students. The Secretary shall carry out such programs directly, or through grants, contracts, or cooperative agreements with public and private entities and individuals, or through agreements with other Federal agencies, and shall coordinate such programs with other appropriate Federal activities. Such programs may include -

(1) the development and demonstration of innovative strategies for the training of school personnel, parents, and members of the community for drug and violence prevention activities based on State and local needs;

(2) the development, demonstration, scientifically based evaluation, and dissemination of innovative and high quality drug and violence prevention programs and activities, based on State and local needs, which may include -

(A) alternative education models, either established within a school or separate and apart from an existing school, that are designed to promote drug and violence prevention, reduce disruptive behavior, reduce the need for repeat suspensions and expulsions, enable students to meet challenging State academic standards, and enable students to return to the regular classroom as soon as possible;

(B) community service and service-learning projects, designed to rebuild safe and healthy neighborhoods and increase students' sense of individual responsibility;

(C) video-based projects developed by noncommercial telecommunications entities that provide young people with models for conflict resolution and responsible decisionmaking; and

(D) child abuse education and prevention programs for elementary and secondary students;

(3) the provision of information on drug abuse education and prevention to the Secretary of Health and Human Services for dissemination;

(4) the provision of information on violence prevention and education and school safety to the Department of Justice for dissemination;

(5) technical assistance to chief executive officers, State agencies, local educational agencies, and other recipients of funding under this part to build capacity to develop and implement high-quality, effective drug and violence prevention programs consistent with the principles of effectiveness in section 7115(a) of this title;

(6) assistance to school systems that have particularly severe drug and violence problems, including hiring drug prevention and school safety coordinators, or assistance to support appropriate response efforts to crisis situations;

(7) the development of education and training programs, curricula, instructional materials, and professional training and development for preventing and reducing the incidence of crimes and conflicts motivated by hate in localities most directly affected by hate crimes;

(8) activities in communities designated as empowerment zones or enterprise communities that will connect schools to community- wide

efforts to reduce drug and violence problems; and

(9) other activities in accordance with the purpose of this part, based on State and local needs.

(b) Peer review

The Secretary shall use a peer review process in reviewing applications for funds under this section.

Sec. 7132. Impact evaluation

(a) Biennial evaluation

The Secretary, in consultation with the Safe and Drug-Free Schools and Communities Advisory Committee described in section 7134 of this title, shall conduct an independent biennial evaluation of the impact of programs assisted under this subpart and of other recent and new initiatives to combat violence and illegal drug use in schools. The evaluation shall report on whether community and local educational agency programs funded under this subpart -

(1) comply with the principles of effectiveness described in section 7115(a) of this title;

(2) have appreciably reduced the level of illegal drug, alcohol, and tobacco use, and school violence and the illegal presence of weapons at schools; and

(3) have conducted effective parent involvement and training programs.

(b) Data collection

The National Center for Education Statistics shall collect data, that is subject to independent review, to determine the incidence and prevalence of illegal drug use and violence in elementary schools and secondary schools in the States. The collected data shall include incident reports by schools officials, anonymous student surveys, and anonymous teacher surveys.

(c) Biennial report

Not later than January 1, 2003, and every 2 years thereafter, the Secretary shall submit to the President and Congress a report on the findings of the evaluation conducted under subsection (a) of this section together with the data collected under subsection (b) of this section and data available from other sources on the incidence and prevalence, age of onset, perception of health risk, and perception of social disapproval of drug use and violence in elementary schools and secondary schools in the States. The Secretary shall include data submitted by the States pursuant to subsection 7116(a) of this title.

Sec. 7133. Hate crime prevention

(a) Grant authorization

From funds made available to carry out this subpart under section 7103(2) of this title the Secretary may make grants to local educational agencies and community-based organizations for the purpose of providing assistance to localities most directly affected by hate crimes.

(b) Use of funds

(1) Program development

Grants under this section may be used to improve elementary and secondary educational efforts, including -

(A) development of education and training programs designed to prevent and to reduce the incidence of crimes and conflicts motivated by hate;

(B) development of curricula for the purpose of improving conflict or dispute resolution skills of students, teachers, and administrators;

(C) development and acquisition of equipment and instructional materials to meet the needs of, or otherwise be part of, hate crime or conflict programs; and

(D) professional training and development for teachers and administrators on the causes, effects, and resolutions of hate crimes or hate-based conflicts.

(2) Application

In order to be eligible to receive a grant under this section for any fiscal year, a local educational agency, or a local educational agency in conjunction with a community-based organization, shall submit an application to the Secretary in such form and containing such information as the Secretary may reasonably require.

(3) Requirements

Each application under paragraph (2) shall include -

(A) a request for funds for the purpose described in this section;

(B) a description of the schools and communities to be served by the grants; and

(C) assurances that Federal funds received under this section shall be used to supplement, and not supplant, non-Federal funds.

(4) Comprehensive plan

Each application shall include a comprehensive plan that contains -

(A) a description of the hate crime or conflict problems within the schools or the community targeted for assistance;

(B) a description of the program to be developed or augmented by such Federal and matching funds;

(C) assurances that such program or activity shall be administered by or under the supervision of the applicant;

(D) procedures for the proper and efficient administration of such program; and

(E) fiscal control and fund accounting procedures as may be necessary to ensure prudent use, proper disbursement, and accurate accounting of funds received under this section.

(c) Award of grants

(1) Selection of recipients

The Secretary shall consider the incidence of crimes and conflicts motivated by bias in the targeted schools and communities in awarding grants under this section.

(2) Geographic distribution

The Secretary shall attempt, to the extent practicable, to achieve an equitable geographic distribution of grant awards.

(3) Dissemination of information

The Secretary shall attempt, to the extent practicable, to make available information regarding successful hate crime prevention programs, including programs established or expanded with grants under this section.

(d) Reports

The Secretary shall submit to Congress a report every 2 years that shall contain a detailed statement regarding grants and awards, activities of grant recipients, and an evaluation of programs established under this section.

Sec. 7134. Safe and Drug-Free Schools and Communities Advisory Committee

(a) Establishment

(1) In general

There is hereby established an advisory committee to be known as the "Safe and Drug Free Schools and Communities Advisory Committee" (referred to in this section as the "Advisory Committee") to -

(A) consult with the Secretary under subsection (b) of this section;

(B) coordinate Federal school- and community-based substance abuse and violence prevention programs and reduce duplicative research or services;

(C) develop core data sets and evaluation protocols for safe and drug-free school- and community-based programs;

(D) provide technical assistance and training for safe and drug-free school- and community-based programs;

(E) provide for the diffusion of scientifically based research to safe and drug-free school- and community-based programs; and

(F) review other regulations and standards developed under this subchapter.

(2) Composition

The Advisory Committee shall be composed of representatives from -

(A) the Department of Education;

(B) the Centers for Disease Control and Prevention;

(C) the National Institute on Drug Abuse;

(D) the National Institute on Alcoholism and Alcohol Abuse;

(E) the Center for Substance Abuse Prevention;

(F) the Center for Mental Health Services;

(G) the Office of Juvenile Justice and Delinquency Prevention;

(H) the Office of National Drug Control Policy;

(I) State and local governments, including education agencies; and

(J) researchers and expert practitioners.

(3) Consultation

In carrying out its duties under this section, the Advisory Committee shall annually consult with interested State and local coordinators of school- and community-based substance abuse and violence prevention programs and other interested groups.

(b) Programs

(1) In general

From amounts made available under section 7103(2) of this title to carry out this subpart, the Secretary, in consultation with the Advisory Committee, shall carry out scientifically based research programs to strengthen the accountability and effectiveness of the State, chief executive officer's, and national programs under this part.

(2) Grants, contracts or cooperative agreements

The Secretary shall carry out paragraph (1) directly or through grants, contracts, or cooperative agreements with public and private entities and individuals or through agreements with other Federal agencies.

(3) Coordination

The Secretary shall coordinate programs under this section with other appropriate Federal activities.

(4) Activities

Activities that may be carried out under programs funded under this section may include -

(A) the provision of technical assistance and training, in collaboration with other Federal agencies utilizing their expertise and national and regional training systems, for Governors, State educational agencies and local educational agencies to support high quality, effective programs that -

(i) provide a thorough assessment of the substance abuse and violence problem;

(ii) utilize objective data and the knowledge of a wide range of community members;

(iii) develop measurable goals and objectives; and

(iv) implement scientifically based research activities that have been shown to be effective and that meet identified needs;

(B) the provision of technical assistance and training to foster program accountability;

(C) the diffusion and dissemination of best practices and programs;

(D) the development of core data sets and evaluation tools;

(E) program evaluations;

(F) the provision of information on drug abuse education and prevention to the Secretary of Health and Human Services for dissemination by the clearinghouse for alcohol and drug abuse information established under section 290aa(d)(16) of title 42; and

(G) other activities that meet unmet needs related to the purpose of this part and that are undertaken in consultation with the Advisory Committee.

Sec. 7135. National Coordinator Program

(a) In general

From funds made available to carry out this subpart under section 7103(2) of this title, the Secretary may provide for the establishment of a

National Coordinator Program under which the Secretary shall award grants to local educational agencies for the hiring of drug prevention and school safety program coordinators.

(b) Use of funds

Amounts received under a grant under subsection (a) of this section shall be used by local educational agencies to recruit, hire, and train individuals to serve as drug prevention and school safety program coordinators in schools with significant drug and school safety problems. Such coordinators shall be responsible for developing, conducting, and analyzing assessments of drug and crime problems at their schools, and administering the safe and drug-free grant program at such schools.

Sec. 7136. Community service grant program

(a) In general

From funds made available to carry out this subpart under section 7103(2) of this title, the Secretary may make grants to States to carry out programs under which students expelled or suspended from school are required to perform community service.

(b) Allocation

From the amount described in subsection (a) of this section, the Secretary shall allocate among the States -

(1) one-half according to the ratio between the school-aged population of each State and the school-aged population of all the States; and

(2) one-half according to the ratio between the amount each State received under section 6334 of this title for the preceding year and the sum of such amounts received by all the States.

(c) Minimum

For any fiscal year, no State shall be allotted under this section an amount that is less than one-half of 1 percent of the total amount allotted to all the States under this section.

(d) Reallotment

The Secretary may reallot any amount of any allotment to a State if the Secretary determines that the State will be unable to use such amount within 2 years of such allotment. Such reallotments shall be made on the same basis as allotments are made under subsection (b) of this section.

(e) Definition

In this section, the term "State" means each of the 50 States, the District of Columbia, and the Commonwealth of Puerto Rico.

Sec. 7137. School Security Technology and Resource Center

(a) Center

From funds made available to carry out this subpart under section 7103(2) of this title, the Secretary, the Attorney General, and the Secretary of Energy may enter into an agreement for the establishment at the Sandia National Laboratories, in partnership with the National Law Enforcement and Corrections Technology Center - Southeast and the National Center for

Rural Law Enforcement in Little Rock, Arkansas, of a center to be known as the "School Security Technology and Resource Center" (hereafter in this section "the Center").

(b) Administration

The Center established under subsection (a) of this section shall be administered by the Attorney General.

(c) Functions

The center established under subsection (a) of this section shall be a resource to local educational agencies for school security assessments, security technology development, evaluation and implementation, and technical assistance relating to improving school security. The Center will also conduct and publish school violence research, coalesce data from victim communities, and monitor and report on schools that implement school security strategies.

Sec. 7138. National Center for School and Youth Safety

(a) Establishment

From funds made available to carry out this subpart under section 7103(2) of this title, the Secretary of Education and the Attorney General may jointly establish a National Center for School and Youth Safety (in this section referred to as the "Center"). The Secretary of Education and the Attorney General may establish the Center at an existing facility, if the facility has a history of performing two or more of the duties described in subsection (b) of this section. The Secretary of Education and the Attorney General shall jointly appoint a Director of the Center to oversee the operation of the Center.

(b) Duties

The Center shall carry out emergency response, anonymous student hotline, consultation, and information and outreach activities with respect to elementary and secondary school safety, including the following:

(1) Emergency response

The staff of the Center, and such temporary contract employees as the Director of the Center shall determine necessary, shall offer emergency assistance to local communities to respond to school safety crises. Such assistance shall include counseling for victims and the community, assistance to law enforcement to address short-term security concerns, and advice on how to enhance school safety, prevent future incidents, and respond to future incidents.

(2) Anonymous student hotline

The Center shall establish a toll-free telephone number for students to report criminal activity, threats of criminal activity, and other high-risk behaviors such as substance abuse, gang or cult affiliation, depression, or other warning signs of potentially violent behavior. The Center shall relay the reports, without attribution, to local law enforcement or appropriate school hotlines. The Director of the Center shall work with the Attorney General to establish guidelines for Center staff to work with law enforcement around the Nation to relay information reported through the hotline.

(3) Consultation

The Center shall establish a toll-free number for the public to contact staff of the Center for consultation regarding school safety. The Director of the Center shall hire administrative staff and individuals with expertise in enhancing school safety, including individuals with backgrounds in counseling and psychology, education, law enforcement and criminal justice, and community development to assist in the consultation.

(4) Information and outreach

The Center shall compile information about the best practices in school violence prevention, intervention, and crisis management, and shall serve as a clearinghouse for model school safety program information. The staff of the Center shall work to ensure local governments, school officials, parents, students, and law enforcement officials and agencies are aware of the resources, grants, and expertise available to enhance school safety and prevent school crime. The staff of the Center shall give special attention to providing outreach to rural and impoverished communities.

Sec. 7139. Grants to reduce alcohol abuse

(a) In general

The Secretary, in consultation with the Administrator of the Substance Abuse and Mental Health Services Administration, may award grants from funds made available to carry out this subpart under section 7103(2) of this title, on a competitive basis, to local educational agencies to enable such agencies to develop and implement innovative and effective programs to reduce alcohol abuse in secondary schools.

(b) Eligibility

To be eligible to receive a grant under subsection (a) of this section, a local educational agency shall prepare and submit to the Secretary an application at such time, in such manner, and containing such information as the Secretary may require, including -

(1) a description of the activities to be carried out under the grant;

(2) an assurance that such activities will include one or more of the proven strategies for reducing underage alcohol abuse as determined by the Substance Abuse and Mental Health Services Administration;

(3) an explanation of how activities to be carried out under the grant that are not described in paragraph (2) will be effective in reducing underage alcohol abuse, including references to the past effectiveness of such activities;

(4) an assurance that the applicant will submit to the Secretary an annual report concerning the effectiveness of the programs and activities funded under the grant; and

(5) such other information as the Secretary determines appropriate.

(c) Streamlining of process for low-income and rural LEAs The Secretary, in consultation with the Administrator of the Substance Abuse and Mental Health Services Administration, shall develop procedures to make the application process for grants under this section more user-friendly, particularly for low-income and rural local educational agencies.

(d) Reservations

(1) SAMHSA

The Secretary may reserve 20 percent of any amount used to carry out this section to enable the Administrator of the Substance Abuse and Mental Health Services Administration to provide alcohol abuse resources and start-up assistance to local educational agencies receiving grants under this section.

(2) Low-income and rural areas

The Secretary may reserve 25 percent of any amount used to carry out this section to award grants to low-income and rural local educational agencies.

Sec. 7140. Mentoring programs

(a) Purpose; definitions

(1) Purpose

The purpose of this section is to make assistance available to promote mentoring programs for children with greatest need -

    (A) to assist such children in receiving support and guidance from a mentor;

    (B) to improve the academic achievement of such children;

    (C) to improve interpersonal relationships between such children and their peers, teachers, other adults, and family members;

    (D) to reduce the dropout rate of such children; and

    (E) to reduce juvenile delinquency and involvement in gangs by such children.

(2) Definitions

In this part:

    (A) Child with greatest need

The term "child with greatest need" means a child who is at risk of educational failure, dropping out of school, or involvement in criminal or delinquent activities, or who lacks strong positive role models.

    (B) Eligible entity

The term "eligible entity" means -

        (i) a local educational agency;

        (ii) a nonprofit, community-based organization; or

        (iii) a partnership between a local educational agency and a nonprofit, community-based organization.

    (C) Mentor

The term "mentor" means a responsible adult, a postsecondary school student, or a secondary school student who works with a child -

(i) to provide a positive role model for the child;

(ii) to establish a supportive relationship with the child; and

(iii) to provide the child with academic assistance and exposure to new experiences and examples of opportunity that enhance the ability of the child to become a responsible adult.

(D) State

The term "State" means each of the several States, the District of Columbia, the Commonwealth of Puerto Rico, the United States Virgin Islands, Guam, American Samoa, and the Commonwealth of the Northern Mariana Islands.

(b) Grant program

(1) In general

The Secretary may award grants from funds made available to carry out this subpart under section 7103(2) of this title to eligible entities to assist such entities in establishing and supporting mentoring programs and activities for children with greatest need that -

(A) are designed to link such children (particularly children living in rural areas, high-crime areas, or troubled home environments, or children experiencing educational failure) with mentors who -

(i) have received training and support in mentoring;

(ii) have been screened using appropriate reference checks, child and domestic abuse record checks, and criminal background checks; and

(iii) are interested in working with children with greatest need; and

(B) are intended to achieve one or more of the following goals with respect to children with greatest need:

(i) Provide general guidance.

(ii) Promote personal and social responsibility.

(iii) Increase participation in, and enhance the ability to benefit from, elementary and secondary education.

(iv) Discourage illegal use of drugs and alcohol, violence, use of dangerous weapons, promiscuous behavior, and other criminal, harmful, or potentially harmful activity.

(v) Encourage participation in community service and community activities.

(vi) Encourage setting goals and planning for the future, including encouragement of graduation from secondary school and planning for postsecondary education or training.

(viii) Discourage involvement in gangs.

(2) Use of funds

(A) In general

Each eligible entity awarded a grant under this subsection shall use the grant funds for activities that establish or implement a mentoring program, that may include -

(i) hiring of mentoring coordinators and support staff;

(ii) providing for the professional development of mentoring coordinators and support staff;

(iii) recruitment, screening, and training of mentors;

(iv) reimbursement to schools, if appropriate, for the use of school materials or supplies in carrying out the mentoring program;

(v) dissemination of outreach materials;

(vi) evaluation of the mentoring program using scientifically based methods; and

(vii) such other activities as the Secretary may reasonably prescribe by rule.

(B) Prohibited uses

Notwithstanding subparagraph (A), an eligible entity awarded a grant under this section may not use the grant funds -

(i) to directly compensate mentors;

(ii) to obtain educational or other materials or equipment that would otherwise be used in the ordinary course of the eligible entity's operations;

(iii) to support litigation of any kind; or

(iv) for any other purpose reasonably prohibited by the Secretary by rule.

(3) Availability of funds

Funds made available through a grant under this section shall be available for obligation for a period not to exceed 3 years.

(4) Application

Each eligible entity seeking a grant under this section shall submit to the Secretary an application that includes -

(A) a description of the plan for the mentoring program the eligible entity proposes to carry out with such grant;

(B) information on the children expected to be served by the mentoring program for which such grant is sought;

(C) a description of the mechanism the eligible entity will use to match children with mentors based on the needs of the children;

(D) an assurance that no mentor will be assigned to mentor so many children that the assignment will undermine the mentor's ability to be an effective mentor or the mentor's ability to establish a close relationship (a one-to-one relationship, where practicable) with each mentored child;

(E) an assurance that the mentoring program will provide children with a variety of experiences and support, including -

(i) emotional support;

(ii) academic assistance; and

(iii) exposure to experiences that the children might not otherwise encounter on their own;

(F) an assurance that the mentoring program will be monitored to ensure that each child assigned a mentor benefits from that assignment and that the child will be assigned a new mentor if the relationship between the original mentor and the child is not beneficial to the child;

(G) information regarding how mentors and children will be recruited to the mentoring program;

(H) information regarding how prospective mentors will be screened;

(I) information on the training that will be provided to mentors; and

(J) information on the system that the eligible entity will use to manage and monitor information relating to the mentoring program's -

(i) reference checks;

(ii) child and domestic abuse record checks;

(iii) criminal background checks; and

(iv) procedure for matching children with mentors.

(5) Selection

(A) Competitive basis

In accordance with this subsection, the Secretary shall award grants to eligible entities on a competitive basis.

(B) Priority

In awarding grants under subparagraph (A), the Secretary shall give priority to each eligible entity that -

(i) serves children with greatest need living in rural areas, high-crime areas, or troubled home environments, or who attend schools with violence problems;

(ii) provides high quality background screening of mentors training of mentors, and technical assistance in carrying out mentoring programs; or

(iii) proposes a school-based mentoring program.

(C) Other considerations

In awarding grants under subparagraph (A), the Secretary shall also consider -

(i) the degree to which the location of the mentoring program proposed by each eligible entity contributes to a fair distribution of mentoring programs with respect to urban and rural locations;

(ii) the quality of the mentoring program proposed by each eligible entity, including -

(I) the resources, if any, the eligible entity will dedicate to providing children with opportunities for job training or postsecondary education;

(II) the degree to which parents, teachers, community-based organizations, and the local community have participated, or will participate, in the design and implementation of the proposed mentoring program;

(III) the degree to which the eligible entity can ensure that mentors will develop longstanding relationships with the children they mentor;

(IV) the degree to which the mentoring program will serve children with greatest need in the 4th through 8th grades; and

(V) the degree to which the mentoring program will

continue to serve children from the 9th grade through graduation from secondary school, as needed; and

        (iii) the capability of each eligible entity to effectively implement its mentoring program.

    (D) Grant to each State

Notwithstanding any other provision of this subsection, in awarding grants under subparagraph (A), the Secretary shall select not less than one grant recipient from each State for which there is an eligible entity that submits an application of sufficient quality pursuant to paragraph (4).

    (6) Model screening guidelines

    (A) In general

Based on model screening guidelines developed by the Office of Juvenile Programs of the Department of Justice, the Secretary shall develop and distribute to each eligible entity awarded a grant under this section specific model guidelines for the screening of mentors who seek to participate in mentoring programs assisted under this section.

    (B) Background checks

The guidelines developed under this subsection shall include, at a minimum, a requirement that potential mentors be subject to reference checks, child and domestic abuse record checks, and criminal background checks.

SUBPART 3 - GUN POSSESSION

Sec. 7151. Gun-free requirements

(a) Short title

This subpart may be cited as the "Gun-Free Schools Act."

(b) Requirements

(1) In general

Each State receiving Federal funds under any subchapter of this chapter shall have in effect a State law requiring local educational agencies to expel from school for a period of not less than 1 year a student who is determined to have brought a firearm to a school, or to have possessed a firearm at a school, under the jurisdiction of local educational agencies in that State, except that such State law shall allow the chief administering officer of a local educational agency to modify such expulsion requirement for a student on a case-by-case basis if such modification is in writing.

(2) Construction

Nothing in this subpart shall be construed to prevent a State from allowing a local educational agency that has expelled a student from such a student's regular school setting from providing educational services to such student in an alternative setting.

(3) Definition

For the purpose of this section, the term "firearm" has the same meaning given such term in section 921(a) of title 18.

(c) Special rule

The provisions of this section shall be construed in a manner consistent with the Individuals with Disabilities Education Act [20 U.S.C. 1400 et seq.].

(d) Report to State

Each local educational agency requesting assistance from the State educational agency that is to be provided from funds made available to the State under any subchapter of this chapter shall provide to the State, in the application requesting such assistance -

(1) an assurance that such local educational agency is in compliance with the State law required by subsection (b) of this section; and

(2) a description of the circumstances surrounding any expulsions imposed under the State law required by subsection (b) of this section, including -

(A) the name of the school concerned;

(B) the number of students expelled from such school; and

(C) the type of firearms concerned.

(e) Reporting

Each State shall report the information described in subsection (d) of this section to the Secretary on an annual basis.

(f) Definition

For the purpose of subsection (d) of this section, the term "school" means any setting that is under the control and supervision of the local educational agency for the purpose of student activities approved and authorized by the local educational agency.

(g) Exception

Nothing in this section shall apply to a firearm that is lawfully stored inside a locked vehicle on school property, or if it is for activities approved and authorized by the local educational agency and the local educational agency adopts appropriate safeguards to ensure student safety.

(h) Policy regarding criminal justice system referral

(1) In general

No funds shall be made available under any subchapter of this chapter to any local educational agency unless such agency has a policy requiring referral to the criminal justice or juvenile delinquency system of any student who brings a firearm or weapon to a school served by such agency.

(2) Definition

For the purpose of this subsection, the term "school" has the same meaning given to such term by section 921(a) of title 18.

SUBPART 4 - GENERAL PROVISIONS

Sec. 7161. Definitions

In this part:

(1) Controlled substance

The term "controlled substance" means a drug or other substance identified under Schedule I, II, III, IV, or V in section 812(c) of title 21.

(2) Drug

The term "drug" includes controlled substances; the illegal use of alcohol and tobacco; and the harmful, abusive, or addictive use of substances, including inhalants and anabolic steroids.

(3) Drug and violence prevention

The term "drug and violence prevention" means -

(A) with respect to drugs, prevention, early intervention, rehabilitation referral, or education related to the illegal use of drugs;

(B) with respect to violence, the promotion of school safety, such that students and school personnel are free from violent and disruptive acts, including sexual harassment and abuse, and victimization associated with prejudice and intolerance, on school premises, going to and from school, and at school- sponsored activities, through the creation and maintenance of a school environment that is free of weapons and fosters individual responsibility and respect for the rights of others.

(4) Hate crime

The term "hate crime" means a crime as described in section 1(b) of the Hate Crime Statistics Act of 1990.

(5) Nonprofit

The term "nonprofit," as applied to a school, agency, organization, or institution means a school, agency, organization, or institution owned and operated by one or more nonprofit corporations or associations, no part of the net earnings of which inures, or may lawfully inure, to the benefit of any private shareholder or individual.

(6) Protective factor, buffer, or asset

The terms "protective factor," "buffer," and "asset" mean any one of a number of the community, school, family, or peer individual domains that are known, through prospective, longitudinal research efforts, or which are grounded in a well- established theoretical model of prevention, and have been shown to prevent alcohol, tobacco, or illegal drug use, as well as violent behavior, by youth in the community, and which promote positive youth development.

(7) Risk factor

The term "risk factor" means any one of a number of characteristics of the community, school, family, or peer- individual domains that are known, through prospective, longitudinal research efforts, to be predictive of alcohol, tobacco, and illegal drug use, as well as violent behavior, by youth in the school and community.

(8) School-aged population

The term "school-aged population" means the population aged five through 17, as determined by the Secretary on the basis of the most recent satisfactory data available from the Department of Commerce.

(9) School based mental health services provider

The term "school based mental health services provider" includes a State-licensed or State-certified school counselor, school psychologist, school social worker, or other State-licensed or -certified mental health professional qualified under State law to provide such services to children and adolescents.

(10) School personnel

The term "school personnel" includes teachers, principals, administrators, counselors, social workers, psychologists, nurses, librarians, and other support staff who are employed by a school or who perform services for the school on a contractual basis.

(11) School resource officer

The term "school resource officer" means a career law enforcement officer, with sworn authority, deployed in community oriented policing, and assigned by the employing police department to a local educational agency to work in collaboration with schools and community based organizations to -

(A) educate students in crime and illegal drug use prevention and safety;

(B) develop or expand community justice initiatives for students; and

(C) train students in conflict resolution, restorative justice, and crime and illegal drug use awareness.

Sec. 7162. Message and materials

(a) "Wrong and harmful" message

Drug and violence prevention programs supported under this part shall convey a clear and consistent message that the illegal use of drugs and acts of violence are wrong and harmful.

(b) Curriculum

The Secretary shall not prescribe the use of specific curricula for programs supported under this part.

Sec. 7163. Parental consent

Upon receipt of written notification from the parents or legal guardians of a student, the local educational agency shall withdraw such student from any program or activity funded under this part. The local educational agency shall make reasonable efforts to inform parents or legal guardians of the content of such programs or activities funded under this part, other than classroom instruction.

Sec. 7164. Prohibited uses of funds

No funds under this part may be used for -

(1) construction (except for minor remodeling needed to accomplish the purposes of this part); or

(2) medical services, drug treatment or rehabilitation, except for pupil services or referral to treatment for students who are victims of, or witnesses to, crime or who illegally use drugs.

Sec. 7165. Transfer of school disciplinary records

(a) Nonapplication of provisions

This section shall not apply to any disciplinary records with respect to a suspension or expulsion that are transferred from a private, parochial or other nonpublic school, person, institution, or other entity, that provides education below the college level.

(b) Disciplinary records

In accordance with the Family Educational Rights and Privacy Act of 1974 (20 U.S.C. 1232g), not later than 2 years after January 8 2002, each State receiving Federal funds under this chapter shall provide an assurance to the Secretary that the State has a procedure in place to facilitate the transfer of disciplinary records, with respect to a suspension or expulsion, by local educational agencies to any private or public elementary school or secondary school for any student who is enrolled or seeks, intends, or is instructed to enroll, on a full- or part-time basis, in the school.

II. GUN-FREE SCHOOL ZONES ACT

18 U.S.C. § 922(q)

(q)(1) The Congress finds and declares that –

(A) crime, particularly crime involving drugs and guns, is a pervasive, nationwide problem;

(B) crime at the local level is exacerbated by the interstate movement of drugs, guns, and criminal gangs;

(C) firearms and ammunition move easily in interstate commerce and have been found in increasing numbers in and around schools, as documented in numerous hearings in both the Committee on the Judiciary of the House of Representatives and the Committee on the Judiciary of the Senate;

(D) in fact, even before the sale of a firearm, the gun, its component parts, ammunition, and the raw materials from which they are made have considerably moved in interstate commerce;

(E) while criminals freely move from State to State, ordinary citizens and foreign visitors may fear to travel to or through certain parts of the country due to concern about violent crime and gun violence, and parents may decline to send their children to school for the same reason;

(F) the occurrence of violent crime in school zones has resulted in a decline in the quality of education in our country;

(G) this decline in the quality of education has an adverse impact on interstate commerce and the foreign commerce of the United States;

(H) States, localities, and school systems find it almost impossible to handle gun-related crime by themselves – even States, localities, and school systems that have made strong efforts to prevent, detect, and punish gun-related crime find their efforts unavailing due in part to the failure or inability of other States or localities to take strong measures; and

(I) the Congress has the power, under the interstate commerce clause and other provisions of the Constitution, to enact measures to ensure the integrity and safety of the Nation's schools by enactment of this subsection.

(2)(A) It shall be unlawful for any individual knowingly to possess a firearm that has moved in or that otherwise affects interstate or foreign commerce at a place that the individual knows, or has reasonable cause to believe, is a school zone.

(B) Subparagraph (A) does not apply to the possession of a firearm –

(i) on private property not part of school grounds;

(ii) if the individual possessing the firearm is licensed to do so by the State in which the school zone is located or a political subdivision of the State, and the law of the State or political subdivision requires that, before an individual obtains such a license, the law enforcement authorities of the State or political subdivision verify that the individual is qualified under law to receive the license;

(iii) that is –

(I) not loaded; and

(II) in a locked container, or a locked firearms rack that is on a motor vehicle;

(iv) by an individual for use in a program approved by a school in the school zone;

(v) by an individual in accordance with a contract entered into between a school in the school zone and the individual or an employer of the individual;

(vi) by a law enforcement officer acting in his or her official capacity; or

(vii) that is unloaded and is possessed by an individual while traversing school premises for the purpose of gaining access to public or private lands open to hunting, if the entry on school premises is authorized by school authorities.

(3)(A) Except as provided in subparagraph (B), it shall be unlawful for any person, knowingly or with reckless disregard for the safety of another, to discharge or attempt to discharge a firearm that has moved in or that otherwise affects interstate or foreign commerce at a place that the person knows is a school zone.

(B) Subparagraph (A) does not apply to the discharge of a firearm –

(i) on private property not part of school grounds;

(ii) as part of a program approved by a school in the school zone, by an individual who is participating in the program;

(iii) by an individual in accordance with a contract entered into between a school in a school zone and the individual or an employer of the individual; or

(iv) by a law enforcement officer acting in his or her official capacity.

(4) Nothing in this subsection shall be construed as preempting or preventing a State or local government from enacting a statute establishing gun free school zones as provided in this subsection.

III. JEANNE CLERY DISCLOSURE OF CAMPUS SECURITY POLICY AND CAMPUS CRIME STATISTICS ACT

20 U.S.C. § 1092(f)

Disclosure of campus security policy and campus crime statistics

(1) Each eligible institution participating in any program under this subchapter and part C of subchapter I of chapter 34 of title 42 shall on August 1, 1991, begin to collect the following information with respect to campus crime statistics and campus security policies of that institution, and beginning September 1, 1992, and each year thereafter, prepare, publish, and distribute, through appropriate publications or mailings, to all current students and employees, and to any applicant for enrollment or employment upon request, an annual security report containing at least the following information with respect to the campus security policies and campus crime statistics of that institution:
(A) A statement of current campus policies regarding procedures and facilities for students and others to report criminal actions or other emergencies occurring on campus and policies concerning the institution's response to such reports.
(B) A statement of current policies concerning security and access to campus facilities, including campus residences, and security considerations used in the maintenance of campus facilities.
(C) A statement of current policies concerning campus law enforcement, including –
(i) the enforcement authority of security personnel, including their working relationship with State and local police agencies; and
(ii) policies which encourage accurate and prompt reporting of all crimes to the campus police and the appropriate police agencies.
(D) A description of the type and frequency of programs designed to inform students and employees about campus security procedures and practices and to encourage students and employees to be responsible for their own security and the security of others.
(E) A description of programs designed to inform students and employees about the prevention of crimes.
(F) Statistics concerning the occurrence on campus, in or on noncampus buildings or property, and on public property during the most

recent calendar year, and during the 2 preceding calendar years for which data are available –

(i) of the following criminal offenses reported to campus security authorities or local police agencies:

(I) murder;

(II) sex offenses, forcible or nonforcible;

(III) robbery;

(IV) aggravated assault;

(V) burglary;

(VI) motor vehicle theft;

(VII) manslaughter;

(VIII) arson; and

(IX) arrests or persons referred for campus disciplinary action for liquor law violations, drug-related violations, and weapons possession; and

(ii) of the crimes described in subclauses (I) through (VIII) of clause (i), and other crimes involving bodily injury to any person in which the victim is intentionally selected because of the actual or perceived race, gender, religion, sexual orientation, ethnicity, or disability of the victim that are reported to campus security authorities or local police agencies, which data shall be collected and reported according to category of prejudice.

(G) A statement of policy concerning the monitoring and recording through local police agencies of criminal activity at off-campus student organizations which are recognized by the institution and that are engaged in by students attending the institution, including those student organizations with off-campus housing facilities.

(H) A statement of policy regarding the possession, use, and sale of alcoholic beverages and enforcement of State underage drinking laws and a statement of policy regarding the possession, use, and sale of illegal drugs and enforcement of Federal and State drug laws and a description of any drug or alcohol abuse education programs as required under section 1011i of this title.

(I) A statement advising the campus community where law enforcement agency information provided by a State under section 14071(j) of title 42, concerning registered sex offenders may be obtained, such as the law enforcement office of the institution, a local law enforcement agency with jurisdiction for the campus, or a computer network address.

(2) Nothing in this subsection shall be construed to authorize the Secretary to require particular policies, procedures, or practices by institutions of higher education with respect to campus crimes or campus security.

(3) Each institution participating in any program under this subchapter and part C of subchapter I of chapter 34 of title 42 shall make timely reports to the campus community on crimes considered to be a threat to other students and employees described in paragraph (1)(F) that are reported to campus

security or local law police agencies. Such reports shall be provided to students and employees in a manner that is timely and that will aid in the prevention of similar occurrences.

(4)(A) Each institution participating in any program under this subchapter and part C of subchapter I of chapter 34 of title 42 that maintains a police or security department of any kind shall make, keep, and maintain a daily log, written in a form that can be easily understood, recording all crimes reported to such police or security department, including-
    (i) the nature, date, time, and general location of each crime; and
    (ii) the disposition of the complaint, if known.

    (B)(i) All entries that are required pursuant to this paragraph shall, except where disclosure of such information is prohibited by law or such disclosure would jeopardize the confidentiality of the victim, be open to public inspection within two business days of the initial report being made to the department or a campus security authority.
    (ii) If new information about an entry into a log becomes available to a police or security department, then the new information shall be recorded in the log not later than two business days after the information becomes available to the police or security department.
    (iii) If there is clear and convincing evidence that the release of such information would jeopardize an ongoing criminal investigation or the safety of an individual, cause a suspect to flee or evade detection, or result in the destruction of evidence, such information may be withheld until that damage is no longer likely to occur from the release of such information.

(5) On an annual basis, each institution participating in any program under this subchapter and part C of subchapter I of chapter 34 of title 42 shall submit to the Secretary a copy of the statistics required to be made available under paragraph (1)(F). The Secretary shall –
    (A) review such statistics and report to the Committee on Education and the Workforce of the House of Representatives and the Committee on Labor and Human Resources of the Senate on campus crime statistics by September 1, 2000;
    (B) make copies of the statistics submitted to the Secretary available to the public; and
    (C) in coordination with representatives of institutions of higher education, identify exemplary campus security policies, procedures, and practices and disseminate information concerning those policies, procedures, and practices that have proven effective in the reduction of campus crime.

(6)(A) In this subsection:
    (i) The term "campus" means –
        (I) any building or property owned or controlled by an

institution of higher education within the same reasonably contiguous geographic area of the institution and used by the institution in direct support of, or in a manner related to, the institution's educational purposes, including residence halls; and

(II) property within the same reasonably contiguous geographic area of the institution that is owned by the institution but controlled by another person, is used by students, and supports institutional purposes (such as a food or other retail vendor).

(ii) The term "noncampus building or property" means-

(I) any building or property owned or controlled by a student organization recognized by the institution; and

(II) any building or property (other than a branch campus) owned or controlled by an institution of higher education that is used in direct support of, or in relation to, the institution's educational purposes, is used by students, and is not within the same reasonably contiguous geographic area of the institution.

(iii) The term "public property" means all public property that is within the same reasonably contiguous geographic area of the institution, such as a sidewalk, a street, other thoroughfare, or parking facility, and is adjacent to a facility owned or controlled by the institution if the facility is used by the institution in direct support of, or in a manner related to the institution's educational purposes.

(B) In cases where branch campuses of an institution of higher education, schools within an institution of higher education, or administrative divisions within an institution are not within a reasonably contiguous geographic area, such entities shall be considered separate campuses for purposes of the reporting requirements of this section.

(7) The statistics described in paragraph (1)(F) shall be compiled in accordance with the definitions used in the uniform crime reporting system of the Department of Justice, Federal Bureau of Investigation, and the modifications in such definitions as implemented pursuant to the Hate Crime Statistics Act. Such statistics shall not identify victims of crimes or persons accused of crimes.

(8)(A) Each institution of higher education participating in any program under this subchapter and part C of subchapter I of chapter 34 of title 42 shall develop and distribute as part of the report described in paragraph (1) a statement of policy regarding-

(i) such institution's campus sexual assault programs, which shall be aimed at prevention of sex offenses; and

(ii) the procedures followed once a sex offense has occurred.

(B) The policy described in subparagraph (A) shall address the following areas:

(i) Education programs to promote the awareness of rape, acquaintance rape, and other sex offenses.

(ii) Possible sanctions to be imposed following the final determination of an on-campus disciplinary procedure regarding rape, acquaintance rape, or other sex offenses, forcible or nonforcible.

(iii) Procedures students should follow if a sex offense occurs, including who should be contacted, the importance of preserving evidence as may be necessary to the proof of criminal sexual assault, and to whom the alleged offense should be reported.

(iv) Procedures for on-campus disciplinary action in cases of alleged sexual assault, which shall include a clear statement that –

(I) the accuser and the accused are entitled to the same opportunities to have others present during a campus disciplinary proceeding; and

(II) both the accuser and the accused shall be informed of the outcome of any campus disciplinary proceeding brought alleging a sexual assault.

(v) Informing students of their options to notify proper law enforcement authorities, including on-campus and local police, and the option to be assisted by campus authorities in notifying such authorities, if the student so chooses.

(vi) Notification of students of existing counseling, mental health or student services for victims of sexual assault, both on campus and in the community.

(vii) Notification of students of options for, and available assistance in, changing academic and living situations after an alleged sexual assault incident, if so requested by the victim and if such changes are reasonably available.

(C) Nothing in this paragraph shall be construed to confer a private right of action upon any person to enforce the provisions of this paragraph.

(9) The Secretary shall provide technical assistance in complying with the provisions of this section to an institution of higher education who requests such assistance.

(10) Nothing in this section shall be construed to require the reporting or disclosure of privileged information.

(11) The Secretary shall report to the appropriate committees of Congress each institution of higher education that the Secretary determines is not in compliance with the reporting requirements of this subsection.

(12) For purposes of reporting the statistics with respect to crimes described in paragraph (1)(F), an institution of higher education shall distinguish, by means of separate categories, any criminal offenses that occur –

(A) on campus;

(B) in or on a noncampus building or property;

(C) on public property; and

(D) in dormitories or other residential facilities for students on campus.

(13) Upon a determination pursuant to section 1094(c)(3)(B) of this title that an institution of higher education has substantially misrepresented the number, location, or nature of the crimes required to be reported under this subsection, the Secretary shall impose a civil penalty upon the institution in the same amount and pursuant to the same procedures as a civil penalty is imposed under section 1094(c)(3)(B) of this title.

(14)(A) Nothing in this subsection may be construed to –

(i) create a cause of action against any institution of higher education or any employee of such an institution for any civil liability; or

(ii) establish any standard of care.

(B) Notwithstanding any other provision of law, evidence regarding compliance or noncompliance with this subsection shall not be admissible as evidence in any proceeding of any court, agency, board, or other entity, except with respect to an action to enforce this subsection.

(15) This subsection may be cited as the "Jeanne Clery Disclosure of Campus Security Policy and Campus Crime Statistics Act."

IV. FEDERAL REGULATIONS IMPLEMENTING THE JEANNE CLERY DISCLOSURE OF CAMPUS SECURITY POLICY AND CAMPUS CRIME STATISTICS ACT

TITLE 34 – EDUCATION

CHAPTER VI – OFFICE OF POSTSECONDARY EDUCATION, DEPARTMENT OF EDUCATION

PART 668 STUDENT ASSISTANCE GENERAL PROVISIONS – Table of Contents

Subpart D Institutional and Financial Assistance Information for Students

Sec. 668.41 Reporting and disclosure of information.

Source: 51 FR 43323, Dec. 1, 1986, unless otherwise noted.

(a) Definitions. The following definitions apply to this subpart:

Athletically related student aid means any scholarship, grant, or other form of financial assistance, offered by an institution, the terms of which require the recipient to participate in a program of intercollegiate athletics at the institution. Other student aid, of which a student-athlete simply happens to be the recipient, is not athletically related student aid.

Certificate or degree-seeking student means a student enrolled in a course of credit who is recognized by the institution as seeking a degree or certificate.

First-time undergraduate student means an entering undergraduate who has never attended any institution of higher education. It includes a student enrolled in the fall term who attended a postsecondary institution for the first time in the prior summer term, and a student who entered with advanced standing (college credit earned before graduation from high school).

Normal time is the amount of time necessary for a student to complete all requirements for a degree or certificate according to the institution's catalog. This is typically four years for a bachelor's degree in a standard term-based institution, two years for an associate degree in a standard term-based institution, and the various scheduled times for certificate programs.

Notice means a notification of the availability of information an institution is required by this subpart to disclose, provided to an individual on a one-to-one basis through an appropriate mailing or publication, including direct mailing through the U.S. Postal Service, campus mail, or electronic mail. Posting on an Internet website or an Intranet website does not constitute a notice.

Official fall reporting date means that date (in the fall) on which an institution must report fall enrollment data to either the State, its board of trustees or governing board, or some other external governing body.

Prospective employee means an individual who has contacted an eligible institution for the purpose of requesting information concerning employment with that institution.

Prospective student means an individual who has contacted an eligible institution requesting information concerning admission to that institution.

Undergraduate students, for purposes of Sec. Sec. 668.45 and 668.48 only, means students enrolled in a bachelor's degree program, an associate degree program, or a vocational or technical program below the baccalaureate.

(b) Disclosure through Internet or Intranet websites. Subject to paragraphs (c)(2), (e)(2) through (4), or (g)(1)(ii) of this section, as appropriate, an institution may satisfy any requirement to disclose information under paragraph (d), (e), or (g) of this section for-

(1) Enrolled students or current employees by posting the information on an Internet website or an Intranet website that is reasonably accessible to the individuals to whom the information must be disclosed; and

(2) Prospective students or prospective employees by posting the information on an Internet website.

(c) Notice to enrolled students.

(1) An institution annually must distribute to all enrolled students a notice of the availability of the information required to be disclosed pursuant to paragraphs (d), (e), and (g) of this section, and pursuant to 34 CFR 99.7 (Sec. 99.7 sets forth the notification requirements of the Family Educational Rights and Privacy Act of 1974). The notice must list and briefly describe the information and tell the student how to obtain the information.

(2) An institution that discloses information to enrolled students as required under paragraph (d), (e), or (g) of this section by posting the information on an Internet website or an Intranet website must include in the notice described in paragraph (c)(1) of this section-

(i) The exact electronic address at which the information is posted; and

(ii) A statement that the institution will provide a paper copy of the information on request.

(d) General disclosures for enrolled or prospective students. An institution must make available to any enrolled student or prospective student, on request, through appropriate publications, mailings or electronic media, information concerning-

(1) Financial assistance available to students enrolled in the institution (pursuant to Sec. 668.42);

(2) The institution (pursuant to Sec. 668.43); and

(3) The institution's completion or graduation rate and, if

applicable, its transfer-out rate (pursuant to Sec. 668.45). In the case of a request from a prospective student, the information must be made available prior to the student's enrolling or entering into any financial obligation with the institution.

(e) Annual security report –

(1) Enrolled students and current employees – annual security report. By October 1 of each year, an institution must distribute, to all enrolled students and current employees, its annual security report described in Sec. 668.46(b), through appropriate publications and mailings, including –

(i) Direct mailing to each individual through the U.S. Postal Service, campus mail, or electronic mail;

(ii) A publication or publications provided directly to each individual; or

(iii) Posting on an Internet website or an Intranet website, subject to paragraphs (e)(2) and (3) of this section.

(2) Enrolled students – annual security report. If an institution chooses to distribute its annual security report to enrolled students by posting the disclosure on an Internet website or an Intranet website, the institution must comply with the requirements of paragraph (c)(2) of this section.

(3) Current employees – annual security report. If an institution chooses to distribute its annual security report to current employees by posting the disclosure on an Internet website or an Intranet website, the institution must, by October 1 of each year, distribute to all current employees a notice that includes a statement of the report's availability, the exact electronic address at which the report is posted, a brief description of the report's contents, and a statement that the institution will provide a paper copy of the report upon request.

(4) Prospective students and prospective employees – annual security report. The institution must provide a notice to prospective students and prospective employees that includes a statement of the report's availability, a description of its contents, and an opportunity to request a copy. An institution must provide its annual security report, upon request, to a prospective student or prospective employee. If the institution chooses to provide its annual security report to prospective students and prospective employees by posting the disclosure on an Internet website, the notice described in this paragraph must include the exact electronic address at which the report is posted, a brief description of the report, and a statement that the institution will provide a paper copy of the report upon request.

(5) Submission to the Secretary – annual security report. Each year, by the date and in a form specified by the Secretary, an institution must submit the statistics required by Sec. 668.46(c) to the Secretary.

(f) Prospective student-athletes and their parents, high school coach and guidance counselor – report on completion or graduation rates for student-athletes. (1)(i) Except under the circumstances described in paragraph (f)(1)(ii) of this section, when an institution offers a prospective student-athlete athletically related student aid, it must provide to the prospective student-athlete, and his or her parents, high school coach, and guidance counselor, the report produced pursuant to Sec. 668.48(a).

(ii) An institution's responsibility under paragraph (f)(1)(i) of this section with reference to a prospective student athlete's high school coach and guidance counselor is satisfied if-

(A) The institution is a member of a national collegiate athletic association;

(B) The association compiles data on behalf of its member institutions, which data the Secretary determines are substantially comparable to those required by Sec. 668.48(a); and

(C) The association distributes the compilation to all secondary schools in the United States.

(2) By July 1 of each year, an institution must submit to the Secretary the report produced pursuant to Sec. 668.48.

(g) Enrolled students, prospective students, and the public – report on athletic program participation rates and financial support data.

(1)(i) An institution of higher education subject to Sec. 668.47 must, not later than October 15 of each year, make available on request to enrolled students, prospective students, and the public, the report produced pursuant to Sec. 668.47(c). The institution must make the report easily accessible to students, prospective students, and the public and must provide the report promptly to anyone who requests it.

(ii) The institution must provide notice to all enrolled students, pursuant to paragraph (c)(1) of this section, and prospective students of their right to request the report described in paragraph (g)(1) of this section. If the institution chooses to make the report available by posting the disclosure on an Internet website or an Intranet website, it must provide in the notice the exact electronic address at which the report is posted, a brief description of the report, and a statement that the institution will provide a paper copy of the report on request. For prospective students, the institution may not use an Intranet website for this purpose.

(2) An institution must submit the report described in paragraph (g)(1)(i) of this section to the Secretary within 15 days of making it available to students, prospective students, and the public.

(Approved by the Office of Management and Budget under control number 1845-0004 and 1845-0010)

(Authority: 20 U.S.C. 1092)

[64 FR 59066, Nov. 1, 1999]

TITLE 34 – EDUCATION

CHAPTER VI – OFFICE OF POSTSECONDARY EDUCATION, DEPARTMENT OF EDUCATION

PART 668   STUDENT ASSISTANCE GENERAL PROVISIONS – Table of Contents

Subpart D Institutional and Financial Assistance Information for Students

Sec. 668.46 Institutional security policies and crime statistics.

(a) Additional definitions that apply to this section.

Business day: Monday through Friday, excluding any day when the institution is closed.

Campus:

(1) Any building or property owned or controlled by an institution within the same reasonably contiguous geographic area and used by the institution in direct support of, or in a manner related to, the institution's educational purposes, including residence halls; and

(2) Any building or property that is within or reasonably contiguous to the area identified in paragraph (1) of this definition, that is owned by the institution but controlled by another person, is frequently used by students, and supports institutional purposes (such as a food or other retail vendor).

Campus security authority:

(1) A campus police department or a campus security department of an institution.

(2) Any individual or individuals who have responsibility for campus security but who do not constitute a campus police department or a campus security department under paragraph (1) of this definition, such as an individual who is responsible for monitoring entrance into institutional property.

(3) Any individual or organization specified in an institution's statement of campus security policy as an individual or organization to which students and employees should report criminal offenses.

(4) An official of an institution who has significant responsibility for student and campus activities, including, but not limited to, student housing, student discipline, and campus judicial proceedings. If such an official is a pastoral or professional counselor as defined below, the official is not considered a campus security authority when acting as a pastoral or professional counselor.

Noncampus building or property:

(1) Any building or property owned or controlled by a student organization that is officially recognized by the institution; or

(2) Any building or property owned or controlled by an institution

that is used in direct support of, or in relation to, the institution's educational purposes, is frequently used by students, and is not within the same reasonably contiguous geographic area of the institution.

Pastoral counselor: A person who is associated with a religious order or denomination, is recognized by that religious order or denomination as someone who provides confidential counseling, and is functioning within the scope of that recognition as a pastoral counselor.

Professional counselor: A person whose official responsibilities include providing mental health counseling to members of the institution's community and who is functioning within the scope of his or her license or certification.

Public property: All public property, including thoroughfares, streets, sidewalks, and parking facilities, that is within the campus, or immediately adjacent to and accessible from the campus.

Referred for campus disciplinary action: The referral of any person to any campus official who initiates a disciplinary action of which a record is kept and which may result in the imposition of a sanction.

(b) Annual security report. An institution must prepare an annual security report that contains, at a minimum, the following information:

(1) The crime statistics described in paragraph (c) of this section.

(2) A statement of current campus policies regarding procedures for students and others to report criminal actions or other emergencies occurring on campus. This statement must include the institution's policies concerning its response to these reports, including –

(i) Policies for making timely warning reports to members of the campus community regarding the occurrence of crimes described in paragraph (c)(1) of this section;

(ii) Policies for preparing the annual disclosure of crime statistics; and

(iii) A list of the titles of each person or organization to whom students and employees should report the criminal offenses described in paragraph (c)(1) of this section for the purpose of making timely warning reports and the annual statistical disclosure. This statement must also disclose whether the institution has any policies or procedures that allow victims or witnesses to report crimes on a voluntary, confidential basis for inclusion in the annual disclosure of crime statistics, and, if so, a description of those policies and procedures.

(3) A statement of current policies concerning security of and access to campus facilities, including campus residences, and security considerations used in the maintenance of campus facilities.

(4) A statement of current policies concerning campus law enforcement that-

(i) Addresses the enforcement authority of security personnel, including their relationship with State and local police agencies and whether those security personnel have the authority to arrest individuals;

(ii) Encourages accurate and prompt reporting of all crimes to

the campus police and the appropriate police agencies; and

(iii) Describes procedures, if any, that encourage pastoral counselors and professional counselors, if and when they deem it appropriate, to inform the persons they are counseling of any procedures to report crimes on a voluntary, confidential basis for inclusion in the annual disclosure of crime statistics.

(5) A description of the type and frequency of programs designed to inform students and employees about campus security procedures and practices and to encourage students and employees to be responsible for their own security and the security of others.

(6) A description of programs designed to inform students and employees about the prevention of crimes.

(7) A statement of policy concerning the monitoring and recording through local police agencies of criminal activity in which students engaged at off-campus locations of student organizations officially recognized by the institution, including student organizations with off-campus housing facilities.

(8) A statement of policy regarding the possession, use, and sale of alcoholic beverages and enforcement of State underage drinking laws.

(9) A statement of policy regarding the possession, use, and sale of illegal drugs and enforcement of Federal and State drug laws.

(10) A description of any drug or alcohol-abuse education programs, as required under section 120(a) through (d) of the HEA. For the purpose of meeting this requirement, an institution may cross-reference the materials the institution uses to comply with section 120(a) through (d) of the HEA.

(11) A statement of policy regarding the institution's campus sexual assault programs to prevent sex offenses, and procedures to follow when a sex offense occurs. The statement must include-

(i) A description of educational programs to promote the awareness of rape, acquaintance rape, and other forcible and nonforcible sex offenses;

(ii) Procedures students should follow if a sex offense occurs, including procedures concerning who should be contacted, the importance of preserving evidence for the proof of a criminal offense, and to whom the alleged offense should be reported;

(iii) Information on a student's option to notify appropriate law enforcement authorities, including on-campus and local police, and a statement that institutional personnel will assist the student in notifying these authorities, if the student requests the assistance of these personnel;

(iv) Notification to students of existing on- and off-campus counseling, mental health, or other student services for victims of sex offenses;

(v) Notification to students that the institution will change a victim's academic and living situations after an alleged sex offense and of the options for those changes, if those changes are requested by the victim and are reasonably available;

(vi) Procedures for campus disciplinary action in cases of an alleged sex offense, including a clear statement that –

(A) The accuser and the accused are entitled to the same opportunities to have others present during a disciplinary proceeding; and

(B) Both the accuser and the accused must be informed of the outcome of any institutional disciplinary proceeding brought alleging a sex offense. Compliance with this paragraph does not constitute a violation of the Family Educational Rights and Privacy Act (20 U.S.C. 1232g). For the purpose of this paragraph, the outcome of a disciplinary proceeding means only the institution's final determination with respect to the alleged sex offense and any sanction that is imposed against the accused; and

(vii) Sanctions the institution may impose following a final determination of an institutional disciplinary proceeding regarding rape, acquaintance rape, or other forcible or nonforcible sex offenses.

(12) Beginning with the annual security report distributed by October 1, 2003, a statement advising the campus community where law enforcement agency information provided by a State under section 170101(j) of the Violent Crime Control and Law Enforcement Act of 1994 (42 U.S.C. 14071(j)), concerning registered sex offenders may be obtained, such as the law enforcement office of the institution, a local law enforcement agency with jurisdiction for the campus, or a computer network address.

(c) Crime statistics-

(1) Crimes that must be reported. An institution must report statistics for the three most recent calendar years concerning the occurrence on campus, in or on noncampus buildings or property, and on public property of the following that are reported to local police agencies or to a campus security authority:

(i) Criminal homicide:

(A) Murder and nonnegligent manslaughter.

(B) Negligent manslaughter.

(ii) Sex offenses:

(A) Forcible sex offenses.

(B) Nonforcible sex offenses.

(iii) Robbery.

(iv) Aggravated assault.

(v) Burglary.

(vi) Motor vehicle theft.

(vii) Arson.

(viii)(A) Arrests for liquor law violations, drug law violations, and illegal weapons possession.

(B) Persons not included in paragraph (c)(1)(viii)(A) of this section, who were referred for campus disciplinary action for liquor law violations, drug law violations, and illegal weapons possession.

(2) Recording crimes. An institution must record a crime statistic in its annual security report for the calendar year in which the crime was

reported to a campus security authority.

(3) Reported crimes if a hate crime. An institution must report, by category of prejudice, any crime it reports pursuant to paragraphs (c)(1)(i) through (vii) of this section, and any other crime involving bodily injury reported to local police agencies or to a campus security authority, that manifest evidence that the victim was intentionally selected because of the victim's actual or perceived race, gender, religion, sexual orientation, ethnicity, or disability.

(4) Crimes by location. The institution must provide a geographic breakdown of the statistics reported under paragraphs (c)(1) and (3) of this section according to the following categories:

(i) On campus.

(ii) Of the crimes in paragraph (c)(4)(i) of this section, the number of crimes that took place in dormitories or other residential facilities for students on campus.

(iii) In or on a noncampus building or property.

(iv) On public property.

(5) Identification of the victim or the accused. The statistics required under paragraphs (c)(1) and (3) of this section may not include the identification of the victim or the person accused of committing the crime.

(6) Pastoral and professional counselor. An institution is not required to report statistics under paragraphs (c)(1) and (3) of this section for crimes reported to a pastoral or professional counselor.

(7) UCR definitions. An institution must compile the crime statistics required under paragraphs (c)(1) and (3) of this section using the definitions of crimes provided in appendix A to this subpart and the Federal Bureau of Investigation's Uniform Crime Reporting (UCR) Hate Crime Data Collection Guidelines and Training Guide for Hate Crime Data Collection. For further guidance concerning the application of definitions and classification of crimes, an institution must use either the UCR Reporting Handbook or the UCR Reporting Handbook: NIBRS EDITION, except that in determining how to report crimes committed in a multiple-offense situation an institution must use the UCR Reporting Handbook. Copies of the UCR publications referenced in this paragraph are available from: FBI, Communications Unit, 1000 Custer Hollow Road, Clarksburg, WV 26306 (telephone: 304-625-2823).

(8) Use of a map. In complying with the statistical reporting requirements under paragraphs (c)(1) and (3) of this section, an institution may provide a map to current and prospective students and employees that depicts its campus, noncampus buildings or property, and public property areas if the map accurately depicts its campus, noncampus buildings or property, and public property areas.

(9) Statistics from police agencies. In complying with the statistical reporting requirements under paragraphs (c)(1) through (4) of this section, an institution must make a reasonable, good faith effort to obtain the required statistics and may rely on the information supplied by a local or

State police agency. If the institution makes such a reasonable, good faith effort, it is not responsible for the failure of the local or State police agency to supply the required statistics.

(d) Separate campus. An institution must comply with the requirements of this section for each separate campus.

(e) Timely warning.

(1) An institution must, in a manner that is timely and will aid in the prevention of similar crimes, report to the campus community on crimes that are –

(i) Described in paragraph (c)(1) and (3) of this section;

(ii) Reported to campus security authorities as identified under the institution's statement of current campus policies pursuant to paragraph (b)(2) of this section or local police agencies; and

(iii) Considered by the institution to represent a threat to students and employees.

(2) An institution is not required to provide a timely warning with respect to crimes reported to a pastoral or professional counselor.

(f) Crime log.

(1) An institution that maintains a campus police or a campus security department must maintain a written, easily understood daily crime log that records, by the date the crime was reported, any crime that occurred on campus, on a noncampus building or property, on public property, or within the patrol jurisdiction of the campus police or the campus security department and is reported to the campus police or the campus security department. This log must include-

(i) The nature, date, time, and general location of each crime; and

(ii) The disposition of the complaint, if known.

(2) The institution must make an entry or an addition to an entry to the log within two business days, as defined under paragraph (a) of this section, of the report of the information to the campus police or the campus security department, unless that disclosure is prohibited by law or would jeopardize the confidentiality of the victim.

(3)(i) An institution may withhold information required under paragraphs (f)(1) and (2) of this section if there is clear and convincing evidence that the release of the information would –

(A) Jeopardize an ongoing criminal investigation or the safety of an individual;

(B) Cause a suspect to flee or evade detection; or

(C) Result in the destruction of evidence.

(ii) The institution must disclose any information withheld under paragraph (f)(3)(i) of this section once the adverse effect described in that paragraph is no longer likely to occur.

(4) An institution may withhold under paragraphs (f)(2) and (3) of this section only that information that would cause the adverse effects described in those paragraphs.

(5) The institution must make the crime log for the most recent 60-day period open to public inspection during normal business hours. The institution must make any portion of the log older than 60 days available within two business days of a request for public inspection.

(Approved by the Office of Management and Budget under control number 1845-0022)

(Authority: 20 U.S.C. 1092)

[64 FR 59069, Nov. 1, 1999, as amended at 65 FR 65637, Nov. 1, 2000; 67 FR 66520, Oct. 31, 2002]

CHAPTER NINE

Forms

Form I-1: Staff Skills Inventory

(To be conducted annually)

Name: _____   Room #: _____

Please check any of the following areas in which you have expertise or training:

Emergency Response:

__ First Aid   __ Search and Rescue   __ Emergency Management

__ CPR   __ Law Enforcement   __ CISD (Critical Incident
                                                        Stress Debriefing

__ EMT   __ CB Radio   __ Other (Specify)

__ Firefighting   __ Ham Radio   _____

Mobile/cellular phone to be used in emergency:

_____

____ I speak the following foreign languages:

_____

_____

_____

_____

Source: Virginia Department of Education

Form I-2: Crisis Team Member List

Position/Name	Work Phone	Cell Phone
Principal _____	_____	_____
Ass't Principal_____	_____	_____
Guidance Director _____	_____	_____
School Nurse _____	_____	_____
Resource Officer _____	_____	_____
School Psychologist _____	_____	_____
Social Worker _____	_____	_____
Secretary _____	_____	_____
Teacher _____	_____	_____
Administrator _____	_____	_____
Counselor _____	_____	_____
Custodian _____	_____	_____

Source: Virginia Department of Education

Form I-3: Authorization to Release Children in Emergency

Dear Parents/Guardians:

Our school has developed an emergency business plan for use in the event of a disaster. The emergency plan is devoted to the welfare and safety of your child during school hours. It is available for inspection in the school office.

We are requesting your assistance at this time:
Should there be an emergency, such as a major fire, tornado or explosion, your child may be required to remain in the care of the school until it is deemed safe by an Emergency Services authority that the child can be released. At that point, children may be released only to properly authorized parents/guardians and/or designees. Therefore, please list as many names (with local telephone numbers and addresses) as possible, of those persons to whom you would allow your child's release in the event of an emergency. Be sure to notify those persons listed that you have authorized their supervision in case of an emergency.

If you are unable to come to school, it is essential that others be designated to care for your child. No child will be released to the care of unauthorized persons.

We appreciate your cooperation in this important matter.

CHILD: _____ **TEACHER:** _____ **GRADE:** _____

You may release my child to any of the persons listed below:

Name	*Phone*	*Address*	*Relationship*
_____	_____	_____	_____
_____	_____	_____	_____
_____	_____	_____	_____
_____	_____	_____	_____
_____	_____	_____	_____

Parent/Guardian: _____ Date:_____
                              Signature

Home Phone: _____ Cell/Work Phone: _____

Source: Virginia Department of Education

Form I-4: Situation Involving Weapon

These are steps for key personnel to take in situations involving a weapon at school.

Staff:
1. Notify principal or other designated individual.

2. Remain calm.

3. Avoid heroics.

4. Don't threaten.

5. Keep a safe, non-intimidating distance.

6. Avoid abrupt, sporadic movements.

7. Look to see whether there is a place you can dive or jump to.

8. Negotiate minimally until the principal, a designee or law enforcement personnel arrive.

Administrator or Designee:

1. Assess the situation and decide whether to call a lockdown or to handle the situation on a need-to-know basis.

2. Call 911.

3. Contact the superintendent at telephone number _____.

4. Inform another administrator or designee of the threat, ensuring classes do not change until an "all clear" has been issued.

5. Provide as much information as possible.

- Be prepared to act as a resource and liaison between school and police.

- Have a map of the school and grounds available for police.

6. Gather as much detailed information as possible and try to determine:

- Location, identity and detailed description of individual.

- Location and description of weapon.

- Any pertinent background information regarding the individual, including possible reason for carrying a weapon.

7. Isolate the individual. If the location of the weapon is known, prevent access to it.

8. Remain calm. Try not to raise your voice. If raising your voice becomes necessary, speak decisively and with clarity. Your tone and demeanor will strongly influence the outcome of the crisis.

9. Avoid heroics. Look for a place where you can dive or jump to, and keep a safe, non-intimidating distance.

10. Do not use force or touch the person or weapon. Avoid sudden moves or gestures.

11. Negotiate minimally until law enforcement arrives.

12. Meet with police when they arrive and follow their instructions.

Source: University of Arkansas System, Criminal Justice Institute, School Violence Resource Center

Form I-5: Violent Situations

These are general guidelines to follow when dealing with a violent or
potentially violent individual at school.

Staff:
1. Notify principal or other designated individual.

2. Follow the following guidelines:

- Be empathetic. Try not to be judgmental regarding the
  person's feelings. They are real and must be attended, even
  if they are not based on reality.

- Clarify messages. Listen to what is really being said. Ask
  reflective questions. Use both silence and restatements.

- Respect personal space. Stand at least 1.5 to 3 feet away
  from the person who is acting out. Encroaching on personal
  space tends to escalate the situation.

- Be aware of your body position. Standing eye to eye and toe
  to toe sends a message of challenge. Standing one-leg length
  away and at an angle off to the side makes it less likely that
  the situation will escalate.

- Permit verbal venting if possible. Allow the individual to
  release as much energy as possible by venting verbally. If
  this cannot be allowed, state directives and reasonable limits
  during lulls in the venting process.

- Set and enforce reasonable limits. If the individual becomes
  belligerent, defensive or disruptive, state limits and
  directives clearly and concisely.

- Remain calm, rational and professional. How you respond
  will directly affect the individual's conduct.

- Use physical techniques only as a last resort. Use the least
  restrictive effective method. Using physical techniques on
  someone who is only acting out verbally can escalate the
  situation.

- Ignore challenge questions, as answering them can fuel a
  power struggle. When the individual challenges your

position, training, etc., redirect the individual's attention to the issue at hand.

• Keep your nonverbal cues non-threatening. Be aware of your body language, movement and tone of voice. The more an individual loses control, the less he listens to your actual words. More attention is paid to nonverbal cues.

-From the National Crisis Prevention Institute

Administrator or Designee:

1. Follow the same above guidelines.

Source: University of Arkansas System, Criminal Justice Institute, School Violence Resource Center

Form II-1: Situation Involving Severe Weather

These are steps for key personnel to take in situations involving severe weather.

Tornadoes, Hurricanes and Thunderstorms

If a tornado watch or severe thunderstorm warning is received during school hours:

1. The principal or a designee should notify all school staff.

2. Teachers continue regular classroom activities.

3. School will dismiss at the normal hour in the regular manner. Drivers will follow regular routes using extra caution.

4. Review school procedures for establishing safe areas.

If there has been a tornado warning stating that a tornado has actually been sighted:

1. The principal or designee will receive the warning by way of radio tuned to a weather channel, a call from the superintendent or a designated representative, or the civil defense office.

2. The principal will inform the staff.

3. Staff and students will immediately proceed to an area predetermined by the school and assume a position protecting the face and head.

4. Teacher will take attendance and notify the principal or a designated representative if anyone is missing.

5. The school secretary or other designated individual will close all vaults and secure important records.

6. All qualified personnel will render first aid if necessary.

7. Staff and students will not return to their classrooms until the principal or a designated representative declares an "all clear."

If no warning has been issued, but a tornado has been sighted and is approaching the school, the principal or a designated representative will direct all individuals to proceed as follows:

Plan 1 - If time permits, take classes to designated areas.

Plan 2 - If time does not permit removal to designated areas:

- Go to the nearest enclosed hallway, not to open corridors.

- Avoid open spaces and outside hallways.

- Avoid areas with large roof expanse such as the gymnasium, cafeteria or auditorium.

Take Cover Procedures

For the protection of all building occupants, it is important that everyone is informed and understands what to do in the event of severe weather that makes it necessary for the school population to take cover. The following take-cover procedures should be taught in each class:

1. Discuss the take-cover warning.

2. Practice the take-cover position.

3. Encourage students to remain calm and not to panic in the event of a crisis situation.

4. Discuss the "all clear" code.

Staff:

1. Take students to a hallway or other approved location. Seat them on the floor in the hall with their backs against the lockers/walls. If necessary, double up against the lockers/walls. If there is no time to move the students, have them get on the floor away from glass.

2. Instruct students to put their heads down against their knees, cover their necks with their hands and their faces with their arms.

TORNADO WATCH OR SEVERE THUNDERSTORMS

Administrators or designee:

1. The superintendent or a designee will decide whether to close the schools based on current weather information.

2. If the schools close early, all procedures for the emergency closing of schools will be in effect.

If the weather becomes severe enough during the night or on the weekends to close the schools, all procedures for the emergency closing of schools will be put into effect.

Source: University of Arkansas System, Criminal Justice Institute, School Violence Resource Center

Form II-2: Sample Notice to Parents
Regarding Lockdown Drill

Date

Dear Parents/Guardians:

In keeping with our ongoing efforts to maintain a safe school, we will be conducting a lockdown drill on _____ (DATE) at _____ (TIME). Your child's teacher will prepare each class for this drill by discussing its specifics with the class ahead of time.

Please talk to your child about this drill.

- Calmly explain that a lockdown is something that the school does to keep students safe when a danger is present, such as when someone gains unauthorized access into the building.

- Assure your child that we hope a lockdown is never needed but that practicing the drill will help keep him or her safe.

- Compare the drill to a school drill they already are familiar with, such as a fire drill or a weather emergency drill.

- Remind your child that by practicing the drill we are better prepared to stay safe.

Form II-3: Gas Leak Response

Gas leaks are often identified by an odor similar to the odor of rotten eggs. If a gas leak is suspected, key personnel should take these steps:

Staff:
1. Notify principal or other designated individual.
2. If you are instructed to evacuate:

- Leave lights on.

- Do not lock doors.

- Instruct students to take with them any items that are easily accessible.

Administrator or Designee:
1. Determine whether you need to evacuate or shelter in place.
2. If evacuation is required:

- Assign staff members to check halls, restrooms, locker rooms and other areas for students.

- If inside, allow fresh air ventilation, if possible.

- If outside, move upwind from any odor.

3. Contact appropriate administrator at telephone number _____.

4. Contact insurance representative at telephone number _____.

5. Determine whether first aid is needed.

6. Establish safe places for classes to reconvene.

Source: University of Arkansas System, Criminal Justice Institute, School Violence Resource Center

Form II-4: Hazardous Spill Response

In the event of a hazardous spill, key personnel should take these steps.

Staff:
1. Notify principal or other designated individual.
2. Avoid direct or indirect contact with material spill.
3. Remove any contaminated clothing.
4. If you are instructed to evacuate:

- Leave lights on.

- Do not lock doors.

- Instruct students to take with them any items that are easily accessible.

Administrator or Designee:
1. Determine whether you need to evacuate or shelter in place.
2. Evacuate the area:

- If spill is outside, move students inside.

- If spill is inside, move students to location with different ventilation system.

- Assign staff members to check halls, restrooms, locker rooms and other areas for students.

- Avoid direct or indirect contact with material spill.

- Remove contaminated clothing.

3. Contact appropriate administrator at telephone number _____.

4. Contact insurance representative at telephone number _____.

5. Determine whether first aid is needed.

6. Establish safe places for classes to reconvene.

Source: University of Arkansas System, Criminal Justice Institute, School Violence Resource Center

Form II-5: Crisis Kit Checklist

Use this checklist to help make sure you have the materials you need to respond to a crisis. Gather and store crisis kit items at strategic locations inside and outside the school. Store the items in a large bag, plastic garbage bag or barrel. Possible storage areas include principals' offices, local fire and police departments, police car trunks, and designated school locations. Update the information in the kits as needed, and make sure you have enough supplies based on your school's size.

- Emergency response telephone numbers.

- Placards with directional words like PARENTS, COUNSELORS, MEDIA, CLERGY, VOLUNTEERS and KEEP OUT.

- Color-coded name tags and sign-in sheets for service personnel.

- Blank white poster board for signs and duct tape to attach signs to tables.

- Notebooks, pens and markers.

- Preprinted referral pads to be given to counselors and clergy indicating name of counselor/clergy, name of person to be referred for follow-up, concerns and date.

- Walkie-talkies to communicate with members of the crisis response team and other emergency personnel. Include extra batteries.

- Ankle bands or wrist bands to identify victims.

- First aid supplies.

- Blankets.

- School site layout, floor plans and aerial maps.

- Current roster of student and staff with pictures, addresses, phone numbers, emergency contacts and medical information.

- Attendance rosters.

- Brief summary of school history, number of teachers and staff, and name of principal.

- District fact sheet with enrollment, number of schools, etc.

- County map with school district bus routes marked.

- Bus rosters and routes.

- Resources list of support personnel, such as a contact person for the local phone company.

- Caution tape.

- Telephone directory for school system.

Source: U.S. Department of Education

Form II-6: Emergency Telephone Numbers

Call 911 in any situation that presents an immediate danger to life and property. In addition, the following is a list of other important numbers.

	PHONE	FAX
Poison Control Center	_____	_____
Police	_____	_____
Sheriff's Office	_____	_____
Superintendent	_____	_____
Assistant Superintendent	_____	_____
Director of Transportation	_____	_____
Bus Transportation	_____	_____
Insurance	_____	_____

Source: University of Arkansas System, Criminal Justice Institute, School Violence Resource Center

Form II-7: Sample Letter Home Following Crisis Event

Date

Dear Parents/Guardians,

We regret to inform you about an unfortunate event affecting our school. Yesterday [provide a brief factual statement regarding the event]. An investigation is under way. Until it is complete, we will not have all the details about this tragedy.

The school's crisis team has begun meeting with students and staff. We anticipate that some may need continuing support for a while to help them deal with the emotional upset that such an event produces. Enclosed are some materials that you may find helpful in talking about the matter at home.

If you have any questions or concerns that you think we can help address, please feel free to call the school at [phone number] and ask for any of the following staff members: [identify staff members].

The following community agencies are ready to help anyone who is feeling overwhelmed by their emotions:

- [Provide name and number of community health center].

- [Provide name and number of other available services provider].

We know events such as this are stressful. We are taking every step we can to be responsive to the needs of our students and their families.

Sincerely,

Principal

Source: U.S. Department of Education

Form II-8: Initial Announcement of Crisis Event

TO:
FROM:

We have just been advised of a tragedy involving a member of our school. I am sad to announce that _____
has died/has been in a serious accident. As soon as we have more information, we will pass it on to you. People will be available in the building to help those of you who need extra support in dealing with this situation. Your teachers will advise you of the location and times available for this support.

As soon as we know the family's/families' wishes regarding _____ we will share that information with you.
We ask that all students remain in their classrooms and adhere to their regular schedules.

Source: Virginia Department of Education

Form II-9: Parent Information Sheet - Post-Disaster

<u>Helping Your Child After a Disaster</u>

Children may be especially upset and express feelings about the disaster. These reactions are normal and usually will not last long. Listed below are some problems you may see in your child:

- Excessive fear of darkness, separation, or being alone

- Clinging to parents, fear of strangers

- Worry

- Increase in immature behaviors

- Not wanting to go to school

- Changes in eating/sleeping behaviors

- Increase in either aggressive behavior or shyness

- Bed-wetting or thumb-sucking

- Persistent nightmares; and/or

- Headaches or other physical complaints.

The following will help your child:

- Talk with your child about his/her feelings about the disaster. Share your feelings, too.

- Talk about what happened. Give your child information he/she can understand.

- Reassure your child that you are safe and together. You may need to repeat this reassurance often.

- Hold and touch your child often.

- Spend extra time with your child at bedtime.

- Allow your child to mourn or grieve over a lost toy, a lost blanket, a lost home.

- If you feel your child is having problems at school, talk to his/her teacher so you can work together to help your child.

Please reread this sheet from time to time in the coming months. Usually a child's emotional response to a disaster will not last long, but some problems may be present or recur for many months afterward.

Your community mental health center is staffed by professionals skilled in talking with people experiencing disaster-related problems.

Source: Virginia Department of Education

Form II-10: Thank You Letter - Faculty/Staff

SCHOOL LETTERHEAD

Dear Faculty and Staff Members:

We would like to thank you for your support during the recent crisis at our school. Your professionalism and dedication were evident as we all worked to quiet and soothe scared students and allay their fears while still tending to instructional responsibilities.

We know that this has been an extremely difficult time for you as well as the students. Without your courage and concern, our school could not possibly have come through this crisis as well as we did.

Thank you once again. Your expertise and commitment have enabled all of us to work together as a team and overcome this tragic situation.

Sincerely,

Principal

Guidance Chair

Source: Virginia Department of Education

Form II-11: Bomb Threat Report Form

Make numerous copies and keep them at the main telephone or switchboard for immediate use.

Questions to Ask

1. When is bomb going to explode?
2. Where is it right now?
3. What does it look like?
4. What kind of bomb is it?
5. What will cause it to explode?
6. Did you place the bomb?
7. Why?
8. What is your address?
9. What is your name?

Caller's Voice

____ Calm   ____ Nasal
____ Angry   ____ Stutter
____ Excited   ____ Lisp
____ Slow   ____ Raspy
____ Rapid   ____ Deep
____ Soft   ____ Ragged
____ Loud   ____ Clearing Throat
____ Laughter   ____ Deep Breathing
____ Crying   ____ Cracking Voice
____ Normal   ____ Disguised
____ Distinct   ____ Accent
____ Slurred   ____ Familiar
____ Whispered

Exact Wording of Threat

_____

_____

_____

If voice was familiar, who did it sound like? _____

Background Sounds

____ Street   ____ Animal Noises
____ PA System   ____ Static
____ Voices   ____ Music
____ Motor   ____ House Noises
____ Local   ____ Office Machines
____ Booth   ____ Long Distance

Time: _____ Date: _____
Sex of caller: ____ Culture: ____
Age: _____ Length of call: ____

Number at which call was received:

_____

Remarks:

_____

_____

_____

Threat Language

____ Well-spoken
____ Foul language
____ Taped
____ Incoherent
____ Message read

Source: Virginia Department of Education

Form II-12: Intruder Response

In the event that an intruder gains unauthorized access to school premises, key personnel should take these steps.

Staff:
1. Notify principal or other designated individual.
2. Take attendance and remain with students.
3. Wait for instructions.

Administrator or Designee:
1. Assess situation and determine threat level.

2. Call 911 if danger is indicated.

3. Contact appropriate administrator at telephone number _____.

4. If lockdown is needed, notify teachers.

5. Keep telephone lines open for emergency use.

6. Provide police with maps of building and grounds.

Source: University of Arkansas System, Criminal Justice Institute, School Violence Resource Center

Form II-13: Students/Staff Needing Special Assistance for Evacuation

Name	Grade/Homeroom	Assistance Needed/Assister

Main Building

_____	_____	_____
_____	_____	_____
_____	_____	_____
_____	_____	_____
_____	_____	_____
_____	_____	_____
_____	_____	_____
_____	_____	_____
_____	_____	_____
_____	_____	_____
_____	_____	_____

Annex A

_____	_____	_____
_____	_____	_____
_____	_____	_____
_____	_____	_____
_____	_____	_____
_____	_____	_____
_____	_____	_____
_____	_____	_____

Source: Virginia Department of Education

Form III-1: Bus Transportation Accident Response

Steps for key personnel to take in the event of a bus transportation accident:

Bus Driver:
1. Notify dispatch using proper procedures.
2. Secure the bus, making sure no passengers leave and no one boards the bus.
3. Set out warning devices such as triangle or cones.
4. Determine whether anyone has been injured.
5. Move the bus to a safer location on the side of the road, if possible.
6. Passenger safety is the most important thing to keep in mind. If the bus is not badly damaged and is not in danger of being struck, keep the passengers on the bus until help arrives.
7. Refer media to administration.

Dispatch:
1. Take control. Remain calm and help the driver make proper decisions.
2. Call designated management staff.
3. Call appropriate law enforcement agency or 911.

Transportation Personnel:
1. Upon arrival, assess for immediate safety concerns.
2. Complete accident reports and take pictures.
3. Refer media to administration.

Schools:
1. Contact parents and relay necessary information.
2. Conduct follow-up on any student who received medical treatment within three days of accident.

Source: University of Arkansas System, Criminal Justice Institute, School Violence Resource Center

Form III-2: Parent Letter - Notice of Bus Accident

Dear Parents,

This morning, prior to school, there was an accident involving a school bus and an automobile. There were known injuries to the passengers of the car. The children on Bus # _____ witnessed the aftermath of the accident but were not involved in it.

The children from the bus involved in the accident were taken to the library by the guidance counselors and administration. The children were asked if they were injured in any way and their parents were then contacted. Because your child was on Bus # ___ he or she may show delayed reaction to the accident. Please be alert over the next several days to symptoms of delayed reaction, including:

- a desire to be alone, unusually quiet

- loss of appetite

- problems with sleeping, nightmares

- difficulty with concentration

- crying

- angry outburst, short temper

- headaches, upset stomach

- depressed, sad

Your child may also exhibit some physical complaints. Please contact (principal's name) to fill out an accident report. The school will be offered support services for students needing help dealing with the accident. We will also provide counseling services to parents in helping their children to cope. Please don't hesitate to call if you have any questions or concerns.

Sincerely,

Principal of School

Source: Virginia Department of Education

Form VI-1: Questionnaire for Chaperones

Thank you for volunteering to serve as a chaperone for the following field trip: [INSERT TRIP DESCRIPTION AND DATE OF TRIP]. We value your willingness to help our school and our students.

Please complete, sign and date this form and return it to _____ no later than _____. Once we review the completed form, we will notify you whether you have been selected to serve as a chaperone on this trip. If the answer to any question below is "Yes," please explain in the space provided.

1. ___ Yes ___ No   Have you ever been disciplined for any type of misconduct in connection with your employment?

2. ___ Yes ___ No   Have you ever been convicted of a criminal offense?

3. ___ Yes ___ No   Are you on probation in any state?

4. ___ Yes ___ No   Have you ever been acquitted or found not guilty of any criminal offense for reasons related to insanity or diminished mental capacity?

5. ___ Yes ___ No   Are any criminal charges currently pending against you?

I certify that I am at least 21 years of age and have completed this form truthfully and to the best of my knowledge.

PRINT NAME: _____   SIGNATURE: _____

DATE: _____

ADDRESS: _____

PHONE: _____

Form VI-2: Guidelines for Chaperones

Thank you for agreeing to serve as a chaperone for the following field trip:
[INSERT TRIP DESCRIPTION AND DATE OF TRIP].

As a chaperone, you serve as a role model and help students learn. The
following guidelines for chaperones apply to this trip. Please review them
carefully. Please sign and date this form and return it to   _____
no later than _____. Once again, thank you for your assistance.

1. Chaperones are required to remain with their assigned group at all times,
   until chaperoning duties are finished.

2. Chaperones agree to continuously monitor their group's activities.

3. Chaperones will not use any alcohol or tobacco products during the trip
   at any time.

4. Chaperones will refrain from using profane or inappropriate language
   at any time during the trip.

5. Chaperones are NEVER to touch a child unless the child is presenting
   an immediate threat to the health or safety of himself or others.

6. Chaperones are not to administer medications to students.

7. Chaperones may not bring along non-student siblings or other children
   on the trip.

8. Chaperones will report any safety or health concerns to a teacher
   immediately.

I have read the above guidelines and agree to abide by them.

NAME: _____

SIGNATURE: _____

DATE: _____

Form VI-3: Field Trip Permission Slip

On _____, your child's class will be taking a field trip to
_____. We will be leaving the school at_____
and returning at _____. The cost of this trip is _____.
If cost is a concern, please contact the school principal.

Please complete and return the bottom portion of this form no later than
_____. Your child will not be permitted to attend if this slip is not
completed and returned.

I give permission for my child, _____, of room ____,
to attend the field trip to _____ on _____
I am enclosing a check or money order in the amount of _____
made payable to _____, to cover the cost of this trip.

I hereby grant permission for school personnel to arrange for the provision
of medical treatment to _____ in the event of a medical
emergency. If such an emergency occurs, please contact
_____ at phone number _____ or
_____ at phone number _____

If your child is allergic to any medications, please list them here (if none,
write "none:"): _____.

NAME: _____

SIGNATURE _____

PHONE: _____

RELATIONSHIP TO STUDENT_____

Form VII-1: Parent Letter Regarding Child with Allergy

Dear Parents,

This letter is to inform you that a student in your child's classroom has a severe peanut/nut allergy. Strict avoidance of peanut/nut products is the only way to prevent a life-threatening allergic reaction. We are asking your assistance in providing the student with a safe learning environment.

If exposed to peanuts/nuts the student may develop a life-threatening allergic reaction that requires emergency medical treatment. The greatest potential for exposure at school is to peanut products and nut products. To reduce the risk of exposure, the classroom will be peanut/nut free. Please do not send any peanut- or nut-containing products for your child to eat during snack-time in the classroom. Any exposure to peanuts or nuts through contact or ingestion can cause a severe reaction. If your child has eaten peanuts or nuts prior to coming to school, please be sure your child's hands have been thoroughly washed prior to entering the school.

Since lunch is eaten in the cafeteria, your child may bring peanut butter, peanut or nut products for lunch. In the cafeteria there will be a designated peanut-free table where any classmate without peanut or nut products can sit. If your child sits at this table with a peanut or nut product, s/he will be asked to move to another table. This plan will help to maintain safety in the classroom while allowing non-allergic classmates to enjoy peanut/nut products in a controlled environment. Following lunch, the children will wash their hands prior to going to recess or returning to the class. The tables will be cleaned with soap, water and paper towels after each lunch.

We appreciate your support of these procedures. Please complete and return this form so that we are certain that every family has received this information. If you have any questions, please contact me.

X _____

Signature of Principal/Teacher/Nurse

I have read and understand the peanut/nut-free classroom procedures. I agree to do my part in keeping the classroom peanut and nut free.

Child's name:_____

Parent's signature: _____

Date: _____

Source: Massachusetts Department of Education

Form VII-2: Substitute Teacher Letter
Regarding Child with Allergy

Dear Substitute Teacher,

The students listed below in this class have life-threatening food allergies.

Please maintain the food allergy avoidance strategies that we have developed to protect these students.

Should a student ingest, touch or inhale the substance to which they are allergic (the allergen), a severe reaction (anaphylaxis) may follow requiring the administration of epinephrine (Epi-pen®).

The Allergy Action Plan, which states who has been trained to administer epinephrine, is located _____.
Epinephrine is a life-preserving medication and should be given in the first minutes of a reaction.

Student   Allergies

_____

_____

_____

_____

_____

Please treat this information confidentially to protect the privacy of the students. Your cooperation is essential to ensure their safety. Should you have any questions please contact the school nurse _____ or the principal _____.

_____
Classroom teacher

Source: Massachusetts Department of Education

Form VII-3: Sample Diabetes Management Plan

Effective Dates: _____

This plan should be completed by the student's personal health care team and parents/guardian. It should be reviewed with relevant school staff and copies should be kept in a place that is easily accessed by the school nurse, trained diabetes personnel, and other authorized personnel.

Student's Name: _____

Date of Birth: _____ Date of Diagnosis: _____

Grade: _____ Homeroom Teacher: _____

Physical Condition: ____ Type 1 Diabetes ____ Type 2 Diabetes _____

Contact Information

Mother/Guardian: _____

Address: _____

Telephone: Home: _____ Work: _____ Cell: _____

Father/Guardian: _____

Address: _____

Telephone: Home: _____ Work: _____ Cell: _____

Other Emergency Contacts:

Name: _____

Relationship: _____

Telephone: Home: _____ Work: _____ Cell: _____

Notify parents/guardian or emergency contact in the following situations:

_____

_____

Blood Glucose Monitoring

Target range for blood glucose: ____ 70-150 ____ 70-180 ____ Other: ____

Usual times to check blood glucose:_____

Times to do extra blood glucose checks (*check all that apply*):

____ before exercise

____ after exercise

____ when student shows signs of hyperglycemia

____ when student shows signs of hypoglycemia

____ other (explain): _____

Can student perform own blood glucose checks? ____ Yes ____ No

Type of blood glucose meter student uses: _____

Insulin

Usual Lunchtime Dose

Base dose of Humalog/Novolog/Regular insulin at lunch (circle type of rapid-/short-acting insulin used) is ____ units or does flexible dosing using ____ units/____ grams carbohydrate. Use of other insulin at lunch: (circle type of insulin used): intermediate/NPH/lente ____ units or basal/Lantus/Ultralente ____ units.

Insulin Correction Doses

Parental authorization should be obtained before administering a correction dose for high blood glucose levels. ____ Yes ____ No

____ units if blood pressure is ____ to ____ mg/dl

____ units if blood pressure is ____ to ____ mg/dl

____ units if blood pressure is ____ to ____ mg/dl

____ units if blood pressure is ____ to ____ mg/dl

____ units if blood pressure is ____ to ____ mg/dl

Can student give own injections? ____ Yes ____ No

Can student determine correct amount of insulin? ____ Yes ____ No

Can student draw correct dose of insulin? ____ Yes ____ No

____ Parents are authorized to adjust the insulin dosage under the following circumstances: _____

_____

For Students with Insulin Pumps

Type of pump: _____ Basal rates: _____ 12 am to _____

_____ _____ to _____

_____ _____ to _____

Type of insulin in pump: _____

Type of infusion set: _____

Insulin/carbohydrate ratio: _____ Correction factor: _____

Student Pump Abilities/Skills	Needs Assistance
Count carbohydrates	_____ Yes _____ No
Bolus correct amount for carbohydrates consumed	_____ Yes _____ No
Calculate and administer corrective bolus	_____ Yes _____ No
Calculate and set basal profiles	_____ Yes _____ No
Calculate and set temporary basal rate	_____ Yes _____ No
Disconnect pump	_____ Yes _____ No
Reconnect pump at infusion set	_____ Yes _____ No
Prepare reservoir and tubing	_____ Yes _____ No
Insert infusion set	_____ Yes _____ No
Troubleshoot alarms and malfunctions	_____ Yes _____ No

For Students Taking Oral Diabetes Medications

Type of medication: _____ Timing: _____

Other medications: _____ Timing: _____

Meals and Snacks Eaten at School

Is student independent in carbohydrate calculations and management? ___ Yes ___ No

Meal/Snack	Time	Food content/amount
Breakfast	_____	_____
Mid-morning snack	_____	_____
Lunch	_____	_____
Mid-afternoon snack	_____	_____
Dinner	_____	_____

Snack before exercise? ____ Yes ____ No

Snack after exercise? ____ Yes ____ No

Other times to give snacks and correct amount: _____

Preferred food snacks: _____

Foods to avoid, if any: _____

Instructions for when food is provided to the class (e.g., as part of a class party or food sampling event):

_____

_____

Exercise and Sports

A fast-acting carbohydrate such as _____ should be available at the site of exercise or sports.

Restrictions on activity, if any: _____

Student should not exercise if blood glucose level is below _____ mg/dl or above _____ mg/dl or if moderate to large urine ketones are present.

Hypoglycemia (Low Blood Sugar)

Usual symptoms of hypoglycemia: _____

_____

Treatment of hypoglycemia: _____

_____

Urine should be checked for ketones when blood glucose levels are above ____ mg/dl.

Treatment for ketones: _____

Supplies to Be Kept at School

____ Blood glucose meter, test strips, batteries   ____ Insulin pump and supplies

____ Lancet device, lancets, gloves, etc.   ____ Insulin pen, needles cartridges

____ Urine ketone strips   ____ Carbohydrate containing snack

____ Insulin vials and syringes   ____ Glucagon emergency kit

Signatures

This Diabetes Medical Management Plan has been approved by:

_____

Student's Physician/Health Care Provider   Date

I give permission to the school nurse, trained diabetes personnel, and other designated staff members of _____ school to perform and carry out the diabetes care tasks as outlined by _____'s Diabetes Medical Management Plan. I also consent to the release of the information contained in this Diabetes Medical Management Plan to all staff members and other adults who have custodial care of my child and who may need to know this information to maintain my child's health and safety.

Acknowledged and received by:

_____   _____

Student's Parent/Guardian   Date

_____   _____

Student's Parent/Guardian   Date

Source: U.S. Department of Health and Human Services

Form VII-4: Parent Letter Regarding MRSA

Dear Parents,

This letter is being sent to provide information regarding Methicillin-Resistant Staphlylococcus Aureus (MRSA) infections in schools.

MRSA infection is a type of staph infection that is resistant to some antibiotics. It has existed for decades but has just recently begun to become more prevalent in non-health care settings, including schools. Although MRSA infection is a cause for some concern, it is completely preventable and completely curable.

Our school district has posted information about MRSA infection and precautions that your child can take on our website at _____. Further information is available from the Centers for Disease Control and Prevention at www.cdc.gov. We are providing additional information in this letter to tell you what we are doing at our schools to guard against an outbreak. We are also offering suggestions you can follow at home.

Steps Being Taken at Our Schools:

School restrooms, locker rooms and team rooms are being disinfected on a daily basis, and the artificial turf on our athletic playing field is being disinfected once per week. We have placed spray bottles with disinfectant as gel disinfectant dispensers in all weight rooms. Supervisory personnel are instructing all students who use the weight room to disinfect weight room equipment before and after use. These students are also being instructed to use the gel disinfectant on their hands whey they leave the weight room.

Steps to Take at Home:

The best way to prevent MRSA infection is to practice good hygiene habits. Keeping hands clean with soap and water or an alcohol-based hand soap is very important. Students should take a shower after engaging in sports activity. Cuts and scrapes must be kept clean and completely covered until they are completely healed. Contact with other people's wounds and bandages is to be avoided, as is the sharing of personal items, such as towels, toothbrushes and razors.

Thank you for your assistance.

Sincerely,

Superintendent

Form VII-5: Model Notification of FERPA Rights

The Family Educational Rights and Privacy Act (FERPA) affords parents and students over 18 years of age ("eligible students") certain rights with respect to the student's education records. These rights are:

1. The right to inspect and review the student's education records within 45 days of the day the School receives a request for access. Parents or eligible students should submit to the School principal [or appropriate school official] a written request that identifies the record(s) they wish to inspect. The School official will make arrangements for access and notify the parent or eligible student of the time and place where the records may be inspected.

2. The right to request the amendment of the student's education records that the parent or eligible student believes are inaccurate or misleading. Parents or eligible students may ask the School to amend a record that they believe is inaccurate or misleading. They should write the School principal [or appropriate official], clearly identify the part of the record they want changed, and specify why it is inaccurate or misleading. If the School decides not to amend the record as requested by the parent or eligible student, the School will notify the parent or eligible student of the decision and advise them of their right to a hearing regarding the request for amendment. Additional information regarding the hearing procedures will be provided to the parent or eligible student when notified of the right to a hearing.

3. The right to consent to disclosures of personally identifiable information contained in the student's education records, except to the extent that FERPA authorizes disclosure without consent. One exception, which permits disclosure without consent, is disclosure to school officials with legitimate educational interests. A school official is a person employed by the School as an administrator, supervisor, instructor, or support staff member (including health or medical staff and law enforcement unit personnel); a person serving on the School Board; a person or company with whom the School has contracted to perform a special task (such as an attorney, auditor, medical consultant, or therapist); or a parent or student serving on an official committee, such as a disciplinary or grievance committee, or assisting another school official in performing his or her tasks. A school official has a legitimate educational interest if the official needs to review an education record in order to fulfill his or her professional responsibility.
[Optional] Upon request, the School discloses education records without consent to officials of another school district in which a student seeks or intends to enroll.

[NOTE: FERPA requires a school district to make a reasonable attempt to notify the parent or eligible student of the records request unless it states in its annual notification that it intends to forward records on request.]

4. The right to file a complaint with the U.S. Department of Education concerning alleged failures by the School to comply with the requirements of FERPA. The name and address of the Office that administers FERPA are:

Family Policy Compliance Office

U.S. Department of Education

400 Maryland Avenue, SW

Washington, DC 20202-5901

[NOTE: In addition, an institution may want to include its directory information public notice, as required by § 99.37 of the regulations, with its annual notification of rights under FERPA.]

Source: U.S. Department of Education

Form VII-6: Dealing with Suicidal Students

These are steps for key personnel to take when it appears that a student is at risk for committing suicide.

Staff:
1. Notify principal or other designated individual.

2. Respond by listening empathetically and gathering information.

3. Refer the student to a guidance counselor.

Guidance:
1. Gather information and check for lethality indicators.

2. Contact the student's parents or guardians.

3. If your assessment indicates the student is currently a suicidal risk, keep the student with you until a parent/guardian arrives for pickup.

4. Contact the school resource officer.

5. Provide the parents/guardians with a list of agencies for referral.

6. If the parents/guardians refuse to accept/seek help, contact the appropriate children and families services agency at phone _____.

7. Document all actions taken by school personnel.

8. Complete these follow-up steps:

   • Try to have the student commit to contact you or another adult if suicidal feelings return.

   • Make guidance appointments for the student on a continuing basis and monitor how the student is coping.

   • Contact parents/guardians to check on progress with referral agencies and to make them aware of student's behavior at school.

   • Keep the principal, other administrators and the student's teachers apprised of the student's situation.

Social Worker:

1. May assist by contacting parents/guardians who cannot be reached by school personnel.

Administrator or Designee:

1. If suicide is attempted at school, contact superintendent or designee at telephone number _____.

2. If suicide is attempted at school, contact insurance representative at telephone number _____.

5. Provide support as needed.

6. Follow up with guidance department.

Source: University of Arkansas System, Criminal Justice Institute, School Violence Resource Center

Form VII-7: Announcement of Student Suicide

(To be read to students by the classroom teacher.)

TO: School Faculty
FROM: Principal
SUBJECT: (Crisis)
DATE:

John Doe committed suicide early Saturday morning. As a faculty, we extend our sympathy to John's family and friends.

We encourage all students to consider the tragic nature of this death and to realize that death is final. John's death is a reminder to us all that the act of taking one's own life is not an appropriate solution to any of life's problems nor is it an act of courage. Please let your teachers know if you would like to talk to a counselor or other staff member.

Funeral services for John will be held in _____ and there will not be a memorial service in this area. Expressions of sympathy may be sent to _____.

Source: Virginia Department of Education

Form VII-8: Announcement - Student Death
From Accident or Illness

As many of you are aware, we were sorry to hear that _____,
a student in the _____ grade of our school, died on _____ from
injuries in a car crash. As soon as we learn the funeral plans, we will
announce them. Those of you who want to discuss your feelings about
_____'s death should obtain a hall pass from your teacher to
go to the library. This help will be available throughout the school day.
Let us have a moment of silence. Thank you for your cooperation today.

Source: Virginia Department of Education

Form VII-9: Parent Letter: Unexpected Student Death

Dear Parents,

Yesterday, we learned that one of our first graders, _____,
died while in the hospital. _____ had his tonsils removed
over the past weekend. Complications set in after his parents took him
home where he died yesterday afternoon.

Today, at school, each teacher read a short message about _____
to his/her class. We discussed what happened and how _____
died. We also stressed that many people have their tonsils out every day
and have no problems with it. Our guidance counselor and our school
psychologist were available throughout the day to talk with any student
that may have had a particularly difficult time dealing with the news.

Any death is difficult for children to understand. _____'s
death is particularly difficult due to his young age and its unexpectedness.
The fact that _____ died while at the hospital and the fact
that it was related to having his tonsils out may also be frightening for
children, especially those who may need to have their own tonsils out in
the future.

We recommend that you take some time to discuss death with your child.
We suggest allowing your child to talk about how he/she feels and any
fears or concerns he/she may have as a result of hearing this news. We are
enclosing a list of suggestions to help you talk with your child about
_____'s death and/or the death of any loved one.

If you feel that your child would benefit from talking with our guidance
counselor or our school psychologist, please call us at the school and
share your concerns.

The faculty, staff and students extend our heartfelt sympathies to the
family and to all their friends. We, at the school, will miss _____
very much. He was our friend and we loved him.

Sincerely,

School Principal

Source: Virginia Department of Education

Form VII-10: Student/Parent Letter - Sudden Student Death

SCHOOL LETTERHEAD

Date

Dear Students and Parents:

On Friday, John Doe, a fifth-grade student at [School] was in a terrible
accident. Apparently, John was hit by a car that was speeding and
had crossed over the median strip to the wrong side of the road. John
died instantly.

John's death is a tragic, emotional loss for the entire [School] family.
I am sure all of us will make every effort to comfort and support
John's family as they attempt to deal with this traumatic loss. There
are no adequate words to express our sense of grief and sympathy for
the family.

Because John's death is felt so deeply by so many, on Monday and
thereafter as needed, we will bring in our crisis team to discuss this
accident and loss with students and faculty.

We encourage each of you to discuss this loss with your child. In order
to help you do so we are holding a parent meeting on [date], and [time],
in the cafeteria of [School]. The topic will be ways to help children
cope with loss and will be presented by _____ , a
local mental health professional.

John's family, friends, and the school are suffering deeply. Please join
us in supporting John's family.

Sincerely,

Principal

(School)

Source: Virginia Department of Education

THE JUDICIAL SYSTEM

In order to allow you to determine the relative importance of a judicial decision, the cases included in *Keeping Your School Safe & Secure: A Practical Guide* identify the particular court from which a decision has been issued. For example, a case decided by a state supreme court generally will be of greater significance than a state circuit court case. Hence a basic knowledge of the structure of our judicial system is important to an understanding of school law.

Almost all the reports in this volume are taken from appellate court decisions. Although most education law decisions occur at trial court and administrative levels, appellate court decisions have the effect of binding lower courts and administrators so that appellate court decisions have the effect of law within their court systems.

State and federal court systems generally function independently of each other. Each court system applies its own law according to statutes and the determinations of its highest court. However, judges at all levels often consider opinions from other court systems to settle issues which are new or arise under unique fact situations. Similarly, lawyers look at the opinions of many courts to locate authority which supports their clients' cases.

Once a lawsuit is filed in a particular court system, that system retains the matter until its conclusion. Unsuccessful parties at the administrative or trial court level generally have the right to appeal unfavorable determinations of law to appellate courts within the system. When federal law issues or constitutional grounds are present, lawsuits may be appropriately filed in the federal court system. In those cases, the lawsuit is filed initially in the federal district court for that area.

On rare occasions, the U.S. Supreme Court considers appeals from the highest courts of the states if a distinct federal question exists and at least four justices agree on the question's importance. The federal courts occasionally send cases to state courts for application of state law. These situations are infrequent and, in general, the state and federal court systems should be considered separate from each other.

The most common system, used by nearly all states and also the federal judiciary, is as follows: a legal action is commenced in district court (sometimes called trial court, county court, common pleas court or superior court) where a decision is initially reached. The case may then be appealed to the court of appeals (or appellate court), and in turn this decision may be appealed to the supreme court.

Several states, however, do not have a court of appeals; lower court decisions are appealed directly to the state's supreme court. Additionally, some states have labeled their courts in a nonstandard fashion.

In Maryland, the highest state court is called the Court of Appeals. In the state of New York, the trial court is called the Supreme Court. Decisions of this court may be appealed to the Supreme Court, Appellate Division. The highest court in New York is the Court of Appeals. Pennsylvania has perhaps the most complex court system. The lowest state court is the Court of Common Pleas. Depending on the circumstances of the case, appeals may be taken to either the Commonwealth Court or the Superior Court. In certain instances the Commonwealth Court functions as a trial court as well as an appellate court. The Superior Court, however, is strictly an intermediate appellate court. The highest court in Pennsylvania is the Supreme Court.

While supreme court decisions are generally regarded as the last word in legal matters, it is important to remember that trial and appeals court decisions also create important legal precedents. For the hierarchy of typical state and federal court systems, please see the diagram below.

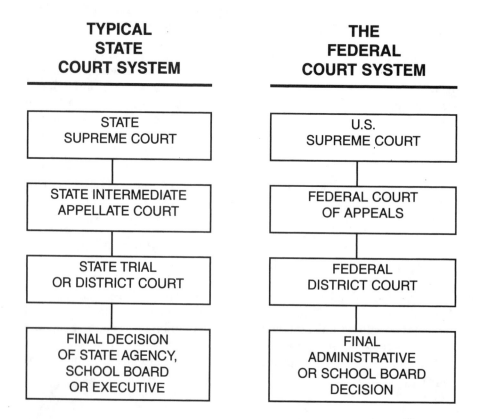

TYPICAL STATE COURT SYSTEM

- STATE SUPREME COURT
- STATE INTERMEDIATE APPELLATE COURT
- STATE TRIAL OR DISTRICT COURT
- FINAL DECISION OF STATE AGENCY, SCHOOL BOARD OR EXECUTIVE

THE FEDERAL COURT SYSTEM

- U.S. SUPREME COURT
- FEDERAL COURT OF APPEALS
- FEDERAL DISTRICT COURT
- FINAL ADMINISTRATIVE OR SCHOOL BOARD DECISION

Federal courts of appeals hear appeals from the district courts which are located in their circuits. Below is a list of states matched to the federal circuits in which they are located.

First Circuit	— Maine, Massachusetts, New Hampshire, Puerto Rico, Rhode Island
Second Circuit	— Connecticut, New York, Vermont
Third Circuit	— Delaware, New Jersey, Pennsylvania, Virgin Islands
Fourth Circuit	— Maryland, North Carolina, South Carolina, Virginia, West Virginia
Fifth Circuit	— Louisiana, Mississippi, Texas
Sixth Circuit	— Ohio, Kentucky, Michigan, Tennessee
Seventh Circuit	— Illinois, Indiana, Wisconsin
Eighth Circuit	— Arkansas, Iowa, Minnesota, Missouri, Nebraska, North Dakota, South Dakota
Ninth Circuit	— Alaska, Arizona, California, Guam, Hawaii, Idaho, Montana, Nevada, Northern Mariana Islands, Oregon, Washington
Tenth Circuit	— Colorado, Kansas, Oklahoma, New Mexico, Utah, Wyoming
Eleventh Circuit	— Alabama, Florida, Georgia
District of Columbia Circuit	— Hears cases from the U.S. District Court for the District of Columbia
Federal Circuit Appeals	— Sitting in Washington, D.C., the U.S. Court of Federal Circuit, hears patent and trade appeals and certain appeals on claims brought against the federal government and its agencies

HOW TO READ A CASE CITATION

Generally, court decisions can be located in case reporters at law school or governmental law libraries. Some cases can also be located on the Internet through legal Web sites or official court websites.

Each case summary contains the citation, or legal reference, to the full text of the case. The diagram below illustrates how to read a case citation.

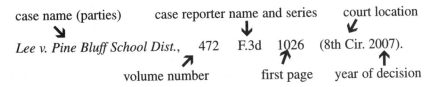

Some cases may have two or three reporter names such as U.S. Supreme Court cases and cases reported in regional case reporters as well as state case reporters. For example, a U.S. Supreme Court case usually contains three case reporter citations.

first reporter   third reporter

Gratz v. Bollinger, 539 U.S. 244, 123 S.Ct. 2411, 156 L.Ed.2d 257 (2003).

second reporter

The citations are still read in the same manner as if only one citation has been listed.

Occasionally, a case may contain a citation which does not reference a case reporter. For example, a citation may contain a reference such as:

case name   year of decision   first page   year of decision

Saxon v. Chapman, No. 266077, 2006 WL 1237036 (Mich. Ct. App. 2006).

court file number   WESTLAW[1]   court location

The court file number indicates the specific number assigned to a case by the particular court system deciding the case. In our example, the Michigan Court of Appeals has assigned the case of *Saxon v. Chapman* the case number of

---

[1]WESTLAW® is a computerized database of court cases available for a fee.

"No. 266077" which will serve as the reference number for the case and any matter relating to the case. Locating a case on the Internet generally requires either the case name and date of the decision, and/or the court file number.

Below, we have listed the full names of the regional reporters. As mentioned previously, many states have individual state reporters. The names of those reporters may be obtained from a reference law librarian.

P.	**Pacific Reporter**
	Alaska, Arizona, California, Colorado, Hawaii, Idaho, Kansas, Montana, Nevada, New Mexico, Oklahoma, Oregon, Utah, Washington, Wyoming
A.	**Atlantic Reporter**
	Connecticut, Delaware, District of Columbia, Maine, Maryland, New Hampshire, New Jersey, Pennsylvania, Rhode Island, Vermont
N.E.	**Northeastern Reporter**
	Illinois, Indiana, Massachusetts, New York, Ohio
N.W.	**Northwestern Reporter**
	Iowa, Michigan, Minnesota, Nebraska, North Dakota, South Dakota, Wisconsin
So.	**Southern Reporter**
	Alabama, Florida, Louisiana, Mississippi
S.E.	**Southeastern Reporter**
	Georgia, North Carolina, South Carolina, Virginia, West Virginia
S.W.	**Southwestern Reporter**
	Arkansas, Kentucky, Missouri, Tennessee, Texas
F.	**Federal Reporter**
	The thirteen federal judicial circuits courts of appeals decisions.
F.Supp.	**Federal Supplement**
	The thirteen federal judicial circuits district court decisions. *See, The Judicial System, p. 689* for specific state circuits.
Fed.Appx.	**Federal Appendix**
	Contains unpublished decisions of the U.S. Circuit Courts of Appeal.
U.S.	**United States Reports**
S.Ct.	**Supreme Court Reporter** > U.S. Supreme Court Decisions
L.Ed.	**Lawyers' Edition**

GLOSSARY

Americans with Disabilities Act (ADA) - The ADA is a federal law that bars discrimination on the basis of disability in several contexts, including employment, access to programs and services provided by public entities, and access to places of public accommodation.

Assumption of Risk - A defense to a claim of negligence, in which the defendant asserts that the injured plaintiff is barred from recovery because he knowingly and voluntarily exposed himself to the hazard that caused his injury.

Biometrics - Methods and techniques used to identify individuals on the basis of a behavioral or physical characteristic or trait.

Class Action Suit - Federal Rule of Civil Procedure 23 allows members of a class to sue as representatives on behalf of the whole class provided that the class is so large that joinder of all parties is impractical, there are questions of law or fact common to the class, the claims or defenses of the representatives are typical of the claims or defenses of the class, and the representative parties will adequately protect the interests of the class. In addition, there must be some danger of inconsistent verdicts or adjudications if the class action were prosecuted as separate actions. Most states also allow class actions under the same or similar circumstances.

Clery Act - see Jeanne Clery Disclosure of Campus Security Policy and Campus Crime Statistics Act.

Crime Prevention Through Environmental Design (CPTED) - An approach to increasing safety in a variety of contexts, including the school context, that recognizes the important role that the design of the built environment can play in reducing the risk of criminal activity.

Cyberbullying - Student bullying that is perpetrated via the Internet, mobile phone or other electronic technology.

Due Process Clause - The clauses of the Fifth and Fourteenth Amendments to the Constitution which guarantee the citizens of the United States "due process of law" (see below). The Fifth Amendment's Due Process Clause applies to the federal government, and the Fourteenth Amendment's Due Process Clause applies to the states.

Due Process of Law - The idea of "fair play" in the government's application of law to its citizens, guaranteed by the Fifth and Fourteenth Amendments. Substantive due process is just plain *fairness*, and procedural due process is accorded when the government utilizes adequate procedural safeguards for the protection of an individual's liberty or property interests.

Enjoin - see Injunction.

Equal Protection Clause - The clause of the Fourteenth Amendment which prohibits a state from denying any person within its jurisdiction equal protection of its laws. Also, the Due Process Clause of the Fifth Amendment which pertains to the federal government. This has been interpreted by the Supreme Court to grant equal protection even though there is no explicit grant in the Constitution.

Establishment Clause - The clause of the First Amendment which prohibits Congress from making "any law respecting an establishment of religion." This clause has been interpreted as creating a "wall of separation" between church and state. The test frequently used to determine whether government action violates the Establishment Clause, referred to as the *Lemon* test, asks whether the action has a secular purpose, whether its primary effect promotes or inhibits religion, and whether it requires excessive entanglement between church and state.

Exclusionary Rule - A rule that allows criminal suspects to have excluded from consideration any evidence that is seized in violation of the Fourth Amendment.

42 U.S.C. §§ 1981, 1983 - Section 1983 of the federal Civil Rights Act prohibits any person acting under color of state law from depriving any other person of rights protected by the Constitution or by federal laws. A vast majority of lawsuits claiming constitutional violations are brought under § 1983. Section 1981 provides that all persons enjoy the same right to make and enforce contracts as "white citizens." Section 1981 applies to employment contracts. Further, unlike § 1983, § 1981 applies even to private actors. It is not limited to those acting under color of state law. These sections do not apply to the federal government, though the government may be sued directly under the Constitution for any violations.

Family Educational Rights and Privacy Act (FERPA) - A federal law that protects the privacy of student education records.

Fourth Amendment - Federal constitutional amendment that protects individuals from unreasonable searches and seizures.

Free Exercise Clause - The clause of the First Amendment which prohibits Congress from interfering with citizens' rights to the free exercise of their religion. Through the Fourteenth Amendment, it has also been made applicable to the states and their sub-entities. The Supreme Court has held that laws of general applicability which have an incidental effect on persons' free exercise rights are not violative of the Free Exercise Clause.

Government Accountability Office (GAO) - A federal agency that acts as the investigative arm of Congress. The GAO examines matters relating to the receipt and payment of public funds.

Incorporation Doctrine - By its own terms, the Bill of Rights applies only to the federal government. The Incorporation Doctrine states that the Fourteenth Amendment makes the Bill of Rights applicable to the states.

Individualized Educational Program (IEP) - The IEP is designed to give children with disabilities a free, appropriate education. It is updated annually, with the participation of the child's parents or guardian.

Individuals with Disabilities Education Act (IDEA) - Also known as the Education of the Handicapped Act (EHA), the Education for All Handicapped Children Act (EAHCA), and the Handicapped Children's Protection Act (HPCA). Originally enacted as the EHA, the IDEA is the federal legislation which provides for the free, appropriate education of all children with disabilities.

Injunction - An equitable remedy (see Remedies) wherein a court orders a party to do or refrain from doing some particular action.

Jeanne Clery Disclosure of Campus Security Policy and Campus Crime Statistics Act - A federal law requiring colleges and universities to disclose information regarding crime on and around campus.

Jurisdiction - The power of a court to determine cases and controversies. The Supreme Court's jurisdiction extends to cases arising under the Constitution and under federal law. Federal courts have the power to hear cases where there is diversity of citizenship or where a federal question is involved.

***Miranda* Warning** - warning that police must provide to an individual in police custody before proceeding with questioning.

MRSA - MRSA, which stands for Methicillin-resistant staphylococcus Aureus, is a type of staph bacteria that is resistant to certain antibiotics.

Negligence per se - Negligence on its face. Usually, the violation of an ordinance or statute will be treated as negligence per se because no careful person would have been guilty of it.

National Incident Management System (NIMS) - a system developed by the Secretary of Homeland Security to provide a national template that helps government, private, and nongovernmental organizations effectively coordinate efforts during crisis events.

Overbroad - A government action is overbroad if, in an attempt to alleviate a specific evil, it impermissibly prohibits or chills a protected action. For example, a law attempting to deal with street litter by prohibiting the distribution of leaflets or handbills could be challenged as overbroad.

Rehabilitation Act - Section 504 of the Rehabilitation Act prohibits employers who receive federal financial assistance from discriminating against otherwise qualified individuals solely on the basis of disability.

Remand - The act of an appellate court in returning a case to the court from which it came for further action.

Remedies - There are two general categories of remedies, or relief: legal remedies, which consist of money damages, and equitable remedies, which consist of a court mandate that a specific action be prohibited or required. For example, a claim for compensatory and punitive damages seeks a legal remedy; a claim for an injunction seeks an equitable remedy. Equitable remedies are generally unavailable unless legal remedies are inadequate to address the harm.

Res Judicata - The judicial notion that a claim or action may not be tried twice or re-litigated, or that all causes of action arising out of the same set of operative facts should be tried at one time. Also known as claim preclusion.

Section 1981 & Section 1983 - see 42 U.S.C. §§ 1981, 1983.

Safe and Drug-Free Schools and Communities Act - Federal law supporting programs that prevent violence in and around schools, prevent illegal alcohol, tobacco and drug use, and foster a safe and drug-free school environment.

Sheltering-in-place - A planned response to the danger presented by the possible release of environmental contaminants that calls for students and personnel to take refuge in a safe interior location.

Sovereign Immunity - The idea that the government cannot be sued without its consent. It stems from the English notion that the "King can do no wrong." This immunity from suit has been abrogated in most states and by the federal government through legislative acts known as "tort claims acts."

Special Relationship Doctrine - A legal doctrine by which a state defendant can be held liable for a person's injury if the state defendant took actions that created a legal duty to protect the person from injury.

Standing - The judicial doctrine which states that in order to maintain a lawsuit a party must have some real interest at stake in the outcome of the trial.

State-Created Danger Doctrine - A legal doctrine by which a state defendant can be held liable for a person's injury if the state's actions either created or significantly increased the danger that caused the injury.

Statute of Limitations - A statute of limitation provides the time period in which a specific cause of action may be brought.

Summary Judgment - Also referred to as pretrial judgment. Similar to a dismissal. Where there is no genuine issue as to any material fact and all that remains is a question of law, a judge can rule in favor of one party or the other. In general, summary judgment is used to dispose of claims which do not support a legally recognized claim.

Supremacy Clause - Clause in Article VI of the Constitution which states that federal legislation is the supreme law of the land.

Title IX - Federal law barring discrimination on the basis of sex under any educational program or activity that receives federal financial assistance.

Title VI - A part of the Civil Rights Act of 1964 that prohibits discrimination based on race, color or national origin in programs or activities that receive federal financial assistance.

Title VII of the Civil Rights Act of 1964 (Title VII) - Title VII prohibits discrimination in employment based upon race, color, sex, national origin, or religion. It applies to any employer having fifteen or more employees. Under Title VII, where an employer intentionally discriminates, employees may obtain money damages unless the claim is for race discrimination. For those claims, monetary relief is available under 42 U.S.C. § 1981.

Vacate - The act of annulling the judgment of a court either by an appellate court or by the court itself. The Supreme Court will generally vacate a lower court's judgment without deciding the case itself, and remand the case to the lower court for further consideration in light of some recent controlling decision.

Writ of Certiorari - The device used by the Supreme Court to transfer cases from the appellate court's docket to its own. Since the Supreme Court's appellate jurisdiction is largely discretionary, it need only issue such a writ when it desires to rule in the case.

INDEX